THE BUSINESS

OF THE

SUPREME COURT

A STUDY IN THE FEDERAL JUDICIAL SYSTEM

BY

FELIX FRANKFURTER

AND

JAMES M. LANDIS

New York

THE MACMILLAN COMPANY

1928

To

Mr. JUSTICE HOLMES

WHO, AFTER TWENTY-FIVE TERMS,
CONTINUES TO CONTRIBUTE HIS
GENIUS TO THE WORK OF A
GREAT COURT.

PREFACE

TO an extraordinary degree legal thinking dominates the United States. Every act of government, every law passed by Congress, every treaty ratified by the Senate, every executive order issued by the President is tested by legal considerations and may be subjected to the hazards of litigation. Other Nations, too, have a written Constitution. But no other country in the world leaves to the judiciary the powers which it exercises over us.

The little community of Euclid Village enacts a zoning ordinance; the Supreme Court has to pass on it. The United States makes a treaty with Germany concluding the Great War; not until the Supreme Court has spoken, in a law-suit nominally between two individuals, do we know the limits and meaning of the treaty. The Senate seeks to investigate the propriety of contributions in senatorial campaigns; the power to pursue such investigation turns on Supreme Court decisions. Everyone conversant with American legal procedure is alive to the need of more competent, more expeditious and more economic means for settlement of controversies. Commercial arbitration and declaratory judgments have long proved themselves effective procedural devices in England. In the United States not only must their utility be related to distinctively American problems of political science, but their adoption must pass barriers in the Constitution not revealed to the unsophisticated eye of the layman. When reforms for the administration of criminal justice are urged in Great Britain, Royal Commissions or Departmental Committees are appointed to explore the situation and to make recommendations for parliamentary enactment. With us, it is not enough to know what wisdom and experience suggest. We are met with the further question: Can we do it under our constitutional system? This is true of every important concern of cities, States and Nation, of business, trade unions and the professions. Most of the problems of modern society, whether of industry, agriculture or finance, of racial interactions or the eternal conflict between liberty and authority, are sooner or later legal problems for solution by our courts and, ultimately, by the Supreme Court of the United States.

Of the part played by important decisions of the Supreme Court in the history of the United States Mr. Charles Warren has told us a good deal; and in his life of John Marshall the late Senator Beveridge made a notable beginning of the biographical study of great judges of the Court which is so essential to an understanding of its history. But the significance of the development of the Court's business since its establishment in 1789 — the steady extension of its jurisdiction as a reflex of the expansion of Federal power, the growth of Federal litigation and the modes of its disposition — has enlisted scant attention. Yet the history of the Supreme Court, as of the Common Law, derives meaning to no small degree from the cumulative details which define the scope of its business, and the forms and methods of performing it —the Court's procedure, in the comprehensive meaning of the term. Not merely is its work of technical adjudication inseparably related to the procedural rules and practices of the Court. The essentially political significance of the Supreme Court's share in the operations of the Union can hardly be overemphasized. The rôle of procedure in the evolution and activity of political institutions has been little heeded by political scientists. But, as Professor Wallace Notestein has recently demonstrated in his " Winning of the Initiative by the House of Commons," the formalities and modes of doing business, which we characterize as procedure, though lacking in dramatic manifestations, may, like the subtle creeping in of the tide, be a powerful force in the dynamic process of government.

Of this truth the history of the Federal judicial system brings striking proof. That the Supreme Court, under Marshall's guidance, was one of the chief promoters of the Federalist philosophy long after the decline of avowed Federalism is familiar enough. But it is no less true that throughout our history the authority conferred upon the Federal Courts represents an important aspect of the struggle between centralization and states' rights. In turn, the mode in which the Federal judiciary, particularly the Supreme Court, exercised the powers entrusted to it by Congress profoundly influenced the balance of forces in the unabated contest between States and National Government, as well as in the conflict between growingly divergent economic interests.

The story of these momentous political and economic issues lies concealed beneath the surface technicalities governing the jurisdiction of the Federal Courts. This book is an attempt to uncover these technicalities, and to fit the meaning of the successive Judiciary Acts into the texture of American history.

Another phase of procedure may here be noted. Beyond the " judicial power " of the Supreme Court which Congress can grant or withhold are those methods and practices in the discharge of its business which are within the Court's own making. The bearing upon their judicial product of the methods and practices of appellate courts, generally, calls for intensive study. There is little doubt, however, that the manner of conducting its business is reflected in the quality of the Supreme Court's work, compared with that of state courts. The volume of litigation that is allowed to come before the Supreme Court is limited by the human limitations of nine judges' working-time. And in the disposition of cases — argument, deliberation, opinion-writing — the Supreme Court operates under the following conditions which are indispensable to a seasoned, collective judicial judgment:

1. Encouragement of oral argument; discouragement of oratory. The Socratic method is applied; questioning, in which the whole Court freely engage, clarifies the minds of the Justices as to the issues and guides the course of argument through real difficulties.

2. Consideration of every matter, be it an important case or merely a minor motion, by every Justice before conference, and action at fixed, frequent and long conferences of the Court. This assures responsible deliberation and decision by the whole Court.

3. Assignment by the Chief Justice of cases for opinion-writing to the different Justices after discussion and vote at conference. Flexible use is thus made of the talents and energies of the Justices, and the writer of the opinion enters upon the task not only with knowledge of the conclusions of his associates, but with the benefit of their suggestions made at the conference.

4. Distribution of draft opinions in print, for consideration of them by the individual Justices in advance of the conference and then their discussion at subsequent conferences. Ample time

is thus furnished for care in formulation of result, for recirculation of revised opinions, if necessary, and for writing dissents. This practice makes for team play, and encourages individual inquiry instead of subservient unanimity.

5. Discouragement of rehearings. Thoroughness in the process of adjudication excludes the debilitating habit of some state courts to be prodigal with rehearing.

6. To these specific procedural habits must be added the traditions of the Court, the public scrutiny which it enjoys, and the long tenure of the Justices. The inspiration that comes from a great past is reinforced by sensitiveness to healthy criticism. Continuity and experience in adjudication are secured through length of service, as distinguished from the method of selection, of judges.

These factors probably play a larger part in the work of the Supreme Court than elevation of station, high responsibility, and the greater ability of the Justices, drawn as they are from the whole country, as compared with state court judges.

The present publication has been made possible by the generous co-operation of the Editors of the Harvard Law Review, in whose pages this study first appeared in serial form. We are greatly indebted to Mr. Chief Justice Taft, former Attorney General Wickersham, and Francis Rawle, Esq., former President of the American Bar Association, for saving us from some errors.

Felix Frankfurter
James M. Landis

Harvard Law School.
August 1, 1927.

CONTENTS

THE BUSINESS OF

THE SUPREME COURT OF THE UNITED STATES

A STUDY IN THE FEDERAL JUDICIAL SYSTEM

INTRODUCTION

FEBRUARY 13, 1925, marks a new chapter in the history of the federal judiciary. The pressure upon Congress for relief from a volume of business that was seriously threatening the Supreme Court's capacity to deal adequately with its appropriate tasks culminated in the enactment of a law,[1] drafted by a Committee of the Justices (hence known as the " Judges Bill ") which drastically redistributes the powers of the courts in the federal system. These changes, which became effective on May 13, 1925, constitute the latest of a body of laws which, since the creation of the federal courts on September 24, 1789, have determined their structure and the content of their business.

Because it is one in a series, full understanding of the latest Judiciary Act depends upon its setting in the series. It is the temporary culmination of a continuous process of empiric legislation by which the federal judiciary has been adapted, more or less, to the changing needs of time and circumstances. The Act of February 13, 1925, will be no more permanent than was its most recent predecessor, the Circuit Courts of Appeals Act. If anything, changes in the future are likely to be more rapid than they have been in the past because the accelerated business pace of the country is reflected in the pace of the business of the

---

[1] Act of Feb. 13, 1925, 43 STAT. 936.

courts. A résumé of the Judiciary Acts of the past is therefore essential not merely to an effective appreciation of what the Judges Bill aimed at and what it is likely to accomplish, but also to help us better to understand old problems left unsolved and new ones that will emerge. We may thus be forehanded in grappling with the problems of practice that will inevitably arise under the new Act, and be prepared for the equally inevitable future legislation making new disposition of the federal judicial power.

The mechanism of law — what courts are to deal with which causes and subject to what conditions — cannot be dissociated from the ends that law subserves. So-called jurisdictional questions treated in isolation from the purposes of the legal system to which they relate become barren pedantry. After all, procedure is instrumental; it is the means of effectuating policy. Particularly true is this of the federal courts. The Judiciary Acts, the needs which urged their enactment, the compromises which they embodied, the consequences which they entailed, the changed conditions which in turn modified them, are the outcome of continuous interaction of traditional, political, social, and economic forces. In common with other courts, the federal courts are means for securing justice through law. But in addition and transcending this in importance, the legislation governing the structure and function of the federal judicial system is one means of providing the accommodations necessary to the operation of a federal government. The happy relation of States to Nation — constituting as it does our central political problem — is to no small extent dependent upon the wisdom with which the scope and limits of the federal courts are determined. What Ex-Justice Curtis said in 1864 holds true for our entire history; it is certainly true today.

" Let it be remembered, also, for just now we may be in some danger of forgetting it, that questions of jurisdiction were questions of power as between the United States and the several States." [2]

We venture another preliminary reminder. The federal judicial system is one. Each member of the hierarchy of its courts

---

[2] Curtis, Notice of the Death of Chief Justice Taney, Proceedings in Circuit Court of the United States for the First Circuit, 9.

has its specialized difficulties. But, in the large, the system articulates as a system. The volume and nature of appellate work depends largely upon the intake of the *nisi prius* courts. The facility with which business is dispatched by the Supreme Court and the quality of its output are only partly determined by the statutory limits of its jurisdiction, its rules of practice and the quality of its membership and of its bar. Its work is largely predetermined by the jurisdictional ambit of the lower courts.

It will be our purpose, therefore, to sketch rapidly the system of " inferior courts " which Congress from time to time established, the authority which was vested in them, and the scope of review over them and the state courts by which Congress conferred " appellate jurisdiction " upon the Supreme Court. This calls for an inquiry into lively issues of politics and policy, which were resolved by legislation bearing on its face no trace of the fierce controversies usually preceding enactment. Varying responses were made to the need for courts as a result of westward expansion. Conflicting views were pressed in devising measures for absorbing the increase in the volume of business due to the general growth of population and to industrial development. In every case controversies were adjusted by compromise rather than by exclusive acceptance of competing conceptions regarding American federalism.

A survey of the workings of the federal courts discloses three broad periods down to the recent enactment. The Civil War marks the close of one era; the establishment of intermediate courts of appeals in 1891 is the second dividing line. In each period the business coming before the Supreme Court is part of the story of the judicial business of the federal courts and will be treated as such. In addition, the litigation before the Supreme Court, the demands made upon the resources and time of that Court and the methods by which they have been met, raise considerations independent of the judicial system as a whole and will be dealt with independently. We shall then be ready to discuss the reviewing power now exercised by the Supreme Court, and the problems implicit in the nature of its business.

CHAPTER I
THE PERIOD PRIOR TO THE CIVIL WAR

I

The First Judiciary Act has been so smothered in praise that its real significance has become obscured. Mr. Charles Warren's recent investigation [3] into its history has happily helped to restore perspective for understanding. One need not resort to the heightened rhetoric of eloquence and characterize the Act of September 24, 1789, as " probably the most important and the most satisfactory act ever passed by Congress." [4] After all, Congress about the same time wrote into law Hamilton's proposals for dealing with the financial needs of the new nation, and not a few " important " and " satisfactory " measures have been passed since 1789. We pay Oliver Ellsworth [5] and his associates ample homage by calling their handiwork a great law. The Act has three claims to greatness. It devised a judicial organization which, with all its imperfections, served the country substantially unchanged for nearly a century. Through supervision over state courts conferred upon the Supreme Court by its famous Section Twenty-five, the Act created one of the most important nationalizing influences in the formative period of the Republic. But the transcendent achievement of the First Judiciary Act is the establishment for this country of the tradition of a system of inferior federal courts.

Familiarity with political institutions breeds indifference to their origin. Never having been without inferior federal courts, we assume their inevitability. To leave the enforcement of rights under the " Constitution and Laws of the United States " wholly to the courts of the states, with appellate review by the Supreme Court, *was* a possible alternative.[6] No other English-speaking

---

[3] See Charles Warren, " New Light on the History of the Federal Judiciary Act of 1789," 37 HARV. L. REV. 49.

[4] See Henry B. Brown, " The New Federal Judicial Code," 36 A.B.A. REP. 339, 345, quoted in Charles Warren, *supra,* 37 HARV. L. REV. at 52.

[5] The Senate committee that drafted the Judiciary Act consisted of Ellsworth of Connecticut, Paterson of New Jersey, Maclay of Pennsylvania, Strong of Massachusetts, Lee of Virginia, Bassett of Delaware, Few of Georgia, and Wingate of New Hampshire. See 1 ANN. CONG. 18 (Apr. 7, 1789).

[6] See Charles Warren, *supra,* 37 HARV. L. REV. at 65. In the Virginia Ratify-

union (not to deal with nations nurtured in legal institutions radically different from our own) has a scheme of federal courts.[7] Most significant of all, the Australian Commonwealth, although it followed the theory of the American Constitution and its details in many instances with " pedantic imitation," [8] has thus far departed from the American example by not availing itself of the power vested in its Parliament to create " other federal courts " [9] than the High Court provided for by its Constitution.

The American judicial experiment — for the Judiciary Act was avowedly experimental [10] — is thus unique in character.

---

ing Convention Pendleton suggested that Congress' " first experiment will be, to appoint the state courts to have the inferior federal jurisdiction." See 2 ELLIOT'S DEBATES, 380. On Mar. 2, 1793, a resolution was introduced in the Senate to amend Article III of the Constitution so as to enable Congress to vest the judicial power of the United States " in such of the State courts as it shall deem fit." See Charles Warren, " Federal Criminal Laws and the State Courts," 38 HARV. L. REV. 545, 550, note 10. Maclay first was of the opinion that not only must the entire grant of the judicial power in the Constitution be vested in a federal judiciary, but also that the very grant excluded state courts from assuming jurisdiction over such subject-matter. See MACLAY, SKETCHES OF DEBATE IN THE SENATE OF THE UNITED STATES, 87.

[7] The British North America Act vests in the Canadian Parliament " the establishment of any additional Courts for the better Administration of the Laws of Canada," besides providing for the organization of a General Court of Appeal for Canada. See 30 & 31 VICT. c. 3, § 101 (1867). It was not until 1875 that a Supreme Court with criminal and civil appellate jurisdiction throughout the Dominion was created. See 38 VICT. (Can.) c. 11 (1875). The Union of South Africa Act provides for a Supreme Court of South Africa, and makes the several supreme and district courts of the Provinces provincial and local divisions of the Supreme Court. See 9 EDW. VII, c. 9, §§ 95, 98 (1909). The Australia Constitution Act provides that " the judicial power of the Commonwealth shall be vested in a Federal Supreme Court, to be called the High Court of Australia, and in such other federal courts as the Parliament creates, and in such other courts as it invests with federal jurisdiction." See 63 & 64 VICT. c. 12, § 71 (1900). The High Court of Australia was organized under the Judiciary Act of 1903. See 1903 COMMONWEALTH ACTS, No. 6. Inferior courts have not been added to the federal system.

[8] See Higgins, J., in Australasian Temperance and General Mutual Life Assurance Society, Ltd. *v.* Howe, 31 C.L.R. 290, 330 (1922). See also HIGGINS, THE AUSTRALIAN COMMONWEALTH BILL, Preface.

[9] See note 7, *supra.*

[10] While the House was debating the Judiciary Act, Madison, writing to Judge Pendleton on Sept. 14, 1789, adverts to defects of the pending measure and continues: " The most I hope for is, that some offensive violations of Southern jurisprudence may be corrected, and that the system may speedily undergo a reconsideration, under the auspices of the judges, who alone will be able, perhaps,

Like the Constitution itself, it was a response to the practical problems and controversies of our early history. In such an intensified form, at least, they were never present in the British federations when, from time to time, they came to construct their judicial systems.[11] Sectionalism is primarily the explanation of the most important solutions and evasions of the dominant problems of American federalism.[11a] Further, the experience under the Articles of Confederation dominated the work of the Constitutional Convention at Philadelphia. The system which was established and the institutions which were derived from the powers granted by the Constitution were methods of dealing with concrete difficulties and fears revealed during the Confederacy. Such considerations and such experience explain the constitutional power to " constitute tribunals inferior to the Supreme Court " and the prompt exercise of this power by the First Congress. All this is usually ascribed to the nationalist philosophy of the Federalist party and the adherence by the opposition to doctrines of local self-government. But it is important to emphasize that the founders did not divide into two schools of

---

to set it to rights." See 3 RIVES, WORKS OF JAMES MADISON, 49–50. On Aug. 2, 1797, Col. Davie wrote to Justice Iredell: " I sincerely hope something will be done at the next session with the Judiciary Act; *it is so defective in point of arrangement, and so obscurely drawn, that, in my opinion, it would disgrace the composition of the meanest legislature of the States.*" 2 McREE, LIFE OF IREDELL, 335. Breckenridge of Kentucky during the debates on the repeal of the Act of 1801 voiced the same sentiment when he expressed the view that the Act of 1789 and all the legislation that followed upon it were but experimental and that these experiments should not be regarded as unalterable. See 11 ANN. CONG. 94 (Jan. 14, 1801).

[11] See, *e.g.*, Higgins, J., in Australasian Temperance and General Mutual Assurance Society, Ltd. *v.* Howe, *supra,* at 330: " If we could consider what is desirable . . . we might think that the jurisdiction given in matters ' between residents of different States ' is a piece of pedantic imitation of the Constitution of the United States, and absurd in the circumstances of Australia, with its State Courts of high character and impartiality." See also Starke, J., at 339: " As a matter of history, this fear [of local influence prejudicial to non-residents seeking redress in the local courts] little grounded in point of fact in Australia, led to the passing of the provision in the Australian Constitution."

[11a] " We must frankly face the fact that in this vast and heterogeneous nation, this sister of all Europe, regional geography is a fundamental fact; that the American peace has been achieved by restraining sectional selfishness and assertiveness and by coming to agreements rather than to reciprocal denunciation or to blows." Frederick J. Turner, " The Significance of the Section in American History," 8 WIS. MAG. HIST. 255, 275. See also TURNER, ESSAYS ON THE WEST, *passim.*

abstract political philosophy. The generalized forms in which their political opinions were expressed were merely a spacious and more authoritative way of furthering the very concrete aims pursued by our early statesmen.

Of all this the First Judiciary Act is a striking illustration. Trade requires dependable laws and courts. Maritime commerce was then the jugular vein of the Thirteen States.[12] The need for a body of law applicable throughout the nation was recognized by every shade of opinion in the Constitutional Convention.[13] From this recognition it was an easy step to entrust the development of such law to a distinctive system of courts, administering the same doctrines, following the same procedure, and subject to the same nationalist influences. The desirability of independent lower federal courts for this limited class of cases

[12] Nine-tenths of the population was engaged in agriculture, and this concentration of interests made the country dependent on foreign markets for manufactured articles. See BASSETT, THE FEDERALIST SYSTEM, 190. See also ADAMS, HISTORY OF THE UNITED STATES, 26; Dawes in the Massachusetts Convention, 1 ELLIOT'S DEBATES, 74–76.

[13] See, e.g., Gorham in the Constitutional Convention: " There are in the States already Federal Courts, with jurisdiction for trial of piracies &c. committed on the seas. No complaints have been made by the States or the courts of the States." See 2 FARRAND, RECORDS OF THE FEDERAL CONVENTION, 46. Randolph in the Virginia Ratifying Convention: " Cases of admiralty and maritime jurisdiction cannot with propriety be vested in particular state courts. As our national tranquility and reputation, and intercourse with foreign nations, may be affected by admiralty decisions, as they ought therefore to be uniform, and as there can be no uniformity if there be thirteen distinct independent jurisdictions, this jurisdiction ought to be in the federal judiciary." See 2 ELLIOT'S DEBATES, 418. It will be remembered that Edmund Randolph had objected to the lack of limitation or definition of the judicial power. See 2 FARRAND, op. cit., 564; WARREN, THE SUPREME COURT IN UNITED STATES HISTORY, 8. Randolph's earlier attitude seems, however, to have been in favor of as broad a basis of federal jurisdiction as the Constitution eventually adopted. See the Ninth Resolution offered to the Philadelphia Convention on May 29, 1787, 4 ELLIOT'S DEBATES, 41. James Wilson in the Constitutional Convention was of the opinion that " the admiralty jurisdiction ought to be given wholly to the National Government, as it related to cases not within the jurisdiction of particular States, and to a scene in which controversies with foreigners would be most likely to happen." See 1 FARRAND, op. cit., 124. See also Hamilton's summary: " The most bigoted idolizers of State authority have not thus far shown a disposition to deny the national judiciary the cognizance of maritime causes. These so generally depend on the laws of nations, and so commonly affect the rights of foreigners, that they fall within the considerations which are relative to the public peace. The most important part of them are, by the present Confederation, submitted to federal jurisdiction." THE FEDERALIST, Lodge ed., 497–498.

found general concurrence or, at least, did not encounter vigorous opposition even from the Anti-Federalists.[14]

A totally different but powerful influence behind the demand for federal courts was due to the friction between individual states which came to the surface after the danger of the common enemy had disappeared. In one aspect it gave rise to lively suspicions and hostilities by the citizens of one state towards those of another as well as towards aliens.[15] This fear of parochial

---

[14] Thus, Richard Henry Lee, who was hostile to the Judiciary Bill drafted by his Committee, upon its introduction in the Senate moved to restrict the jurisdiction of the federal courts to maritime cases. See MACLAY, JOURNAL, 85. Tucker of South Carolina in the House moved an amendment restricting the power of Congress to appoint inferior courts to courts of admiralty. See 1 ANN. CONG. 762, 778 (Aug. 18 and 22, 1789). The 14th Amendment proposed by the Virginia Ratifying Convention limited the power of Congress in creating inferior federal courts to Courts of Admiralty. See 2 ELLIOT'S DEBATES, 485. This was copied by the North Carolina Convention. See 3 ELLIOT'S DEBATES, 214. The New York Convention proposed an amendment to limit the power of Congress to establish inferior courts with original jurisdiction to cases of admiralty and maritime jurisdiction and for the trial of piracies and felonies committed on the high seas. See 1 ELLIOT'S DEBATES, 353. See also AMES, AMENDMENTS TO THE CONSTITUTION, 1896 AM. HIST. ASSN. REP. 153.

[15] See, *e.g.*, Madison in the Virginia Convention: "It may happen that a strong prejudice may arise in some states, against the citizens of others, who may have claims against them. We know what tardy, and even defective administration of justice, has happened in some states." See 2 ELLIOT'S DEBATES, 391. Davie in the North Carolina Convention: "The security of impartiality is the principal reason for giving up the ultimate decision of controversies between citizens of different states. . . . The tedious delays of judicial proceedings at present in some states, are ruinous to creditors. In Virginia many suits are twenty or thirty years spun out by legal ingenuity, and the defective construction of their judiciary. A citizen of Massachusetts or this country might be ruined before he could recover a debt in that state. It is necessary therefore in order to obtain justice, that we recur to the judiciary of the United States, where justice must be equally administered, and where a debt may be recovered from the citizen of one state as soon as from the citizen of another." See 3 ELLIOT'S DEBATES, 144. The opponents hotly contested the wisdom of this clause, arguing as they did that it cast discredit upon the State judiciaries: "Cannot we trust the state courts with disputes between a Frenchman, or an Englishman, and a citizen; or with disputes between two Frenchmen? This is disgraceful: it will annihilate your state judiciary: it will prostrate your legislature." Mason in the Virginia Convention, 2 ELLIOT'S DEBATES, 387. The fear of prejudicial action by state courts is strikingly indicated by Section 11 of the First Judiciary Act. It gave the circuit courts jurisdiction of any civil suit where "an alien is a party." See 1 STAT. 73, 78. This grant, broader than that of the Constitution, was later confined by judicial interpretation to require that the other party be a United States citizen. Hodgson *v.* Burbank, 5 Cranch (U. S.) 303 (1809).

prejudice, dealing unjustly with litigants from other states and foreign countries, undermined the sense of security necessary for commercial intercourse. Here was a situation which greatly concerned men of business. But mercantile and creditor classes were not crudely seeking to feather their own nests; their devotion to country was enlisted in an effort to fashion instruments of government adequate to secure and promote those individual rights for which independence had been won.[16] One remedy was a system of national courts. The whole matter was put with candor and authority in the Pennsylvania debates on the Constitution by James Wilson:

" But when we consider the matter a little further, is it not necessary, if we mean to restore either public or private credit, that foreigners as well as ourselves, have a just and impartial tribunal to which they may resort? I would ask how a merchant must feel to have his property lay at the mercy of the laws of Rhode Island? I ask further, how will a creditor feel who has his debts at the mercy of tender laws in other states? It is true, that under this constitution, these particular iniquities may be restrained in future; but sir, there are other ways of avoiding payment of debts. There have been instalment acts, and other acts of a similar effect. Such things, sir, destroy the very sources of credit.

" Is it not an important object to extend our manufactures and our commerce? This cannot be done unless a proper security is provided for the regular discharge of contracts. This security cannot be obtained, unless we give the power of deciding upon those contracts to the general governments [*sic*]." [17]

But the comprehensive scope of action involved in this proposal — the vast field of litigation and of influence which the federal courts would draw unto themselves in the diversity of citizenship cases — encountered the opposition of those forces in the various states which, in pursuit of their interests as they saw them, favored restraint upon the commercial classes, both domestic and foreign. Here, then, was another phase of the central fight waged by those who wanted vigorous and extensive national

---

[16] See E. S. Corwin, " The Progress of Constitutional Theory Between the Declaration of Independence and the Meeting of the Philadelphia Convention," 30 AM. HIST. REV. 511.

[17] See 3 ELLIOT'S DEBATES, 282.

authority, not because of any *a priori* notions of political science but as a practical remedy for the ineffectiveness of the Confederacy and the disintegrating tendencies of state governments.[18] Finding the mind of Congress prepared for the creation of federal courts, at least for maritime purposes, it was not too difficult for Ellsworth and his nationalist collaborators to achieve enlargement for the jurisdiction of courts, the need for whose existence was recognized.[19]

The fiscal necessities of the Union constituted one of the powerful factors for the inclusion in the Constitution of the authority to establish inferior federal courts.[20] When the Constitution enabled the central government to secure ways and means for its subsistence by going directly against the individual citizen instead of depending on the largess of the states, it was inevitable that power should be written into the Constitution whereby the Federal Government could fashion its own judicial machinery for enforcing its claims and safeguarding its agents against the obstructions and prejudices of local authorities.[21]   Reliance on

---

[18] See E. S. Corwin, *supra*, 30 AM. HIST. REV. at 521.

[19] See Charles Warren, *supra*, 37 HARV. L. REV. at 53.

[20] The Ninth Resolution proposed by Edmund Randolph to the Constitutional Convention included a clause extending the jurisdiction of the inferior federal tribunals to cases " which respect the collection of the national revenue." See 4 ELLIOT'S DEBATES, 42. Such a resolution was moved by Madison and Randolph and agreed to by the Convention on June 13, 1787. See 1 FARRAND, RECORDS OF THE FEDERAL CONVENTION, 223. A similar resolution was introduced by Paterson of New Jersey. See 1 FARRAND, *op. cit.*, 244. Hamilton's proposition to the Federal Convention contained a similar proposal for the extension of the federal judicial power to " all causes in which the revenues of the General Government . . . are concerned." See 1 HAMILTON, WORKS, Lodge ed., 333. In the discussion upon the Act of 1801 in the House it was urged that " it became the Government of the United States to organize the Judiciary in such a way as to insure an obedience to its laws, and to insure the faithful collection of revenue; that this last object could only be attained by the institution of Federal courts . . ." 10 ANN. CONG. 878 (Jan. 5, 1800).

[21] See, *e.g.*, Luther Martin before the Maryland House of Representatives on Nov. 29, 1787: " They may lay direct Taxes by assessment, Poll Tax, Stamps, Duties on Commerce, and excise everything else — all this is to be collected under the direction of their own Officers . . . and should any individual dare to dispute the conduct of an Excise Man, ransacking his Cellars, he may be hoisted into the Federal Court from Georgia to vindicate his just rights, or to be punished for his impertinence. In vain was it urged that the State Courts ought to be competent to the decision of such cases: The advocates of this System thought State Judges would be under State influence and therefore not sufficiently independent." See 3 FARRAND, RECORDS OF THE FEDERAL CONVENTION, 156.

its own courts for the assertion of the federal authority was treated as a correlative to the substantive powers of government given to the new United States. This field of jurisdiction, however, was not explicitly occupied until a little later.[22] The resistance to a powerful judiciary was too formidable to secure at the outset as broad a base of authority as the Federalists desired. To press for too much might have endangered what was for them an essential minimum.

Thus, the most significant resultant of the conflicting forces which produced the Act of 1789 was a system of federal courts distributed throughout the nation. Congress, as is well known, divided the country into thirteen districts.[23] Rhode Island and North Carolina were still not members of the Union. For all the other states a United States district court was established, coterminous with the boundaries of each state, save that Massachusetts and Virginia were divided into two districts.[24] This restriction of district courts to respective state lines has been followed ever since, with one negligible exception.[25] A second tier of courts was provided for by dividing the country into three circuits in each of which a court, consisting of two Supreme Court Justices and one of the district judges of the circuit, was to sit twice a year in the various districts comprising the circuit.[26] This gave

---

[22] See Act of Feb. 4, 1815, § 8, 3 STAT. 195, 198. This section provided for the removal of suits from the state courts in cases against federal, military, customs, and other civil officers acting under the authority of the Act, which provided for the collection of customs duties. It was to continue in force only for the period of the War. The Act of Mar. 3, 1815, § 6, 3 STAT. 231, 233, made similar provision for the removal of suits against customs officials for one year. The Act of Mar. 3, 1817, § 2, 3 STAT. 396, extended for four years the provisions of the above, restricting, however, the power to remove before final judgment in state courts. The Act of Mar. 2, 1833, § 3, 4 STAT. 632, 633, authorized removal of all suits against officers of the United States on account of any acts done by them under the revenue laws. This section is part of the "Force Bill" passed in reply to South Carolina's threats of nullification.

[23] Act of Sept. 24, 1789, § 2, 1 STAT. 73.

[24] *Ibid.*, § 3.

[25] By the Act of Feb. 13, 1801, § 21, 2 STAT. 89, 96, a district was created out of territory embracing the District of Columbia and certain portions of the states of Maryland and Virginia. This Act was repealed on Mar. 8, 1802. See 2 STAT. 132. The bill introduced by Harper of South Carolina on Mar. 11, 1800, provided for a similar disregard of state lines in the establishment of federal judicial districts. See note 66, *infra*.

[26] See Act of Sept. 24, 1789, § 4, 1 STAT. 73, 74.

us our system of circuit courts which, with successive changes, persisted till January 1, 1912.[27] A Supreme Court, with a Chief Justice and five associates, headed the system.[28]

The content of jurisdiction conferred on the new judiciary was very limited in comparison with what it now exercises. The substance of the business of the lower courts concerned admiralty matters [29] and the miscellaneous litigation depending upon the citizenship of litigants.[30] They also had jurisdiction over penalties and forfeitures under the laws of the United States,[31] together with a small number of criminal cases,[32] which was still more curtailed after the Supreme Court denied them jurisdiction over common-law offenses.[33] Broadly speaking, to the circuit courts were allotted cases resting on diversity of citizenship, while the district courts became the admiralty courts for the country. A limited appellate jurisdiction over the district courts was also conferred upon the circuit courts.[34] The volume of this appellate business compared with their original jurisdiction is not disclosed by available data.[35] It could not have been very con-

---

[27] See Act of Mar. 3, 1911, § 301, 36 STAT. 1087, 1169.

[28] See Act of Sept. 24, 1789, § 1, 1 STAT. 73.

[29] *Ibid.*, § 9.

[30] *Ibid.*, § 11.

[31] *Ibid.*, § 9.

[32] *Ibid.*, §§ 9, 11.

[33] United States *v.* Hudson, 7 Cranch (U. S.) 32 (1812); United States *v.* Coolidge, 1 Wheat. (U. S.) 415 (1816).

[34] See Act of Sept. 24, 1789, §§ 21, 22, 1 STAT. 73, 83.

[35] This, of course, cannot be accurately estimated until the dockets of the federal district courts are studied and the results published. The figures submitted by Jefferson to Congress on Feb. 26, 1802, are the only available data, so far as we know, as to the total business of the circuit courts. See 1 AM. STATE PAPERS, Misc., 319. The tabulation includes the cases docketed term by term in the circuit courts and those other courts exercising circuit jurisdiction from their establishment to the close of 1801. The totals follow:

Court	Causes Instituted	Causes " Depending "
New Hampshire	114	7
Rhode Island	275	10
Massachusetts	323	41
Maine	9	3
Connecticut	354	38
Vermont	278	64
New York and Albany	106	0
New Jersey	104	14
Pennsylvania	1061	174

siderable if later figures are a dependable guide to the earlier period.[36] The district and circuit courts were in practice two *nisi prius* courts dealing with different items of litigation. To the Supreme Court Congress gave appellate jurisdiction over all classes of cases which constitutionally could be reviewed, in addition to the controversies arising under the " original jurisdiction" conferred by the Constitution itself.[37] This appellate jurisdiction was fed by two streams, one running from the lower federal courts, the other from the state courts. We find not a trace at this early day of a suggestion for an appellate tribunal intermediate between the circuit courts and the Supreme Court. The volume of appellate business did not yet call for relief of the Supreme Court by limiting its appellate jurisdiction; and not till later did the circuit courts arouse hostility and fear because the vast power which they exercised was largely uncontrolled. These are problems which did not have to be met because they had not yet arisen. Legislation concerning judicial organization throughout our history has been a very empiric response to very definite needs.

Delaware	163	16
Maryland	279	69
Kentucky	870	246
Virginia	2162	331
North Carolina	629	134
South Carolina	495	261
Georgia	897	147
Eastern and Western Tennessee	239	74

Ohio and the western districts of Virginia and Pennsylvania were reported as unorganized.

TOTALS	8358	1629

These totals are a correction of an earlier memorandum submitted by Jefferson. See note 79, *infra*.

[36] In 1820 a Senate Report gives a list of causes pending in the various circuit and district courts on October 1, 1819. See SEN. DOC. No. 134, 16th Cong., 1st Sess., Ser. No. 27. The total causes pending in the district courts were 1167, and in the circuit courts 2176, effectively illustrating the ratio between the original and the appellate business of the circuit courts. An interesting comparison in the growth of the circuit court business is given by figures for the May and October terms of 1837 of suits on the trial docket of the circuit courts and district courts exercising circuit court jurisdiction. The figure in this instance is 5492. No returns are given for Connecticut, Delaware, Ohio, Michigan, and Indiana, and the District Court for the Northern District of Alabama failed to have a term for that year. See SEN. DOC. No. 50, 25th Cong., 3rd Sess., Ser. No. 339.

[37] See Act of Sept. 24, 1789, §§ 13, 25, 1 STAT. 73, 80, 85.

The system thus established hardly became operative before it was subjected to criticism. The controversy which began immediately and continued till 1869 [38] centered round the circuit system. The core of the problem lay in the fact that three tiers of courts were operated by two sets of judges. The whole system pivoted on circuit riding by the Justices. This involved the very serious question of the capacity of the Justices effectively to discharge their duties both at Washington and on circuit; it no less seriously concerned the adaptability of such a system to the territorial expansion of the country. More territory implied more circuits. More circuits meant either more circuit riding for the Justices or more Justices for circuit riding.

2

The House of Representatives ordered an inquiry into the workings of the new federal judicial system immediately after it had been set up. To the Attorney General were referred " such Matters relative to the Administration of justice under the Authority of the United States, as may require to be remedied, and such Provisions in the respective cases, as he should deem advisable." [39] The task fell to Edmund Randolph, Washington's Attorney General. He made his report on December 27, 1790.[40] The most serious problem submitted in his " enumeration of what I [Ran-

---

[38] See Act of Apr. 10, 1869, 16 STAT. 44.

[39] See House Resolution of Aug. 5, 1790, HOUSE JOURNAL, 289.

[40] This Report was printed as a separate document. It is also contained in I AM. STATE PAPERS, MISC., 21. The Report was received by the House on Dec. 31, 1790. HOUSE JOURNAL, 346. On November 3, 1791, the House resolved to take up the consideration of the Report in a Committee of the Whole. 3 ANN. CONG. 154. On November 4, 1791, it was referred to a special committee for consideration. 3 ANN. CONG. 156. On November 9, 1791, a resolution to the effect that the Attorney General be directed to report " such further information as he may be in possession of, relative to the operation of the Judicial System," was agreed to. 3 ANN. CONG. 166. This resolution was discharged on November 30, 1791, when the Speaker laid before the House a letter from the Attorney General. HOUSE JOURNAL, 465. The nature of this letter is not disclosed. On the same day the committee to whom the Report had been referred for consideration was discharged and another committee was appointed. 3 ANN. CONG. 216. On January 6, 1792, Ames and Sturges were added to this committee. HOUSE JOURNAL, 489. See also, CONWAY, EDMUND RANDOLPH, 143.

dolph] conceived to be the principal defects,"[41] is involved in the circuit duties of the Justices. The arguments, *pro* and *con*, which he summarized constitute the stuff of a controversy lasting eighty years. They have never been stated more impressively nor more pithily than in Randolph's report.

Randolph argued that the work of the Supreme Court, if discharged to the full measure of its requirements, demands the entire energy and talent of its judges:

" Those who pronounce the law of the land without appeal, ought to be pre-eminent in most endowments of the mind. Survey the functions of a judge of the supreme court. He must be a master of the common law in all its divisions, a chancellor, a civilian, a federal jurist, and skilled in the laws of each state. To expect that in future times this assemblage of talents will be ready, without farther study, for the national service, is to confide too largely in the public fortune. Most vacancies on the bench will be supplied by professional men, who perhaps have been too much animated by the contentions of the bar, deliberately to explore this extensive range of science. In a great measure then, the supreme judges will form themselves after their nomination. But what leisure remains from their itinerant dispensation of justice? Sum up all the fragments of their time, hold their fatigue at naught, and let them bid adieu to all domestic concerns, still the average term of a life, already advanced, will be too short for any important proficiency."[42]

Randolph heeded little the contention that circuit riding contributed to the equipment of the members of the Supreme Court by immersing them in the laws of the various states, which made for more vivid understanding of state legislation coming before the Supreme Court. To this day, the difficulties presented by the variety of state laws, embodying, as they frequently do, far-reaching state policies not revealed by a mere reading of session laws, are among the most subtle problems of Supreme Court adjudication.[43] The argument that circuit riding assured inti-

---

[41] Rep. Atty. Gen. i.

[42] *Ibid.*, 7–8.

[43] The effect that familiarity with local problems has upon decisions of the Supreme Court can, of course, only be guessed at. An interesting instance is afforded by United States *v.* Grimaud, 220 U. S. 506 (1911), in the Court. The case involved the validity of a delegation of legislative power to the Secretary of Agricul-

macy between the Supreme Court and the bar of the country and
thus made for a cohesive administration of justice Randolph
passed over in silence — an argument urged with increasing vigor
as the country moved westward and left Washington less and
less at the center.[44]   All these considerations in support of the
advantage of circuit work to the Supreme Court, were cavalierly

---

ture in permitting him to establish rules for the regulation of the public forests.
The statute had been held invalid by the District Court. 170 Fed. 205 (S. D. Cal.,
1909). The case was affirmed by a divided Court on appeal. 216 U. S. 614 (1910).
Upon reargument the former decision was reversed without a dissenting vote. 220
U. S. 506 (1911). Between the dates of the two decisions it is to be noted that Mr.
Justice Van Devanter of Wyoming became a member of the Court. One can only
surmise that his unusual familiarity with the actual problems involved in the administration of the public domain had its effect upon the later decision. Every
body of laws has undisclosed assumptions and emphases not spelled out in words
but familiar to those living under it. What the Supreme Court has said in cases
arising under a system founded on Spanish law is, in varying degree, applicable to
the views of outsiders on the legislation of the individual states. See, *e.g.,* Holmes,
J.: " This Court has stated many times the deference due to the understanding of
the local courts upon matters of purely local concern. . . . This is especially true
in dealing with the decisions of a Court inheriting and brought up in a different
system from that which prevails here. When we contemplate such a system from
the outside it seems like a wall of stone, every part even with all the others, except
so far as our own local education may lead us to see subordinations to which we are
accustomed. But to one brought up within it, varying emphasis, tacit assumptions,
unwritten practices, a thousand influences gained only from life, may give to the
different parts wholly new values that logic and grammar never could have got
from the books." Diaz *v.* Gonzales, 261 U. S. 102, 105–106 (1923). How unfortunate unfamiliarity with local traditions can be is illustrated by the decision
of the Supreme Court in Panama R. R. Co. *v.* Rock, 266 U. S. 209 (1924), criti-
cized in 38 HARV. L. REV. 499. See also Porter in the House of Representatives,
23rd Cong., 2nd Sess., Feb. 23, 1835, 1 CONG. GLOBE, 280.

[44] See, *e.g.,* Buchanan in the Senate on April 7, 1826: " The importance of a
full knowledge of the local law is greater in the Western States, than in the rest
of the Union. . . . By compelling the Judges of the Supreme Court to hold the
Circuits, the knowledge they have acquired of the local laws will be retained and
improved, and they will thus be enabled, not only the better to arrive at correct
results themselves, but to aid their brethren of the Court who belong to different
Circuits, and are, of course, deprived of an opportunity to acquire such information, except in that manner." 2 CONG. DEB. 416. In 1866 the editor of the
American Law Review repeats the same sentiments: " The bill for re-organizing
the Circuit Courts, we are rejoiced to say, did not pass. . . . The great objection
to it is, that it relieves the supreme judges of all *nisi prius* duties. . . . It [this
duty] must keep each judge's knowledge of practice and evidence much more
fresh and serviceable than it could ever be, were he never to preside at a jury
trial. . . . The consequent mingling and association with the bar all over the
circuit keeps up an acquaintance and understanding between it and the bench

disposed of by Gouverneur Morris some time after Randolph's report:

" I am not quite convinced that riding rapidly from one end of this country to another is the best way to study law. I am inclined to believe that knowledge may be more conveniently acquired in the closet than in the high road." [45]

To the extent that the federal system mingled appellate and *nisi prius* work for the same judges it followed, of course, English judicature.[46] Randolph next attacked evils which to him were inherent in the conflicting functions of such a system:

" The detaching of the judges to different circuits, defeats the benefit of an unprejudiced consultation. The delivery of a solemn opinion in court, commits them; and should a judgment rendered by two, be erroneous, will they meet their four brethren unbiassed? May not human nature, thus trammelled, struggle too long against conviction? And how few would erect a monument to their candor, at the expense of their reputation for firmness and discernment?

---

which we should be sorry to see at all lessened." 1 AM. L. REV. 207. The same demand for association between the bench and bar is voiced again as late as 1922. See Henry C. Clark, " Circuit Riding as a National Asset," 8 A. B. A. JOUR. 772.

[45] In the Senate on January 14, 1802, 11 ANN. CONG. 82. Stanley in the House on February 18, 1802, speaks to the same effect: " Nine-tenths of the decisions of our State courts and Federal courts turn on questions of common law; yet has it ever been suggested that an American judge was incompetent to decide on common law questions, because he had not studied in England? " 11 ANN. CONG. 573.

[46] Randolph urged an essential difference between the situations confronting the two systems, concluding that the assize scheme " cannot safely be the ground-work of our reasoning on the judiciary of the United States," REPORT, 8–9. Webster in the House on January 4, 1826, recognizes that the scheme " seems to have been borrowed from the English Courts of Assize and *Nisi Prius*," but he adds: " It was founded on a false analogy. . . . The English Judges at *Nisi Prius*, so far as civil causes are concerned, have nothing to do but try questions of fact by the aid of a jury, on issues or pleadings already settled in the Court from which the record proceeds. . . . Here suits are brought, proceeded with, through all their stages, tried, and finally determined. . . . The Courts, indeed, were called Circuit Courts; which seemed to imply an itinerant character; but, in truth, they resembled much more, in their power and jurisdiction, the English Courts sitting in bench, than the Assizes, to which they appear to have been likened." 2 CONG. DEB. 873–874. It is of interest to note that many of the criticisms levelled at this time against the American judicial organization, were urged against the English circuit system in 1863. See Frederick Lawrence, " The Circuit System: Its Influence on the Administration of Justice and on the Interests of the Bar," 2 JUR. SOC. P. 735.

" Jealousy among the members of a court is always an evil; and its malignity would be double, should it creep into the supreme court, obscure the discovery of right, and weaken that respect which the public welfare seeks for their decrees. But this cannot be affirmed to be beyond the compass of events to men agitated by the constant scanning of the judicial conduct of each other.

" If this should not happen, there is fresh danger on the other side; lest they should be restrained by delicacy and mutual tenderness, from probing without scruple, what had been done in the circuit courts." [47]

But Randolph exhausted neither the objections to the newly established judiciary nor did he do full justice to its merits. It was strongly urged that the personnel of the circuit courts made them ill-balanced tribunals.[48] The quality of the new district judges aroused wide scepticism.[49] The superiority and prestige

---

[47] REPORT, 8. See also Bayard in the House on February 19, 1802: " It is possible that a judge of the Supreme Court would not be influenced by the *esprit de corps,* that he would neither be gratified by the affirmance, nor mortified by the reversal of his opinions; but this, sir, is estimating the strength and purity of human nature upon a possible, but not on its ordinary sçale." 11 ANN. CONG. 618.

[48] See, *e.g.,* Bayard in the House on February 19, 1802: " I have ever considered it, also, as a defect in this court, that it was composed of judges of the highest and lowest grades. This, sir, was an unnatural association; the members of the court stood on ground too unequal to allow the firm assertion of his opinion to the district judge. . . . In the district court he was everything, in the circuit court he was nothing. Sometimes he was obliged to leave his seat, while his associate reviewed the judgment which he had given in the court below. . . . No doubt in some instances the district judge was an efficient member of this court, but this never arose from the nature of the system but from the personal character of the man." 11 ANN. CONG. 621–622. See also Griswold on February 25, 1802: " Experience had confirmed the opinion, which has been long entertained, that such an association was unnatural, and whilst it destroyed the dignity of the district judge, necessarily lessened the respectability of the court itself." 11 ANN. CONG. 769.

[49] Mason, in a letter to Webster of December 29, 1823, writes intimately about the quality of the district judges: " For the business that ought to be done in the national courts, the present establishment does not afford a sufficient number of judges. I make no account of the district judges. When brought to act in matters of serious importance, as members of the circuit court, none of them, as far as I know, have been, or are of any value. Out of their own district courts they do nothing." HILLARD, MEMOIR OF JEREMIAH MASON, 279. Talbot in the Senate on April 26, 1824, reverts to the same subject: " The salaries that had been given to them [the district judges] had not always brought men of the first legal talents into the office of district judge; and he feared that, in many instances, they would not be competent to the performance of the duties." 41 ANN. CONG. 575–576.

of the Justices, so ran the argument, would overawe their associate district judges. On the other hand, their professional
equipment for circuit business was questioned because of the
constant shifting of the Justices from circuit to circuit. An
itinerant bench was called upon to administer local law from
New Hampshire to Georgia. Local law was in great danger of
being expounded by Justices unfamiliar with local needs and
local policies and by rotating interpreters.[50] The minimum
requirements of uniformity and stability were thus greatly
jeopardized.

The circuit system had its vigorous defenders. The strongest
claim, perhaps, was founded on the by-products of these federal
courts as educative agencies. They served as symbols of the new
nation, which would evoke and foster the attachments of the
people to the still tenuous Union. This was a claim which
Randolph could not ignore:

" It may be urged that it will tend to impress the citizens of the
United States favorably towards the general government, should the
most distinguished judges visit every state." [51]

But he was unpersuaded:

" Will not the judges of the circuit courts be adequate to their
stations?

" The supreme judges themselves who ride the circuits, will (if
indeed such a circumstance can be of much avail) be soon graduated
in the public mind, in relation to the circuits; will soon be considered
as circuit judges, and will not be often appreciated as supreme judges.
When a discomfited party looks up to the highest tribunal for redress,

---

[50] See, *e.g.*, Bayard in the House on February 19, 1802: "It was supposed
that the presiding judges of the circuit courts, proceeding from the same body,
would tend to identify the principles and rules of decision in the several districts.
In practice, a contrary effect has been discovered to be produced by the peculiar
organization of these courts. In practice we have found not only a want of
uniformity of rule between the different districts, but no uniformity of rule in
the same district. No doubt there was uniformity in the decisions of the same
judge; but as the same judge seldom sat twice successively in the same district,
and sometimes not till after an interval of two or three years, his opinions were
forgotten or reversed before he returned. . . . The law ceased to be a science.
To advise your client it was less important to be skilled in the books than to be
acquainted with the character of the judge who was to preside." 11 ANN. CONG.
619, 621.   [51] REPORT, 8.

he is told by the report of the world that in it every quality is centered necessary to justice. But how would his sanguine hopes be frustrated, if among six judges, two are most probably to repeat their former suffrages, or to vindicate them with strenuous ability; or if to avoid this, the wisdom of a third of the number must be laid aside? " [52]

In fact, the Justices carried out the hopes that were entertained for them as inculcators of national patriotism.[53] They utilized charges to the grand juries as opportunities for popular education. Jay, Cushing, Wilson, Iredell, all indulged in the practice.[54] These " elegant " and " eloquent " speeches received wide publicity. Having a Federalist flavor with more or less pungency, they promptly aroused political opposition. That the Circuit Justices helped to further the Federalist cause there can hardly be doubt. That they helped to consolidate the opposition is no less clear.[55] Criticism against the judiciary was accumulating

---

[52] *Ibid.*

[53] See 1 WARREN, THE SUPREME COURT IN UNITED STATES HISTORY, 59–61.

[54] See 1 WARREN, *op. cit.*, 59, note; BROWN, LIFE OF OLIVER ELLSWORTH, 245. See Charge to Richmond Grand Jury, 3 CORRESPONDENCE AND PAPERS OF JOHN JAY, 478; Charge to Grand Juries of the Eastern Circuit, 3 *ibid.*, 387, to which a reply from the Grand Jury is appended: " The very Excellent Charge given to the Grand Jury of this District by his Honor the Chief Judge of the Federal Court, demands our thanks and particular attention; and that it may be more influential and impress the mind of our fellow citizens at large beg leave to ask a Copy of it for the press." 3 *ibid.*, 395. Numerous charges to grand juries by Mr. Justice Iredell with responses by the grand jury, invariably requesting a copy of the charge for publication, are to be found in 2 McREE, LIFE OF IREDELL, 347, *et seq.*

[55] Following an animated charge by Mr. Justice Iredell on May 22, 1797, the grand jury for the District of Virginia presented " as a real evil the circular letter of several members of the late Congress, and particularly letters with the signature of Samuel J. Cabell, endeavoring at a time of real public danger to disseminate unfounded calumnies against the happy government of the United States . . . and to increase or produce a foreign influence ruinous to the peace, happiness, and independence of the United States." This presentment was made without any reference to the court's power to punish this as an offense but in accordance with a prevalent custom of making presentments of matters they esteemed public grievances. This action produced a retort from Cabell and the other Anti-Federalists attacking the entire judiciary. See 2 McREE, *op. cit.*, 510. Jefferson contemplated an appeal to the Virginia House of Delegates to punish this action as a crime and drafted a petition to this effect. See 7 JEFFERSON, WRITINGS, Ford ed., 158, 166, 171. Iredell replied by a vindication of his action in the press, — conduct that even his friend, Governor Johnston of North Carolina, characterized as inappropriate in a Supreme Court Justice. See 2 McREE, *op. cit.*, 511, 515.

from friends, as well as enemies, of a strong federal bench. Ardent Federalists with increasing vigor urged Randolph's proposal for separate circuit judges; the emerging Jeffersonian Party came to regard the federal courts as a political adjunct of the hated Federalists. The judicial system was drawn into the vortex of politics.

The history of the federal bench in these early days is thus part and parcel of a fierce party strife. And yet the second major Judiciary Act — the law of the " Midnight Judges " — is apt to be treated too exclusively by historians merely as a piece of stupendous jobbery. Jobbery it was,[56] but by no means the design only of hungry politicians, or the effort of a party to entrench itself on the bench after the country had sent it into the wilderness.[57] Behind the Act lay the pressure of solid professional conceptions regarding a judicature appropriate for the new country, reinforced by defects unmistakably revealed in the workings of the initial system. Randolph was prophetic. The evils which he anticipated the Justices experienced. Jay and his associates, as is well known, found impossible the circuit duties which the Act of 1789 imposed and demanded relief in unmis-

---

[56] The entire list of appointments was as follows: *First Circuit* — John Lowell of Massachusetts, Jeremiah Smith of New Hampshire, Benjamin Bourne of Rhode Island; *Second Circuit* — Egbert Benson of New York, Oliver Wolcott of Connecticut, Samuel Hitchcock of Vermont; *Third Circuit* — William Tilghman of Pennsylvania, Richard Bassett of Delaware, William Griffith of New Jersey; *Fourth Circuit* — Philip Barton Key of Maryland, George Keith Taylor and Charles Magill of Virginia; *Fifth Circuit* — Thomas Bee of South Carolina, John Sitgreaves of North Carolina, Joseph Clay, Jr., of Georgia; *Sixth Circuit* — William McClung of Kentucky. Charles Lee of Virginia was appointed to the Fourth Circuit, and Jared Ingersoll to the Third Circuit but they both declined the appointments. See " The United States and the New Court Bill," 10 Am. L. Rev. 398, 403. The partisan character of such appointments as Richard Bassett, Jeremiah Smith, Charles Lee, Jared Ingersoll, Oliver Wolcott, and Philip Barton Key is only too obvious. See Carpenter, Judicial Tenure in the United States, 56. Richard Bassett, who had voted as presidential elector for Adams in 1797, secured his appointment through the influence of James Ashton Bayard, the great sponsor of the Act in the House. See Papers of James A. Bayard, 1913 Am. Hist. Assn. Rep. 124, 125, 130, 143. As to the political affiliations of the appointees under the First Judiciary Act, see Beard, Economic Origins of Jeffersonian Democracy, 103.

[57] See, *e.g.*, the critical study made by Professor Max Farrand and his correction of the errors into which such historians as Channing, McMaster, and Tyler had fallen. " The Judiciary Act of 1801," 5 Am. Hist. Rev. 682, 686.

takable language. " We really, sir," they addressed Washington,
" find the burdens laid upon us so excessive that we cannot forbear
representing them in strong and explicit terms. . . . That the task of
holding twenty-seven Circuit Courts a year, in the different States,
from New Hampshire to Georgia, besides two sessions of the Supreme
Court at Philadelphia, in the two most severe seasons of the year, is
a task which, considering the extent of the United States and the small
number of Judges, is too burdensome." [58]

In response to this memorial, transmitted to Congress by Washington,[59] the Act of March 2, 1793,[60] was passed, affording at
least partial relief. Thereafter, only one Justice was required to
attend each circuit.[61] Six Justices were thus available for three
circuits. They were called on circuit, therefore, only once a
year. This palliative eased matters very little.[62] The conditions of the country still left this reduced circuit riding an

---

[58] See 1 AM. STATE PAPERS, Misc., 52.

[59] This letter was laid before the Senate and the House by Washington on
November 7, 1792. See 3 ANN. CONG. 611, 671.

[60] On November 21, 1792, a Senate Committee, consisting of Ellsworth, Strong,
Monroe, Johnston and King, was appointed to consider the judiciary system.
See 3 ANN. CONG. 616. On January 3, 1793, Ellsworth reported a bill from this
Committee which was debated the following day. See 3 ANN. CONG. 625, 626.
This bill, the basis of the Act of 1793, was passed by the Senate on January 8,
1793, and placed before the House on the same day. See 3 *ibid.*, 627, 802. The
House amended the bill on February 18, and passed it in this amended form on
February 20. See 3 *ibid.*, 881, 884. The Senate again amended the bill on February
25, and reported it back to the House. See 3 *ibid.*, 655, 894. The nature of these
amendments is not disclosed; but on February 27 the House agreed to the new
Senate amendments and again amended the first section so as to allow one Supreme Court Justice to hold the circuit court where the district judge had been
disqualified by having been of counsel in the case or having had an interest in it.
See 3 *ibid.*, 896. This amendment was agreed to again by the Senate. See 3 *ibid.*,
659, 899. That this measure was a direct response to the complaint of the
Justices is evidenced by the fact that the House Committee to whom the letter
was referred on November 8, 1792, was discharged from further consideration
upon the report of the Senate bill in the House. See 3 *ibid.*, 675; HOUSE JOURNAL,
665. Mr. Warren holds a contrary opinion. See 1 WARREN, THE SUPREME COURT
IN UNITED STATES HISTORY, 89.

[61] See 1 STAT. 333.

[62] It did, however, induce Chief Justice Jay to remain on the bench. On
February 17, 1794, the Justices again complained to the President. See 1 AM.
STATE PAPERS, Misc., 77. This letter was placed before both Houses of Congress
on February 19. See 4 ANN. CONG. 45, 457. In the House it was tabled, but in
the Senate it was referred to a Committee who, however, reported that the matter
be postponed to the next session. See 4 *ibid.*, 109.

intolerable hardship.[63] The growing volume of the Supreme Court's appellate business only intensified the conflicting drain which Supreme Court and circuit court work made upon the energies and capacities of the Justices. Time made Randolph's analysis of the weakness of the circuit system more and more true. Dissatisfaction with the existing system was also fed by the desire of influential opinion to extend the scope of federal jurisdiction. The interference of local prejudices with the enforcement of federal laws stimulated the proponents of a more comprehensive federal judiciary.[64] But no serious attempt look-

[63] Rev. A. Iredell in a letter to his brother, Justice Iredell, concludes that a "Junior Judge must lead the life of a Postboy." See 2 McREE, LIFE OF IREDELL, 306. This picturesque phrase is often attributed to the Justice. See, *e.g.,* 1 WARREN, *op. cit.,* 86. On the other hand, when the circuit system was reëstablished by the repeal of the Act of 1801 the capacity of the Justices to attend to both their duties on circuit and in Washington is defended by a partisan pamphlet of the time: "To decide upon the ability of the judges to perform the service, let us consider the labours of one judge — judge Cushing for instance. The law requires of him to hold annually, in conjunction with the district judges, two sessions of a circuit court in each of the states of N. Hampshire, Massachusetts and Rhode-Island. — Ten days may fairly be computed the full length of a session. — The courts will then require sixty days. — His travel in going to and returning from those courts cannot exceed 480 miles, which allowing one day for each 20 miles amounts to 24 days more. — A session of the supreme court will not require more than 21 days. His residence does not exceed 480 miles distance from the seat of government. — At the above moderate rate of travelling, there must be added 48 days more, making the whole time while on expense and in public service, 153 days, or a little over five months, for which service he receives $3,500 in each year. A less portion of time than he devoted to the public service while a judge of the state courts of Massachusetts. As to the sufficiency of an annual supreme court it cannot be doubted, when it is known that for ten years that court decided but 43 causes, and that at its last session the dockets consisted of 8 only, 3 of which were decided." See PLAIN TRUTH AND ALGERNON SIDNEY, A VIEW AND VINDICATION OF THE MEASURES OF THE PRESENT ADMINISTRATION, 11–12 (1802).

[64] See Wolcott to Ames on December 29, 1799: "The steady men in Congress will attempt to extend the judicial department and I hope that their measures will be very decided. It is impossible, in this country, to render an army an engine for government, and there is no way to combat the state opposition but by an efficient and extended organization of judges, magistrates, and other civil officers." 2 GIBBS, ADMINISTRATIONS OF WASHINGTON AND ADAMS, 316. Hamilton in a letter to Dayton in 1799 suggested the extension of the federal judicial system so as to provide for the appointment of justices of peace in each county of a state. See 6 HAMILTON, WORKS, J. C. Hamilton ed., 385. *Per contra,* criticism of the decisions of the federal courts became particularly marked during the period beginning with 1798 when a *de facto* state of war existed with France, and the courts in their decisions were suspected by the Anti-Federalists as having an anti-French bias. See 1 WARREN, *op. cit.,* 156–167.

ing towards drastic reform appears until John Adams, in 1799, brought the matter before Congress.[65] His recommendation culminated in the notorious Act of February 13, 1801.[66]   This

---

[65] See Message of December 3, 1799: "To give energy to the government, it appears indispensable that the judicial system of the United States should be revised. It cannot but happen that numerous questions respecting the interpretation of the laws and the rights and duties of officers and citizens must arise in this extensive country; on the one hand it is necessary that the laws be executed, on the other that individuals should be guarded against oppression; neither of these objects can be assured under the present organization of the judicial department." See 1 MESSAGES AND PAPERS OF THE PRESIDENTS, 279; 10 ANN. CONG. 188. That the desire for judicial reform was claiming the attention of the Federalists is evident from the fact that prior to this time proposals had already been made on the floor of Congress. See the letter of Iredell to Mrs. Iredell of Mar. 31, 1796, 2 McREE, *op. cit.*, 465. On December 24, 1797, Allen proposed a resolution in the House to amend the judiciary system, which resulted in a bill's being reported by Bayard on March 1, 1798, supplementary to the Judiciary Act. See 7 ANN. CONG. 757, 1116. This bill, providing for the trial of causes between two states in a neighboring state, was rejected by the House on March 15, 1798. See 8 ANN. CONG. 1267. On May 28, 1798, a bill from the Senate "altering and extending the Judicial Courts of the United States" was referred to a committee but consideration was postponed until the next session. See 8 ANN. CONG. 1835, 1876.

[66] See 2 STAT. 89. In the House, Harper from the committee, to which was referred so much of the President's speech as related to a "revision and amendment of the Judiciary system" on March 11, 1800, made a report and at the same time presented a bill "for the better establishment and regulation of the courts of the United States." See 10 ANN. CONG. 623. This bill provided for the division of the United States into twenty-nine districts, that disregarded both state boundaries and state names. It was said to have been prepared by Hamilton. See 1 WARREN, *op. cit.*, 186. The bill was debated in the House for three consecutive days. On March 28, upon a motion to strike out the seventh section of this bill, whereby was raised a decisive vote, John Marshall "entered into a lengthy defence of the new system." The motion, however, was carried. See 10 *ibid.*, 646. On the following day the proponents, realizing that the pivotal section of the bill had been defeated and wishing to avert the failure of the bill, secured the discharge of the consideration of the bill by the Committee of the Whole. See 10 *ibid.*, 649. On March 31, another bill was reported from the same committee by Harper. See 10 *ibid.*, 650. Upon Kitchell's objection that the bill contained the same principles that had been embodied in the former one, its consideration was postponed until the next session. See 10 *ibid.*, 666. However, on May 1, another bill was reported from the same committee by Harper, which was ordered to be printed. See 10 *ibid.*, 694. During this session no attempt was made in the Senate to secure a complete revision of the judicial system.

In the next session of Congress, on December 19, 1800, the bill which later became the Act of 1801 was reported in the House by Griswold of Connecticut. See 10 ANN. CONG. 837. Consideration of the bill by the Committee of the Whole began on January 5, 1801, when the motion of Eggleston to strike out that part of the bill dividing Virginia into two districts was lost. See 10 *ibid.*, 891. On

measure combined thoughtful concern for the federal judiciary with selfish concern for the Federalist party.

What was proposed and what prevailed was the entire elimination, in accordance with Randolph's view, of circuit riding by the Justices,[67] the creation of sixteen new circuit judges for the six circuits,[68] and an expansion of the authority of the federal courts to the full limit of constitutional power.[69] The stuff of Randolph's report was voluminously repeated in long debates both in the Senate and House.[70] His speculative considerations were reinforced by arguments from ten years' experience with the system. The opposition countered heavily with charges of spoils, politics, extravagance, and judicial entrenchment of discredited political doctrines.[71] Moreover, by this time party lines were compactly

---

January 7, a motion reducing the jurisdictional amount to $400 was lost by the deciding vote of the Speaker. The object of this provision was avowedly to defeat the jurisdiction of the federal courts by placing the jurisdictional amount in excess of the quit rents alleged to be due to the assignees of the confiscated Fairfax estates. See 10 *ibid.*, 897. On January 8, a motion of Nicholas to add a clause limiting the jurisdiction of the federal courts in suits by assignees upon promissory notes or choses in action to cases where jurisdiction could be assumed as if no assignment had been made, was carried. See 10 *ibid.*, 899. Upon the motion of Harper certain sections which established a number of district courts with admiralty jurisdiction were struck out, and an amendment was prepared by Harper to establish additional district courts " with admiralty powers " " in the most maritime positions." See 10 *ibid.*, 899. On January 9 and 12, the House debated the salary that was to be paid to the various judges. See 10 *ibid.*, 900, 906. On January 13, the action taken on January 7 was rescinded and the jurisdictional amount reduced to $400. See 10 *ibid.*, 907. Consideration was again resumed on January 16, and on January 20, 1801, the bill passed the House by a vote of 51 to 43. See 10 *ibid.*, 912, 915. On January 21, the bill was reported to the Senate, where it was referred to a committee on the following day. See 10 *ibid.*, 734, 735. On January 29, it was reported from the committee without amendment. See 10 *ibid.*, 737. Debate was begun on February 4, and on February 5, motions to reduce the salaries of the circuit judges were lost. See 10 *ibid.*, 738–740. On February 6, a motion to strike out the whole of the bill and insert provisions calling for the division of the United States into four circuits and the retention of the present circuit duties of the Supreme Court Justices was lost. See 10 *ibid.*, 741. On February 7, the bill passed the Senate without amendment. See 10 *ibid.*, 742.

[67] See Act of Feb. 13, 1801, §§ 1–3, 2 STAT. 89.

[68] See Act of Feb. 13, 1801, § 7, 2 STAT. 89, 90. For the appointments to these circuits see note 56, *supra*.

[69] See Act of Feb. 13, 1801, § 11, 2 STAT. 89, 92.

[70] See, *e.g.*, the use made of Randolph's report on February 23, 1802, in the House, 11 ANN. CONG. 674–678.

[71] See, *e.g.*, Claiborne in the House on January 9, 1800, expostulating against

formed; opposition to an enhancement of the authority of the federal judiciary was a concrete manifestation of a more far-reaching political division between the proponents and opponents of extension of federal power. Identifying the fate of party with the country's salvation, as is the way of politicians, the Federalists regarded the impending election of Jefferson (not to speak of the alternative of an Aaron Burr) as the triumph of the mob.[72] Their best minds sought to insure the country's safety by putting the country's laws, at least for judicial administration, into the hands of worthy Federalists.[73] Panic, politics, and sound professional instincts had a brief victory. The law was doomed to repeal by the Jeffersonian Party,[74] so far as it was constitutionally possible for them to undo the mischief.[75] The behavior of

this " shameful profusion of public money." See 10 ANN. CONG. 900. See also Nicholas of Virginia, 10 *ibid.*, 904.

[72] The election of Jefferson, which occurred on February 17, 1801, was then impending in the House. See 10 ANN. CONG. 1028.

[73] See, *e.g.,* Gen. Gunn to Hamilton on December 13, 1800: " With this view of the subject, permit me to offer for your consideration, the policy of the federal party *extending the influence of our Judiciary;* if neglected by the federalists, the ground will be occupied by the enemy the very next session of Congress, and, sir, we shall see ―――― and many other scoundrels, placed on the seat of Justice." See 6 HAMILTON, WORKS, J. C. Hamilton ed., 483, quoted in 2 BEVERIDGE, LIFE OF JOHN MARSHALL, 548. For the partisan character of the appointments see note 56, *supra.*

[74] Intimations that one of the first measures of the incoming administration would be the repeal of the Act of 1801 are scattered through the correspondence of this period. See 1 WARREN, THE SUPREME COURT IN UNITED STATES HISTORY, 193; CARPENTER, JUDICIAL TENURE IN THE UNITED STATES, 60.

[75] The constitutionality of the repeal was, of course, the great point of discussion in both Houses. That the objection prevailed but little against party solidarity is evident from the fact that only one member of the Jeffersonian Party, Eustis of Boston, deserted the ranks to vote against the repeal. See PAPERS OF JAMES A. BAYARD, 1913 AM. HIST. ASSN. REP. 150. The argument advanced by Breckenridge, who led the fight for the repeal in the Senate, was that the courts being themselves only creatures of the legislature could be abolished as well as created at will. He denied the imperative duty of Congress to create inferior courts, and emphasized the point that Congress being able to abolish the court must also be able to abolish the judgeship. " It is a principle of our Constitution, as well as of common honesty, that no man shall receive public money but in consideration of public services. Sinecure offices, therefore, are not permitted by our laws or Constitution. By this construction, complete sinecure offices will be created." 11 ANN. CONG. 28. Mason summed up what he conceived to be the constitutional checks upon the independence of the judiciary in these words: " A judge may say, I am not to be turned out of office by the President on the one hand, or starved by the Legislature on the other. He may say to the Legislature, or to the Presi-

dent, and to both of them combined, you shall not turn me out of this office as long as it exists, to gratify your enmity to me, or your favoritism to another person; so long as the interest and convenience of the people require this institution, they are entitled to my services." 11 ANN. CONG. 64. The Jeffersonians also pointed to a precedent in this matter, namely, the abolition of the district courts of Kentucky and Tennessee by the twenty-fourth section of the Act of 1801. It was admitted that the judges in this instance were promoted to circuit judges, but nevertheless the district courts were abolished. Gouverneur Morris tried in vain to stem the effect of this argument: "If the law be only defective, why not amend? And if unconstitutional, why repeal? In this case no repeal can be necessary; the law is in itself void; it is a mere dead letter." 11 ANN. CONG. 81. In the House a novel construction was introduced: "I am free to declare, that if the intent of this bill is to get rid of the judges, it is a perversion of your power to a base purpose; it is an unconstitutional act. If, on the contrary, it aims not at the misplacing one set of men, from whom you differ in political opinion, with a view to introducing others, but at the general good by abolishing useless offices, it is a Constitutional Act. The *quo animo* determines the nature of this act, as it determines the innocence or guilt of other acts." 11 ANN. CONG. 658. The constitutional as well as the political arguments make this debate one of the liveliest in the legislative history of the judiciary. At the time the chief speeches for and against the repeal were printed in pamphlet form and given great currency. They were published by Collier & Stockwell (Albany, 1802), E. Bronson (Philadelphia, 1802), and Munroe & Francis (Boston, 1802). The leaders of the Federalist Party felt that the effect of the repeal was not only to turn the administration of justice over to the Jeffersonian rabble, but also to put the Constitution and its principles at the mercy of the legislature. In the Senate the debate had taken the turn of denying power in the judiciary to review the constitutionality of legislation. 11 ANN. CONG. 179–182. The repeal was generally lamented by the Federalists as the passing of the Union. Bayard wrote to Bassett on March 3, 1802: "This day the constitution has numbered 13 years and in my opinion has recd. a mortal wound." See PAPERS OF JAMES A. BAYARD, 1913 AM. HIST. ASSN. REP. 150. Tracy of Connecticut during the Senate debate remarked: "I apprehend that the repeal of this act will be the hand-writing on the wall, stamping *Mene Tekel* upon all we hold dear and valuable in our Constitution." 11 ANN. CONG. 58. Stanley in the House made an equally dire prophecy: "This measure will be the first link in that chain of measures which will add the name of America to the melancholy catalogue of fallen Republics." 11 ANN. CONG. 579. For an excellent review of the congressional debates, unfortunately marred by a partisan interpretation, see CARPENTER, JUDICIAL TENURE IN THE UNITED STATES, 58–78. During the summer of 1802 the circuit judges who had been deprived of their commissions protested to Congress. These protests were given wide publicity, the document penned by Bassett being published in pamphlet form and widely distributed. On January 27, 1803, Griswold of Connecticut in the House moved to submit the petition of the judges for compensation to judicial decision but, despite the impassioned oratory of the Federalists, the motion was lost. 12 ANN. CONG. 427, 431, 439. See 1 WARREN, THE SUPREME COURT IN UNITED STATES HISTORY, 224–226. On Jan. 27, 1803, the memorials of the judges were presented to the Senate by Ross and referred to committee. 12 ANN. CONG. 31. Morris on the following day made a report submitting a resolution that the President cause "an information, in the nature

some of the " Midnight Judges " during the summer of 1801,[76] together with the preliminary decision in *Marbury* v. *Madison*,[77] served only to intensify Jefferson's ire.[78] The repeal came promptly on March 8, 1802.[79]

---

of a *quo warranto*, to be filed by the Attorney-General against Richard Bassett, one of the said petitioners, for the purpose of deciding judicially on their claims." See 1 AM. STATE PAPERS, Misc., 340. The resolution was hotly debated on Feb. 3, 1803, and failed of adoption by a vote of 15 to 13. 12 ANN. CONG. 78. The constitutionality of the repeal was, of course, never settled judicially. Story expresses an opinion that the measure was unconstitutional. 2 STORY, THE CONSTITUTION, 4 ed., 427–429. Bayard, however, in a letter to Hamilton of April 25, 1802, quotes Marshall, then Chief Justice, as being of the opinion that the repeal was " operative." 6 HAMILTON, WORKS, J. C. Hamilton ed., 544. See also BROWN, PLUMER'S MEMORANDUM OF PROCEEDINGS IN THE UNITED STATES SENATE: 1803–1807, 103. The correspondence between Paterson and Marshall, when the latter inquired of him whether they should undertake the circuit duty that was imposed upon them under the Act of April 29, 1802, has been lately revealed by Mr. Warren and illustrates that Marshall did possess doubts as to the constitutionality of requiring the attendance of the members of the Supreme Court on circuit. 1 WARREN, *op. cit.*, 269–272. These doubts were resolved by the unanimous opinions of his associates that the constitutionality of this question must be regarded as settled by the contemporaneous usage of 1789 — an opinion that was later embodied into judicial doctrine. Stuart *v.* Laird, 1 Cranch (U. S.) 299 (1803).

[76] 1 WARREN, *op. cit.*, 194–200.

[77] 1 Cranch (U. S.) 137 (1803). This was a preliminary motion for rule to show cause why a writ of *mandamus* should not be granted to require Madison, then Secretary of State, to deliver the commissions which he withheld from William Marbury, William Harper, Robert Hooe, and Dennis Ramsay.

[78] See BROWN, *op. cit.*, 101; 1 WARREN, *op. cit.*, 200–208.

[79] See 2 STAT. 132. Jefferson in his message of December 8, 1801, called attention to the judiciary system. " The Judiciary system of the United States, and especially that portion of it recently erected, will, of course, present itself to the contemplation of Congress; and that they may be able to judge of the proportion which the institution bears to the business it has to perform, I have caused to be procured from the several States, and now lay before Congress, an exact statement of all the causes decided since the first establishment of the courts, and of those which were depending when additional courts and judges were brought in to their aid." See 1 MESSAGES AND PAPERS OF THE PRESIDENTS, 319. These figures were subjected to severe and searching scrutiny both in Congress and in the press. See, *e.g.*, the Lucius Crassus letters of Hamilton commenting on Jefferson's message. 8 HAMILTON, WORKS, Lodge ed., 271. On February 26, 1802, during the debate in the House on the repeal Jefferson submitted a message correcting certain errors that he had made in his original statement. 11 ANN. CONG. 798; 1 MESSAGES AND PAPERS OF THE PRESIDENTS, 325. See also note 35, *supra*. On January 4, 1802, Randolph in the House moved a resolution to go into a Committee of the Whole and consider what alterations should be made in the judicial system. After a debate this resolution was referred to a special committee. 11 ANN. CONG. 362, 364. On January 6, 1802, Breckenridge in the Senate moved for

Short-lived as was the Second Judiciary Act, the ideas which it embodied, both as to the organization of the courts and the scope of their jurisdiction, long persisted and finally prevailed. It contained a program which for decades was intermittently

---

the repeal of the Act of 1801, and his motion was seconded by S. T. Mason. 11 *ibid.*, 23. The consideration of the motion began on January 8 (11 *ibid.*, 25), continued through January 12 (11 *ibid.*, 46–58), January 13 (11 *ibid.*, 59–74), January 14 (11 *ibid.*, 75–99), January 15 (11 *ibid.*, 99–116), January 19 (11 *ibid.*, 116–145). On that day Chipman of Vermont moved to have a committee appointed to inquire into what alterations were necessary in the federal judicial system, which, upon the motion of Dayton, was put in the form of an amendment to Breckenridge's original motion. The amendment was lost and Breckenridge's motion was passed by a vote of 15 to 13, and a committee consisting of Anderson, Baldwin, and Breckenridge appointed to draft a bill for repeal. 11 ANN. CONG. 145. Such a bill was reported by Anderson on January 22. 11 *ibid.*, 146. The debate was resumed on January 27, when a motion made by Dayton the day before, to refer the bill to a select committee to determine what alterations might be necessary in the judicial system, was carried by the deciding vote of the Vice-President upon division by the House. 11 *ibid.*, 148. On February 2, Ross presented a memorial from the Philadelphia bar against repeal. 11 *ibid.*, 152. On the same day Breckenridge having given notice that he would move for the discharge of the select committee on the day before, introduced his motion, and the committee was discharged by a vote of 16 to 14. 11 ANN. CONG. 152, 154, 160. On February 3, Ross' motion to amend the repealing Act so as to exclude the third district was defeated and the final vote on the bill carried by 16 to 15. 11 *ibid.*, 160, 183. The bill, as thus passed, was received by the House on February 4 and, upon the motion of John Randolph, referred to the Committee of the Whole. 11 *ibid.*, 476, 480. On February 8, a petition of sundry merchants of Philadelphia was presented praying for repeal. 11 *ibid.*, 483. The debate began on February 15, when a motion for postponement by Bayard was defeated. 11 *ibid.*, 518. A similar motion by Dennis for postponement was likewise defeated. 11 *ibid.*, 521. On February 16, memorials against repeal were presented from the merchants and traders of Philadelphia and the Corporation of the Chamber of Commerce of the City of New York. 11 *ibid.*, 522. A memorial of the New Jersey Bar against repeal was presented on February 17. 11 *ibid.*, 545. A memorial for repeal by sundry inhabitants of Philadelphia was presented on February 18. 11 *ibid.*, 568. A similar memorial was also presented on February 20. 11 *ibid.*, 629. The debate continued throughout the days of February 16 (11 *ibid.*, 523–545), February 17 (11 *ibid.*, 546–568), February 18 (11 *ibid.*, 569–602), February 19 (11 *ibid.*, 603–628), February 20 (11 *ibid.*, 629–665), February 23 (11 *ibid.*, 665–721), February 24 (11 *ibid.*, 721–746), February 25 (11 *ibid.*, 746–797), February 27 (11 *ibid.*, 798–814), February 28 (11 *ibid.*, 814–854), March 1 (11 *ibid.*, 854–949). On that day a motion to strike out the first section of the bill was lost. On March 2 Bayard introduced several amendments, but they were all negatived. Griswold introduced an amendment which was also lost. 11 *ibid.*, 950–958. On March 3, Lowndes' motion to postpone the consideration of the bill was lost. 11 *ibid.*, 981. And on the same day the bill passed the House, without amendment, by a vote of 59 to 32. 11 *ibid.*, 982.

pressed for reënactment.[80] The Federalists would have found vindication in the Act of 1869 [81] which drastically curtailed circuit riding, in the Act of 1875 [82] which vastly extended the domain of the federal courts, and the Act of 1891 [83] which created a new class of circuit judges. But these changes come at the end of a continuous process of tinkering, minor adaptations, temporary expedients, proposals for major reforms giving rise to influential debates — all the reflexes of the creaking of the judicial machinery because of its inadequacy to cope with the demands made upon it by changing circumstances.

3

The Jeffersonians repealed the Act of February 13, 1801, but they could not rest there. They had to face the same conditions that had moved the Federalists to reorganize the judicial system. They, too, had to provide for the needs of new territory; they, too, had to relieve the Justices from excessive circuit burdens; they, too, had to pass " an Act to amend the judicial system." [84]

---

[80] The persistence of the 1801 scheme is seen not only in the numerous times in which the measure appeared in the form of a bill before both houses of Congress, but also in the attitude of professional minds of a later era toward the proposal. Mason on December 29, 1823, writes thus to Webster: " But I prefer the second project in the report, which is to create circuit courts on the plan of those of 1801. The only objection against that mentioned in the report, is that those courts were tried and abolished. This rests wholly on party feelings. Whether these feelings have subsided sufficiently to do away the force of this reason, I cannot judge." HILLARD, MEMOIR OF JEREMIAH MASON, 279. Van Buren also remarks upon the persistence of the scheme: " Several plans were considered one of which I will notice here because I think it involves a principle of great importance and because after repeated ineffectual efforts for its establishment it seems yet to have supporters in and out of Congress and will in all probability be again proposed. This arrangement separates the Justices of the Supreme Court from the performance of circuit duties and devolves them upon circuit Judges, to be appointed for that purpose, or upon the district Judges." AUTOBIOGRAPHY OF VAN BUREN, 1918 AM. HIST. ASSN. REP. 218.

[81] Act of April 10, 1869, 16 STAT. 44.

[82] Act of Mar. 3, 1875, 18 STAT. 470.

[83] Act of Mar. 3, 1891, 26 STAT. 826. The Act of April 10, 1869, also created nine circuit judges, but the definite demarcation between circuit and district judges is more marked by the later Act.

[84] Act of April 29, 1802, 2 STAT. 156, as amended by Act of Mar. 3, 1803, 2 STAT. 244. This bill originated in the Senate on March 18, 1802, when, upon a

This Act divided the country into six circuits with a circuit court in each, composed as before of one Justice and one district judge, who were required to hold two annual sessions of the circuit

---

motion to appoint a committee to inquire " whether any, and what, amendments are necessary to be made in the acts to establish the judicial courts of the United States," the matter was referred to a committee consisting of Anderson, Brown, Bradley, Nicholas, and Jackson. 11 ANN. CONG. 201. All the members of this committee had voted for the repeal of the Act of 1801. On March 21, Anderson reported the bill. 11 *ibid.*, 205. Upon its second reading on April 2, the bill was amended and recommitted. Breckenridge was appointed to take the place of Brown. 11 *ibid.*, 251. On April 5, the bill was again reported from committee with amendments. 11 *ibid.*, 252. On April 8, after an unsuccessful attempt to insert an amendment providing for the appointment of commissioners in bankruptcy, the bill passed the Senate by a vote of 16 to 10. No one who had voted against the repeal of the Act of 1801 voted for its passage, but Bradley, who had voted for repeal, voted against its passage. 11 *ibid.*, 256–257. The bill was received by the House on April 9 and referred to a select committee. 11 *ibid.*, 1160. It was reported from committee on April 13 by Giles, who had been most active in the House in urging the repeal of the Act of 1801. 11 *ibid.*, 1163–1164. On April 19, the debate on the bill opened. Bayard objected to a provision reducing the two sessions of the Supreme Court to one, urging that it would result in undue delay to suitors in that Court. He was supported by Griswold and Dennis. The practice of the supreme courts of the states was referred to as being an unbroken precedent for two sessions. To this Elmendorf of New York replied: " It appears to me that the arguments of the gentlemen do not apply to the Supreme Court. It is not pretended that this court is calculated for the trial of original causes, but barely for the correction of errors. . . . The number of causes actually tried will depend much more on the length than the frequency of terms." 11 *ibid.*, 1208. Bayard's amendment was lost. 11 *ibid.*, 1211. A further amendment by Bayard to strike out the provision for continuance of suits from term to term in the Supreme Court was defeated. 11 *ibid.*, 1211. On April 20, Davis' motion for the addition of a seventh circuit consisting of Kentucky and Tennessee was carried. 11 *ibid.*, 1212. On April 21, Davis' amendment was again debated and on its resubmission lost. The same day Bayard introduced an amendment providing for certification of points upon which a circuit court should be divided. 11 *ibid.*, 1213–1215. It was carried the next day. 11 *ibid.*, 1219. Leib of Pennsylvania then moved an amendment to prevent the clerks of the circuit courts from returning special juries and placing this duty upon the marshal. This was opposed by Bayard on the ground that the marshal being an appointee of the executive — " proceeding from the nostrils of the Executive " — the measure was designed to increase executive influence and the opportunities of executive patronage. Giles retorted by pointing to the abolition of over four hundred offices, dependent upon executive patronage, which had been the work of his party since it came in office. The motion was carried. 11 *ibid.*, 1223. Dennis moved to strike out the fifteenth section, which vested in the President power to appoint commissioners in bankruptcy. His motion failed by one vote. 11 *ibid.*, 1227. Bayard's amendment to prevent the Act from going into operation until the " first day of July next " was lost. 11 *ibid.*, 1230. On April 23, the motion to strike out the fifteenth section was again made and, after a final appeal by

court in each of the seventeen districts.[85] But it allowed the
circuit court to be held by a single judge.[86] With the growth
of the country and the corresponding increase in circuit court
business, the latter provision was constantly invoked if circuit
courts were to be held at all. Increasingly it became impossible
for the Justices to attend circuit in all the districts at all sessions,
and the circuit courts devolved more and more into the hands of
single district judges.[87]

The backbone of the 1802 structure, however, was the re-
established circuit riding system. Circuit courts did not require
the attendance of circuit Justices; but every new circuit required
the creation of a new Justice. New circuits, in view of the westward push of the population, were on the horizon. According to
the rejected Federalist scheme of legislation, new circuit courts
were to be taken care of by new circuit judges, without necessarily
changing the make-up of the Supreme Court. It was a flexible
organization. The Act of 1802, however, rigidly tied the Supreme Court to the circuit system. More circuits again meant
more Justices. This was bound to encounter opposition because
there is no necessary correlation between the needed number of
circuit courts of the country and the effective size of the Supreme
Bench. Yet this is the system under which we operated until
1869.

Bayard, was passed by a vote of 46 to 30. 11 *ibid.*, 1232–1236. Not a single
member who had not voted for the repeal of the Act of 1801 voted for the passage of this bill; but four members, Thomas T. Davis, Ebenezer Elmer, Thomas
Moore, and James Mott, who had voted for the repeal, voted against this Act.
On April 26, the Senate voted to concur in all the amendments made by the House
save that which struck out the fifteenth section. 11 *ibid.*, 291. On April 26, the
House receded from this amendment. 11 *ibid.*, 1248.

That partisan motives played a prominent part in the passage of this Act and
in the framing of its specific provisions is plain from the history of its passage
and the debates that accompanied it. Bayard was particularly vituperative in
his language, referring to the bill as "this mighty potchery of legislation" and
again as a "miserable piece of patchwork." 11 *ibid.*, 1211, 1235. It was charged
that the change in the sessions of the Supreme Court was made to prevent the
usual session in June, when it was hoped that the constitutionality of the repeal
of the Act of 1801 would be taken up. The opposition, the Federalists charged,
postponed the next sitting of the Supreme Court for fourteen months so as to
prevent any decision until the new system had become well established. 11 *ibid.*,
1236. See 1 WARREN, THE SUPREME COURT IN UNITED STATES HISTORY, 222–224.

[85] Act of April 29, 1802, § 4, 2 STAT. 156, 157.   [86] *Ibid.*, § 4, proviso.
[87] See, *e.g.*, HILLARD, MEMOIR OF JEREMIAH MASON, 278.

The demand for a new circuit in the new West, insistent for some time, led in 1807 to the establishment of a new circuit composed of new territory, outside of the original thirteen states. Kentucky had become a state in 1792,[88] but its remoteness made it orphan territory under the federal judicial system. No Justice was assigned to it for circuit duty. The district judge presided over both district and circuit courts held in the district of Kentucky.[89] Tennessee shared a similar fate after attaining statehood in 1796,[90] and the note of discontent arising from this situation steadily swelled. A proposal to include Kentucky and Tennessee in a fourth circuit to be presided over by two new circuit Justices, was made by Senator Humphrey Marshall of Kentucky.[91] On her admission to statehood[92] Ohio became an added

---

[88] Act of Feb. 4, 1791, 1 STAT. 189.

[89] Act of Sept. 24, 1789, § 10, 1 STAT. 73, 77. The disadvantages attending the fusion of district court with circuit court jurisdiction in the district judge are best illustrated by the Report of Berrien of South Carolina from the Senate Judiciary Committee on January 26, 1829: " These beneficial provisions are not extended to the citizens of those States where a District Judge alone presides in the *quasi* Circuit Courts, of which we have spoken. His single opinion is decisive of the controversy in every matter of law. If the amount exceed two thousand dollars, the party who can sustain the expense of prosecuting an appeal, or writ of error, may indeed have his cause reviewed by the Supreme tribunal — but every suitor cannot sustain this expense, and to him the doom is final. In many instances, too, the counsels of an Associate would probably have changed the result, and have rendered this appeal unnecessary; and in those cases, where, from the smallness of the amount in controversy, the right of appeal is not allowed, the injury resulting from the error of this single Judge, is remediless. The evil is more striking in criminal cases. The fiat of an individual, which dooms the accused to imprisonment, or to death, is irresistible, irreversible. No appeal is allowed — no writ of error provided by law; and, from the constitution of the Court, no disagreement can arise to invoke the protective interposition of the supreme tribunal." 20th Cong., 2nd Sess., Ser. No. 181, SEN. DOC. 50, p. 5.

[90] Act of June 1, 1796, 1 STAT. 491; Act of Jan. 31, 1797, § 2, 1 STAT. 496. Vermont was admitted into the Union in 1791. Act of Feb. 18, 1 STAT. 191. But upon its creation into a judicial district it was annexed to the eastern circuit and thereby was provided with a circuit court. Act of Mar. 2, 1791, § 3, 1 STAT. 197.

[91] On April 26, 1798, a motion to this effect was made by Marshall in the Senate. 7 ANN. CONG. 550. The motion was referred to a select committee on May 2. A bill was reported on May 8. 7 *ibid.*, 553, 556. The bill was recommitted after a debate on May 16. 7 *ibid.*, 559. It was again reported with amendments on May 22 and passed the Senate on May 25. 7 *ibid.*, 561, 564. On May 28, this bill was referred by the House to a committee. 8 ANN. CONG. 1835. On June 7, 1798, its consideration was postponed until the next session. 8 *ibid.*, 1876.

[92] Act of April 30, 1802, 2 STAT. 173. By the Act of Feb. 19, 1803, § 2, 2

source of grievance, but not until February 24, 1807,[93] were the accumulated demands satisfied by the erection of a seventh circuit comprising Kentucky, Tennessee, and Ohio. Automatically this called for the appointment of a sixth Associate Justice who was required to reside in the seventh circuit.[94] Thus begins the periodic increase in the membership of the Supreme Court as the territorial needs of the country for more circuit courts were met.

The forces which made for the discontent that gave rise to the Act of 1807 continued. The country pushed westward. A new state is formed out of Louisiana.[95] New territory brings new judicial needs coincident with a rise in the volume of judicial business in the old districts and circuits. More business in the circuit and district courts means more business for the Supreme Court. In addition, a perennial maw of circuit work eats up the Supreme Court Justices. The stress and strain of the circuit-riding system are a constant source of complaint. Conditions compel the Justices either to slight their Supreme Court work with an undue delay in the disposition of appeals or to slight their circuit court work by insufficient attendance on circuit, or both. Thus the attention of the House was called to the " considerable delay and injury " " occasioned to suitors " " from the increased business of the Supreme Court." [96] From fifty-one cases dock-

---

STAT. 201, Ohio was created a judicial district with a district court and a district judge who, as in the case of Kentucky, exercised circuit court jurisdiction.

[93] 2 STAT. 420, amended by the Act of Mar. 22, 1808, 2 STAT. 477, and the Act of Feb. 4, 1809, 2 STAT. 516. Upon a resolution of Henry Clay in the Senate on Jan. 2, 1807, a committee was appointed to provide for the circuit system in Kentucky, Tennessee, and Ohio. 16 ANN. CONG. 27, 28. Such a measure passed the Senate on Jan. 26, 1807. 16 ibid., 46. On February 13, it was reported to the House from committee with several amendments. 16 ibid., 485. It passed the House on February 16 by a vote of 82 to 7. 16 ibid., 500. On February 20, the Senate concurred in the House amendments. 16 ibid., 74.

[94] Thomas Todd of Kentucky was appointed by Jefferson to fill this position. See 1 WARREN, op. cit., 299–301. The necessity of bringing into the Supreme Court a member familiar with the land law of the western states was keenly felt.

[95] Act of Feb. 20, 1811, 2 STAT. 641; Act of April 8, 1812, 2 STAT. 701. By Section 3 of the latter Act Louisiana was created a judicial district, and such jurisdiction and powers as formerly belonged to the district judge of the territory of Orleans were vested in the new federal district judge.

[96] On February 24, 1812, Gold of New York adverted in the House to these delays and submitted a resolution for the appointment of a committee to investigate what alterations were necessary in the judicial system of the United States. The resolution was agreed to and a committee of five appointed. 24 ANN. CONG. 1086; 11 NILES REG. 479.

eted in the February Term, 1803, the business of the Supreme
Court rose to ninety-eight in the February Term, 1810.[97]   The
legislative calendar shows the recurring effort to divorce the
Supreme Court from the circuit courts.   Bills to this effect were
introduced in both the Senate and House.[98]   But Congress

[97] The figures for 1803 are taken from HOUSE REPORT, No. 942, 50th Cong.,
1st Sess., Ser. No. 2600, which in turn quotes Mr. Justice Harlan. The figures
for 1810 are taken from HOUSE REPORT, No. 45, 44th Cong., 1st Sess., Ser. No.
1708.

[98] On December 24, 1813, Ingersoll in the House proposed a resolution to alter
the judicial system. 26 ANN. CONG. 805. On March 1, 1814, Ingersoll, for the
Judiciary Committee, reported a bill extending the jurisdiction of the circuit
courts to " all actions, suits, controversies, matters and things, of whatsoever
nature, which are cognizable by the judicial authority of the United States under
the Constitution." 27 ANN. CONG. 1768. This bill was indefinitely postponed by
the House on April 5, 1814. 27 *ibid.*, 1958. At the next session of the same
Congress, Ingersoll again reported the bill, but no action was taken upon it. 28
ANN. CONG. 412. This Congress, however, passed the Act of Mar. 3, 1815, 3 STAT.
244, vesting in the state courts jurisdiction of " all complaints, suits, and prosecutions, for taxes, duties, fines, penalties, and forfeitures " arising and payable under
any act of Congress for the collection of direct taxes or internal revenues. On
December 23, 1816, Nelson of Virginia from the House Judiciary Committee reported a bill abolishing the circuit duties of the Supreme Court Justices and
providing for the appointment of a circuit judge for each district. 30 ANN.
CONG. 357; 11 NILES REG. 294. On February 6, 1817, the Committee of the
Whole was discharged from further consideration of this bill and it was committed to the Judiciary Committee. 30 ANN. CONG. 873. On February 7, Nelson
reported another bill which, however, did not get beyond a second reading. 30
ibid., 915. In the Senate on February 27, 1817, Chace of the Judiciary Committee
reported a similar bill. 30 *ibid.*, 181. Attempts to secure its passage failed and
on the closing day of the session, upon the motion of Jeremiah Mason, its further
consideration was postponed. 30 *ibid.*, 206. In the next Congress Talbot of
Kentucky on January 27, 1818, submitted a motion calling for the consideration
of a scheme for the reduction of the membership of the Supreme Court, the
abolition of circuit duties, and the creation of circuit courts, which motion was
agreed to. 31 ANN. CONG. 135, 138. In the next session Tichnor of Vermont
renewed Talbot's motion on November 30, 1818. 33 ANN. CONG. 30. On December 1, 1818, Daggett of Connecticut introduced a bill for extending the judicial
system. 33 *ibid.*, 31. This bill provided for the division of the country into nine
circuits, and for the appointment of nine circuit judges, who with the district
judge were to hold the circuit courts. The Supreme Court was also to be reduced
to five members. See Webster in the House on January 4, 1826, 2 CONG. DEB. 875.
Tichnor's motion was withdrawn, and on December 7, 1818, Daggett's bill was
referred to the Judiciary Committee. 33 ANN. CONG. 34, 40. It was reported
back to the Senate without amendment on January 6. 33 *ibid.*, 100. The bill
passed the Senate on January 26, 1819. 33 *ibid.*, 186. In the House the bill was
referred to the Judiciary Committee who reported it without amendment on
February 2, 1819. 33 *ibid.*, 831, 935. No further action, however, was taken in
the House.

ignored the workings of the provision it made in 1807 for the seventh circuit. The size of this circuit, it was complained, led Mr. Justice Todd practically to eliminate Tennessee from his circuit attendance.[99] These efforts to make the structure better adapted to the country's needs coincided with proposals to enlarge the duties of the federal courts. The ambitious Story was the author of a " Judges Bill "[100] in 1816, which sought to confer on the circuit courts the full sweep of judicial power contained in the Constitution.[101] But nothing happened. Congressional preoccupation with judicial organization is extremely tenuous all through our history except after needs have gone unremedied for so long a time as to gather compelling momentum

[99] On December 9, 1817, Claiborne of Tennessee, in submitting a resolution for alterations in the judicial system, called the attention of the House to the plight of the Seventh Circuit: " One circuit judge was assigned to Kentucky, Tennessee, and Ohio; the labors of that circuit were too Herculean for the constitution of any man whatever. The consequence was, that in Tennessee, being the last district in the judge's circuit, where the cases before the court are numerous and important, there were no trials — for the past five years there had not been perhaps twenty causes disposed of. The time of the judge was so divided that it made it impossible for him to devote the necessary time to the court in Tennessee. Unless some remedy was provided, there was in that State an operative denial of justice as to the laws of the United States." 31 ANN. CONG. 419. The Seventh Circuit's grievance is dwelt on by Buchanan in the House on Jan. 9, when, quoting from a memorial from the bar of Nashville, " Such has been the delay of justice in the State of Tennessee, that some of the important causes now pending in their Circuit Courts, are older than the professional career of almost every man at the bar." 2 CONG. DEB. 918. Wright in the House on Jan. 19, 1826, comparing the dockets of the circuits shows that the suits per year in the Seventh Circuit totalled 1700 as against 130, the highest for any other circuit. 2 CONG. DEB. 1047. This extraordinary volume of business consisted in the main of land cases. See BROWN, PLUMER'S MEMORANDUM OF PROCEEDINGS IN THE UNITED STATES SENATE: 1803–1807, 254. It will be recalled that Mr. Justice Todd's death was accelerated by the strain of sitting twice a year in the three distant Western states and once a year at Washington. See 1 WARREN, op. cit., 301.

[100] Story's explanation of the manner in which this bill was prepared is reminiscent of the Judges Bill of 1925: " The printed bill was originally prepared by myself, and submitted to my brethren of the Supreme Court. It received a revision from several of them, particularly Judges Marshall and Washington, and was wholly approved by them, and indeed, except as to a single section, by all the other Judges." 1 W. W. STORY, LIFE AND LETTERS OF JOSEPH STORY, 300.

[101] An exposition of his bill by Mr. Justice Story is to be found in his son's life, 1 W. W. STORY, op. cit., 293. We have not been able to discover a copy of the text of the bill. It was this bill that was advocated by Chace in the Senate on February 27, 1817. See note 98, supra.

for action, or when some unusually dramatic litigation arouses widespread general interest.

The continuing expansion of the country kept impairing the ability of this judicial organization to cope effectively with its business. A series of new states are admitted during this period. Louisiana was followed by Indiana in 1816,[102] Mississippi in 1817,[103] Illinois in 1818,[104] Alabama in 1819,[105] Maine in 1820,[106] Missouri in 1821.[107] From 7,239,881 in 1810 the population increased to 9,638,453 in 1820.[108] The business corporation began to emerge,[109] adding substantially to the litigious traffic that found its way into the federal courts.

After a short subsidence, a substantial effort to move Congress to action is again made. New states asked for an extension of the circuit system;[110] the Seventh Circuit complained of the breakdown of that system.[111] The situation reached the stage of Congressional concern. Memorials to Congress led to an investi-

---

[102] Act of April 19, 1816, 3 STAT. 289; Res. of Dec. 11, 1816, 3 STAT. 399. By the Act of Mar. 3, 1817, § 2, 3 STAT. 390, Indiana was erected into one judicial district with a district judge who exercised circuit court jurisdiction.

[103] Act of Mar. 1, 1817, 3 STAT. 348; Res. of Dec. 10, 1817, 3 STAT. 472. By the Act of April 3, 1818, § 2, 3 STAT. 413, Mississippi was erected into one judicial district with a district judge who exercised circuit court jurisdiction.

[104] Act of April 18, 1818, 3 STAT. 428; Res. of Dec. 3, 1818, 3 STAT. 536. By the Act of Mar. 3, 1819, § 2, 3 STAT. 502, Illinois was erected into one judicial district with a district judge who exercised circuit court jurisdiction.

[105] Act of Mar. 2, 1819, 3 STAT. 489; Res. of Dec. 14, 1819, 3 STAT. 608. By the Act of April 21, 1820, § 2, 3 STAT. 564, Alabama was erected into one judicial district with a district judge who exercised circuit court jurisdiction.

[106] Act of Mar. 3, 1820, 3 STAT. 544. By the Act of Mar. 30, 1820, Maine was made part of the First Circuit. Prior to that time the district court of Maine had exercised circuit court jurisdiction.

[107] Act of Mar. 6, 1820, 3 STAT. 545; Res. of Mar. 2, 1821, 3 STAT. 645. By the Act of Mar. 16, 1822, § 2, 3 STAT. 653, Missouri was erected into one judicial district with a district judge who exercised circuit court jurisdiction.

[108] ROSSITER, A CENTURY OF POPULATION GROWTH, 1790-1900, U. S. BUREAU OF CENSUS, 80.

[109] HENDERSON, POSITION OF FOREIGN CORPORATIONS IN AMERICAN CONSTITUTIONAL LAW, 36.

[110] *E.g.*, Indiana communicated a memorial to Congress praying for a different organization of the courts in that state. 40 ANN. CONG. 146, 649; 41 *ibid.*, 49, 804.

[111] On February 23, 1824, a petition of practitioners in the court of the United States for the Seventh Circuit in the Kentucky district praying for reorganization was referred to the House Judiciary Committee. 41 ANN. CONG. 1619. See also Buchanan in the House on January 9, 1826, 2 CONG. DEB. 918-919. See note 99, *supra.*

gation and a report by the Judiciary Committee of the House
testified to the existence of real evils.[112]   The Committee submitted alternative proposals for consideration " in order that
the next Congress may be prepared to decide whether . . . and
what changes are necessary."   These alternatives, soon to be
embodied in bills,[113] were for many years before Congress.
The Federalist scheme of 1801 was revived by Webster, as
Chairman of the House Judiciary Committee, in a bill reported
by him on February 28, 1824.[114]   A less radical remedy was
sought in a bill calling for separate circuit judges for the western
circuits.[115]   The third expedient was the familiar device of increasing the membership of the Supreme Court.[116]   The need for
legislation was vigorously put by Monroe in his Annual Message
to the Second Session of the Eighteenth Congress on December
7, 1824:

" Some of our arrangements, and particularly the judiciary establishment, were made with a view to the original thirteen States only.
Since then the United States have acquired a vast extent of territory;

---

[112] See HOUSE REPORT, No. 105, 17th Cong., 2nd Sess., Ser. No. 87.   The
report, which was made by Plumer of New Hampshire, was made upon the
reference of the memorial of the Indiana Legislature to the Judiciary Committee.
See 40 ANN. CONG. 1173–1175.

[113] In the Senate on December 12, 1822, Johnson of Louisiana submitted a
resolution to alter the judicial system " so as to make it uniform throughout the
Union, by establishing circuit courts in the new States." 40 ANN. CONG. 29.
The resolution was referred to the Judiciary Committee, but on February 27,
1823, the committee was discharged from further consideration of the matter. 40
ibid., 31, 287. Van Buren, however, on the same day submitted a resolution that
the Attorney General be requested to submit such suggestions and modifications
as he might deem would improve the system. 40 *ibid.*, 293. After discussion the
resolution was not agreed to. 40 *ibid.*, 298.

[114] 42 ANN. CONG. 1701. The revived circuit judges' scheme differed from the
Act of 1801 in that a circuit judge was to be appointed for each district who,
with the district judge, was to constitute the circuit court. It also provided
for eleven circuits. On May 14, 1824, Webster, despairing of getting anything
done that session, moved for the postponement of the bill. 42 *ibid.*, 2617.

[115] See comment of Mason upon this project in a letter to Webster of December 29, 1823, and his decided preference for " circuit courts on the plan of those in
1801." HILLARD, MEMOIR OF JEREMIAH MASON, 278–279.

[116] Such a scheme was proposed by Owen of Alabama on December 8, 1823.
41 ANN. CONG. 805, 810. This proposal was the basis of the bill reported from
the House Judiciary Committee by Webster on December 22, 1825. 2 CONG.
DEB. 845.

eleven new States have been admitted into the Union, and Territories have been laid off for three others, which will likewise be admitted at no distant day. An organization of the Supreme Court which assigns to the judges any portion of the duties which belong to the inferior, requiring their passage over so vast a space under any distribution of the States that may now be made, if not impracticable in the execution, must render it impossible for them to discharge the duties of either branch with advantage to the Union. The duties of the Supreme Court would be of great importance if its decisions were confined to the ordinary limits of other tribunals, but when it is considered that this court decides, and in the last resort, on all the great questions which arise under our Constitution, involving those between the United States individually, between the States and the United States, and between the latter and foreign powers, too high an estimate of their importance can not be formed. The great interests of the nation seem to require that the judges of the Supreme Court should be exempted from every other duty than those which are incident to that high trust." [117]

This Congress, however, failed to take any action.[118] President Adams in his opening message to the new Congress made no mention of the matter,[119] but the proposals for reform now had sufficient impetus to put the movement under way. Opposition to a new panel of circuit judges was unabated; [120] the only road to relief lay through an extension of the existing system. A bill providing for three new circuits and three new Associate Justices was reported from the House Judiciary Committee on December

---

[117] 2 MESSAGES AND PAPERS OF THE PRESIDENTS, 829–830.

[118] In this session of Congress debates upon the bill and the suggestions advanced in the forms of resolutions are numerous in the Senate. 43 ANN. CONG. 527–535, 582–589, 603–616. The House failed to reach the matter during this session.

[119] 2 MESSAGES AND PAPERS OF THE PRESIDENTS, 865.

[120] See, *e.g.*, Buchanan in the House on Jan. 10, 1826: " Next to doing justice, it is important to satisfy the People that justice has been done. The confidence on their part, in the Judiciary of their country, produces that contentment and tranquility which is the best security against sudden and dangerous political excitements. The Judges of the Supreme Court now enjoy this confidence in an eminent degree. . . . No suspicion has ever arisen against their personal or judicial integrity. Would the Supreme Court have enjoyed the same good fortune, if the judges had been entirely secluded from public observation, and had been confined, in the discharge of their important duties, to a room in this Capitol? " 2 CONG. DEB. 931.

22, 1825, by Webster.[121]   He himself was only lukewarm in
its support,[122] but the measure found a vigorous sponsor in
Buchanan.[123]   The latter, though alive to the handicaps under
which the circuit system was laboring, was an ardent believer in
the benefits incident to circuit riding:

" The time will come when the Judges of the Supreme Court shall
not be able to perform both their appellate and circuit court duties;
necessity will then compel their separation. The day, however, I trust
is far distant. I am willing to delay that event as long as possible —
not to anticipate its arrival." [124]

After a three weeks' debate,[125] the bill passed the House on January 25, 1826.[126]   In the meantime the Senate had also been
active. The inequality of justice produced by the existing system
was pressed by Western senators,[127] and on January 9, 1826, Van

---

[121] 2 CONG. DEB. 845.

[122] Webster, in the House on January 4, 1826, admits a change of opinion,
supporting an extension of the present system rather than the creation of separate
circuit judges. 2 CONG. DEB. 877. His earlier attitude was manifested by his bill
of 1824. Note 114, *supra*. The same sentiment is revealed in a letter to Mason
of January 15, 1824. HILLARD, MEMOIR OF JEREMIAH MASON, 281. See also
8 J. Q. ADAMS, MEMOIRS AND CORRESPONDENCE, 84. His speech in the House,
though the ablest of the debate, and his conduct of the bill in its stormy course,
illustrates that his conversion to the new scheme was skin-deep.

[123] " This system has continued without alteration, addition, or complaint, for
a period of eighteen years; and the question for the committee now to decide is,
whether the country shall now go on in this happy judicial course, extending the
present well tried system to meet the wants of the People, or whether we shall
commence a career of new and untried and hazarded experiments." In the House,
Jan. 9, 1826, 2 CONG. DEB. 917.

[124] 2 CONG. DEB. 925.

[125] This is, probably, one of the most distinguished debates dealing with judicial organization. Beginning on January 4, 1826, it continued without interruption
until January 25, 1826. See 2 CONG. DEB. 872–880 (Jan. 4), 883–892 (Jan. 6),
892–925 (Jan. 9), 927–939 (Jan. 10), 940–953 (Jan. 11), 953–970 (Jan. 12), 970–
988 (Jan. 13), 988–998 (Jan. 16), 999–1018 (Jan. 17), 1020–1040 (Jan. 18), 1042–
1054 (Jan. 19), 1061–1075 (Jan. 20), 1081–1095 (Jan. 23), 1095–1116 (Jan. 24),
1119–1149 (Jan. 25). Mr. Warren has partially summarized the debate. 2 WAR-
REN, THE SUPREME COURT IN UNITED STATES HISTORY, c. 17.

[126] The vote was 132 to 59. 2 CONG. DEB. 1149.

[127] Eaton of Tennessee on December 13, 1825, in proposing a resolution for
amending the judicial system so that all the states should participate equally in its
benefits, called attention to the complaint of the West: " The Western country
had not had a fair dealing on the subject, and, until they should be placed on the
same footing with the other States of this Union, as respected their Judiciary, they

Buren of the Judiciary Committee reported a bill for the same increase in circuits but redistricting the states that comprised them.[128] The debate in the Senate reveals the conflicting views of Senators as to the methods by which judicial organization should be kept abreast of national development. Opposition to an increase in the personnel of the Supreme Court was marked.[129] Strong fear was expressed, among others by Levi Woodbury, a future Justice, that increasing numbers would decrease individual responsibility.[130] The Federalist scheme of 1801 was also suggested.[131] A new note creeps in with the proposal to reduce federal jurisdiction by its transference to the state courts.[132] Finally the Senate passed the House bill in an amended form so as to correspond in substance with Van Buren's measure.[133] The bill, thus amended, came before the House.[134] Its Judiciary Committee reported unanimously against accepting the Senate organization of the circuits.[135] The Senate, equally obstreperous,

---

would never cease to complain, and to ask redress." 2 CONG. DEB. 13. A similar resolution was pressed by Johnston of Louisiana on December 15. See 2 CONG. DEB. 14.

[128] 2 CONG. DEB. 30.

[129] See, *e.g.*, Woodbury of New Hampshire on April 11 and 12, 1826, 2 CONG. DEB. 463–488, 508–509; Robbins of Rhode Island on April 11, 1826, 2 CONG. DEB. 497–507; Harper of South Carolina on April 14, 1826, 2 CONG. DEB. 548–555.

[130] "Any labor to be performed jointly by ten, naturally appears to impose less upon each, than if it was to be performed by seven. Each one, also, in his conduct, stands out in less bold relief to the public eye. Each is, from the well known frailty of man, inclined to think he may nod with greater safety while so many others watch. . . . This is human nature; and we can as easily escape from ourselves as escape from its influence, though under much greater checks and responsibilities as legislators than judges." Woodbury in the Senate on April 11, 1826, 2 CONG. DEB. 478.

[131] See, *e.g.*, Holmes of Maine in the Senate on April 13, 1826, 2 CONG. DEB. 537–543.

[132] A bill to this effect was introduced in the Senate by Dickerson of New Jersey and received the endorsement of Findlay of Pennsylvania on April 13, 1826. See 2 CONG. DEB. 547–548.

[133] A motion by Mills of Massachusetts to reduce the number of judges to seven was defeated on April 14. 2 CONG. DEB. 570. The bill passed the Senate on April 15 by a vote of 31 to 8. 2 *ibid.*, 571.

[134] The Senate's amendments, on motion of Webster, were referred to the Judiciary Committee. 2 CONG. DEB. 2303.

[135] On April 24, Webster reported from committee a resolution that the House disagree with the amendments. 2 CONG. DEB. 2514. The two objections were the new classification of districts into circuits and the requirement that the Justices

stood firm and even rejected the House resolution for a conference.[136] Further attempt at compromise was made in the House,
but the Judiciary Committee resisted.[137] The deadlock could not
be broken.

To what extent judicial reform foundered on the political hostility between Van Buren and Webster is largely surmise.[138] The
part played by prospective candidates for the new seats on the
Supreme Bench is also speculative. One brute fact is incon-
testable: the need for judicial reorganization was recognized by
all parties and its fulfillment was indefinitely postponed. At
least one explanation for the failure may be ventured. Legislation affecting judicial structure, unless it calls for wholesale
appointments, is without the driving force of a powerful, concentrated economic, political, or social interest.[139]

---

reside within their circuits. Webster felt that this would make the Justices judges
of circuits rather than judges of the Supreme Court — it would tend to make them
local rather than national in significance. 2 *ibid.,* 2515. After debate on April 28,
1826, the question of disagreeing to the Senate's amendment was decided in the
affirmative by a vote of 110 to 59. 2 *ibid.,* 2578–2586.

[136] On May 3, 1826, Van Buren advocated the adherence of the Senate to their
amendment, and the motion was carried. 2 CONG. DEB. 668–671. On May 4, the
House referred the question of the Senate's adherence to the Judiciary Committee.
2 *ibid.,* 2601–2603. The Judiciary Committee on May 5 reported, requesting a
conference with the Senate; a motion to this effect was carried. 2 CONG. DEB.
2603–2605. On May 8, the Senate Judiciary Committee reported that " no good "
would result from such a conference and that the invitation of the House be refused. 2 CONG. DEB. 691.

[137] On May 12, 1826, Webster from the Judiciary Committee reported in favor
of adherence to disagreement with the Senate. 2 CONG. DEB. 2628. See also Report of Webster, HOUSE REPORT, No. 207, 19th Cong., 1st Sess., Ser. No. 142. This
report was reprinted by order of the House on February 8, 1828. HOUSE REPORT,
No. 134, 20th Cong., 1st Sess., Ser. No. 177. On May 15, 1826, Webster moved
again to recommit the bill to the Judiciary Committee to see whether there was
anything in the amendment of the Senate which could not be altered by subsequent
legislation. The motion was negatived. 2 CONG. DEB. 2632. On May 16, 1826,
Letcher moved an identical resolution which the House voted to consider, but a
motion for the indefinite postponement of the bill was carried by a vote of 99 to
89. The reporter of the Congressional debate parenthetically remarks that this was
equivalent to rejection. 2 CONG. DEB. 2647.

[138] AUTOBIOGRAPHY OF VAN BUREN, 1918 AM. HIST. ASSN. REP. 219; 2 WAR-
REN, THE SUPREME COURT IN UNITED STATES HISTORY, 143. The inaccessibility
of the Van Buren Manuscripts, lodged in the Library of Congress, has rendered
further investigation of this phase of the subject impracticable.

[139] " In letters from Washington, I am told there is considerable talk of doing

While Congress was threshing over schemes for judicial expansion to keep pace with the country's growth, a powerful drive was afoot to cut down materially the jurisdiction of the Supreme Court.[140] This movement was wholly unrelated to the general issues of judicial reform. It represented the stubborn convictions of extreme State-Righters. They did not aim to reduce the burdens of the Supreme Court or to facilitate its labors; they aimed to reduce the powers of the National Government. We refer, of course, to the fight which centered around Section Twenty-five of the Judiciary Act,[141] subjecting state court decisions to Supreme Court review. The story need not detain us; it has been admirably narrated by Mr. Warren.[142] Suffice it to say that this proposal, with its serious bearing on the size of the

---

something on this subject, but that the result is very uncertain. In one of them is repeated a saying of A. Burr, 'that every legislature, in their treatment of the judiciary, is a d——d Jacobin club.' There is certainly nothing in a good judiciary likely to attract the favorable regards of a Legislature in turbulent party times. The dominant party in such times can expect no aid in furtherance of some of their measures from the judiciary. Indeed, both parties have unreasonable expectations of aid from the judiciary, are usually disappointed, and are apt to view it with jealousy. And as it has nothing to offer to appease or attract either party, neither will hazard much for it." Mason to Story on January 15, 1818, HILLARD, MEMOIR OF JEREMIAH MASON, 185–186, quoted in 2 WARREN, *op. cit.*, 132.

[140] The movement for the repeal of Section Twenty-five of the Judiciary Act assumes proportions after Cohens *v.* Virginia, 6 Wheat. (U. S.) 264 (1821). Resolutions denying the jurisdiction of the Supreme Court were passed in the Virginia Legislature. 19 NILES REG. 340, 417; 20 *ibid.*, 118. After the decision, the "Algernon Sidney" Papers of Judge Roane echoed the widespread protest against the right of review asserted by the Supreme Court. See W. E. Dodd, "Chief Justice Marshall and Virginia, 1813–1821," 12 AM. HIST. REV. 776. In 1822 Stevenson of Virginia had moved for the repeal of the section in Congress, and in 1824 Wickliffe of Kentucky again urged repeal. See 25 NILES REG. 302. This sentiment for repeal resulted in the report of a bill from the Senate Judiciary Committee, by Van Buren in 1824, requiring the assent of five of the seven Justices in any decision holding invalid a state law. See 41 ANN. CONG. 28, 336. Webster himself was not opposed to the idea. 2 WARREN, *op. cit.*, 124. During the debates on the revision of the judicial system there are constant echoes of this controversy. On April 8, 1826, Rowan in the Senate offered an amendment to the circuit court act requiring the concurrence of seven Justices of the proposed nine to hold state legislation unconstitutional. 2 CONG. DEB. 423. Forsythe in the House, on June 25, 1826, moved a similar amendment. 2 *ibid.*, 1119.

[141] Act of Sept. 24, 1789, § 25, 1 STAT. 73, 85.

[142] Charles Warren, "Legislative and Judicial Attacks on the Supreme Court of the United States — A History of the Twenty-Fifth Section of the Judiciary Act," 47 AM. L. REV. 1, 161.

Supreme Court docket and its even greater bearing upon the relation of the States to the Nation, failed in 1825 as it has always failed in its later revivals.[143]

4

The legislative activity from 1816 to 1826 thus spent itself in talk. It did serve, however, to disseminate knowledge concerning the work and the needs of the federal courts. So far as the judiciary itself was concerned, the upshot was the retention of all of its business, only more of it. Having denied organic relief, Congress could not resist some corrective for the arrears of cases in the Supreme Court, increasing from term to term. The rather leisurely tempo of the Supreme Court's work was accelerated by adding a month to its " session." [144] For a hundred years, as occasion demanded, Congress has resorted to this device for extending the Court's working time by lengthening its term. Barring this administrative change (which, while it helped to alleviate Supreme Court arrears, further decreased circuit court attendance by the Justices) another decade of legislative sterility followed. But the old grievances are again

---

143 On January 24, 1831, a bill for the repeal of the Twenty-fifth Section was favorably reported from the House Judiciary Committee by Davis of South Carolina.   At the same time a minority report was submitted by Buchanan, W. W. Ellsworth, and E. D. White.   This report, one of the famous documents of American constitutional law, of which six thousand copies were ordered printed by the House, adds to the factitious argument of Story, J., in Martin *v.* Hunter's Lessee, 1 Wheat. (U. S.) 304 (1816), a realization of the essentially practical problems that are involved in the maintenance of such a right of review over state decisions by the Supreme Court as part of the mechanism of adjustment needful for our federal system.   See 7 CONG. DEB. lxxvii, lxxxi; HOUSE REPORT, No. 43, 21st Cong., 2nd Sess., Ser. No. 210.   The bill suffered a severe defeat in the House by the overwhelming vote of 138 to 51.   See Charles Warren, *supra,* 47 AM. L. REV. 164.

144 Act of May 4, 1826, 4 STAT. 160.   The use of the word " term " instead of " session " does not occur in legislation respecting this subject prior to the Act of July 23, 1866, 14 STAT. 209.   Under the Act of 1789, § 1, 1 STAT. 73, the Supreme Court held two sessions, one beginning on the first Monday in February and the other on the first Monday in August.   Under the Act of February 13, 1801, § 1, 2 STAT. 89, there were also two stated sessions beginning on the first Monday in June and the first Monday in December.   By the Act of April 29, 1802, § 1, 2 STAT. 156, one stated session was provided for, beginning on the first Monday in February.

stirred out of Congress and, therefore, in it. Moreover the old grievances increase and multiply. Arkansas reached statehood [145] and joined the vast domain already outside the circuit system. Trade and commerce, finance, insurance, inland transportation, began to weave their interstate network.[146] Professor Turner thus summarizes the forces of economic transformation dominating this period:

" In the industrial field transportation was revolutionized by the introduction of the steamboat and by the development of canals and turnpikes. The factory system, nourished by the restrictions of the embargo and the war, rapidly developed until American manufactures became an interest which, in political importance, outweighed the old industries of shipping and foreign commerce. The expansion of cotton-planting transformed the energies of the south, extended her activity into the newer regions of the Gulf . . ." [147]

In the vernacular of today, the country's business showed a steady upward curve, and the country's business meant business for the courts. And so we find the thrice-told tale of memorials to Congress, resolutions in Congress, references to the Judiciary Committees, reports painting the familiar picture of a circuit system that did not work — its general inadequacies and its special injustice to a huge section of the country. Thus, on January 26, 1829, Berrien of South Carolina on behalf of the Senate Judiciary Committee tells the Senate what they have heard for many years:

" The most casual survey of the system has convinced the Committee of the existence of that inequality, which is assumed by the resolution, in an extent which it will be their duty to exhibit to the Senate; and a very careful consideration of the subject has not enabled them to discover any motives to its continuance, deduced either from

---

[145] Act of June 15, 1836, 5 Stat. 50. Section Four of this Act erected the state into one judicial district with a district judge who exercised circuit court jurisdiction.

[146] See Davis, Essays in the Earlier History of American Corporations, *passim;* Henderson, Position of Foreign Corporations in American Constitutional Law, c. 3.

[147] Turner, Rise of the New West, 4. See also Frederick J. Turner, " The Significance of the Frontier in American History," 1893 Am. Hist. Assn. Rep. 199.

an examination of the system itself, or from the condition of the country which is subjected to its operation." [148]

Everyone agrees to the truth of this picture. There is general concurrence on diagnosis. But conflicting views as to remedy cannot be resolved. "Thus far," concludes Berrien's report,

" a majority of the Committee have been enabled to concur in opinion: beyond this, they have been unable to reconcile the various and conflicting views which they individually entertain. In this state of things, all that is left to them to do, after having ascertained the existence of that inequality in the administration of the public justice, to which the resolution of inquiry was directed, is to present a brief view of the several remedies which have at different times been suggested, and then to commit the subject to the determination of the Senate.

" These various plans are as follows:

1. To continue the present system of Circuit Courts in the States to which it extends, and to appoint Circuit Judges for the six new States, with a provision for their elevation to the Supreme Court, as vacancies may occur on that bench.

2. To provide for the appointment of three or two additional Judges of the Supreme Court, and by this means to extend the Circuit Courts, as they are now constituted, to all the States.

3. To revive the system of 1801, by the appointment of Circuit Judges, distinct from those of the Supreme bench, and thus to extend an uniform system to all the States.

4. To direct the Circuit Courts in the several States, to be held by the District Judges, allotting three to a circuit; and in this, and in the preceding case, to relieve the Justices of the Supreme Court from the performance of circuit duties.

5. To keep the Supreme Court as it now is, both as to the numbers of which it shall consist, and the duties to be performed by the Judges; providing only, that whenever a vacancy shall occur, the Judge to be appointed shall be allotted to one of the circuits to be created in the new States: and to create three new circuits, and appoint Circuit Judges, to hold with the District Judges the Circuit Courts therein, leaving the Circuit Courts in the other States to be held, as at present, by the Justices of the Supreme Court and the District Judges in the said States respectively." [149]

---

[148] SEN. REP. No. 50, 20th Cong., 2nd Sess., Ser. No. 181, p. 1.
[149] *Ibid.*, pp. 6–7.

The grievance of the West bulks largest in the dissatisfaction with the federal judiciary. In Congress the Western representatives clamor most insistently for relief. They find a vigorous supporter in the new President, himself an ardent Westerner. In four successive messages Jackson urged action. In his message of 1831 he pointed out that " one fourth of the States in the Union do not participate in the benefits of a Circuit Court." [150] A year later he returned to the attack:

" Nothing can be more obvious than the obligation of the General Government to place all the States on the same footing in relation to the administration of justice, and I trust this duty will be neglected no longer." [151]

Neglected it was. In 1834 and 1835 he renewed his demand for legislation.[152] After two years came relief. The Senate Judiciary Committee early in 1835 reported a bill which would have secured one of the Justices for circuit duty in the unprovided territory by consolidating into a single circuit the two circuits which then comprised New Jersey and Pennsylvania, Delaware, and Maryland.[153] The bill encountered fatal Western opposi-

---

[150] 3 MESSAGES AND PAPERS OF THE PRESIDENTS, 1121.

[151] Message of Dec. 4, 1832, 3 ibid., 1168.

[152] Message of Dec. 1, 1834, 3 ibid., 1336; Message of Dec. 7, 1835, 3 ibid., 1396.

[153] On April 3, 1834, a bill was reported from the House Judiciary Committee providing for two new Supreme Court Justices and for the establishment of an eighth and a ninth circuit. HOUSE REPORT, No. 429, 23rd Cong., 1st Sess., Ser. No. 262. Frelinghuysen of New Jersey in the Senate on Feb. 4, 1835, offered a resolution to annex the Fourth to the Third Circuit and thus, without the addition of a new member to the Supreme Court, extend the circuit system to all the states. Indiana was to be attached to the Seventh Circuit, Alabama to the Sixth, and a new circuit created of Louisiana, Mississippi, Illinois, and Missouri. The resolution was adopted. 11 CONG. DEB. 287. A bill to this effect was reported from the Judiciary Committee on Feb. 23, 1825. 11 CONG. DEB. 584–594. At the same session of Congress Reynolds of Illinois in the House on January 17, 1835, had offered a resolution to extend the benefits of the circuit system to all the states, but he withdrew it upon being informed that the matter was already before the Judiciary Committee. 11 CONG. DEB. 1001. A bill extending the system without adding a Supreme Court Justice was reported by the Committee but withdrawn on February 5 upon a point of order. 11 ibid., 1192. On March 3, the House again took up the bill, amended it, and then laid it aside. 11 ibid., 1645. Objection that 12 o'clock had arrived and that the functions of the House had ceased, prevented Clay from getting any further consideration for the bill. 11 ibid., 1655.

tion. It was successfully urged that the proposed new circuit was too unmanageable for one Justice.[154] The proposed inclusion of Louisiana intensified the objections. The Supreme Court, it was insisted, ought to contain a civilian.[155] Buchanan renewed his 1826 proposal for the creation of two new circuits for the Western states.[156] His plan, involving the addition of a member to the Supreme Court, prevailed in the Senate, February 24, 1835.[157] The House did not reach consideration of the measure till the closing day of the session, and it died with the death of that Congress.[158] Finally, by the Act of March 3, 1837,[159] Congress divided the United States into nine circuits, and added two members to the Supreme Court. The scheme of nine circuits, with a court of nine,[160] has survived the transformation of the

---

[154] Benton of Missouri in the Senate on February 23, 1835, vented his sarcasm upon the proposed measure: " It gave them a judicial circuit which extended from the Gulf of Mexico to lake Michigan — from the torrid to the frigid zone, and proposed to give them one term in a year. The gentlemen had better have made it like those planets whose circles are once in twenty years. . . . Louisiana is at one end of it, and then you are to take a huge leap over Tennessee and Kentucky, the Cumberland and Ohio Rivers, and then alight on the borders of lake Michigan. . . . We ought to wait for organizing this circuit till we have arrived at a greater art in aerial navigation." 1 Cong. Globe, 279.

[155] Thus, Porter of Louisiana in the Senate on February 23, 1835: " In Louisiana, the whole of our jurisprudence is based upon the civil law; but what is her situation? When her cases are tried and brought to the Supreme Court there is not a judge on the bench who has any knowledge of it. The requisite knowledge can not be acquired from books, but only by applying its principles to the affairs of men." 1 Cong. Globe, 280. See also note 43, supra.

[156] Upon Buchanan's motion the bill was recommitted to the Judiciary Committee with instructions to create two instead of one circuit out of these Western states. 1 Cong. Globe, 281.   [157] 1 Cong. Globe, 286.   [158] 1 Cong. Globe, 330.

[159] 5 Stat. 176. On December 8, 1836, a bill was introduced in the Senate by Grundy of Tennessee to amend the judicial system. 3 Cong. Globe, 10. Upon its second reading it was referred to the Senate Judiciary Committee on December 15. 3 ibid., 27. It was reported out by Grundy on December 26. 3 ibid., 51. On February 13, 1837, it was amended in the Committee of the Whole. 3 ibid., 185. It passed the Senate on February 15 without debate. 3 ibid., 197. On February 17, it was referred to the House Judiciary Committee and reported back on February 22, without amendment. 3 ibid., 209, 243. On February 24, Thomas of the House Judiciary Committee reported the bill again to the House with sundry amendments and proposing a different division of circuits. 3 ibid., 251. On March 3, 1837, the bill was debated. Robertson moved to substitute the House amendments, but the motion was defeated and the bill was passed. 3 ibid., 280.

[160] By the Act of March 2, 1855, 10 Stat. 631, a tenth circuit (but without a circuit Justice) consisting of California was added, and by the Act of March 3, 1863, 12 Stat. 794, amended by the Act of February 19, 1864, 13 Stat. 4, Oregon

country into a continent and has been adapted to the needs of a population which increased from seventeen million in 1840 to a hundred and ten million in 1920. The Act of 1837 gave the West and the Southwest two circuits. Eight states — Alabama, Arkansas, Illinois, Indiana, Louisiana, Michigan, Mississippi, and Missouri — were at last added to the circuit system.[161] But, as so frequently happens, a long delayed plan for relief had become antiquated by events. What may have been adequate to the situation in 1825 was found wholly inadequate for 1837. The rapid increase of Supreme Court and circuit work was too much for the Justices. A circuit system no longer could work. Responding to a Senate inquiry in 1838 [162] the Justices reported the number of miles travelled by them in doing circuit duty. The summary carries its own comment:

Justice	Miles Travelled	Circuit	States in Circuit [163]
Taney	458	Fourth	Dela., Md.
Barbour	1498	Fifth	Va., N. C.
Story	1896	First	Mass., Me., N. H., R. I.
Baldwin	2000	Third	Pa., N. J.
Wayne	2370	Sixth	S. C., Ga.
McLean	2500	Seventh	Ill., Ohio, Ind., Mich.
Thompson	2590	Second	N. Y., Conn., Vt.
Catron	3464	Eighth	Tenn., Ky., Mo.
McKinley	10,000	Ninth	Ala., La., Miss., Ark.

and California were organized into a tenth circuit and an additional Justice was added to the Supreme Court. But by the Act of July 23, 1866, 14 STAT. 209, the Supreme Court was again reduced to seven and the districts reorganized into nine circuits. By the Act of April 10, 1869, 16 STAT. 44, the membership of the Supreme Court was again increased to nine. Again on February 10, 1891, Hoar of the Senate Judiciary Committee reported out a bill for increasing the number of judicial circuits from nine to ten. HOUSE REPORT, No. 2179, 21st Cong., 2nd Sess., Ser. No. 2827. On September 21, 1890, Dolph of Oregon in the Senate moved an amendment to the bill, which later became the Circuit Courts of Appeals Act of 1891, for the addition of a tenth circuit to consist of Oregon, Washington, Montana, and Idaho, but his amendment was defeated. 21 CONG. REC. 10287.

161 Act of Mar. 3, 1837, § 1, 5 STAT. 176. The growth of the circuits is charted in 1 Fed. Cas. x.

162 A resolution to this effect was introduced by Clay of Alabama on March 13, 1838, 6 CONG. GLOBE, 237. On Jan. 10, 1839, Clay also introduced a resolution to inquire into the expediency of equalizing the amount of labor to be performed by the Supreme Court Justices. 7 *ibid.*, 112.

163 SEN. DOC. No. 50, 25th Cong., 3rd Sess., Ser. No. 339. McKinley, J., added to his report: " I have never yet been at Little Rock, the place of holding the court

Thus starts again the long treadmill of discussion and attempted legislation to amend or abolish the circuit system.[164] With the increase in its business, the Supreme Court again fell seriously in arrears.[165] More time for its work was devised. Again a month was added to the Court's time by providing for its commencement on the first Monday of December instead of

---

in Arkansas; but from the best information I can obtain, it could not be conveniently approached in the spring of the year, except by water, and by that route the distance would be greatly increased." *Ibid.*, 39. Even Taney, whose circuit was the smallest and not remote, had his difficulties: " In Baltimore he [Taney] was present nearly every April and November, at the terms of Court, though occasionally, the length of the term of the Supreme Court kept him in Washington too long to permit him to sit in the April term." STEINER, LIFE OF ROGER B. TANEY, 451. An interesting comparison is afforded by the distances travelled by the judges prior to the increase from seven to nine circuits:

Circuit	Distances Travelled by Justices
First	1940
Second	1500
Third	116
Fourth	450
Fifth	1000
Sixth	1950
Seventh	2600

These figures are taken from the speech of Wright in the House on January 19, 1826, 2 CONG. DEB. 1047.

[164] On February 27, 1841, the Senate took up the consideration of a bill to amend the judicial system that had been reported from the Senate Judiciary Committee. In the discussion that followed, Burton of Missouri advocated an increase in the membership of the Supreme Court to twelve in order to extend properly the circuit system. 7 CONG. GLOBE, 213. Walker called especial attention to the fact that the present system was " virtually denying to the Southwest her full participation in the blessings of the judicial system." 7 *ibid.*, 215. The bill passed the Senate but was not taken up in the House. 7 *ibid.*, 216. By the Act of August 16, 1842, 5 STAT. 507, the circuits were reorganized but no extension was made. The Fifth Circuit was absorbed into the Fourth and Sixth Circuits, and Alabama and Louisiana were carved out of the huge Ninth Circuit to form an independent Fifth Circuit.

[165] The capacity of the Supreme Court to dispose of litigation during this period is revealed by the figures contained in SEN. Doc. No. 91, 29th Cong., 1st Sess., Ser. No. 473:

Term	Cases Pending	Cases Disposed of
1841.................	106	42
1842.................	107	52
1843.................	118	36
1844.................	168	46
1845.................	173	64

the second Monday of January,[166] and the Justices were relieved from attending " more than one term of the circuit court within any district of said circuit in any one year." [167]   The condition of the Supreme Court calendar made urgent still more drastic relief.   In the 1845 " session " a hundred and seventy-three cases were docketed, and a hundred and nine were left undecided at its close.[168]   In 1848 it was proposed in the House to relieve the Justices of circuit duty for one year.[169]   This opened the sluices to the old debates of 1825 and 1826.   The bill passed the House but the Senate had its own notions for reform.   It rejected the House measure and in its place passed a bill relieving the Justices of this duty for two years, which the House in its turn promptly rejected.[170]   The Supreme Court was thrown back upon

---

[166] Act of June 17, 1844, 5 STAT. 676.   On January 3, 1844, a bill introduced by Crittenden of Kentucky to change the session of the Supreme Court was referred to the Senate Judiciary Committee.   12 CONG. GLOBE, 96.   On February 27, it was reported back by Berrien without amendment.   12 *ibid.*, 326.   On March 25, an amendment was moved and adopted in the Committee of the Whole.   See 12 *ibid.*, 440.   It passed the Senate on March 28.   12 *ibid.*, 451.   On May 15, the House Judiciary Committee reported it without amendment.   12 *ibid.*, 600.   It passed that body on the last day of the session.   12 *ibid.*, 693.

[167] Act of June 17, 1844, § 2, 5 STAT. 676.

[168] See note 165, *supra*.

[169] On Feb. 29, 1848, Ingersoll of Missouri from the House Judiciary Committee reported a bill relieving the Supreme Court Justices of circuit duty for two years.   Bowlin of Missouri moved a substitute bill that gave the district judges in the first instance the same jurisdiction as the circuit courts, and contemplated an intermediate court of appeals consisting of the district judges and one member of the Supreme Court.   18 CONG. GLOBE, 398–399.   On March 6, the House debated the measure at length.   Thompson of Mississippi moved an amendment to cut down the relief from two years to one, and the amendment was adopted.   Bowlin's substitute bill was rejected, and the original bill as amended was passed.   See 18 *ibid.*, 432–433.   The Senate Judiciary Committee reported the bill to the Senate without amendment.   18 *ibid.*, 446, 453.   Benton of Missouri spoke in opposition to the bill on March 9.   18 *ibid.*, 581.   The debate in the Senate occurred on April 7.   The bill received the hearty support of Dayton and Crittenden.   Allen of Ohio voiced the prevailing sentiment of the opponents: " I would admonish those gentlemen, who do not think as I do on these points, but wish to maintain this Judiciary in its present features, that if they do not wish to sound the tocsin, they had better not separate the judges for an hour from circuit duties, and direct intercourse with the people of the States."   18 *ibid.*, 595.   The vote to engross the bill failed by 19 to 17.   18 *ibid.*, 581–598; 19 *ibid.*, App. 582–590.   On April 12 a vote to reconsider the bill passed, and after further debate on April 17, the bill was finally defeated.   18 *ibid.*, 623, 640, 642.

[170] On April 20, 1848, Badger in the Senate reported a bill for relieving the Supreme Court of circuit duty for two terms and repealing the second section of

self-help through its control over practice before it.   Up to this
time argument before the Court was unconfined.[171]   By a rule
promulgated on December 1, 1849, a divided Court limited
argument of counsel to two hours a side.[172]

This rule did something, but not much.   The machinery was
carrying a load beyond its capacity.   The existing judicial structure was unequal to the volume and the range of litigation coming to the federal courts.   There is a steady growth of business
before the Supreme Court.[173]   The actual volume of business in
the various district and circuit courts, the manner of its disposition, the waste and cost which congestion has involved, we shall
not know until pride in the history of individual federal courts
and an appreciation of the significance of their records leads to
an illuminating writing of their story.[174]   But we know enough

---

the Act of June 17, 1844.   18 CONG. GLOBE, 656.   On April 28 it was reported back
from the Judiciary Committee without amendment.   18 *ibid.*, 700.   On June 24
" after a brief explanation " the bill passed the Senate.   18 *ibid.*, 872.   In the House
it was referred to the Judiciary Committee and reported back with an amendment
on Aug. 8, 1848, when it was finally rejected by a vote of 98 to 61.   18 *ibid.*,
882, 1049.

[171] In the February Term, 1812, a rule was adopted permitting only two counsel to argue upon each side of the case.   See 1 Wheat. (U. S.) xviii (1816).   This
was interpreted by the Court to deny two counsel the opportunity of arguing upon
each point that the case involved.   See Fitzsimmons v. Ogden, 7 Cranch (U. S.)
2 (1812).

[172] 7 How. (U. S.) v (1849).   Wayne and Woodbury, JJ., took specific pains
to have their dissent to the adoption of this rule recorded.   8 How. (U. S.) v
(1850).

[173] In 1840 the number of cases docketed was 92.   In 1850 the number had
increased to 253, and in 1860 to 310.   See Davis in the Senate on May 1, 1882,
13 CONG. REC. 3464.

[174] Our national history will not have been adequately written until the history of our judicial systems can be adequately told through monograph studies of
individual courts.   Such a barren compilation as Thomas Speed's History of the
United States Courts in Kentucky has to be supplanted by studies that tell and
interpret.   Judge Charles P. Daly's " History of the New York Court of Common
Pleas," 1 ed. (Smith, N. Y.) xvii, and, even more so, Roscoe's " History of the
English Prize Courts " are examples for extensive emulation.   The notable edition
just published by Judge Hough of " Cases in Vice Admiralty and Admiralty,
New York, 1715–1788," with his vivid introductory picture of the Vice-Admiralty
of the Province and the Court of Admiralty of New York prior to the Constitution, shows to what scholarly uses the neglected old files, particularly of our earlier
federal courts, may be put.

Nor shall we be able to know how our courts function until an effective system of judicial statistics becomes part of our tradition.   Something is told in the

now to know that only inertia and the usual slowness of response to the need for judicial reform maintained the system. One more vigorous effort for thoroughgoing reorganization was made before the Civil War. In his message to Congress of December 5, 1853, President Pierce echoed the old criticisms.[175] Conditions had made them more valid than ever. Congress again starts the familiar round. In answer to a Senate Resolution [176] Pierce transmitted the report of his Attorney General on the circuit system.[177] Caleb Cushing in a notable document canvassed the various plans for improvement and concluded with a proposal which, while it formally retained circuit duties for the Justices, called for the appointment of a set of circuit judges.[178] The time was not yet ripe for agreement on

figures furnished in the Annual Reports of the Attorney General beginning with 1875; but not enough. A very modest beginning has been made by Mr. Ernest Knaebel, the Reporter of the Supreme Court, in giving a " Summary Statement of Business of the Supreme Court." See *e.g.*, 265 U. S. 599. But a much more detailed analysis of the business of the Court is needed if we are to have what might be called a social audit of our political institutions comparable to the financial audit of our business institutions. What is needed is an annual detailed analysis of litigation, the courts whence cases come, the dispositions made of them, the nature of the questions involved, etc., etc., etc. In this connection, see " Final Report of Departmental Committee to Revise Judicial Statistics of Scotland," REPORT ON JUDICIAL STATISTICS OF SCOTLAND FOR 1897, 7–9. Dealing with a very specialized court Mr. E. S. Roscoe, the Registrar of the British Prize Court, has shown what can be done. THE ORGANIZATION AND WORK OF THE BRITISH PRIZE COURT (1914–1923). The annual judicial statistics of England and Wales, Scotland, and Ireland, are a challenging commentary on our own lack of self-critique. For the function of statistics in the administration of justice, see, generally, Georg von Mayr, " Theoretische Statistik " and " Statistik und Gesellschaftslehre," in MARQUARDSEN, HANDBUCH DES OEFFENTLICHEN RECHTS; MAYO-SMITH, STATISTICS AND SOCIOLOGY, c. 1; ROBINSON, HISTORY AND ORGANIZATION OF CRIMINAL STATISTICS IN THE UNITED STATES, *passim*. *Cf.* Dean (now Mr. Justice) Harlan F. Stone: " The statistical method of dealing with social problems often cannot be relied on as mathematical demonstration leading to specific conclusions, but it may be used to indicate tendencies, to mark out the boundaries of a problem and to point the direction which should be given to a particular investigation of a non-statistical character." Review of " Criminal Justice in Cleveland," 35 HARV. L. REV. 967–968.

[175] 5 MESSAGES AND PAPERS OF THE PRESIDENTS, 217–218. His second message of December 4, 1854, returned to the subject. 5 *ibid.*, 292.

[176] Res. of Dec. 7, 1853, 32 CONG. GLOBE, 14.

[177] Ex. Doc. No. 41, 33rd Cong., 1st Sess., Ser. No. 698. The report was also transmitted to the House and printed as Ex. Doc. No. 73, 33rd Cong., 1st Sess., Ser. No. 723. See also 2 FUESS, CALEB CUSHING, 180.

[178] " It is to have, at present, nine, and prospectively, ten circuits; to rearrange

so ambitious a program.   Profounder issues were absorbing the
energies and arousing the emotions of Congress.   The lesser issue
of judicial reform was side-tracked and partly engulfed by its
political and personal relations to the transcendent controversy of
slavery.   Everything was subordinated to the impending conflict.
Even so, something had to be done about California.[179]   A whole

the existing nine circuits, so as to comprehend within them all the judicial districts
except those of California; to appoint nine assistant circuit judges, one for each
circuit; to preserve unimpaired the existing jurisdiction of the circuit courts, in all
the districts, as well as those now within the circuits as those without; to withdraw the circuit powers from the district judges, and revest them in the proper
circuit court exclusively; to have the ordinary circuit court holden as it is in each
judicial district, and composed of the justice of the Supreme Court residing in the
circuit, as now, but to associate with him an assistant circuit judge, so that the
court shall be holden by a justice of the Supreme Court and the assistant circuit
judge the latter being left to his proper district duties, and there being a real and
effective circuit court even in the case of the necessary occasional absence of the
justice of the Supreme Court." Ex. Doc. No. 41, *supra*, p. 9. It is to be noted
how closely the Act of April 10, 1869, 16 STAT. 44, achieved Cushing's plan in
detail. His survey of the merits and demerits of the existing system deserves
notice: " The general system, thus cursorily sketched, has now stood the test of
the controversies and criticism of two generations; its practical working has become
familiar to the whole community; the adjudications of a long succession of eminent
judges have regulated its forms and imparted precision to its action; and no other
theory of judicial decision presents itself, which promises any advantages com-
mensurate with the experimental uncertainties which a radical change of organization would introduce into the administration of justice throughout the Union. The
district courts, with jurisdiction limited by the boundaries of the respective States;
the circuit courts, with concurrent jurisdiction, or with original, superior, and
appellate jurisdiction; and the Supreme Court, with its constitutional power, seem
together to constitute a judicial system of inherent adaptation to the federative
political system of the United States. Accordingly, while Congress has in its wisdom seen fit, as the occasion seemed to require, to make changes in secondary
matters, such as the number of judges of the Supreme Court, or the number and
limits of the several circuits, or the personality of the circuit courts, or the quality
or degrees of the relative or absolute jurisdiction of the district and circuit courts,
— it has left the great monumental parts of the system as they were constructed
by the same wise men who framed the Constitution." Ex. Doc. No. 41, *supra*,
p. 4.

   [179] Given of California in the Senate on February 7, 1855, called attention to
the flood of land cases in the district courts of California, the necessity for a
prompt and adequate adjudication of these highly important claims, and the impossibility of the courts' coping with their crowded dockets. See 36 CONG. GLOBE,
605. See also Cushing's Report, Ex. Doc. No. 41, *supra*, p. 5. By the Act of
September 28, 1850, § 2, 9 STAT. 521, California was divided into two districts with
district judges exercising circuit court jurisdiction. By the Act of August 31, 1852,
10 STAT. 76, 84, the district judge of the northern district was also made judge of
the southern district. By the Act of January 18, 1854, 10 STAT. 264, a judge was
provided for the southern district.

new empire had been opened up, bringing in its train a mass of highly important litigation. Almost over night law had to be made wholesale.[180] It was imperative to have a judge to make it. While the general system was left untouched, California was provided for *ad hoc*. By the Act of March 2, 1855,[181] California was erected into a circuit with a separate circuit judge. The process of divorcing circuit courts from the Supreme Court had begun.[182]

The Civil War put out of men's minds such placid concerns as judicial organization, but the Civil War is also a turning-point in the history of the federal judiciary. The Northern victory released new conceptions of nationalism and new economic forces. Their reflex is seen in the structure of our judiciary. In a few years they altered profoundly the system that had prevailed since 1789.

---

[180] See McAllister (U. S. C. C.) Rep., *passim*, containing the opinions of California's first circuit judge, the well-known Marshall Hall McAllister. The conditions out of which the litigious difficulties of early California arose are vividly sketched by Judge Field in his Early Days in California, 121 *et seq*. See also J. N. Pomeroy's introductory sketch to Legislative and Judicial Works of Judge Field, 22 *et seq*., and the revealing story of Dr. Mary Floyd Williams in her San Francisco Vigilance Committee of 1851, particularly Chapter 7, The Failure to Establish Social Control.

[181] 10 STAT. 631.

[182] On February 5, 1855, a bill to this effect was reported from the Senate Judiciary Committee. See 36 CONG. GLOBE, 567. A similar bill was reported to the House on February 8, 1855. 36 *ibid.*, 630. On February 7, the bill was debated in the Senate. Judah P. Benjamin of Louisiana and Stephen A. Douglas of Illinois both objected to the bill in that it introduced an innovation in the circuit system. 36 *ibid.*, 604, 606. Seward rejoined that the force of such a precedent was certainly very slight. 36 *ibid.*, 608. On February 12, Benjamin's motion to recommit the bill to the judiciary so that the circuit courts of California would be organized in conformity with the other circuit courts of the United States was defeated, and the bill was passed. 36 *ibid.*, 680–681. The bill passed the House on February 27, with little discussion. 36 *ibid.*, 715, 971.

CHAPTER II

FROM THE CIVIL WAR
TO
THE CIRCUIT COURTS OF APPEALS ACT

I

THROUGHOUT the history of the federal courts their business has come from the interests that at different periods have been predominant in our national life. The range and intensity of governing political, social, and economic forces are accurately reflected in the volume and variety of federal litigation. This is markedly illustrated by the era beginning with the defeat of the Confederacy. The years of the Civil War were years of preoccupation with military victory. Just as in the World War, this meant stimulation of some economic forces and repression of others. Peace brought with it an accelerated industrial development, partly because normal processes, which had been pent up during the War, were released, and partly because of their intensification by the War. The transcontinental railroad systems increased domestic commerce enormously.[1] The railroads steadily pushed the frontier westward.[2] They brought economic penetration of the Northwest and Southwest.[3] Popula-

---

[1] The following mileage figures indicate the pace of railroad development:

1850	9,021	miles
1860	30,626	"
1870	52,922	"
1880	93,922	"
1890	166,654	"

See BEARD, CONTEMPORARY AMERICAN HISTORY, 29; Louis B. Schmidt, "Some Significant Aspects of the Agrarian Revolution in the United States," 18 IA. JOURN. OF HIST. & POL. 371, 379. See also Robert E. Riegel, "Trans-Mississippi Railroads during the Fifties," 10 MISS. VALLEY HIST. REV. 109.

[2] See Arthur C. Cole, "The Passing of the Frontier," 5 MISS VALLEY HIST. REV. 288; Paxson, "The Pacific Railroads and the Disappearance of the Frontier in America," 1907 AM. HIST. ASSN. REP. I, 105.

[3] See R. S. Cotterill, "The Beginnings of Railroads in the Southwest," 8 MISS. VALLEY HIST. REV. 318.

tion and politics followed in their wake. The public domain became territories and the territories states.[4] Even more significant, perhaps, was the repercussion of railroad development upon our foreign trade. America became a great food exporter.[5] Contemporaneous advances in steam navigation furthered this industrial expansion. The clipper ship was supplanted by vessels less picturesque but assuring greater speed and ampler tonnage.[6]

The Civil War gave impulse to these powerful new economic forces; it also released political ideas of nationalism no less important in their practical consequences. The supremacy of national authority, the extension of federal activities, the resort to federal agencies, were vindicated both in theory and practice to the mind of the dominant North. The Federal Government not the individual states had won the War. Therefore it was expected to preserve the fruits of victory. National authority had to liquidate the institution of slavery, hitherto recognized by all the leading parties as the local concern of the states. By an easy transition other interests previously left to state action were absorbed by federal authority. The central government exerted power in fields which, in the past, would have aroused bitter opposition as encroachment upon the states. Transportation,[7] education,[8] commerce,[9] were actively promoted

[4] From 1850 to 1868 the following territories were organized: New Mexico (1850), Utah (1850), Washington (1853), Nebraska (1854), Kansas (1854), Colorado (1861), Nevada (1861), Dakota (1861), Arizona (1863), Idaho (1863), Montana (1864), Wyoming (1868); admitted as states in the following order: Kansas (1861), Nevada (1864), Nebraska (1867), Colorado (1876), North and South Dakota (1889), Montana (1889), Washington (1889), Idaho (1890), Wyoming (1890), Utah (1896). See FARRAND, LEGISLATION OF CONGRESS FOR THE GOVERNMENT OF THE ORGANIZED TERRITORIES IN THE UNITED STATES, 55. Admission to statehood was made more difficult by the Act of Feb. 2, 1872, § 5, providing that no state should be admitted without a population sufficient to entitle it to one Representative in Congress. See 17 STAT. 29.

[5] See Louis B. Schmidt, *supra*, 18 IA. JOURN. OF HIST. & POL. 371.

[6] "The Civil War merely hastened a process that had already begun, the substitution of steam for sail." MORISON, MARITIME HISTORY OF MASSACHUSETTS, 369. See WELLS, RECENT ECONOMIC CHANGES, 29–31.

[7] The legislation, during this period, dealing with land grant aids to railroad and telegraph lines, is particularly voluminous. By the Act of July 1, 1862, government aid was given to the construction of a railroad and telegraph line from the Missouri River to the Pacific Ocean. See 12 STAT. 489, amended by Act of July 2, 1864, 13 STAT. 356; the Act of Mar. 3, 1865, 13 STAT. 504; the Act of July 3, 1866, 14 STAT. 79; and the Act of June 20, 1874, 18 STAT. 111.

by the Federal Government.   It became the political receiver of
the southern states, and drastic limitations against the states were

---

By the Act of July 25, 1866, lands were granted for the construction of a railroad between California and Oregon.   See 14 STAT. 239, amended by Act of
June 25, 1868, 15 STAT. 80; and the Act of April 10, 1869, 16 STAT. 47.   By
the Act of July 27, 1866, government aid was afforded for the construction of
a railroad and telegraph line from Missouri and Arkansas to the Pacific Coast.
See 14 STAT. 292.   By the Act of Mar. 3, 1871, the Texas and Pacific Railroad
Company was incorporated and given extensive land grants.   See 16 STAT. 573,
amended by Act of May 2, 1872, 17 STAT. 59; and the Act of June 22, 1874, 18
STAT. 197.   By the Act of July 24, 1866, telegraph companies were permitted to
construct and maintain their lines along post-roads.   See 14 Stat. 221.   Land
grants were made to Minnesota for the construction of railroads by the Act of
May 5, 1864, 13 STAT. 64; the Act of July 4, 1866, 14 STAT. 87; and the Act of
July 13, 1866, 14 STAT. 97; to Wisconsin by the Act of May 5, 1864, 13 STAT. 66;
to Iowa by the Act of May 12, 1864, 13 STAT. 72; to Kansas by the Act of July
1, 1864, 13 STAT. 339; the Act of July 23, 1866, 14 STAT. 210; the Act of July
25, 1866, 14 STAT. 236; and the Act of July 26, 1866, 14 STAT. 289; to Missouri
and Arkansas by the Act of July 4, 1866, 14 STAT. 83; to California by the Act
of July 13, 1866, 14 STAT. 94; and the Act of Mar. 2, 1867, 14 STAT. 548; to
Oregon by the Act of May 4, 1870, 16 STAT. 94.   See Sanborn, " Congressional
Grants of Land in Aid of Railways," 2 UNIV. OF WIS. BULL., No. 3.

   8 See Charles K. Burdick, " Federal Aid Legislation," 8 CORN. L. Q. 324, 326.
The Morrill Act of 1862 — " An Act donating Public Lands to the several States
and Territories which may provide Colleges for the Benefit of Agriculture and the
Mechanic Arts " (12 STAT. 503) — had been vetoed by President Buchanan in 1859.
The veto message illustrates the feeling of opposition to extension of federal power:
" The Constitution is a grant to Congress of a few enumerated but most important powers, relating chiefly to war, peace, foreign and domestic commerce,
negotiation, and other subjects which can be best or alone exercised beneficially
by the common Government.   All other powers are reserved to the States and
to the people.   For the efficient and harmonious working of both, it is necessary
that their several spheres of action should be kept distinct from each other.
This alone can prevent conflict and mutual injury."   5 RICHARDSON, MESSAGES AND
PAPERS OF THE PRESIDENTS, 545.   Similar enactments prevailed in the years
that followed.   See Act of Mar. 30, 1867, 15 STAT. 13; Act of July 4, 1866, 14
STAT. 85.   See STEPHENSON, POLITICAL HISTORY OF THE PUBLIC LANDS, c. 15.

   9 Legislation from 1862 to 1875 reflects the increased commercial activity of
the country and the promotion of various aspects of foreign and domestic commerce by the government.   The Homestead Act of May 20, 1862 (12 STAT.
392, amended by Act of Mar. 21, 1864, 13 STAT. 35) was followed by the Act
of June 21, 1866, 14 STAT. 66, permitting homestead settlement of the public
domain in Mississippi, Louisiana, Arkansas, Alabama, and Florida.   Appropriations
totalling $70,000 were made to insure the safety of emigrants on the overland
routes to the West.   See Act of Feb. 7, 1863, 12 STAT. 642; Act of Mar. 3, 1864,
13 STAT. 14.   See TREAT, NATIONAL LAND SYSTEM, passim.   By the Act of May
17, 1864, 13 STAT. 76, the postal money order system was established.   By the
Act of May 28, 1864, 13 STAT. 93, the Post Office was authorized to establish
direct mail communications with Brazil by means of a monthly line of first-class

written into the Federal Constitution. The nation, distinct from the states, became a permeating conception.[10]

The history of the federal courts is woven into the history of the times. The factors in our national life which came in with reconstruction are the same factors which increased the business of the federal courts, enlarged their jurisdiction, modified and expanded their structure. The problems, to be sure, are the recurring problems which began with the First Judiciary Act and are active today; they are the enduring problems of the relation of states to nation. But their incidence and intensity have varied, as they are bound to vary at different epochs. For law

---

American steamships. By the Act of Feb. 17, 1865, 13 STAT. 430, the establishment of a mail steamship service between the United States and China was authorized. By the Act of Mar. 2, 1867, 14 STAT. 543, provision was made for the establishment of an ocean mail steamship service between the United States and the Hawaiian Islands. The federal government lent extensive aid to the construction of harbor and ship canals between Lake Superior and Lake Huron. See Act of Mar. 3, 1865, 13 STAT. 519, as supplemented by the Act of July 3, 1866, 14 STAT. 81; Res. of Mar. 2, 1871, 16 STAT. 599; and the Act of Mar. 27, 1872, 17 STAT. 44. By the Act of May 5, 1866, 14 STAT. 44, exclusive privileges for fourteen years were granted to the International Ocean Telegraph Company to lay cables between the United States and Cuba, the Bahamas, and islands of the West Indies. By the Act of Mar. 29, 1867, 15 STAT. 10, privileges for twenty years were granted to the American Atlantic Cable Telegraph Company to construct a submarine cable to Europe. The Act of July 4, 1864, 13 STAT. 385, provided substantial encouragement to immigration. By the Act of May 10, 1872, 17 STAT. 91, as amended by the Act of Feb. 18, 1873, 17 STAT. 465, the development of the mining resources of the West was promoted. Similar encouragement was afforded the growth of timber on the western prairies by the Act of Mar. 3, 1873, 17 STAT. 605.

10 " A number of things conspired to introduce a new economic and social order into American life in the sixties and the seventies. The high war tariffs caused men of capital to invest their money in manufacturing; and government contracts for war supplies gave impetus to this development. The state and national governments embarked on a policy of making vast grants of land and credit to railroad enterprises, thus laying the foundations for the modern era of railway development. The passage of the free homestead law of 1862 caused a rush of population toward the West, a movement that was vastly stimulated by the opening up of the less accessible regions by the railroads. These various factors reacted upon each other. . . . The unprecedented activity along all lines of economic endeavor imposed fresh demands upon American inventive genius to which it responded with countless new appliances and machines for farm and factory." SCHLESINGER, NEW VIEWPOINTS IN AMERICAN HISTORY, 248. See BEARD, CONTEMPORARY AMERICAN HISTORY, 28; EMERY, ECONOMIC DEVELOPMENT OF THE UNITED STATES (7 CAMBRIDGE MODERN HISTORY SERIES), c. 22, 696–698.

and courts are instruments of adjustment, and the compromises by which the general problems of federalism are successively met determine the contemporaneous structure of the federal courts and the range of their authority.

The judicial statistics tell a deal of the tale. In 1850 two hundred and fifty-three cases were pending before the Supreme Court;[11] in 1860 they had increased only to three hundred and ten;[12] within the next decade they more than doubled. The Court began its 1870 Term with six hundred and thirty-six cases on its docket.[13] This number nearly doubled within ten years. The October Term of 1880 begins with twelve hundred and twelve cases;[14] the number steadily mounts in the years following, reaching a total of eighteen hundred and sixteen cases at the beginning of the October Term, 1890.[15] But the inflow of Supreme Court cases, we have seen, is conditioned by the volume of litigation in the lower courts. And so we find an enormous increase in the business of the district and the circuit courts. In 1873 the number of cases pending in the circuit and district courts was twenty-nine thousand and thirteen, of which five thousand one hundred and eight were bankruptcy cases.[16] In 1880, despite the fact that the repeal of the Bankruptcy Act had dried up that source of business, the number had increased to thirty-eight thousand and forty-five.[17] The year 1890 brings the total to fifty-four thousand one hundred and ninety-four.[18]

This swelling of the dockets was due to the growth of the country's business, the assumption of authority over cases heretofore left to state courts, the extension of the field of federal activity. The great commercial development brings its share of litigation to the courts; booms and panics alike furnish grist for the courts. The vigorous stimulus of invention occasions

---

[11] Davis in the Senate on May 1, 1882, 13 Cong. Rec. 3464.

[12] *Ibid.*

[13] *Ibid.*

[14] Ten of these were on the original docket. Rep. Atty. Gen. for 1881, 5.

[15] Sixteen of these were on the original docket. Rep. Atty. Gen. for 1891, iv.

[16] Rep. Atty. Gen. for 1873. These are the earliest comprehensive figures given in the Reports of the Attorney General.

[17] Rep. Atty. Gen. for 1880.

[18] Rep. Atty. Gen. for 1890.

many and complicated patent controversies.[19]   The new sea-
borne traffic also carries a heavy cargo of admiralty business.[20]   These are items that add greatly to the work of the
courts without any enlargement of their jurisdiction.   They were
the natural increment of the country's growth.   But the Civil
War also marks the beginning of vast extensions of federal jurisdiction.   As part of the war legislation and limited to the period
of the Rebellion, the Act of March 3, 1863,[21] permitted removal
into the federal courts from state courts of cases brought against
United States officials for acts committed during the Rebellion
and justified under the authority of the President or of Congress.
This is the first of a series of enactments providing for the removal of cases from state courts into federal courts, either when
the defendant asserts some federal immunity or seeks relief from
local prejudice.[22]   A new body of federal laws widely touched the

---

[19] The stimulus given to invention is illustrated by the increasing number
of patents issued during these years. Up to 1870 the total number of patents
issued was 120,573; from 1871 to 1911 there were 902,478.   The figures by
decades follow:

Years	Applications Received	Patents Issued.
1850	2,193	993
1860	7,653	4,778
1870	19,171	13,333
1880	23,012	13,947
1890	41,048	26,292

See H. R. Doc., No. 1110, 62nd Cong., 3rd Sess., App. 1, pp. 502–506. An increase
was made in the force of the Patent Office by the Act of Mar. 29, 1867, 15 STAT.
10. "It was not until after 1845, however, that patent cases began to come
before the United States Supreme Court in any number." WARREN, HISTORY OF
THE AMERICAN BAR, 458.

[20] Mr. Justice Miller in 1872 calls attention to the great increases in litigation — "an increase of which very few persons have any just conception" —
especially in admiralty cases and in bankruptcy. See Miller, "Judicial Reforms,"
2 U. S. JURIST 1. The growing commerce on the Great Lakes was also bringing
admiralty business into circuits that theretofore had known nothing of this
branch of litigation. See 1 Dillon (U. S. C. C.) vi.

[21] § 5, 12 STAT. 756. This was amended by the Act of May 11, 1866, §§ 3, 4, 14
STAT. 46, permitting removal after the appearance of the defendant and at any
subsequent term of court before a jury was empanelled. By the Act of Feb. 5,
1867, 14 STAT. 385, *habeas corpus* was to issue upon removal wherever the defendant was in actual custody under state process.

[22] By the Act of Mar. 7, 1864, § 9, 13 STAT. 17, the provisions of the Act
of Mar. 2, 1833, § 3, 4 STAT. 633, permitting the removal of suits against United
States officials on account of acts done under the revenue laws, were extended

business of the country and correspondingly affected the business of the courts. The National Bank Acts of the sixties brought before the Supreme Court many new variations and applications

---

to the collection of all internal duties. By the Act of June 30, 1864, § 50, 13 STAT. 241, the substance of the former provision as to the extension of the Act of 1833 to internal revenue was repealed. By the Act of July 13, 1866, § 67, 14 STAT. 98, 171, Section 50 of the Act of 1864 was repealed and the Act of 1833 was no longer to apply to cases arising under the internal revenue provisions of the Act of 1864. Insurance Co. *v.* Ritchie, 5 Wall. (U. S.) 541 (1866); City of Philadelphia *v.* Collector, 5 Wall. (U. S.) 720 (1866). However, Section 67 of the Act of 1866 permitted the removal of cases arising from the internal revenue laws against United States officials, so that the effect of this extraordinary series of legislative enactments was to deprive the circuit courts of jurisdiction of cases originally commenced in those courts against revenue officials under the internal revenue laws, unless the parties were citizens of different states, but in a similar case removed from a state court, on petition of the defendant, the circuit court had jurisdiction irrespective of the citizenship of the parties. The Assessors *v.* Osbornes, 9 Wall. (U. S.) 567 (1869).

By the Act of April 9, 1866, § 3, 14 STAT. 27, the removal of cases arising under the Civil Rights Act was permitted.

The Act of July 27, 1866, 14 STAT. 306, introduced the now well-known " separable controversy " provision, permitting removal in cases where $500 was involved and where suit was brought against a citizen of the same state together with a citizen of another state or an alien. If it appeared to the court that there could be a final determination of the controversy, so far as it concerned the defendants of diverse citizenship, without the presence of the other defendants, the suit could be removed as to them.

By the Act of Mar. 2, 1867, 14 STAT. 558, removal was permitted in controversies where diversity of citizenship existed and $500 was involved, upon the petition of either plaintiff or defendant, by the filing of an affidavit as to the existence of prejudice or local influence in the state court.

By the Act of July 27, 1868, 15 STAT. 227, suits against all corporations, other than banking corporations, organized under a law of the United States, for any liability of such a corporation or of its members, could be removed from the state courts.

By the Act of Jan. 22, 1869, 15 STAT. 267, removal was permitted as to all suits brought against common carriers for loss or damage to goods through the hostilities of the Civil War.

By the Act of May 31, 1870, § 18, 16 STAT. 144, the removal provisions of the Civil Rights Act of 1866 were extended to offenses under the former Act — the Force Bill.

By the Act of Feb. 28, 1871, § 16, 16 STAT. 438, prosecutions to prevent racial discrimination in voting could be removed from the state courts. This was repealed by the Act of Feb. 8, 1894, 28 STAT. 36.

By the Act of Mar. 30, 1872, 17 STAT. 44, prosecutions by aliens against United States officials, who were not residents of the states in which the suits were brought, could be removed from the state courts into the circuit courts for the districts involved.

By the Act of Mar. 3, 1875, § 8, 18 STAT. 401, the removal provisions of

of *McCulloch* v. *Maryland*.[23] For a decade, the Bankruptcy Act of 1867 [24] added considerably to the business of the district courts and the Supreme Court. War claims against the government led to the establishment of the modern Court of Claims.[25] Soon appeals from the Court of Claims began to swell the Supreme Court docket.[26] Finally, the political issues of the War begot legislation that for a time flooded the lower courts, and constitutional amendments that to this day are among the main sources of the Supreme Court's business.[27] In the Southern federal courts,

---

the Act of 1866 were made applicable to suits against any officer of either house of Congress acting under its authority.

The Act of Mar. 3, 1875, § 2, 18 STAT. 470, summed up the separate provisions for removal, and attempted to make the jurisdiction of the federal courts in the original instance analogous to their jurisdiction upon removal from the state courts.

[23] See 3 WARREN, THE SUPREME COURT IN UNITED STATES HISTORY, 136, n. 3.

[24] Act of Mar. 2, 1867, 14 STAT. 517. This was repealed to take effect on Sept. 1, 1878. Act of June 7, 1878, 20 STAT. 99. The pressure on the district judges of this bankruptcy jurisdiction was very marked. See 1 Bond (U. S. C. C.) iv; Mr. Justice Miller, "Judicial Reforms," 2 U. S. JURIST, 1.

[25] By the Act of Feb. 24, 1855, 10 STAT. 612, the Court of Claims was established to investigate claims against the government, report its findings and opinions to Congress, and, in case Congress approved the claim, to prepare a bill for its payment. By the Act of Mar. 3, 1863, 12 STAT. 765, the court was authorized to render judgment on those claims subject to an estimate by the Secretary of the Treasury of the amount required to pay for judgment. An appeal lay from the judgment of the Court of Claims to the Supreme Court. This provision was held unconstitutional in Gordon *v.* United States, 2 Wall. (U. S.) 561 (1864), s. c. 117 U. S. 697 (1885), whereupon Congress repealed that portion of the statute authorizing the Secretary of the Treasury to revise the judgment. Act of Mar. 17, 1866, 14 STAT. 9; and see Act of June 25, 1868, 15 STAT. 75. See RICHARDSON, HISTORY OF COURT OF CLAIMS, passim.

[26] Rules for appeals from the Court of Claims were promulgated by the Supreme Court in the 1866 Term. See 3 Wall. (U. S.) vii–viii. The first case to reach the Supreme Court upon appeal was De Groot *v.* United States, 5 Wall. (U. S.) 419 (1866). In 1871 the appeals upon the Supreme Court docket from the Court of Claims numbered twenty-two. See REP. ATTY. GEN. FOR 1871, 3. The original jurisdiction of the Court of Claims as well as the appellate jurisdiction of the Supreme Court was limited by the decision in United States *v.* Alire, 6 Wall. (U. S.) 573 (1867), denying the court the power to render a judgment other than one for money. See also United States *v.* Jones, 131 U. S. 1 (1889).

[27] William M. Evarts in his "Eulogy on Chief Justice Chase" refers to the "crowd of causes bred by the Civil War, which pressed the court with novel embarrassments, and loaded it with unprecedented labors." 3 EVARTS, ARGUMENTS AND SPEECHES, 59, 82.

prosecutions under the Force Bills broke of their own weight;[28] the *Slaughter-House Cases*[29] introduced a steady torrent of cases under the Fourteenth Amendment.[30]

Thus, from many sources flowed new and deeper streams of business to the federal courts. All of them were powerfully reinforced by the Removal Act of 1875. From 1789 down to the Civil War the lower federal courts were, in the main, designed as protection to citizens litigating outside of their own states and thereby exposed to the threatened prejudice of unfriendly tribunals. Barring admiralty jurisdiction, the federal courts were subsidiary courts. The Act of 1875 marks a revolution in their function. Sensitiveness to " states' rights ", fear of rivalry with state courts and respect for state sentiment, were swept aside by the great impulse of national feeling born of the Civil War. Nationalism was triumphant; in national administration was sought its vindication. The new exertions of federal power were no longer trusted to the enforcement of state agencies. Slavery in the South had furnished a dramatic exposition of subordination of national interests to state authority. The clash of

---

28 The Federal Enforcement Act of 1870 opened " the door to a torrent of litigation." CONG. GLOBE, 41st Cong., 2nd Sess., 36–56. Two more acts followed in the next year: Act of Feb. 28, 1871, 16 STAT. 433; Act of April 20, 1871, 17 STAT. 13. The busy years for the federal courts were 1871 to 1875. " The very extent of the litigation under the enforcement acts soon overtaxed the capacity of the twenty-four district courts in the South." See William H. Davis, " The Federal Enforcement Acts," Essay IX, COLUMBIA STUDIES IN SOUTHERN HISTORY AND POLITICS, 225.

29 16 Wall. (U. S.) 36 (1872).

30 The Supreme Court itself called attention to the increasing tendency of counsel to raise questions under the Fourteenth Amendment in order to seek review by the Court. " In fact, it would seem, from the character of many of the cases before us, and the arguments made in them, that the clause under consideration is looked upon as a means of bringing to the test of the decision of this court the abstract opinions of every unsuccessful litigant in a State court of the justice of the decision against him, and of the merits of the legislation on which such a decision may be founded." Davidson v. New Orleans, 96 U. S. 97, 104 (1877). " It is hardly necessary to say, that the hardship, impolicy, or injustice of State laws is not necessarily an objection to their constitutional validity; and that the remedy for evils of that character is to be sought from State legislatures. Our jurisdiction cannot be invoked unless some right claimed under the Constitution, laws, or treaties of the United States is invaded. This court is not a harbor where refuge can be found from every act of ill-advised and oppressive State legislation." Missouri Pac. Ry. Co. v. Humes, 115 U. S. 512, 520 (1885).

economic interests in the North, the risks to which absentee capital was exposed in the state legislation of the Granger Movement,[31] furnished new occasions for federal protection against adverse state action.

In the Act of March 3, 1875, Congress gave the federal courts the vast range of power which had lain dormant in the Constitution since 1789. These courts ceased to be restricted tribunals of fair dealing between citizens of different states and became the primary and powerful reliances for vindicating every right given by the Constitution, the laws, and treaties of the United States. Thereafter, any suit asserting such a right could be begun in the federal courts; any such action begun in a state court could be removed to the federal courts for disposition.[32] The old jurisdiction in cases of diverse citizenship was retained. It had been enormously extended in practice through the developing doctrine of corporate citizenship,[33] as well as by legislation prior to 1875. To the increasing volume of litigation due to diversity of citizenship, the Act of 1875 opened wide a flood of totally new business for the federal courts. This development in the federal judiciary, which in the retrospect seems revolutionary, received hardly a contemporary comment.[34]

---

[31] The Granger Movement, beginning in the early seventies, reveals the restlessness of the West against constitutional restraints and the growing unwillingness of absentee capital to rely upon state courts for the vindication of constitutional rights. " The corporations uniformly fell back on their constitutional guaranties. . . . In Illinois the corporations sought shelter behind the Constitution of the United States and the decision in the Dartmouth College Case." C. F. Adams, Jr., " The Granger Movement," 120 N. Am. Rev. 395, 413. See Buck, The Granger Movement, *passim.* See also Matt H. Carpenter in the Senate on June 15, 1874, 2 Cong. Rec. 4986.

[32] Act of Mar. 3, 1875, 18 Stat. 470.

[33] The growth of the fiction as to the citizenship of a corporation from a mere presumption in the early days of Bank of United States *v.* Deveaux, 5 Cranch (U. S.) 61 (1809) to a substantive doctrine of our constitutional law, occurred chiefly during these years of commercial expansion. See Henderson, Position of Foreign Corporations in American Constitutional Law, c. 5. See also A. H. Garland in the Senate on May 5, 1882, 13 Cong. Rec. 3637.

[34] Contemporary legal periodicals disclose no material either before or after the enactment of this legislation. Histories of the period are equally barren. The view that the Act of 1875 was one aspect of a wide general trend of federal legislation is supported by an anonymous writer in the year of its passage, who explains it as the culmination of a movement which began with the removal legislation of 1864 to strengthen the Federal Government against the states. His

The Act has an interesting legislative history, although it evoked little debate on the floor of Congress, save as to its details. In its original form the Act applied only to controversies involving diversity of citizenship and not to substantive federal rights. In the *Case of the Sewing Machine Companies* [35] the Supreme Court, in 1874, had held that the Removal Act of 1867 [36] was declaratory of the traditional doctrine that the federal courts can assume jurisdiction only when there is no identity of citizenship between any of the plaintiffs and any of the de-

is a voice of protest against the extension of federal jurisdiction and the wisdom of the Act of 1875. See A. I., "Our Federal Judiciary," 2 CENT. L. J. 551. Judge Dillon in 1881 reviews the steady increase in federal jurisdiction: "The history of the Federal jurisdiction is one of constant growth; slow, indeed, during the first half-century and more, but very rapid within the last few years. From various causes, which we need not stop to trace, the small tide of litigation that formerly flowed in Federal channels has swollen into a mighty stream. Certain it is that of late years the importance of the Federal courts has rapidly increased, and that much, perhaps most, of the great litigations of the country is now conducted in them." DILLON, REMOVAL OF CAUSES, 4 ed., 3. Judge Cooley attributed this increase partly to the desire of politicians to increase the number of judicial offices whose appointment would thus come under their control. See COOLEY, MICHIGAN, 361–362.

[35] 18 Wall. (U. S.) 553 (1873). Another important case in which the Supreme Court limited the scope of its jurisdiction was decided during the same term of court. Murdock *v.* City of Memphis, 20 Wall. (U. S.) 590 (1874). By the Act of Feb. 5, 1867, § 2, 14 STAT. 385, Section 25 of the Judiciary Act of Sept. 24, 1789, 1 STAT. 85, was reënacted with the omission of the clause restricting the examination by the Supreme Court of a state court's findings to errors involving a federal right. Interpreting this omission as a repeal of the original clause obviously would have increased enormously the jurisdiction of the Supreme Court. That such was the intention of Congress seemed arguable in view of the general tendency of the period to extend the scope of the national judiciary. The realization of the importance of the issues at stake led the court to call for a re-argument. Former Justice Curtis, at the request of the Court, filed a brief as *amicus curiae,* in which he argued that it was the intention of Congress to repeal the original clause in the Judiciary Act and that such a construction was constitutional. See CURTIS, JURISDICTION OF THE UNITED STATES COURTS, 54. The re-argument occurred on April 2 and 3, 1873, and the case was decided on Jan. 11, 1874. While it was pending, Carpenter of the Senate Judiciary Committee, on Dec. 9, 1873, moved a resolution that the Judiciary Committee be instructed to inquire whether the Act of 1867 did repeal the twenty-fifth section. The resolution was agreed to, but no report was made. 2 CONG. REC. 103. Mr. Justice Miller, speaking for the Court, held that no such repeal had been intended. Three justices, Swayne, Clifford, and Bradley, dissented, and Chief Justice Waite took no part in the decision.

[36] Act of Mar. 2, 1867, 14 STAT. 558.

fendants to a litigation. This result was reached despite important changes in the phraseology of the earlier removal Acts, and over the dissent of two such powerful members of the Court as Justices Miller and Bradley. The decision was promptly followed by a bill, reported from the House Judiciary Committee by Chairman Poland, which sought specifically to write into law what the Supreme Court did not find in the Act of 1867.[37] This provision formed Section 1 of the bill; [38] Section 2 dealt with minor changes of procedure upon removal. Ebenezer Rockwood Hoar had been the successful counsel in the *Sewing Machine Case,* having urged constitutional difficulties against the claim that the Act of 1867 gave the federal courts jurisdiction whenever two opposing parties to a litigation (regardless of other parties to the same litigation) were of diverse citizenship. It so happened that Poland's bill was introduced during Judge Hoar's only term of membership in the House.[39] Accordingly we find him repeating on the floor of the House the constitutional arguments which he had urged before the Supreme Court. To his mind constitutionality and policy alike admonished against the transfer of jurisdiction from state to federal courts which was proposed by Poland's bill:

"I cannot be in favor of extending all over this country a system which takes from State tribunals and from State domination what properly belongs to it, for the purpose of remedying what I hope is to be a temporary evil. We are in danger always of sacrificing great principles of government, of violating the lines which are drawn be-

---

[37] 2 CONG. REC. 4301 (May 27, 1874). It is of interest to note that Poland, scarcely a month before, had been winning counsel in a case where the Supreme Court again affirmed the construction that it had placed upon the Act of 1867 in the Sewing Machine Companies Case, Knapp *v.* Railroad Co., 20 Wall. (U. S.) 117 (1873).

[38] The bill is to be found in full in 2 CONG. REC. 4300. The first section is best described in the words of Poland: " The first section . . . changes the law in this: under the old judiciary act if a suit was brought against a defendant who resided in the State and another defendant who resided out of the State, the defendant who lived out of the State had no right to remove the cause from the State court into the circuit court. The substance of this section, the change that it would make in the existing law if passed, is this: that it authorizes the defendant who resides out of the State where the suit is brought to remove the case into the courts of the United States, although there may be another defendant who lives in the State." 2 CONG. REC. 4301.

[39] Poland, in introducing the bill into the House, intimated that Hoar was of the opinion that the bill was unconstitutional. See *ibid.* 4302.

tween State and national authority by reason of some temporary and particular exigency." [40]

On motion of Eldredge of Wisconsin, who for a decade was an alert opponent of the enlargement of federal judicial power, the first section of the bill was struck out [41] and the bill left the House merely as minor amendments to the procedure governing removal proceedings.[42] In the Senate, Matthew H. Carpenter, on behalf of the Judiciary Committee, proposed as a substitute for the House Bill the Act of 1875 in its present form, altered only in details as it went through the legislative mill.[43] These details alone aroused discussion.[44] Carpenter's bill passed the Senate the day of its introduction by a vote of thirty-three to twenty-two.[45] At the next session came conferences [46] resulting in capitulation by the House,[47] final passage by Congress,[48] and approval by the President on March 3, 1875.[49]

---

[40] *Ibid.* 4303.

[41] *Ibid.* 4302, 4304. McCrary of Iowa also objected to the bill on the ground that the federal judges were already swamped with litigation. *Ibid.* 4303.

[42] *Ibid.* 4304.

[43] On June 15, 1874, the bill was reported from committee. It is found in full in 2 CONG. REC. 4979. Carpenter, in reply to an attack by Bayard of Delaware, reflects the persistence of Story's dictum in Martin *v.* Hunter's Lessee, 1 Wheat. (U. S.) 304, 328 (1816), arguing that the First Judiciary Act of 1789, in failing to give the full scope of judicial power granted by the Constitution to the lower federal courts, was " substantially in contravention of the Constitution." *Ibid.* 4986.

[44] Thurman of Ohio made a motion to strike out the eleventh section of the bill that authorized service of process upon agents of corporations or other persons doing business within a state. *Ibid.* 4980. This motion, supported by Bayard of Delaware, was vigorously opposed by Conkling. Merrimon of North Carolina agreed that the section should be retained and that it was valid as applied to corporations, but he moved to strike out the words " or other person " on the ground that the section was invalid as applied to agents of ordinary persons. *Ibid.* 4982. *Cf.* Flexner *v.* Farson, 248 U. S. 289 (1919). Merrimon's motion was lost.

[45] *Ibid.* 4987.

[46] The House disagreed to the Senate amendments and proposed a conference. Poland, Tremain, and Eldredge were named as managers on the part of the House. HOUSE JOURNAL, 43 Cong., 2nd Sess., Ser. No. 1633, p. 611. The Senate, on Mar. 1, 1875, voted to adhere to its amendments but agreed to the proposed conference, naming Carpenter, Conkling, and Thurman as its managers. SEN. JOURNAL, 43 Cong., 2nd Sess., Ser. No. 1628, p. 372.

[47] The House, in the main, agreed to the Senate amendments. Certain other amendments were made in conference. HOUSE JOURNAL, *supra*, p. 647.

[48] 3 CONG. REC. 2168, 2240.   [49] *Ibid.* 2275.

Congress thus vastly extended the domain of the federal courts. The Supreme Court still further widened this domain by the construction it placed upon the legislation. In the *Pacific Railroad Removal Cases*,[50] the court held that, inasmuch as a federal charter of incorporation is a " law of the United States," every litigation, irrespective of its nature, brought by or against a federally chartered corporation is a suit arising under the " laws of the United States." Soon negligence suits against the Pacific railroads and like litigation cluttered the federal courts and aroused strong local animosities.[51]

All these forces, by successive steps, led to immense expansion in the business of the federal courts. Because of the tasks which have been entrusted to it during the last fifty years, the federal judiciary has exercised an influence which makes it a far more pervasive institution in the life of our country than it was during the first hundred years.

2

The steady growth of old business and the development of their authority found the federal courts wholly ill-equipped, as we have seen, to discharge adequately even their pre-Civil War duties. The new tasks could not be absorbed by the old machinery, and familiar evils became accentuated. The Supreme Court docket became a record of arrears. Justices could not attend circuit; circuit work lapsed more and more into the unrestrained power of a single district judge; new states were added to the old circuit system.[52] The long cycle of grievances and remedies to meet them, which we have traced from 1789 down to the Civil War, again starts its dreary round. The period between 1865 and 1891 spans the struggle

---

[50] 115 U. S. 1 (1885).

[51] 3 WARREN, THE SUPREME COURT IN UNITED STATES HISTORY, 407–408.

[52] By the Act of July 15, 1862, 12 STAT. 576, the district courts of Texas, Florida, Wisconsin, Minnesota, Iowa and Kansas were deprived of their circuit jurisdiction; the circuits were again reorganized, and these states absorbed into the circuit system. By the Act of Feb. 27, 1865, 13 STAT. 440, Nevada was added to the Tenth Circuit. By the Act of July 23, 1866, 14 STAT. 209, the circuits were again reorganized and reduced to nine. By the Act of Mar. 25, 1867, 15 STAT. 5, Nebraska was added to the Eighth Circuit.

for the elimination of the circuit duties of the Justices and the establishment of an intermediate appellate tribunal to relieve the country from injustices due to inadequate judicial resources. Again it became manifest that the federal judiciary articulates as an entirety. The efficacy of the Supreme Court was seen to depend upon the distribution of federal judicial power and the system of courts devised for its exercise. A drastic reorganization of the whole judicial structure had thus become imperative.

Direct relief of the Supreme Court was the focal point of Congressional discussion. Every one agreed that the labors of the Justices must be lightened. As early as 1848 the suggestion of an intermediate appellate court had emerged.[53] Again in 1854 Douglas sponsored the idea as part of a comprehensive scheme for judicial reorganization.[54] These proposals were premature. But the overwhelming demands of the post-war period brought the plan to the forefront of discussion. On motion of Lyman Trumbull, then chairman of the Judiciary Committee,

---

[53] Bowlin of Missouri, upon the introduction of a bill by Ingersoll of Missouri, from the House Judiciary Committee, contemplating relief of the Supreme Court Justices from circuit duty for two years, moved a substitute bill on Feb. 29, 1848, that gave the district courts the same jurisdiction as the circuit courts and provided for an intermediate court of appeals consisting of the district judges and one member of the Supreme Court. See 18 CONG. GLOBE, 398–399.

[54] On April 17, 1854, the Senate Judiciary Committee, through Senator Butler, reported a bill based upon the report of Attorney General Cushing. See 33 CONG. GLOBE, 924, and p. 53, supra. On May 18, 1854, Senator Douglas offered a bill providing for an intermediate court of appeals as a substitute to the Senate bill. 33 CONG. GLOBE, 1210. Douglas' bill continued the existing district courts but conferred on them all the jurisdiction and powers then possessed by the circuit courts. The district judges were to assemble once a year, and, with one Justice of the Supreme Court presiding, were to hear all the appeals from the several district courts within the circuit. "If all the district judges in a circuit could come together once a year to review their own decisions, it would tend to bring about uniformity of thought and uniformity of practice within those districts. To secure this object, my substitute provides that the Court of Appeals in each circuit shall prescribe the rules of practice for the District Courts within the circuit. You thus infuse uniformity into all the District Courts within the same circuit, acting under the same rules, and the consequence would be that very few appeals would be taken from the Court of Appeals to the Supreme Court of the United States." SHEAHAN, LIFE OF STEPHEN A. DOUGLAS, 279. (The bill was rejected in the Senate by a vote of 26 to 19.)

the Senate on April 4, 1864,[55] called upon the Secretary of the Interior [56] to report the volume of business in the district and circuit courts as of January 1, 1864. The Secretary's figures proved what every one knew, but they served to stimulate legislative activity.[57] Lyman Trumbull himself started the ball rolling by a bill which coalesced the district and the circuit courts into a single court of first instance and established nine intermediate courts of appeals with final jurisdiction in a large class of cases. Trumbull did not expect immediate action on his bill. " I desire to say that I introduce it with the view of bringing the subject before the Senate and the country. . . . The amount of business accumulating in the Supreme Court amounts almost to a denial of justice, and some legislation is necessary, and will become more necessary as the business accumulates in that court, to relieve it." [58] Other plans came before Congress [59] but, as Trumbull wisely foresaw, the subject had only reached the discussion stage.

In the next Congress, Senator Ira Harris of New York renewed Trumbull's proposal.[60] His bill, very similar to the Douglas Bill, fused the circuit and district courts, and provided for intermediate appellate courts for each circuit, consisting of the Circuit Justice and the district judges, any three of whom were

[55] SEN. JOURNAL, 38th Cong., 1st Sess., Ser. No. 1175, p. 296.

[56] By the Act of Mar. 3, 1849, § 4, 9 STAT. 395, the Department of the Interior was given a supervisory power over the accounts of marshals, clerks, and other officers of the courts of the United States, and thus was the medium of communication with the clerks of these courts. These powers had been transferred to the Interior Department from the Treasury Department. See Act of May 18, 1842, 5 STAT. 488. With the establishment of the Department of Justice, the powers were lodged with the Attorney General. See Act of June 22, 1870, § 15, 16 STAT. 164; U. S. REV. STAT. § 368.

[57] The report showed 11,930 cases pending in the circuit and district courts and 1040 cases in the territorial courts. From many districts no returns were made. See SEN. EX. DOC., No. 1, 38th Cong., 2nd Sess., Ser. No. 1209. The report was submitted to the Senate on Dec. 8, 1864. CONG. GLOBE, 38th Cong., 2nd Sess., 8.

[58] CONG. GLOBE, 38th Cong., 2nd Sess., 292 (Jan. 17, 1865).

[59] A bill to amend the judicial system was introduced by Henderson of Missouri on Feb. 20, 1865, but on Mar. 3, 1865, the Judiciary Committee asked to be discharged from further consideration of the subject. CONG. GLOBE, 38th Cong., 2nd Sess., 915, 1338. In the House, a similar bill was introduced by Wilson of Iowa on Jan. 16, 1865. *Ibid.* 275.

[60] CONG. GLOBE, 39th Cong., 1st Sess., 2 (Dec. 4, 1865).

to constitute a quorum. An appeal lay from the courts of appeals
to the Supreme Court only on questions of law where more
than $10,000 was involved, or when the adjudication concerned
the Constitution, a treaty, or a revenue law of the United
States. Important questions could also be certified to the Supreme Court from the courts of appeals.[61] The bill was reported
out of the committee on March 16, 1866,[62] and debated for three
days.[63] All the speakers agreed that the docket of the Supreme
Court was congested.[64] Senator George H. Williams of Oregon
(afterwards named by Grant as Chief Justice only to be rejected
by the Senate) dwelt on the necessity of reorganizing the federal
judiciary in order to cope with the flow of litigation inevitably
arising out of the War.[65] The opposition urged that the establishment of nine courts of appeal would produce a conflict of decision in cases where their jurisdiction was final.[66] But the bill
prevailed by a vote of twenty-three to six, on April 4, 1866.[67]
The House did not even consider the measure. No relief came
until 1869. On the contrary, for a time the Supreme Court had
to pay part of the price of the bitterness of Congress towards
Andrew Johnson by reduction of its membership. Fear of
Johnson appointees led Congress to provide that no vacancy on
the Court should be filled " until the number of associate justices
shall be reduced to six." [68] From July 5, 1867, to February 18,
1870, after the death of Wayne, it was a Court of eight.

This animosity between the President and Congress was undoubtedly a potent factor in postponing judicial reorganization.
Relief for the Supreme Court foreshadowed the appointment of
additional judges for inferior courts, and Congress was unwilling
to place this patronage in Johnson's hands. Moreover Con-

---

[61] The bill will be found, section by section, in CONG. GLOBE, 39th Cong.,
1st Sess., 1712–1714.

[62] *Ibid.* 1436.

[63] *Ibid.* 1711–1719 (April 2), 1738–1742 (April 3), 1762–1764 (April 4).

[64] Hendricks of Indiana called particular attention to the congestion of the
federal courts, enforcing his plea for the bill by the remark that " Speedy justice is
almost as important as it is to have justice itself." *Ibid.* 1738.

[65] *Ibid.* 1740.

[66] *Ibid.* 1718. See also the comment in 2 NATION, 488.

[67] *Ibid.* 1764.

[68] Act of July 23, 1866, § 1, 14 STAT. 209.

gress was none too friendly towards the Supreme Court itself. The Radical leaders suspected in the Court considerable hazard to their Reconstruction program.[69] Congress, as is well known, went so far as to withdraw a pending litigation from the Court by an exercise of its power to regulate the Court's appellate jurisdiction.[70] It did so, of course, to avoid judicial questioning of the Reconstruction legislation involved in the *McCardle* case.[71] These factors of political hostility, together with customary inertia toward legislation for judicial organization, combined to delay measures of reform, the necessity for which everyone conceded.

With the doom of Johnson and the advent of Grant, the forces of active opposition to judicial reorganization were dissipated and mounting arrears overcame legislative inertia.   Toward the end of the Johnson régime, Trumbull again introduced a proposal for court relief.[72] He no longer pressed for intermediate appellate tribunals. The failure of the Harris Bill evidently convinced him of what subsequent history confirmed, namely, that the creation of intermediate courts of appeal was still too sudden a wrench from the past. Habit and sentiment engendered by a system in force since 1789 are not readily displaced by a recognition of changing circumstances which demand change of institutions.   To Trumbull it seemed possible both to ease the circuit work of the Justices without radical departure and to meet the growing complaints that circuit courts were largely presided over by single district judges. A new panel of nine circuit

---

[69] See 3 WARREN, *op. cit.* c. 30.   The radical opposition to the Court, engendered by the fear that the Reconstruction Acts might be declared unconstitutional, also found expression in the passage of a bill by the House of Representatives in the month of January, 1868, by a vote of 116 to 39, requiring the concurrence of six Justices in holding unconstitutional a federal law. See 6 NATION, 44, 82, 85, 146. The Senate, however, dropped the bill. Another measure proposed by Thaddeus Stevens in the House, and introduced into the Senate by Lyman Trumbull, forbade the Supreme Court to take jurisdiction in cases arising under the Reconstruction Acts, but neither house took action upon this proposal. See 3 WARREN, *op. cit.* 193.

[70] Act of Mar. 27, 1868, 15 STAT. 44. The full story of this legislation has been told by Mr. Warren. See 3 WARREN, *op. cit.,* c. 30.

[71] *Ex parte* McCardle, 7 Wall. (U. S.) 506 (1868).

[72] CONG. GLOBE, 40th Cong., 3rd Sess., 414 (Jan. 18, 1869). The bill was reported from the Judiciary Committee on Feb. 3, 1869. *Ibid.* 813.

judges was his solution.[73] The Justices were still to go on circuit, but the requirement was cut down to attendance at each circuit court for a single term every two years. Thus we see the reëmergence of the Federalist scheme of 1801 as modified by Caleb Cushing's proposal in 1854. But the old objections against creating circuit judges and withdrawing the Justices from circuit duty, or even greatly limiting their attendance, still had vitality. Senator Edmunds of Vermont echoed the arguments which triumphed in earlier attempts to establish circuit judges. To him Trumbull's compromise measure still involved an "entire change" in the practical operation of the judicial system of the United States.[74] But since he recognized that something had to be done to relieve the dockets, he joined Henry Wilson of Massachusetts in proposing a Supreme Court of fifteen, of whom seven (to be drawn by lot) were to sit in Washington and the rest to go on circuit.[75] The Wilson scheme was overwhelmingly defeated.[76] Trumbull's bill passed the Senate on February 23, 1869,[77] and the House on the last day of the session.[78] It failed of Johnson's signature, we are told, by accident.[79]

The new Congress met on the fourth of March, 1869,[80] and Trumbull promptly reintroduced his bill.[81] Edmunds renewed his opposition, joining Williams of Oregon who advocated a Supreme Court of eighteen, nine for the circuits and nine for Washington, with three shifting every year. This, he argued,

---

[73] The bill is printed in full in Cong. Globe, *supra,* 1366.

[74] *Ibid.* 1366.

[75] Wilson's suggestions were presented by Drake in the form of an amendment to the original bill. It is to be found printed in full, *ibid.* 1484.

[76] By a vote of 39 to 6. *Ibid.* 1487. An amendment by Davis, providing for the retirement of judges upon reaching seventy, was defeated. Grimes' amendment, prohibiting the removal of clerks of the circuit courts without the concurrence of the Supreme Court Justice assigned to the circuit, was rejected. Howe withdrew his amendment providing that the opinion of the presiding judge should prevail whenever the circuit court was divided. *Ibid.* 1488–1489.

[77] *Ibid.* 1489.

[78] *Ibid.* 1895. (Mar. 3, 1869.)

[79] See Henry B. Adams, "The Session," 108 N. Am. Rev. 610, 621.

[80] By the Act of Jan. 22, 1867, 14 Stat. 378. This was repealed by the Act of April 20, 1871, § 30, 17 Stat. 12.

[81] Cong. Globe, 41st Cong., 1st Sess., 29 (Mar. 8, 1869). It was reported from the Judiciary Committee on Mar. 15, and considered on Mar. 22. *Ibid.* 62, 192.

would keep the Supreme Court from becoming isolated from the circuits and prevent it from turning into a " fossilized institution." [82] Thurman of Ohio favored a court, like the French Court of Cassation, of twenty-four judges with three sections, but thought such a scheme unconstitutional.[83] Conkling, on the other hand, thought Trumbull's bill an ineffective improvisation, which would relieve the congestion neither of the Supreme Court nor of the lower courts, while its enactment would check future relief by Congress.[84] Conkling urged postponement in the hope that time would mature a scheme to fit his diagnosis of the real evils of the existing judicial organization. But the Senate was bent on action and passed Trumbull's bill.[85] In the House the debate centered largely around a House amendment providing for the retirement of judges.[86] At least one member, Woodward of Pennsylvania, struck at the core of problems of judicial organization in admonishing the House that congestion of the judicial business was inevitable and bound to increase if the scope of the jurisdiction of the federal courts was uncritically extended.[87] The bill passed the House on March 29, 1869,[88]

---

[82] *Ibid.* 209. Edmunds prophesied that the effect of cutting the Supreme Court loose from the circuit courts would be to change it into a Star Chamber. *Ibid.* 214.

[83] *Ibid.* 210.

[84] *Ibid.* 211.

[85] *Ibid.* 219. Drake of Missouri had offered the Harris Bill with certain innovations as an amendment to the Senate bill. *Ibid.* 151. This bill, drawn by a district judge after consultation with his associate judges, is printed in full. *Ibid.* 192. A motion to postpone the Senate bill so as to consider this and the other substitutes was defeated by a vote of 44 to 11. *Ibid.* 218. A further amendment by Drake to require the Supreme Court to render no decision when it was equally divided, but to have a rehearing when an odd number of Justices was present, was also rejected, 39 to 15. *Ibid.* 219. Sumner's amendment for the retirement of judges at seventy was defeated. *Ibid.* 219.

[86] The bill was reported from committee by Bingham of Ohio on Mar. 29, with amendments providing for the retirement of judges when seventy, and for their forced retirement when they were incompetent to discharge their duties. *Ibid.* 337. Kerr of Indiana moved in vain to increase the age of retirement from seventy to seventy-five. *Ibid.* 344.

[87] *Ibid.* 339.

[88] By a vote of 90 to 53. *Ibid.* 345. Poland's amendment to prevent a Supreme Court Justice from sitting on his own case upon appeal was defeated. *Ibid.* 344.

and, after an extended wrangle between the two houses over the provision for the retirement of judges,[89] became law on April 10, 1869.[90]

The Act of 1869 accomplished as little as Conkling had prophesied. It did not help the Supreme Court to keep up with its business, nor did it materially help at *nisi prius*. In 1872 Mr. Justice Miller began to arouse opinion for the relief of his overburdened Court.[91] Whatever time was saved from curtailed circuit work was more than absorbed by the increasing volume of business which came to the Supreme Court. War litigation, bankruptcy, admiralty, patents, appeals from the District of Columbia and the territories, all combined to put the Supreme Court two years in arrears. By way of relief Miller suggested not increase in personnel but limitations upon jurisdiction. Restricted review from the courts of the District of Columbia and the territories, review in admiralty and equity not on facts but on matters of law, review in no case involving less than $5,000 but permitting certification of difficult questions of law from all courts — these were the Miller proposals. He started the discussion[92] at which he aimed, but provoked opposition to his scheme. The chief attack was against the $5,000 limit. The

---

[89] The bill, as amended by the House, was reported from the Senate Judiciary Committee on April 7, 1869. This permitted the retirement of judges upon full salary, but, as distinguished from the House bill, required judges upon such retirement to resign their offices, and thus sought to prevent a retired judge from sitting in the same court as that to which his successor had been appointed. These amendments were agreed to by the Senate. *Ibid.* 574–576. The House again received the bill on April 8, 1869. Bingham then objected to the Senate's omission of the House requirement that the judge should have had ten years' previous service before becoming eligible to retire at seventy. Consequently, Schenck of Ohio proposed concurrence in the Senate amendments without the requirement of ten years' previous service, and the House agreed. *Ibid.* 650. This new amendment was concurred in by the Senate. *Ibid.* 630. As to retirement of judges, *cf.* 10 Mass. L. Q. 99; *ibid.* 80.

[90] Fear was expressed by contemporary writers as to the wisdom of vesting President Grant with the power to appoint a corps of judges. See 1 ALBANY L. J. 188; 9 NATION, 477. The following were named as circuit judges: *First Circuit* — George Foster Shepley; *Second Circuit* — Lewis B. Woodruff; *Third Circuit* — William McKennan; *Fourth Circuit* — Hugh Lennox Bond; *Fifth Circuit* — William Burnham Woods; *Sixth Circuit* — Halmor Hull Emmons; *Seventh Circuit* — Thomas Drummond; *Eighth Circuit* — John Forrest Dillon; *Ninth Circuit* — Lorenzo Sawyer. See 1 Fed. Cas. xiii–xiv.

[91] See Mr. Justice Miller, "Judicial Reforms," 2 U. S. JURIST, 1.

[92] See, *e.g.*, "The Law's Delay in the Federal Courts," 5 ALBANY L. J. 22.

Supreme Court ought not to be a rich man's court! In opposition to the Miller plan the scheme of buffer appellate tribunals was revived. Each of these plans was pressed upon Congress. Mr. Justice Miller's remedies were in part adopted by Congress in the Act of Feb. 16, 1875,[93] — limited review in admiralty and patent cases and increase of the money limit of appeals from $2,000 to $5,000. The much more far-reaching remedy of intermediate appellate courts for diverting business from the Supreme Court had to wait until 1891 for acceptance.

For the next fifteen years the interest of bench, bar and Congress in the working of the federal judiciary is the story of the vicissitudes of the proposal for intermediate courts of appeal and its encounter with competitive plans for remodelling the Supreme Court.

3

The movement for a comprehensive reorganization of the judicial system made no headway in the Congress which provided the limited relief of the Act of February 16, 1875, but professional opinion began to assert itself. The legal periodicals of that time are alive with discussion.[94] The congestion of the dockets became more and more ominous. Three years were required for an equity suit to reach final hearing in the Southern District of New York. In almost every circuit, to the great complaint of suitors, the circuit court was held by a single judge, and in many instances the circuit judge was unable to sit in all his districts.[95] Moreover, these defects, it was soon

---

[93] 18 STAT. 315. The bill was introduced by Senator Edmunds of Vermont, on Jan. 5, 1875, reported from the Judiciary Committee on Jan. 20, and passed with practically no discussion on Jan. 26. 3 CONG. REC. 238, 599, 730. It passed the House on Feb. 4, 1875. *Ibid.* 984. Criticism of the bill was based upon its failure to deal with appeals from the District of Columbia and the territories. See 2 CENT. L. J. 101.

[94] See, *e.g.,* 6 ALBANY L. J. 365; 2 CENT. L. J. 2; J. M. McCorkle, 2 CENT. L. J. 512; W. L. Nugent, 2 CENT. L. J. 545; A. I., "Our Federal Judiciary," 2 CENT. L. J. 551; 3 CENT. L. J. 68; 9 AM. L. REV. 668.

[95] See HOUSE REPORT, No. 45, 44th Cong., 1st Sess., Ser. No. 1708. The circuit judge in Arkansas attended only once a year for a week, whereas the court sat for a month. In Iowa the three judges when they attended sat separately; in the Circuit Court of the Northern District of Illinois three-fourths of the cases were disposed of by a single judge; the circuit judge never attended the Eastern

realized, would be enormously accentuated by the extensive new jurisdiction conferred by the Act of March 3, 1875.[96] That Act, it was now seen, added voluminously to the business of the federal courts without equipping them to discharge it.

Conditions by this time were ripe for promising legislative effort. Judge McCrary [97] of Iowa was the new leader of reform. On February 2, 1876, McCrary's bill was reported out of the House Judiciary Committee.[98] It aimed to meet the two great failures of the existing system, namely, lack of speedy justice in the courts of first instance and lack of reasonable and prompt review. To remove these central defects, Judge McCrary proposed to give the district and circuit courts concurrent jurisdiction, to eliminate the appellate jurisdiction of the circuit courts, to establish nine new courts, one in each circuit, as intermediate appellate tribunals, and to limit the right of review by the Supreme Court to cases involving more than $10,000 or to questions of construction under the Constitution, laws or treaties of the United States. Further relief was provided for the Justices by putting an end to compulsory attendance on circuit. The Circuit Justice, the circuit judge, and the district judges of the circuit were to be drawn on for the proposed courts of appeals. Any three of these constituted a quorum of the court.[99] The Supreme Court's business would doubtless have kept the Justices in Washington and the practice of circuit attendance, as subsequent experience shows,[100] would have become atrophied. The require-

---

District of Michigan, his time being occupied with the Southern District; in Massachusetts, the judges all held separate sessions; in the Southern District of New York, three and sometimes four sessions of the Circuit Court were held simultaneously.

[96] See A. I., "Our Federal Judiciary," 2 CENT. L. J. 551.

[97] George Washington McCrary was a member of the House of Representatives from Mar. 4, 1869 to Mar. 3, 1877, later was Secretary of War, under President Hayes, from Mar. 12, 1877 to Dec. 10, 1879, and was then appointed United States Circuit Judge for the Eighth Circuit. He resigned to return to practice in 1884.

[98] 4 CONG. REC. 837. The bill had been introduced on Jan. 6, 1876, and referred to the Judiciary Committee. On Jan. 25, Knott from the committee reported a bill modelled upon that of McCrary, which was ordered printed and recommended. *Ibid.* 299, 618.

[99] The bill is printed in full in 4 CONG. REC. 1125.

[100] Under the Act of Mar. 3, 1891, § 3, 26 STAT. 827, the Justices of the Supreme Court are made "competent to sit as judges of the circuit court of ap-

ment of $10,000 for review by the Supreme Court[101] and the restriction of the sittings of the new courts of appeals to a single city in each circuit encountered strenuous opposition,[102] but the bill passed on February 21, 1876, by a vote of one hundred and forty-three to one hundred and two.[103] In the Senate the bill was referred to the Judiciary Committee[104] from which it never emerged.

After a short lull the old grievances again became articulate, this time in an intensified form. Thus, complaint is made of the inequalities in the amount required for review by the Supreme Court — namely, for circuit courts, $5,000; the Court of Claims, $3,000; the Supreme Court of the District of Columbia, $2,500; the Supreme Court of Washington Territory, $2,000; the Supreme Courts of the other territories, $1,000.[105] More important, the density of litigation left about two-thirds of the circuit work to the disposition of district judges, and thus made the single district judges to a considerable extent ultimate courts of appeal.[106] This condition was felt acutely in criminal cases.[107]

peals within their respective circuits," but, in recent years attendances on circuit are very rare. Mr. Justice Holmes presided and wrote the opinion in Johnson *v.* United States, 163 Fed. 30 (1st Circ., 1908); Mr. Justice Day presided in Patterson *v.* United States, 222 Fed. 599 (6th Circ., 1915) and Mr. Chief Justice Taft in Wire Wheel Co. *v.* Budd Wheel Co., 288 Fed. 308 (4th Circ., 1923). See also, Lindsey *v.* Allen, 269 Fed. 656 (D. Mass. 1920).

[101] 4 CONG. REC. 1165.

[102] The Detroit Bar sent a petition to Congress requesting that the McCrary Bill be changed so as to require the new courts of appeals to hold one term in every state embraced by a circuit, in order thereby to avoid the inconvenience and expense caused suitors by requiring them to travel from one end of a circuit to the other. *Ibid.* 1575. This proposal was favorably commented on by "The Nation," which suggested, however, that Congress was ashamed to require judges to hold courts at distant points without paying them sufficient salaries. See 22 NATION, 152. The "Central Law Journal" in reply adverts to the itinerant character of such a court: "The decisions of a court on wheels can never be as stable and uniform as those of a court which sits permanently at one place." 3 CENT. L. J. 185.

[103] 4 CONG. REC. 1206.   [104] *Ibid.* 1249.

[105] See George A. King, 31 NATION, 441.

[106] See G. W. McCrary, "Needs of the Federal Judiciary," 13 CENT. L. J. 167.

[107] The Supreme Court had no jurisdiction of a writ of error from a Circuit Court in a criminal case. United States *v.* More, 3 Cranch (U. S.) 159 (1805). The only means of getting a review was upon a certificate of a division of opinion in the circuit court. U. S. REV. STAT. § 697. See CURTIS, JURISDICTION OF THE UNITED STATES COURTS, 82. It was not until 1889 that review was allowed in a

The district judges thus accumulated intense disfavor. The circuit judges fared no better. According to a correspondent in *The Nation*,[108] in discussing the need for judicial reform, "the greatest despot of the land is the United States circuit judge."[109] The veritable empires over which some of them had to travel made attendance in the various districts sporadic and discriminatory.[110] Moreover, removal of state litigation to distant federal courts made litigation costly as well as slow, and thus doubly harassing.

And so bills are introduced renewing, in substance, the attempts for the reorganization of the judiciary which had been before Congress since the Civil War. Intermediate courts of appeal,[111] additional Supreme Court Justices,[112] an enlarged Su-

---

capital case. Act of Feb. 6, 1889, 25 STAT. 655. See, in general, United States *v.* Sanges, 144 U. S. 310, 319–322 (1892).

[108] Professor Haines' admonition against the quotation of contemporary newspaper criticism as authoritative of contemporary opinion is a needed caution. See Charles G. Haines, "Histories of the Supreme Court of the United States Written from the Federalist Point of View," 3 SOUTHWESTERN POL. & SCI. QUART. 1, 7. Of "The Nation," however, Bryce's characterization may be recalled, "*The Nation* . . . was read by the two classes which in America have most to do with forming political and economic opinion, editors and University teachers." RAIT, MEMORIALS OF ALBERT VENN DICEY, 74.

[109] 32 NATION, 9.

[110] The Eighth Circuit, for example, embraced seven states in which twenty-nine terms of the circuit court were held: — Minnesota (2), Iowa (8), Missouri (6), Arkansas (4), Kansas (3), Nebraska (2), Colorado (4). Further, it possessed a population of eight millions, as compared with the three and a half millions embraced within the entire country at the establishment of the judiciary system in 1789. The territory that comprised this circuit was larger by 175,000 square miles than the original thirteen states. See G. W. McCRARY, *supra*, 13 CENT. L. J. at 168. Judge Dillon estimated that he travelled "not less than 10,000 miles a year." See "The Need of Reform in our Federal Judicial System," 17 ALBANY L. J. 9.

[111] On Dec. 11, 1877, Davis introduced a bill for intermediate appellate courts. 7 CONG. REC. 119. On May 6, 1879, Lapham introduced a bill in the House to provide for courts of review. 9 CONG. REC. 1091. On Jan. 6, 1880, Davis again introduced his bill for intermediate courts of appeals. 10 CONG. REC. 194. On Jan. 26, 1880, Warner introduced a bill in the House for the establishment of one intermediate court of appeals to be known as the superior court of the United States. 10 CONG. REC. 528. On Jan. 10, 1881, Geddes introduced into the House a bill for the establishment of a superior court of the United States. 11 CONG. REC. 493.

[112] On Dec. 6, 1880, Springer, in the House, proposed a bill for an increase in the Supreme Court Justices. 11 CONG. REC. 11. On Dec. 17, 1880, Blaine,

preme Court sitting in divisions,[113] relief of the Justices from circuit duty,[114] limitations upon jurisdiction,[115] — these are the remedies urged.[116]   For four successive years Attorney General Devens pressed the need for action upon the attention of Congress.[117]   McCrary by this time had left the House, and the sponsorship for reorganization through the establishment of intermediate appellate tribunals fell naturally to Senator David Davis of Illinois in view of his interest and equipment, as a former member of the Supreme Court.   Davis' proposal was in effect the McCrary Bill.[118]   The time intervening between the two measures necessitated a still further increase in the judicial force, if the scope of the judicial business was to be retained. Davis' bill called for two additional circuit judges for each circuit, and the intermediate courts in each circuit required a quorum of four instead of McCrary's three.   The Supreme Court Justices were again left free to determine their attendance on circuit by the demands of Supreme Court business.

The Davis Bill met three rival schemes with different variants, appearing from time to time under different authorship.   Senator John T. Morgan of Alabama urged a measure, devised by

---

in the Senate, offered a resolution that the Judiciary Committee be required to report as to the expediency of increasing the number of Justices of the Supreme Court to thirteen. *Ibid.* 209. On Dec. 21, 1880, Whyte introduced a joint resolution, proposing a constitutional amendment defining the number of Justices who should constitute the Supreme Court and what number of them should constitute a forum. *Ibid.* 286. This was a reply to Blaine's resolution and initiated by a fear that with an increase in the number of judicial circuits the Supreme Court would become too large. Whyte also expressed a fear that a political party, by increasing the number of Justices, would be able to destroy the independence of the judiciary. Thus he supported the proposal permanently to limit the number of Justices on the ground that the era of territorial expansion was now at an end, and it was possible to fix the number for at least a century.

[113] Manning on Jan. 26, 1880, introduced into the House his bill to reorganize the Supreme Court into sections. 10 CONG. REC. 528.

[114] On Jan. 21, 1881, McDonald in the Senate introduced a bill to revise Section 610 of the Revised Statutes and thereby relieve the Justices from their circuit duties. 11 *ibid.* 810.

[115] See note 155, *infra.*

[116] A summary of the various plans is to be found in Davis' speech in the Senate on May 1, 1882, 13 CONG. REC. 3464–3466.

[117] See REPORTS OF ATTORNEY GENERAL from 1877–1880.

[118] It is printed in full in the REPORT OF ATTORNEY GENERAL FOR 1885, 37.

William A. Maury,[119] establishing a single court of federal appeals, composed of two divisions, each of five judges.[120]   This proposal, while recognising the need for curtailing review by the Supreme Court, tried to avoid the conflict of decisions inherent in nine co-ordinate tribunals.   The Maury Bill reappeared later in a scheme of the Philadelphia Law Association,[121] which favored a National Court of Appeals composed of seven judges with four annual sessions to be held at New York, New Orleans, Chicago, and San Francisco.[122]   The Maury and Philadelphia plans were primarily devised as life-dikes against the flood of diversity of citizenship litigation which reached the Supreme Court. Another device, involving the idea of a single intermediate tribunal, called for the enlargement of the Supreme Court to eighteen.   From this panel of eighteen Justices as many were to be selected for an intermediate appellate court as seemed to be justified by the amount of the business of the two courts — the Supreme Court and the proposed court of appeals.[123]   A totally different approach was made in a House bill by Manning of Mississippi.   He urged a division of the Supreme Court into three sections of three members each.[124]   The court was to

---

[119] William Arden Maury was an experienced practitioner before the Supreme Court.   He was Assistant Attorney General under President Harrison from 1889 to 1893, and subsequently became a member of the Spanish Treaty Claims Commission.

[120] The bill is printed in full in 13 CONG. REC. 3501.

[121] The bill is printed in full in the Report of the Committee of the Law Association of Philadelphia, 6 AM. BAR ASSN. REP. 313, 324.

[122] The court was to have appellate jurisdiction of all cases involving diversity of citizenship, and an appeal lay to the Supreme Court in these cases only where more than $20,000 was involved or where a constitutional question or the construction of a treaty or a federal law was raised, in which case this question alone was to be certified to the Supreme Court.

[123] See letter of Clifford A. Hand to Everett P. Wheeler, of May 11, 1882, " Current Topics," 28 ALBANY L. J. 101.   Judge Sawyer, of the Ninth Circuit, sought to combine this plan with the Davis scheme.   In his pamphlet advocating his own bill, he provided for the addition of nine more Justices to the Supreme Court.   These eighteen Justices were to constitute a " National Court of Appeals " to consist of two divisions and to hear all the appeals from the circuits.   Above this was to be the enlarged Supreme Court, only for the hearing of causes involving more than $100,000, and appeals transferred to it from the National Court of Appeals or on error from the state courts.   See " Majority Report on the Relief of the United States Courts," 5 AM. BAR ASSN. REP. 343, 348.

[124] Manning's first bill, introduced into the Forty-sixth Congress, contem-

sit *in banc* on all questions involving the construction of the Constitution and of treaties. All other cases were to be dealt with by the divisional courts having charge respectively of common law, equity, admiralty and revenue.

These measures kept judicial reorganization at the forefront of legislative business during the Forty-seventh Congress. Powerful forces and great ability were now behind the need for legislation.[125] The bar throughout the country petitioned Congress for action.[126] By common consent something had to be done, and yet again it all ended in futility.

Davis launched his bill in a very able speech on May 1, 1882,[127] and the debate continued through May 12th.[128] Senator Morgan, as we have seen, urged that nine new appellate tribunals would beget further confusion; he also thought eighteen new judges were a needless addition to the judiciary and violently

plated increasing the Supreme Court to twenty-one, to be divided into three divisions of seven members each. The bill introduced by him on Dec. 16, 1881, provided for three divisions of three Justices. Each division was to sit by itself and determine the causes assigned to it. There was no right of review, but the Court had power to order a rehearing in general session. The principle of this scheme was adopted by the "Minority Report of the American Bar Association," presented by Edward J. Phelps, Cortlandt Parker, William M. Evarts, and Richard T. Merrick. See 5 AM. BAR ASSN. REP. 363. An early suggestion for the division of the Supreme Court into sections appears in 1876. See "The Supreme Court," 9 AM. L. REV. 668.

[125] One of the most widely quoted articles was by former Justice Strong, "The Needs of the Supreme Court," 132 N. AM. REV. 437, reprinted in 15 WEST. JUR. 193, 9 WASH. L. REP. 24, 1 OHIO L. J. 400, 412.

[126] Petitions were presented to Congress by lawyers of Rockford, Springfield, Peoria, and Chicago, Illinois, by the Illinois Bar Ass'n, by the Chicago Law Institute, by the Chicago Bar Ass'n, by the Indiana Bar Ass'n, by members of the bar of the eastern district of Wisconsin, by the New York Bar Ass'n, by the New Orleans Law Ass'n, by the bar of Leavenworth, Kansas, by the Mobile Bar Ass'n, by the lawyers of the eighth judicial district of Pennsylvania, by the Missouri Bar Ass'n, by "sundry citizens" of the United States, by four hundred members of the Missouri Bar, by H. Hitchcock "and others," by members of the bar of Ottawa, Kansas. A resolution in favor of an intermediate court of appeals was also passed by the Wisconsin Legislature and presented to both houses of Congress. See 13 CONG. REC. *passim.*

[127] 13 CONG. REC. 3464–3466. The bill had been introduced by Davis on Dec. 12, 1881, and reported by Davis from the Judiciary Committee on Mar. 13, 1882, with amendments. *Ibid.* 69, 1824.

[128] 13 CONG. REC. 3464–3466 (May 1), 3501–1510 (May 2), 3541–3550 (May 3), 3596–3605 (May 4), 3634–3642 (May 5), 3696–3703 (May 8), 3745–3753 (May 9), 3785–3794 (May 10), 3826–3834 (May 11), 3866–3875 (May 12).

opposed the inclusion in the proposed appellate courts of district judges, whom he charged with political partisanship.[129]   Jonas of Louisiana had his own remedy for the " present enormous glut of business " with which the federal judges were unable to grapple:

" The proper course is to go to the root of the evil, and to ascertain whether the jurisdiction of the United States courts has been providently increased, whether the amendments which have been enacted in the last few years, and which have increased their business to such enormous proportions, were wisely adopted, and whether it is not better for us to go back in our work of legislation and to withdraw a portion of the jurisdiction which has been conferred upon the circuit courts. . . ." [130]

Other Senators,[131] particularly from the South, joined him in urging a reduction of federal jurisdiction instead of an expansion of the federal judiciary.   But the bill prevailed by a vote of thirty-two to eighteen.[132]   Despite heavy memorializing from the bar and pressure from its own membership the House paid no attention to the Davis Bill.   Neither that measure nor any of the numerous proposals [133] which originated in the House ever

---

[129] *Ibid.* 3504.   " . . . in the State where I live district judges since the close of the war have been the mere tools of the party.   I do not wish to see men of that class put upon the court of appeals."

[130] *Ibid.* 3601.

[131] Jones of Florida, George of Mississippi, Williams of Kentucky, Call of Florida.   *Ibid.* 3791, 3827, 3830, 3835.

[132] 13 CONG. REC. 3876.   On May 3, the advisability of making the decision of the courts of appeals final in patent cases was debated.   *Ibid.* 3541–3545.   On May 4, an amendment preventing a judge from sitting on his own cause on appeal was adopted.   *Ibid.* 3597.   On May 8, Jones of Florida reaffirmed Morgan's distrust in the character of the district judges.   Davis defended them and called attention to the efficiency of the rotatory system in New York as a precedent for the scheme whereby district judges were to be members of the intermediate court.   *Ibid.* 3699.   On May 9, Morgan, after calling attention to the fact that no report accompanied the bill and that the Judiciary Committee was divided upon it, denounced it as " a bill gotten up in the interests of the rich, in the interests of the great corporations and capitalists of the country."   *Ibid.* 3751.   After a motion to recommit the bill had failed, it passed on May 11.   *Ibid.* 3836.

[133] On Jan. 12, 1882, McCook introduced a bill for the reorganization of the judiciary.   *Ibid.* 387.   On Feb. 6, Rosecrans introduced a bill for additional appellate courts.   *Ibid.* 923.   Page introduced a similar bill on the same day. *Ibid.* 923.   On Feb. 20, Prescott introduced a bill for the reorganization of the

came out of its Judiciary Committee.[134] Congressional preoccupation with more popular issues, the inevitable drags upon legislative machinery, the potent factor of inertia, all had their share in this persistent postponement of some measure of relief for the federal courts, particularly for the Supreme Bench.

But deeper causes were at work. The reorganization of the federal judiciary did not involve merely technical questions of judicial organization, nor was it the concern only of lawyers. Beneath the surface of the controversy lay passionate issues of power as between the states and the Federal Government, involving sectional differences and sectional susceptibilities. These were the deep lines of cleavage which aroused strong feeling in the Senate and were even more active in the House. Stubborn political convictions and strong interests were at stake which made the process of accommodation long and precarious.[135]

---

judiciary. *Ibid.* 1302. On Jan. 9, Payson introduced a bill to establish a court of appeals. *Ibid.* 278. On April 3, Robeson introduced a bill to modify the appellate jurisdiction of the Supreme Court. *Ibid.* 2530. On June 19, Moore introduced a bill to establish courts of appeals. *Ibid.* 5090. Petitions were also presented to the second session of this Congress by the Kansas Bar, the Illinois Bar, the Ohio Bar, and the Chicago Law Institute. 14 *ibid.* 664, 1212, 1421, 2760.

[134] The majority of the House Judiciary Committee was reported to be in favor of the Davis Bill. See Culberson in the House on Jan. 16, 1883, 14 Cong. Rec. 1245.

[135] See, *e.g.*, Moulton of Illinois in the House on June 7, 1884, speaking of the increase of jurisdiction after the Civil War: " The increase of this jurisdiction evidently grew out of the then anomalous condition of the country and was largely influenced by the passions and prejudices of the times. Up to that time there had been no demand or attempt to increase the jurisdiction of the Federal courts; but at that time and since the theory and practice of the party in power was to concentrate as much power as possible in the executive and judicial departments of the Government, and by consequence lessen the jurisdiction of the State courts and the powers and rights of the States. . . . There is a theory that is attempted to be maintained by those who favor centralization of Federal power, that the Federal courts are the safeguards of the rights of the people; that in these courts alone the ultimate rights and liberties of the citizen can be maintained. This theory is a great mistake and its prevalence tends to many evils. Among others it lessens respect for State courts, State rights, and State protection." 15 Cong. Rec. App. 286–287.

4

The history of the relations between Congress and the Supreme Court during the twenty-five years following the Civil War is most telling proof that the various organs of government are not mechanically set apart from each other. In the language of the present Chief Justice, " The fact is that the Judiciary, quite as much as Congress and the Executive, is dependent on the co-operation of the other two that government may go on." [136] The practical workings of the Supreme Court in the scheme of our national life may be as decisively determined by the extent of appellate jurisdiction allotted to it by Congress, the issues open on review, the range of jurisdiction of the inferior courts, and the machinery available for the disposition of business, as by the learning and the outlook of the Justices, the quality and the training of the bar. The conditions under which the Supreme Court labored from 1850 to 1890 show what happens when Congress, the Judiciary, and the President are entangled in political passions and represent conflicting conceptions about the rôle of the federal courts in the national polity.

The Supreme Court docket got beyond all control. The October Term of 1884 opened with 1315 cases; the 1885 Term brought the number to 1340; the 1886 Term increased it to 1396; 1887 showed 1427; in 1888 there were 1563; in 1889, 1635; in 1890 they reached the absurd total of 1800.[137] The lower courts showed the same break-down of judicial organization. They were staggering under a load which made speedy and effective judicial administration impossible. An overburdened tribunal in any form of judicial organization proves the truism that justice delayed is justice denied. It was so in the case of the inferior federal courts during this period. But peculiar evils in the administration of justice grew out of the particular structure of the federal courts. Territorial expansion before the Civil War had already exposed the difficulties of adapting the circuit system to the country's needs. Further territorial expansion and the tremendous increase in litigation accentuated the inadequacies

---

[136] *Ex parte* Grossman, 267 U. S. 87, 120 (1925).

[137] These figures relate to the appellate docket only. See REPORTS OF ATTORNEY GENERAL for the corresponding years.

of the old system. The eighties mark its debacle. This situation was most acute in the Eighth and Ninth Circuits.[138] By the later eighties, eight-ninths of the litigation in the circuit courts was disposed of by single judges, for the most part district judges.[139] The circuit system contemplated a court of two judges, presided over either by a Circuit Justice or a circuit judge. In providing for a set of circuit judges, the Act of 1869 attempted to save the original circuit system by the appointment of additional judges to hold circuit courts. But by 1890 the statutory duty of the Justices to attend circuit was practically a dead letter.[140] Equally impossible was it for nine circuit judges, and, after 1887,[141] ten, to hold circuit courts in sixty-five districts. Two important features governing the federal judicial system at this time must be kept in mind to appreciate how it worked. The circuit courts exercised partly an appellate jurisdiction. Frequently, therefore, the district judge sitting in the circuit court would sit in sole judgment upon himself as judge of the district court. As we are told in an influential contemporary paper before the American Bar Association:

" Such an appeal is not from Philip drunk to Philip sober, but from Philip sober to Philip intoxicated with the vanity of a matured opinion and doubtless also a published decision." [142]

We have suffered in this country from the folly of multiplicity of appeals, but the federal judicial system, at this time, too often erred in the opposite direction, for the decisions of the circuit court were final in all cases involving less than $5,000. Therefore, in cases arising in the district court appeals in numerous

---

[138] REP. ATTY. GEN. FOR 1890, xviii.

[139] See Walter B. Hill, " The Federal Judicial System," 12 AM. BAR ASSN. REP. 289, 304.

[140] " The Circuit Justice is engaged in term with the full bench from October until May. Allowing the usual time of vacation, the statute requires of the Circuit Justice in the three remaining months of each year duties which he could not possibly perform in thrice that time. It may well be doubted whether it is a wholesome example for Congress to pass laws relative to the highest judicial tribunal in the land which can only be intended in a Pickwickian sense." Walter B. Hill, *supra*, 12 AM. BAR ASSN. REP. at 302.

[141] By the Act of Mar. 3, 1887, 24 STAT. 492, an additional circuit judge was appointed for the Second Circuit.

[142] Walter B. Hill, *supra*, 12 AM. BAR ASSN. REP. at 307.

instances were empty form; in cases begun in the circuit court, unless the amount exceeded $5,000, there was no opportunity of appeal even to " Philip intoxicated." The hazards of litigation were amplified by the conscious reduction of the *ad damnum* below the appealable requirement.[143] No wonder that extravagant language, descriptive of tyranny, was employed by responsible lawyers to characterize the powers wielded at this time by a single federal judge! [144]

Congress was not indifferent to the situation; indeed no one disputed the need for relief. But there was a fierce clash over remedies, because of differences over the purposes which federal courts should subserve. Throughout the post-war period the legislative history affecting judicial organization is in no small measure a story of strife between those who sought to curtail the jurisdiction of the federal courts and those who aimed merely to increase the judicial force to cope with the increase of judicial business. The immense accession of power that came to the federal courts by the legislation of 1875 reflected the attitude of what was the last overwhelmingly Republican post-war Congress. After 1875 the House frequently was Democratic and the Senate ceased to be sweepingly Republican.[145] With this shift in party fortunes, reflecting not only the full reëntry of the South into

---

[143] This practice was sanctioned by the decision in Gibson *v.* Shufeldt, 122 U. S. 27 (1887).

[144] *E.g.,* " As things now stand, each man is a law unto himself in matters not exceeding $5000, and the admittedly illegal exaction is sanctified by disclaimer of all beyond that sum ! ! ! ". R. C. M., " The Supreme Court of the United States and the Schemes for Relieving It," 2 Cur. Comm. 11, 17.

[145] " Mr. Jonas. What has politics got to do with this matter? What difference does it make whether the House was Democratic or the Senate was Democratic? Is there a question of politics in the amendment I have offered?

" Mr. Frye. It makes this difference, if the Senator will allow me, and he knows the difference it makes as well as I do, that the provisions conferring new jurisdiction upon the United States courts have been ingrafted upon our law through and following the war, from the necessities of the war, from the circumstances of the war and the years following the war; and, therefore, it is perfectly natural that Senators and Representatives in Congress from the South should be the Senators and Representatives desiring the repeal of these sections. That is why to a certain extent politics comes in. I never have heard Senators and Representatives from the North demanding the repeal of these sections. I have heard, and I know, and I myself concur with the Senator from Louisiana that that jurisdiction needs amendment in very many respects." 13 Cong. Rec. 3639 (May 5, 1882).

the national legislature but also the appearance of new economic interests in Congress, a continuous effort to pull in the reins on federal judicial power began. In each house bills were sponsored seeking to curtail the business of the federal courts and more particularly the multitudinous litigation involving corporations doing business outside their chartering states.[146] The political conflict which was aroused by the federal courts was augmented by the clash in the two houses. The popular House was for curtailment of power; the successive Senate majorities, whether Republican or Democratic, resisted.

In the Forty-fourth Congress (following the passage of the Act of March 3, 1875) bills were introduced in the House of Representatives to cut down jurisdiction on removal.[147] Half a dozen bills with a like object appeared at the next Congress.[148]

---

[146] The extent to which the fiction of corporate citizenship added to the litigation in the federal courts is illustrated by contemporary debates in Congress. " Fully one-half the litigation in the circuit courts is supplied by corporations, and it is estimated that one-third of the cases in the Supreme Court are those in which corporations are either plaintiffs or defendants." Culberson in the House on Jan. 16, 1883. 14 CONG. REC. 1247. " In 1879, out of two hundred and forty-five cases on what is called the common-law side of the docket of the United States court at Little Rock, one hundred and twenty-three cases were of this character." Garland in the Senate on May 5, 1882. 13 CONG. REC. 3636.

[147] On Dec. 15, 1875, Woodworth of Ohio introduced a bill to prohibit " removal of causes from State to United States courts upon application by parties after appearance in State courts." 4 CONG. REC. 227. On Jan. 6, 1876, Philips of Missouri introduced a bill to amend the Act of Mar. 3, 1875. *Ibid.* 293. A similar bill was introduced by Mackey of Pennsylvania on Jan. 31, 1876. *Ibid.* 770. On Feb. 7, 1876, Ross of Pennsylvania introduced a bill to amend the Act of 1866. *Ibid.* 915. On the same day another bill to amend the Act of 1875 was introduced by W. B. Williams of Michigan. *Ibid.* 918. On Feb. 24, 1876, Durand of Michigan introduced a bill to limit the transfer of cases from state to federal courts. *Ibid.* 1267. On Mar. 9, 1876, Hurd of Ohio from the House Judiciary Committee reported out a substitute bill for the bill introduced by Woodworth. This provided that the application for removal had to be made prior to the time when the defendant filed an appearance in the state court, that there could be no removal upon the application of the plaintiff, and that in all cases there could be no removal from the state courts unless the sum in controversy exceeded $2,000. The bill passed the House, was referred to the Senate Judiciary Committee, and there lost. *Ibid.* 1593–1594, 1617.

[148] On Oct. 29, 1877, Townshend of Illinois introduced a bill " to repeal certain sections of the Revised Statutes and to amend certain sections of the Statutes at Large relating to the removal of causes from State courts." 6 CONG. REC. 186. See " The Proposed Amendments to the Law Relating to the Federal

This time the period of legislative incubation was accelerated by a Supreme Court decision, accentuating the power of foreign corporations to resort to the federal courts and deepening popular hostility.   As a result of *Ex parte Schollenberger*,[149] it was clear that a corporation came within the provisions of the removal statutes so as to give jurisdiction to the circuit court in every state in which the corporation transacted business through an agent.   This decision was rendered on May 13, 1878, and on June 1, 1878, the Judiciary Committee of the House reported a bill which, apart from other serious restrictions upon removal jurisdiction, entirely eliminated corporate citizenship as a means of access to the federal courts.[150]   The bill was in charge of David B. Culberson of Texas,[151] " one of the best lawyers in the House of Representatives ",[152] who for the next ten years pertinaciously urged this drastic measure.   In this Congress the bill did not come to a vote, but he promptly reintroduced it in the next Congress.[153]   Thereafter the House passed it in three successive Congresses, in 1880,[154] 1883,[155] and 1884;[156] three successive Senates buried it.

Judiciary," 1 MONTHLY JURIST, 641. On Nov. 6, 1877, Bouck of Wisconsin introduced a bill to repeal sub-division 3 of Section 639 of the Revised Statutes. 6 CONG. REC. 250. On Nov. 12, 1877, McKenzie of Kentucky introduced a bill to repeal parts of Sections 563 and 629 of the Revised Statutes. *Ibid.* 356. On the same day Tipton of Illinois introduced a bill to amend Section 1 of the Act of 1875. *Ibid.* 357. On Dec. 4, 1877, Cobb of Indiana introduced a similar bill. 7 *ibid.* 13. On Jan. 14, 1878, Keightley of Michigan introduced a bill to regulate the removal of causes from the state courts. *Ibid.* 317.

[149] 96 U. S. 369 (1877).

[150] 7 CONG. REC. 4000. The bill is found in full in 10 CONG. REC. 681; 14 *ibid.* 1244; 15 *ibid.* 4879.

[151] Culberson was a member of Congress from 1875 to 1897 and in 1897 was appointed by President McKinley a commissioner to codify the laws of the United States. He was the father of the late Senator Charles A. Culberson.

[152] So characterized by no less an authority than Senator Frye of Maine. See 13 CONG. REC. 3639 (May 5, 1882).

[153] On Dec. 9, 1879, 10 CONG. REC. 43. On Jan. 15, 1880, Knott from the Judiciary Committee reported a substitute bill which was read and recommitted. *Ibid.* 350. The bill was again reported out by Culberson on Feb. 3, 1880. *Ibid.* 681.

[154] Culberson's bill was debated in 1880 for nine days. *Ibid.* 699–703 (Feb. 4), 723–725 (Feb. 5), 813–820 (Feb. 11), 846–850 (Feb. 12), 950–954 (Feb. 17), 990–993 (Feb. 18), 1010–1015 (Feb. 19), 1082–1084 (Feb. 24), 1276–1281 (Mar. 3), 1304–1305 (Mar. 4). Among those who supported the measure were Knott of Kentucky, Weaver of Iowa, New of Indiana, Herbert of Alabama, Waddill of

The debates in the House, and particularly the vivid speeches in 1880, leave no doubt about the economic and political factors which determined men's votes. Traditional southern sentiment in favor of state institutions and against extension of federal power was undoubtedly alive. But new forces and new. factors had come into play and gave new pungency to old feelings. The effort to curb the federal courts was not a distinctly southern measure. A contest between eastern capital and western and southern agrarianism was at stake. The debate is significant because the real issues were put with candor. The case of the eastern investor was stated with great force by George D. Robinson [157] of Massachusetts:

Missouri, Lapham of New York, and Townshend of Illinois. The most bitter opponent of the bill was Robinson of Massachusetts. The bill passed the House on Mar. 4, 1880, by a vote of 162 to 74, after Robinson's proposal to reduce the jurisdictional amount from $2,000 to $500 was defeated by a vote of 98 to 62, and his proposal to strike out the section dealing with corporate citizenship was also defeated by a vote of 167 to 68. 10 CONG. REC. 1304–1305. It was referred to the Senate Judiciary Committee on Mar. 5, 1880, whence it never emerged. *Ibid.* 1340.

[155] Culberson introduced his bill on Jan. 16, 1882. 13 CONG. REC. 427. It was reported by him from the Judiciary Committee on Mar. 9, 1882. 13 CONG. REC. 1754. No action was taken upon the bill during this session, for the Senate was then considering the Davis Bill together with proposals in the form of amendments to that bill curtailing the jurisdiction of the federal courts. See notes 129, 130, *supra.* In the second session, however, Culberson, on Jan. 5, 1883, moved to take up the bill, but the following day the House refused to consider it, by a vote of 103 to 84. 14 CONG. REC. 904, 924. The bill was debated on Jan. 16, 1883, and passed the same day by a vote of 134 to 67. *Ibid.* 1244–1255. It was again referred to the Senate Judiciary Committee from which it never emerged. *Ibid.* 1270.

[156] The bill was introduced by Culberson on Dec. 11, 1883, and reported out of the Judiciary Committee on Feb. 5, 1884. 15 CONG. REC. 118, 896; HOUSE REPORT, No. 196, 48th Cong., 1st Sess., Ser. No. 2253. It was debated on June 7, 1884, and passed without a roll call. *Ibid.* 489. Only " leave to print " speeches were delivered for and against the bill. See 15 CONG. REC. APP. 276, 286, 360. A resolution of the Iowa legislature advocating an increase in the amount necessary for the jurisdiction of the federal courts was presented to Congress on April 14, 1884, and referred to the Judiciary Committee. 15 CONG. REC. 2917, 2939, 2955. Again the bill was referred to the Senate Judiciary Committee and again it was buried. *Ibid.* 4909.

[157] For Robinson, who afterwards became the well-known Governor of Massachusetts, see 1 HOAR, AUTOBIOGRAPHY, 356–359; LODGE, ADDRESS COMMEMORATIVE OF THE LIFE AND SERVICES OF GEORGE D. ROBINSON.

"In all parts of the country there occur times of excitement. You say that if a corporation shall go into a State to do business, let it abide by the law of the people where it seeks to do business. Yes, gentlemen, in times of peace and harmony and when there is no prejudice or excitement. But no State is always free from that. Massachusetts has had its periods of jealousy and prejudice; and there have been times in my recollection when some gentlemen of the South, if they belong to incorporated companies, could not have gone to Massachusetts and submitted their cases to the State juries and obtained the judgments that they ought to have obtained on the law and the facts.

"And in the West there have been granger laws and granger excitements that have led people to commit enormities in legislation and extravagances in practice; and in the South — why, sir, history is too full for me to particularize.

"Capital is needed to restore the waste places of the South and to build up the undeveloped West; it must flow largely from the old States of the East and from foreign lands. But it will not be risked in the perils of sectional bitterness, narrow prejudices, or local indifference to integrity and honor.

"I say then, let us stand by the national courts; let us preserve their power." [158]

This view was effectively entrenched in the Senate. The numerous appeals to that body from manufacturers, from business organizations and their lawyers [159] found a ready response among

---

[158] 10 CONG. REC. 850 (Feb. 12, 1880).

Compare the penetrating analysis of Charles Francis Adams, Jr. in 1875:

"Thus about the year 1870 the Western mind began to appreciate the fact that its railroad system was secured. Not unnaturally it now began also to count its cost, and to realize that, though the West had the use of this magnificent railroad development, and could not be deprived of it, yet she did not own it, and was, moreover, bound to pay for its use according to the bonds given anterior to its construction. In other words, exactly what might have been anticipated now began to appear. In her over-eagerness the West had made an improvident bargain; she had given for her longed-for-railroads all that she had, all that any one asked; and now she had them, and began to shrewdly suspect that her bargain had after all been somewhat of the hardest. It was, indeed, a case of absentee ownership, with all that those words imply; and when that is said one great cause of the near-impending trouble is disclosed." "The Granger Movement," 120 N. AM. REV. 394.

On the pervasive influence of sectionalism in American politics at this time, see Hannah Grace Roach, "Sectionalism in Congress (1870–1890)," 19 AM. POL. SCI. REV. 500.

[159] After the House had passed the Culberson Bill for the third time and

Senators who in other fields of legislation resisted the economic policies of the West.[160] Instead of withdrawing power from the federal courts, the Senate, as we have seen, sought to provide them with more efficient machinery and more judges to dispose of their increased business. The two houses were deadlocked. The Senate passed the Davis Bill and rejected all proposals seeking to contract the jurisdiction of the federal courts. After the Davis Bill passed the Senate, it was buried in the House Judiciary Committee; while the House passed the Culberson Bill, enacting the proposals rejected by the Senate.[161]

5

Meanwhile the plight of the courts steadily grew worse. The exigency of the situation is put before another Congress in a weighty report [162] by the new Attorney General, A. H. Garland, who, as Senator from Arkansas, had for many years intimately grappled with the problem. On the Judiciary Committee in the Senate, Garland had sought to combine the Davis Bill with curtailment of jurisdiction.[163] He returned to this view in a detailed

---

it was before the Senate, petitions against its passage were presented to the Senate by " Goodbar, White & Co., Tennent, Walker & Co., and other business men and merchants of Saint Louis, Mo."; by the Board of Trade and Transportation of the city of Cincinnati; by Alms & Doepke, " one of the most extensive establishments in Cincinnati, Ohio "; by " business men, lawyers, and others " of Toledo, Ohio; by the Diamond Match Co., of Akron, Ohio; by the John Shillito Co., of Cincinnati, Ohio. 15 CONG. REC. 5171, 5324, 5378, 5469, 5513, 5611.

160 Thus, Senator Cullom has described the influences at work in the Senate which for a time successfully defeated attempts to pass legislation regulating railroad abuses. See CULLOM, FIFTY YEARS OF PUBLIC SERVICE, 329. On the general power of corporate influence in the Senate, see 2 BRYCE, MODERN DEMOCRACIES, 59; HAYNES, ELECTION OF SENATORS, 176–179; ROOSEVELT, AUTOBIOGRAPHY, 471–472, in connection with the famous Archbold-Foraker correspondence, 2 FORAKER, NOTES OF A BUSY LIFE, 328, *et seq.;* and *N. Y. Times,* Sept. 22, 25, 1908.

161 See notes 129, 130, 151, *supra.*

162 REP. ATTY. GEN. FOR 1885.

163 Garland in the debate on the Davis Bill supported the amendments of the southern Senators seeking to curtail the jurisdiction of the federal courts. He nevertheless believed that despite such proposed curtailment, the increase in their litigation required the changes proposed by the scheme for courts of appeals. " I say that if this amendment of the Senator from Louisiana [Jonas] should be adopted, yet the legitimate and proper business arising before the

plan, which " while preserving the general idea of what is known as the Davis Bill " [164] proposed several changes and modifications therein, largely in the direction of curtailed jurisdiction. " There is no concealing the fact," he tells Congress, " that something should be done and that without further delay." [165] Congress did do something but only a part of what Garland asked. A Democratic House found it congenial to adopt Garland's recommendations in so far as he urged a restriction of the right of removal of cases from state courts into federal courts. Culberson took the lead in the House in acting on the Garland report, and for the fifth time introduced his proposals.[166] On March 17, 1886, the House Judiciary Committee reported out his bill.[167] It provided (1) an increase from $500 to $2,000 in the jurisdictional amount, (2) a limitation of the right of an assignee of negotiable paper to sue only when the original holder could sue, (3) elimination of the plaintiff's right to remove from the state courts, save in cases where local prejudice was shown, (4) withdrawal of jurisdiction based solely upon federal incorporation as well as in cases between a foreign corporation doing business within a state and a citizen of that state.[168] The bill passed this time without debate and without division, on January 13, 1887.[169] In the Senate the bill was reported from the Judiciary Committee with serious changes.[170] Remission to the state courts of the heavy item of business that came to the federal courts at the suit of foreign and federal corporations was still too much for the Senate. It retained this large source of litigation, compromising with the House only to the extent of withdrawing the national banks from the stream of federal litigation by declaring them to be " deemed citizens of the States

---

Federal tribunals, confined within their jurisdiction as it was originally, before the innovations of the act of 1875, is of sufficient importance and sufficient weight and so exacting as to require additional force in the United States tribunals." 13 Cong. Rec. 3635 (May 5, 1882).

[164] Rep. Atty. Gen. for 1885, 41.

[165] *Ibid.* 37.

[166] 17 Cong. Rec. 487 (Jan. 6, 1886).

[167] *Ibid.* 2454. The accompanying report is House Report, No. 1078, 49th Cong., 1st Sess., Ser. No. 2438.

[168] The bill is found in full in 18 Cong. Rec. 613.

[169] *Ibid.* 614.

[170] By Wilson of Iowa on Feb. 24, 1887. *Ibid.* 2542–2546.

in which they are respectively located " and thus subjecting them to the exclusive jurisdiction of the state courts.[171] The House swallowed this compromise [172] and the bill became law on March 3, 1887.

This legislation eased the pressure upon the lower courts. To a degree it restrained the inflow of litigation, although the gain was in part offset by cases brought under the new Tucker Act.[173] But the effect of the legislation upon the Supreme Court was negligible. The elimination of national bank litigation cut off a minor feeder of the Supreme Court docket. But inasmuch as appeals to the Supreme Court from the lower courts were limited to controversies involving more than $5,000, lifting the bar for

---

[171] The attitude of the Senate Judiciary Committee toward the Culberson Bill is best illustrated by the remarks of Senator Edmunds, then a member of the Committee: " The bill as it came from the House of Representatives was altogether extreme, and the gentlemen of the committee who felt the inconvenience and wrong of subjecting mere local affairs to the great expense of national jurisdiction, diminished their desires so that the committee at last agreed upon the bill as it now stands, which is much less extreme than the one the other House proposed, and which, on the whole, if we correctly understand it, does not do any injustice to any of the people who have national interests in the States where they do not live other than carrying the right to go to the United States courts from $500 to $2,000." 18 CONG. REC. 2544. The Bill passed the Senate on Mar. 2, 1887, by a vote of 44 to 6, with an amendment providing for an increase in judicial salaries. At the same time a conference with the House was requested, Wilson, Hoar, and Pugh being appointed as conferees. *Ibid.* 2546.

[172] On Mar. 3, 1887, the House agreed to a conference, naming Culberson, Tucker, and Parker as conferees. *Ibid.* 2721. At the same time the Senate recalled the bill, reconsidered the amendment for increasing judicial salaries, and rejected it. *Ibid.* 2618, 2624. The conference committee then reported that the House should recede, and their report was approved by the House. *Ibid.* 2727.

[173] By the Act of Mar. 3, 1887, 24 STAT. 505, the district courts were given concurrent jurisdiction with the Court of Claims in cases where the amount did not exceed $1,000, and the circuit courts were given a similar concurrent jurisdiction where the claim was not in excess of $10,000. This Act also changed the wording of the statutes defining the nature of claims against the government over which the Court of Claims was given jurisdiction. This change was held not to extend the jurisdiction of the Court of Claims beyond claims for money arising out of equitable, maritime, or legal demands, and thus the Court had no power to render decrees for specific performance or for the delivery of property recovered in kind. United States *v.* Jones, 131 U. S. 1 (1889). From the years 1887 to 1892 the cases brought under this Act in the circuit and district courts number 991, of which twenty-two were appealed to the Supreme Court. See REP. ATTY. GEN. FOR 1892, Ex. 3, pp. 10–11.

resort to the federal courts from $500 to $2,000 left wholly untouched the appeals of the Supreme Court. Thus bills for intermediate appellate tribunals continued to be introduced into Congress at the same time that this determined effort to curtail jurisdiction was being made.[174]

The fact that the Act of 1887 scarcely touched the Supreme
Court naturally led Garland in his last two reports, in 1887 and
1888, to repeat his plaintive appeal " that something be done " to
relieve the Supreme Court.[175] " Almost every mail," wrote Garland, " brings me one or more letters about this matter from
people of such legal or other standing as entitles them to a hearing." [176] Bar and bench were again articulate.[177] Even the mem-

---

[174] Bills for the establishment of courts of appeals were introduced into the
House by Rosecrans on Dec. 10, 1883, by Payson on the same day, by Springer
on Feb. 4, 1884, by Dorsheimer on Feb. 18, by Herbert on Feb. 18. 15 CONG.
REC. 60, 64, 866, 1194, 1199. In the Senate similar bills were introduced by
Lapham on Dec. 10, 1883, by Mitchell on Mar. 4, 1884, and by Bayard on the
same day. *Ibid.* 51, 1577, 1578. The Senate Judiciary Committee reported them
back adversely, and reported their own bill on April 14, 1884. *Ibid.* 2919. In
the next session this bill, similar to the Davis Bill, was debated very shortly.
Senator Hoar spoke in support of it, but no action was taken. 16 *ibid.* 880–883.
In the House on Dec. 4, 1884, Oates introduced a bill to establish courts of
appeals. *Ibid.* 56. In the Forty-ninth Congress bills for the establishment of a
circuit court of appeals were introduced in the Senate by Hoar on Dec. 8, 1885,
by Wilson on Jan. 20, 1886, and by Gray on Feb. 16, 1886. 17 CONG. REC.
122, 768, 1467. In the House similar bills were introduced by Wheeler on
Dec. 21, 1885, and by Payson on Dec. 21, 1885. *Ibid.* 366, 377. During the
First Session of the Fiftieth Congress bills for intermediate appellate courts were
introduced by Senator Gray on Dec. 13, 1887, and by Senator Pugh (by request) on Jan. 9, 1888. 19 *ibid.* 47, 287. In the same session of the House
bills of this nature were introduced by Wheeler and Payson on Jan. 4, 1888,
and by Springer on Jan. 16, 1888. *Ibid.* 205, 209, 483. On Mar. 7, 1888,
these bills were reported back adversely by Rogers of the Judiciary Committee,
together with a substitute bill. HOUSE REPORT, Nos. 941, 942, 50th Cong., 1st
Sess., Ser. No. 2600. A bill was also introduced by Phelan for the appointment
of a commission to inquire into the organization of the federal judiciary on
Jan. 4, 1888, which was reported back adversely from the Judiciary Committee.
19 CONG. REC. 231, 1192; HOUSE REPORT, No. 390, 50th Cong., 1st Sess., Ser.
No. 2599. In the second session Payson of the House introduced a bill for
courts of appeals on Feb. 4, 1889. 20 CONG. REC. 1474.

[175] REP. ATTY. GEN. FOR 1887, xv; *ibid.* FOR 1888, xiv.

[176] REP. ATTY. GEN. FOR 1887, xv.

[177] See William Strong, " Relief for the Supreme Court," 151 N. AM.
REV. 567; Walter B. Hill, " The Federal Judicial System," 12 AM. BAR ASSN.
REP. 289, reprinted in 22 CHI. LEG. NEWS, 9; Walter B. Hill, " Report of
the Committee on Federal Legislation," 1889 GA. BAR ASSN. REP. 69; Walter

bers of the Supreme Court felt impelled to speak. Chief Justice Waite,[178] Mr. Justice Harlan,[179] and Mr. Justice Field [180] in turn sought to enlist public opinion to secure Congressional action. Attorney General Miller in 1889 and 1890 repeated the urgings of his predecessor for reorganization of the Judiciary.[181] With strong division of opinion as to the means for the relief of the Supreme Court, the American Bar Association was united in urging the need for some action, and was instrumental in securing consideration of the matter in the President's annual message.[182] His professional interest [183] made President Harrison unusually alert to the needs of the federal bench:

" The plan of providing some intermediate courts having final appellate jurisdiction of certain classes of questions and cases has, I think, received a more general approval from the bench and bar of the country than any other. Without attempting to discuss details, I recommend that provision be made for the establishment of such courts." [184]

At last on April 7, 1890, a bill introduced by Congressman John H. Rogers [185] came out of the House Committee on Ju-

---

B. Hill, " Relief of Suitors in Federal Courts," 66 ATLANTIC MONTHLY, 671; Samuel Maxwell, " Relief of the United States Supreme Court," 23 AM. L. REV. 958; Alfred C. Coxe, " Relief of the Supreme Court," 6 FORUM 567; William M. Meigs, " Relief of the Supreme Court of the United States," 23 AM. L. REG. (N. S.) 360; J. H. Raymond, " Relief of the Federal Court's Docket," 1889 ILL. BAR ASSN. REP. 65; Robert M. Hughes, " Reorganization of the Federal Courts," 10 VA. L. J. 193; W. H. Rossington, " Federal and State Jurisdiction," 1888 KAN. BAR ASSN. REP. 34; R. C. M., " The Supreme Court of the United States and the Schemes for Relieving It," 2 CUR. COMM. 11.

[178] " Remarks of Chief Justice Waite," 36 ALBANY L. J. 318.

[179] Mr. Justice Harlan, " The United States Supreme Court," 20 CHI. LEG. NEWS 208.

[180] Address of Mr. Justice Field, " The Centenary of the Supreme Court of the United States," 24 AM. L. REV. 351.

[181] " I call special attention to the recommendations upon this subject of my predecessor in each one of his annual reports . . ." REP. ATTY. GEN. FOR 1889, xix. See also *ibid.* for 1890, xviii.

[182] Report of the Committee on the Relief of the Supreme Court, 13 AM. BAR ASSN. REP. 338.

[183] See CULLOM, FIFTY YEARS OF PUBLIC SERVICE, 248.

[184] First Annual Message of Dec. 3, 1889; 9 RICHARDSON, MESSAGES AND PAPERS OF THE PRESIDENTS, 42-3.

[185] The bill was introduced on April 4, 1890, 21 CONG. REC. 3049.

diciary.[186]   The bill, in effect, repeated the Davis proposals. District and circuit courts were fused; nine intermediate courts of appeals were created with final decision in cases arising solely through diversity of citizenship, subject, however, to certification; two additional circuit judges for each circuit were to provide the necessary additional judicial force, wholly relieving the Justices from circuit duty.[187]

The debate upon the bill threshed over old straw.   The opposition repeated the arguments of the 1882 debate.[188]   Nine appellate courts, it was urged, would lead to diversity of decisions within the courts' area of finality.[189]   On the other hand, the whole assumption of securing relief by adding to existing machinery was challenged.   Complete elimination of all jurisdiction based on diverse citizenship was the counter proposal.[190] The upshot was the passage of the bill by an overwhelming vote.[191]   In the Senate the clash of opinion of 1882 was still alive.   William M. Evarts was now a powerful member of its Judiciary Committee.   In 1882 he had led the fight before the American Bar Association against the Davis Bill and for the Manning scheme of dividing the Supreme Court into three divisions.[192]   He had since become a convert to the proposal for intermediate appellate courts.   On August 5, 1890, Evarts reported out of committee a substitute for the House bill,[193] which retained the central proposal of nine courts of appeals.[194]

---

[186] *Ibid.* 3130.

[187] The bill is to be found in full in 21 CONG. REC. 3402.

[188] Culberson supported the bill because it would put an end to the "judicial despotism exercised by circuit and district judges." *Ibid.* 3403.

[189] Breckenridge of Kentucky also argued that it would be impossible to limit the number of appellate courts to nine. *Ibid.* 3407.

[190] Oates in closing said, "It behooves every lover of this country to cut down Federal jurisdiction instead of enlarging it, if he would preserve and perpetuate our Government." *Ibid.* 3407.

[191] After the defeat of a motion to recommit the bill, it passed by a vote of 131 to 13. *Ibid.* 3410.

[192] See "Minority Report on the Relief of the United States Courts," 5 AM. BAR ASSN. REP. 363.

[193] 21 CONG. REC. 8133. On motion of Cockrell, 500 additional copies of Rogers' bill were printed, 750 on the motion of Evarts, and 750 on Manderson's motion. SEN. JOURNAL, 51st Cong., 1st Sess., Ser. No. 2677, pp. 268, 453, 472.

[194] The bill is printed in full in 21 CONG. REC. 10218. Save for very minor literary changes, the alteration of allowing direct review by the Supreme Court

Otherwise his bill made important modifications. It retained the district and circuit courts, but abolished the appellate jurisdiction of the circuit courts; it provided for direct appeals from the district and circuit courts to the Supreme Court in defined classes of cases, and routed all other cases to the courts of appeals for final disposition.[195] On a careful forecast of the probable volume of business likely to come before the courts of appeals as well as of the demands on the district and circuit judges, in view of the redistribution of jurisdiction, Evarts felt that a single additional circuit judge for each circuit would be ample to carry the load.[196] The important modification of Evarts upon the House bill was that Evarts bifurcated the appellate stream from the district and circuit courts by sending one branch of intrinsically more important issues straight to the Supreme Court and diverting the more numerous but less difficult issues to the nine new appellate courts. These proposals originated in part with a strong committee of the American Bar Association, and were worked out in conference between this committee and a sub-committee of the House and Senate Judiciary Committees, presided over by Senator Evarts.[197] The ingenuity of Evarts

in capital cases and other infamous crimes, the addition of Sections Thirteen and Fifteen providing for appeals from the United States Court in the Indian Territory and the other territorial supreme courts, the bill, as introduced by Senator Evarts, became law by the Act of Mar. 3, 1891, 26 STAT. 829.

[195] Subject to certification or *certiorari* to the Supreme Court.

[196] 21 CONG. REC. 10220–10222. Evarts pointed out how jurisdiction based upon diversity of citizenship increased, and jurisdiction based on subject-matter decreased, as one moved westward.

[197] The committee of the American Bar Association consisted of David Dudley Field, Henry Hitchcock, Francis Rawle, J. Randolph Tucker, George H. Bates, Edward Otis Hinkley, William Allen Butler, Thomas J. Semmes, J. Hubley Ashton, and Walter B. Hill. The hearing was held on Feb. 13, 1890, at which was presented the draft of a bill " which embodied the characteristic feature of the legislation adopted, viz., the provision retaining in the appellate jurisdiction of the Supreme Court constitutional and all Federal questions and diverting to the new appellate court those cases which for the most part involve municipal law and which principally are brought into the courts of the United States by the mere fact of citizenship of the parties." " Report of the Committee on Judicial Administration and Remedial Procedure," 17 AM. BAR ASSN. REP. 336, 337. The differences between this draft and the bill reported to the Senate by Mr. Evarts were (1) that the draft provided for a writ of error from the lower court to the Supreme Court in only one class of criminal cases, namely, capital cases; (2) that the draft gave the right of exception to an interlocutory decree appointing a

and his associates proposed the relief of the Supreme Court and at the same time the retention of as much of the traditional structure as was possible.   Evarts' device satisfied the most powerful impetus behind the proposal for intermediate appellate tribunals, in that it shut off from the Supreme Court the type of litigation which the proponents of the Davis Bill and its successors most aimed at withdrawing; and yet it satisfied traditionalists like Evarts by retaining the old courts and by providing immediate Supreme Court review of their decisions upon those vital issues which were appropriate for Supreme Court review. Again, while Evarts hardly expected any more circuit attendance by the Justices in the future than in the past, he did not disturb the deep sentiment behind the old tradition by explicitly eliminating them, as did the House bill, from the composition of the circuit courts of appeals.   But he did not satisfy the extremists who still thought of the pioneer days when the Justices were active on circuit and thus, supposedly, kept the common touch. This feeling cut across party lines, for its leading sponsors were Edmunds of Vermont [198] and Vest of Missouri.[199]   The minority supported the old Manning scheme for a tripartite division of the Supreme Court.   But on September 24, 1890,[200] the Evarts

---

receiver; (3) that the draft transferred all the circuit court jurisdiction to the district courts; (4) that the draft contemplated that circuit courts of appeals should be composed of three circuit judges, which would require the appointment of two additional circuit judges for each circuit.

[198] On Aug. 8, 1890, Edmunds from the Judiciary Committee submitted the report of the minority advocating the divisional scheme for relieving the Supreme Court.   See 21 Cong. Rec. 8307.   For the minority report see Sen. Rep., No. 1571, 51st Cong., 1st Sess., Ser. No. 2711.

[199] 21 Cong. Rec. 10223–10224: "I do not want to say anything disrespectful about the judges of the Supreme Court or the circuit and district courts of the United States, but they are men — that is no criticism on them — with like motives, passions, instincts, whatever you may term them, as ourselves and as other men, and when you put a man into an office with a life tenure, and, if I might use the expression, put him on a sort of pedestal above the rest of the people, he then thinks that leisure is the first element of his new position."

[200] The debate began on Sept. 18 and continued for six days.   See *ibid.* 10193–10194 (Sept. 18), 10217–10232 (Sept. 19), 10278–10288 (Sept. 20), 10302–10318 (Sept. 22), 10335 (Sept. 23), 10363–10365 (Sept. 24).   Dolph of Oregon called attention to the imperative need for relief, remarking: "We want a system which is adequate to the business of to-day and sufficient to meet the demands of the future." *Ibid.* 10227.   He favored the House bill rather than the Senate amendment, but was willing to support the latter because of the immediate need

Bill finally prevailed with only six dissenting votes.[201] The differences between the two houses threw the bill into conference at the next session.[202] In conference the House yielded to the Senate amendments.[203] Rogers, however, held out against agreement because the Senate bill did not abolish the circuit courts, failed to provide relief for the Supreme Court over its existing docket by allowing transfers of pending causes to the new circuit courts of appeals, increased the appellate jurisdiction of the Supreme Court in criminal cases, did not relieve the Justices of circuit duty, and made shifting courts of the circuit courts of appeals.[204] Culberson led for acceptance of the conference report,[205] which prevailed.[206] The bill which established the circuit courts of appeals received the President's approval on March 3, 1891.[207]

The remedy was decisive. The Supreme Court at once felt its benefits. A flood of litigation had indeed been shut off. While

---

of reform. On Sept. 20, Ingalls' amendment, now Section Thirteen of the Act, relative to appeals from the Indian Territory, was adopted. *Ibid.* 10279. Then Dolph's amendment, now Section Fifteen of the Act, giving the circuit courts of appeals appellate jurisdiction from the territorial courts where they would have final jurisdiction of appeals from the circuit and district courts, was adopted. *Ibid.* 10282. Dolph's amendment for a tenth circuit comprised of Oregon, Washington, Montana, and Idaho, was defeated. *Ibid.* 10287. A bill for increasing the number of circuits from nine to ten was favorably reported from the Judiciary Committee by Senator Hoar, on Feb. 10, 1891. See Sen. Rep., No. 2179, 51st Cong., 2nd Sess., Ser. No. 2827. On Sept. 22, 1890, Vest offered his divisional bill in the form of an amendment which was rejected by a vote of 36 to 10. 21 Cong. Rec. 10316. Pasco of Florida offered an amendment to prohibit the district judges from sitting on the intermediate court of appeals, but this was rejected. *Ibid.* 10311. Gorman's amendment to remove the circuit court of appeals from Richmond to Baltimore was defeated. *Ibid.* 10364.

[201] The vote was 44 to 6. *Ibid.* 10364.

[202] On Sept. 30, 1890, the House received the Senate bill and referred it to the Judiciary Committee. *Ibid.* 10678–80, 10759. At the next session on Feb. 21, 1891, the House voted not to concur in the Senate amendments, and appointed as conferees Taylor, Caswell, and Rogers. 22 *ibid.* 3087. The Senate at its former session had appointed Evarts, Hoar, and Pugh. Sen. Journal, 51st Cong., 1st Sess., Ser. No. 2677, p. 543.

[203] The conference report was made to both houses on Feb. 28, 1891. 22 Cong. Rec. 3535, 3583.

[204] *Ibid.* 3584–3585.

[205] *Ibid.* 3585. Breckenridge, who had opposed the House bill, was won to the support of the Senate bill. *Ibid.* 3586. Oates opposed the report, proposing one national court of appeals at Washington. 22 Cong. Rec. App. 248.

[206] No tellers were ordered. *Ibid.* 3587.

[207] *Ibid.* 3760.

in the October Term, 1887, 482 new cases were docketed; in 1888, 550, in 1889, 489, and in 1890, 623; in 1891 (with the new Act only a few months in operation) new business dropped to 379 cases and in 1892 to 275 cases.[208]

---

[208] These figures deal only with the appellate docket. See REPORTS OF ATTORNEY GENERAL for the years mentioned.

CHAPTER III

FROM THE CIRCUIT COURTS OF APPEALS ACT
TO
THE JUDICIAL CODE

I

EXCEPT the abortive Federalist Act of 1801, the Circuit Courts of Appeals Act [1] was the first structural modification in the federal judicial system since its creation a hundred years before. The Act issued after long legislative travail, and its authors hoped for their handiwork a permanence not unlike that of the First Judiciary Act. Their hopes were amply realized. Two decades elapsed before a drastic change in the federal judicial organization again occurs; and another fifteen years, before the distribution of power between the Supreme Court and the circuit courts of appeals is radically modified. The Circuit Courts of Appeals Act enjoyed this long life partly, at least, because it increased the competence of the federal courts, but only partly so. Inertia and habit are more far-reaching explanations of the survival of the Act of 1891, intact, for twenty years. Its framers, wise though they were, were not wiser than the architects of the original federal judicial system, and no more prophetic.

From the beginning, all legislation dealing with the organization of the United States courts has been subjected to two limitations. First, no matter what the structure of the courts or the distribution of the judicial power, the business of the courts is determined by the nature and extent of the predominant activities of contemporary life. Secondly, legislation affecting courts, like all other legislation, discloses in practice aptitudes or consequences not contemplated by its framers and wholly absent from the intention of law-makers. The Circuit Courts of Appeals Act did not escape these limitations; it in fact strikingly illustrates them.

---

[1] Act of Mar. 3, 1891, 26 STAT. 826.

Evarts and his associates were of course aware of the enormous industrial development and mounting export trade of the country. Their legislative plans were directed to the growth of the business of the courts corresponding to the expected growth of the business of the country. But they did not anticipate the great legislative energy throughout the country, both national and state, expressive of the vast increase in the regulatory functions of government. To be sure, the Granger legislation, the Interstate Commerce Act, and the Sherman Law gave hints of what was to follow. But these enactments were intimations of the hindsight of the historian, rather than the foresight of the legislator — especially those legislators who fashioned the Circuit Courts of Appeals Act.[2] The Interstate Commerce Act was put on the statute books in 1887. But not until 1903 did its vitality register itself on the dockets of the courts. Evarts was a member of the Senate which passed the Sherman Law as a response to the growing concern over what Roosevelt later denominated " Big Business." It was eight years before the *Knight* case [3] brought the Sherman Law for the first time before the Supreme Court, and then only to evoke a decision which, in the opinion of President Cleveland [4] and his Attorney General,[5] practically put the law to sleep. Thus we find only three anti-trust cases instituted under President McKinley's administration as against forty-four under President Roosevelt and eighty under President Taft.[6] Following McKinley's election, business had an enormous boom, inaugurating the modern era of large scale industry, with its consolidations, mergers and financial concentration and their counterpart of unionization.

The Spanish-American War brought an immediate aftermath of litigation.[7] Much more important, however, was the fact that

---

[2] Senator Evarts, for example, during the debates on the Interstate Commerce Act, in 1887, contended that the Act was unconstitutional, because a restriction upon, rather than a " regulation " of, commerce. See CULLOM, FIFTY YEARS OF PUBLIC SERVICE, 230; 18 CONG. REC. 603–609.

[3] United States *v.* E. C. Knight Co., 156 U. S. 1 (1895).

[4] See Fourth Annual Message of Dec. 7, 1896, 9 RICHARDSON, MESSAGES AND PAPERS OF THE PRESIDENTS, 745.

[5] REP. ATTY. GEN. FOR 1896, Ex. I.

[6] THE FEDERAL ANTITRUST LAWS (Gov't publ.), 69–102.

[7] The number of cases brought in the Court of Claims during the period of the War show a marked increase. On the other hand, the number of appeals

the war coöperated with the forces of domestic expansion to hasten American economic penetration abroad. McKinley's administration also marked the end of the period of *laissez faire*. Roosevelt's " big stick " was wielded largely to secure from Congress legislation to control " Big Business ", and to promote modern social legislation. With differences of emphasis and detail, the path of regulation entered upon by Roosevelt has persisted to this day, and has been trodden by every succeeding President. Wilson, who, before he was President, inveighed against government by commission,[8] as President, after 1913, added his signature to more enactments to regulate business and conduct through boards and commissions than did Roosevelt. All this extended inordinately the bounds of judicial action. The Safety-Appliance Act,[9] the Hours of Service Law,[10] the Food and Drugs Act,[11] the Insecticide Act,[12] the Meat Inspection Law,[13] the Animal Quarantine Law,[14] the Anti-Narcotic Act,[15] the Mann Act,[16] the Lacey Game Act,[17] the Federal Employers' Liability Act,[18] the Packers and Stockyards Act,[19] the Grain Futures

---

from the Court of Claims to the United States Supreme Court show a decrease. The figures, according to the Attorney General's Reports, follow:

Year	Cases Pending in Court of Claims	Appeals Determined by Supreme Court
1897	2,081	26
1898	2,144	19
1899	2,309	29
1900	2,948	8
1901	3,124	16
1902	1,774	13
1903	2,792	12

[8] See, *e.g.*, 2 WILSON, COLLEGE AND STATE, 24, 26–27.

[9] Act of Mar. 2, 1893, 27 STAT. 531, as amended by Act of April 1, 1896, 29 STAT. 85; Act of Mar. 2, 1903, 32 STAT. 943; and Act of April 14, 1910, 36 STAT. 298.

[10] Act of Mar. 4, 1907, 34 STAT. 1415.

[11] Act of June 30, 1906, 34 STAT. 768.

[12] Act of April 26, 1910, 36 STAT. 331. See also Act of Mar. 3, 1905, 33 STAT. 1269, as amended by Act of Aug. 20, 1912, 37 STAT. 314.

[13] Act of June 30, 1906, 34 STAT. 674.

[14] Act of Mar. 3, 1905, 33 STAT. 1264.

[15] Act of Feb. 9, 1909, 35 STAT. 614, as amended by Act of Jan. 17, 1914, 38 STAT. 275.

[16] Act of June 25, 1910, 36 STAT. 825.

[17] Act of May 25, 1900, 31 STAT. 187.

[18] Act of April 22, 1908, 35 STAT. 65.

[19] Act of Aug. 15, 1921, 42 STAT. 159.

Act,[20] the Elkins Act,[21] form only a part of the legislative product of a brief period.   Taxation was resorted to as a means of social control with increasing impact.   During the same time important administrative machinery was established or extended with large power over individual freedom and enterprise.   An invigorated Interstate Commerce Commission, the Federal Trade Commission, the Federal Reserve Board, the Farm Loan Board, the Tariff Commission, the Federal Water Power Commission, the Railway Labor Board, followed each other in quick succession.

The states were equally active in asserting control in fields open to them.   Some form of regulation appeared promptly in the wake of railroad building, but it was largely innocuous until Wisconsin in 1905, and New York, under Governor Hughes, in 1907, began the present effective supervision of construction, rates and practices, finances and management.   This mode of state intervention is steadily extending itself over other forms of business covered by the flexible conception of " public interest." In 1911 the New York Court of Appeals denounced the Workmen's Compensation Law as violative of the fundamental assumptions of American constitutional law; [22] during the next ten years all but half a dozen states enacted such a measure [23] — with the sanction of the Supreme Court of the United States.[24] Anti-trust laws, hours-of-labor acts, truck acts, weekly-payment-of-wages laws, child-labor legislation, pure-food-and-drug acts, factory laws, blue-sky laws, banking laws, illustrate only the more important topics with which American state legislation has busied itself during the last twenty years.

The momentum of these forces was immeasurably accelerated by the World War.   War means control all along the line.   The incidence of the Selective Service Act,[25] the Espionage Laws,[26]

---

[20] Act of Sept. 21, 1922, 42 STAT. 998.

[21] Act of Feb. 19, 1903, 32 STAT. 847.

[22] Ives v. South Buffalo Ry. Co., 201 N. Y. 271, 93 N. E. 431 (1911).

[23] See " Comparison of Workmen's Compensation Laws of United States," BULL. OF U. S. BUREAU OF LABOR STATISTICS, No. 379, Jan. 1, 1925, in connection with Bulletins, Nos. 332 and 240.

[24] N. Y. Central R. R. Co. v. White, 243 U. S. 188 (1916); Mountain Timber Co. v. Washington, 243 U. S. 219 (1917); Arizona Employers' Liability Cases, 250 U. S. 400 (1919); Ward & Gow v. Krinsky, 259 U. S. 503 (1922).

[25] Act of May 18, 1917, 40 STAT. 76.

[26] Act of June 15, 1917, 40 STAT. 217, as amended by Act of May 16, 1918, 40 STAT. 553.

the Lever Act,[27] Trading with the Enemy Act,[28] the Federal Control Act,[29] the Merchant Marine Act,[30] the War Tax measures, is fresh in memory. The Prohibition Amendment, followed by the Volstead Act,[31] belongs to the War era. The post-War period is in many ways one of relaxation; controls are either loosened or abandoned. But the " normalcy " to which we have returned is not characterized by *laissez faire* but by that intricate regulation with which the War found us. Thus the statesmen who shaped the Circuit Courts of Appeals Act were at the threshold of an era which transformed the whole political and legal picture of the United States but of which even the wisest were only dimly aware.

2

Framers of judiciary acts are not required to be seers; and great judiciary acts, unlike great poems, are not written for all time. It is enough if the designers of new judicial machinery meet the chief needs of their generation. The authors of the Circuit Courts of Appeals Act certainly satisfied the exigent requirements of the federal judicial business through the establishment of intermediate appellate courts. The division of the country into nine circuits with nine circuit courts of appeals has remained, despite insistent pressure for further sub-division.[32] The new business

---

[27] Act of Aug. 10, 1917, 40 STAT. 276.

[28] Act of Oct. 6, 1917, 40 STAT. 411.

[29] Act of Mar. 21, 1918, 40 STAT. 451.

[30] Act of June 5, 1920, 41 STAT. 988.

[31] Act of Oct. 28, 1919, 41 STAT. 305.

[32] While the Act of 1891 was under discussion in the Senate, a bill was reported out of the Judiciary Committee by Senator Hoar to increase the number of circuits to ten. SEN. REP., No. 2179, 21st Cong., 2nd Sess., Ser. No. 2827. Since the Act of 1891 bills to establish a tenth circuit have been persistently introduced into both houses, — in the House by Terry on Feb. 5, 1892 (23 CONG. REC. 892), by Lanham on April 11, 1892 (*ibid.* 3182), by Terry on Sept. 9, 1893 (25 *ibid.* 1360), by King on Feb. 4, 1898 (31 *ibid.* 1467), by Brownlow of Tennessee on Dec. 16, 1903 (38 *ibid.* 306), by Brownlow again on Dec. 4, 1905 (40 *ibid.* 46); in the Senate on Aug. 5, 1892, by Sanders (23 *ibid.* 7068), on Jan. 18, 1898, by Wolcott to which Shoup submitted an amendment (31 *ibid.* 718, 3409), by Wolcott again on Dec. 6, 1899 (33 *ibid.* 88), on Dec. 5, 1900, by Thurston (34 *ibid.* 57), on Jan. 11, 1904, by Bate (38 *ibid.* 598), by Clark of Montana on Dec. 6, 1905 (40 *ibid.* 140), by Clark again on Feb. 6, 1906 (*ibid.* 2123). None of these bills was reported from the judiciary committee to which it was referred. A memorial of the Idaho legislature requesting a tenth circuit, presented to the

coming to the Supreme Court was, as we have seen, drastically
reduced, and the arrears steadily decreased. The volume of work
was brought within the compass of the capacity of nine judges.
On one major issue — the retention of the circuit courts and the
resulting waste and confusion of two courts of first instance —
the traditionalist point of view of Senator Evarts had triumphed
over the House bill, but only for a time. This feature of the
Act of 1891 was a deliberate choice; it was a definite rejection
of the counsel of experience as well as of some of the weightiest
professional judgments. The element of time in important legislative changes had not yet played its full force. But there were
features of the Act of 1891 which had to be undone because
their implications had not been adequately considered.[33] One

Senate by Wilson of Idaho on Jan. 4, 1900, also failed to secure action. 33 *ibid.*
659.

[33] The circumstances attending the passage of the Act of March 3, 1891, shed
light on some of the difficulties to which it gave rise. " The parliamentary situation," we are told by Chief Justice Taft, " with respect to the bill had been such
that if a measure of that kind was to pass in the last days of the 50th Congress,
it had to pass exactly as it was reported by the Senate Judiciary Committee.
It was not, therefore, subjected to as full and free discussion as was desirable,
and was not freed from gaps and obscurities which more careful consideration
would have avoided. The Supreme Court in its interpretation has had difficulty
in clarifying it." William Howard Taft, " The Jurisdiction of the Supreme Court
under the Act of February 13, 1925," 35 YALE L. J. 1. For the history of the
Act of March 3, 1891, from the stage of report by the Senate Judiciary Committee to final enactment, see, *supra*, pp. 93 *et seq.;* also the remarks by Anthony
Higgins, United States Senator from Delaware on the first meeting of the Circuit
Court of Appeals for the Third Circuit: " It will not be out of place to recall a
word of the history of the enactment of the statute under which this Court has
been organized. As the bill passed the House of Representatives, it was struc-
turally different from its final shape. The Judiciary Committee of the Senate
entertained profound differences of opinion as to the true form that the Act
should take, and it ended in being left substantially with Mr. Evarts and Mr.
Hoar to determine what that should be, and especially to Mr. Evarts; and the
bill in the shape as they approved of it with the minor amendments was enacted
by the Senate, and then through circumstances that are measurably obscure and
need not further be referred to, final action was postponed until a few days
before the end of the session, when the only possibility of the bill becoming an
Act rested in the adoption of the bill as it passed the Senate by the House, and
in that form it was passed, and so it came about that this most important Act
received its final shape from the hands of one of the most eminent members of
the American Bar." Proceedings at Organization of United States Circuit Court
of Appeals for the Third Circuit at Philadelphia, June 16, 1891, 12–13, for which
we are indebted to Francis Rawle, Esq., of the Philadelphia Bar and former
President of the American Bar Association.

item concerned the scope of review by the Supreme Court in criminal cases; another affected the Supreme Court's appellate jurisdiction over litigation in the District of Columbia; a third arose from the lack of all review over the action of a single judge in denying interlocutory injunctions and on applications for receiverships.

For a full hundred years there was no right of appeal to the Supreme Court in criminal cases. Until 1889 even issues of life or death could reach that Court only upon a certificate of division of opinion.[34] As the practice became more prevalent for a single judge to hold circuit court (until in the eighties it became the rule rather than the exception), the finality of power of the single judge became particularly open to criticism in criminal cases. The growing feeling of injustice finally ripened into the Act of February 6, 1889,[35] by which, in all cases of conviction for a capital crime, final judgment against the accused might be reviewed by the Supreme Court. Originally the bill which became the Act of 1891 restricted resort to the Supreme Court in criminal cases to capital crimes. But the history of criminal justice is largely the story of emotional extremes in the attitude of the public toward the accused. In the nineties, feeling was swinging most vigorously in the direction of leniency. When the Evarts bill reached the floor of the Senate, ardent individualists like John W. Daniel of Virginia [36] urged that the door of appeal be widely opened. The proposed formulation of this view would have carried to the Supreme Court practically every case in which a fine had been imposed by a United States court. This latitudinarian attitude was satisfied by enlarging the right of review by the Supreme Court to all cases of " infamous crimes." [37] Un-

---

[34] See United States *v.* Sanges, 144 U. S. 310, 319–322 (1892).

[35] 25 STAT. 655.

[36] He offered an amendment providing for direct review by the Supreme Court in all cases of conviction of felony and in all cases where the matter in dispute was the right to personal liberty or the right to the custody of a child. See 21 CONG. REC. 10287. The amendment was rejected without division. *Ibid.* 10308.

[37] Senator Gray of Delaware offered an amendment allowing for direct review by the Supreme Court in all cases of conviction of crime the punishment whereof provided by law was death or imprisonment. *Ibid.* 10309. When attention was called to the breadth of review under this provision, Gray indicated a readiness to accept Senator Vest's suggestion that his amendment be limited to cases where the law prescribed imprisonment in a penitentiary. Evarts interrupted by suggest-

fortunately Senator Evarts, who suggested the use of "infa-mous crimes" (a phrase drawn from the Constitution),[38] was not familiar with the meaning which the Supreme Court had already attached to this phrase [39] and which, according to familiar canons of construction, was carried into the enactment. As a House Report in 1896 put it, the amendment "inadvertently" enlarged the right of appeal because it was "not the carefully digested result of committee consideration, but was effected in debate on the floor." [40]   The Supreme Court promptly revealed the unintendedly broad scope of review implicit in this pro-vision.[41]   As construed, the new Act brought to the Court all criminal cases in which, according to Chief Justice Fuller, "the accused might be sentenced to imprisonment in a penitentiary, even if the punishment actually imposed is a fine only." [42]   The practical consequence was a substantial addition to the docket. Attorney General Harmon reported that at the close of the 1895 Term, 123 criminal cases had been docketed of which less than half — 51 — were capital cases.[43]

As soon as Congress became aware of the effect of *In re*

---

ing the limitation of "infamous crimes." "I call attention," said Evarts, "to the constitutional phrase which is ' a capital or other infamous crime,' which is understood to mean the State's present penalty, where the head is shaved and all that, whereas in jail nothing of that kind takes place, and some penitentiaries may have greater gravity of punishment in some States than in others." Evarts' suggestion was accepted by Gray and the amendment passed in that form. *Ibid.* 10309–10310.

[38] Amendment V.

[39] See, *e.g., Ex parte* Wilson, 114 U. S. 417 (1885); United States *v.* Petit, 114 U. S. 429 (1885); Mackin *v.* United States, 117 U. S. 348 (1886); Parkinson *v.* United States, 121 U. S. 281 (1887). Recent decisions (United States *v.* Moreland, 258 U. S. 433; Brede *v.* Powers, 263 U. S. 4) have brought further ambiguity into the phrase "infamous crimes." See Reuben Oppenheimer, "In-famous Crimes and the Moreland Case," 36 Harv. L. Rev. 299.

[40] House Report, No. 666, 54th Cong., 1st Sess., Ser. No. 3459. See also Hoar in the Senate on April 18, 1892, 23 Cong. Rec. 3377.

[41] *In re* Claasen, 140 U. S. 200 (1891).

[42] See letter of Chief Justice Fuller to Senator Hoar in response to the latter's inquiry concerning the working of the Act of 1891, 23 Cong. Rec. 3285.

[43] See letter of Judson Harmon to Senator Hoar on Feb. 1, 1896, Sen. Rep., No. 265, 54th Cong., 1st Sess., Ser. No. 3362. A statement of James H. Mc-Kenney, then Clerk of the Supreme Court, shows that during the 1894 Term there were on the docket of the Supreme Court 65 criminal cases of which only 17 were capital cases. See House Report, No. 666, 54th Cong., 1st Sess., Ser. No. 3459.

Claasen,[44] the effort to remedy the inadvertence began. Evarts was gone from the Senate, and George Frisbie Hoar, one of his active collaborators on the Act of 1891, was now filling the Chairmanship of the Senate Judiciary Committee. Seeking to shut the door more tightly on criminal cases, Hoar took advantage of this revealed defect in the actual operation of the Act of 1891 to propose other restrictions upon access to the Supreme Court. Evarts had succeeded in defeating a provision passed by the House in 1890 whereby the arrears of the Supreme Court would be reduced by transfer of causes to the new circuit courts of appeals. Hoar revived this expedient. His bill,[45] introduced on March 28, 1892,[46] further restricted cases coming from the Court of Claims under the Indian Depredations Act, a new and voluminous item of business threatening the Supreme Court, appeals from the new Court of Private Land Claims, and appeals from the Supreme Court of the District of Columbia. Hoar's bill passed both Houses. In the course of its passage, the proposal affecting the appeals from the District of Columbia was eliminated, because contemporaneously a bill for the establishment of the Court of Appeals for the District was going through Congress,[47] and the reviewable judgment in criminal cases was fixed at fines not less than $1,000 or imprisonment for not less than twelve months.[48] President Harrison vetoed the bill partly because the allowance of appeal in criminal

---

[44] 140 U. S. 200 (1891).

[45] The text of the bill appears in 23 CONG. REC. 5116.

[46] *Ibid.* 2600.   [47] *Ibid.* 3284.

[48] On April 18, 1892, Morgan's suggestion to preserve direct appeals to the Supreme Court in cases where the validity or construction of an act of Congress was involved, was adopted, and the amendment of Senator Palmer of Massachusetts to reduce the fine from $5,000 to $1,000 was also accepted. The bill passed on the same day without division. *Ibid.* 3379. It was reported back from the House Judiciary Committee on May 3, 1892. *Ibid.* 3898; HOUSE REPORT, No. 1258, 52nd Cong., 1st Sess., Ser. No. 3045. The amendments by the House provided for direct appeals from sentences of imprisonment for more than one year without regard to fines; the provision for direct appeals in cases involving the construction or validity of a law was stricken out on the theory that it was unnecessary; an additional section dealing with the printing of the record in these cases was added. The bill passed the House on June 7, 1892, 23 CONG. REC. 5117. The Senate on June 27, 1892, voted to non-concur in the House amendments and named Mitchell, Platt, and Pugh as conferees. *Ibid.* 5488. The House named Culberson, Oates, and Ezra B. Taylor. *Ibid.* 5572. In conference the House receded from its first amendment and the Senate accepted the second and

cases without prison sentences still left too broad a review for
the Supreme Court.   But his controlling objection was the
finality of decision under the Indian Depredations Act in the
Court of Claims, subject only to *certiorari* by the Supreme Court.
Suits involving about thirty million dollars had already been filed
under this Act.   These damages were to be paid out of Indian
trust funds or out of the Treasury of the United States.   Many
" novel and difficult questions " were likely to arise, and President
Harrison, while agreeing that some limitations as to amount
would be reasonable for review by the Supreme Court, insisted
that " neither the claimants, the Indians, nor the Government of
the United States should be absolutely denied opportunity to
bring their exceptions to review by some appellate tribunal." [50]
There was not enough momentum behind Hoar's proposals to
survive this veto.

The undue demand upon the Supreme Court's time by relatively unimportant criminal cases was persistently brought to the
attention of Congress.[51]   Proposals for relief were urged by successive Attorneys General [52] and by the American Bar Association [53] seeking a more drastic reform than the Hoar bill.   The
objective was to eliminate the extension of review over " infamous
crimes " made by the Evarts Act, and to give finality in all
criminal cases, except capital offenses, to the circuit courts of
appeals.   Richard Olney in his first report as Attorney General
summarized the argument which eventually prevailed:

" The statutes as now existing authorize writs of error to the Supreme
Court of the United States in cases of conviction of capital or other-

third House amendments.   The conference report was concurred in by the Senate
on July 1, and by the House on July 2, 1892. *Ibid.* 5704, 5742. A similar
bill had been introduced into the Senate by Wilson on Feb. 17, 1892, which was
reported back adversely from the Senate Judiciary Committee after Hoar's bill
had passed the Senate. *Ibid.* 1225, 3466.

[49] See 23 CONG. REC. 6392; 9 RICHARDSON, MESSAGES AND PAPERS OF THE
PRESIDENTS, 244.   [50] 9 RICHARDSON, *op. cit.* 245.

[51] Chief Justice Fuller in his reply to Senator Hoar remarked that " Experience has shown that such cases, and especially capital cases, though often argued
at great length, rarely present questions of law of peculiar difficulty." 23 CONG.
REC. 3285.

[52] REP. ATTY. GEN. FOR 1893, xxv; *ibid.* FOR 1894, xxix; *ibid.* FOR 1895, 12;
ibid. FOR 1896, xviii.

[53] Report of Committee on Judicial Administration and Remedial Procedure
(for 1894), 17 AM. BAR ASSN. REP. 336, 340.

wise infamous crimes. The sentiment that in cases involving the death penalty the accused should have the right to have the legal merits of his case examined by the highest appellate court may be perhaps worth regarding. But there is no reason why the same right should be accorded in cases punishable by fine and imprisonment only. All the demands of justice will be reasonably satisfied if in cases of that class a review of the proceedings of the trial court were limited to the circuit courts of appeals. As the speedy disposition of such cases would be thereby facilitated and the crowded docket of the Supreme Court be somewhat relieved, the propriety of legislation to that end would seem to be unquestionable." [54]

Not until January 13, 1897, is the reform achieved; and " otherwise infamous crimes " is amended out of the Circuit Courts of Appeals Act.[55]

Neglect of details by the framers of this Act resulted in excessive opportunities for appeal to the Supreme Court in criminal cases; it also shut off resort to the Supreme Court in a nationally important type of criminal litigation. Through inadvertence, the decision of a single judge in a criminal case was allowed to nullify an act of Congress or to construe it out of existence. Up to the Act of 1891 the constitutionality or

---

[54] REP. ATTY. GEN. FOR 1893, xxv.

[55] On Feb. 16, 1895, Vilas in the Senate introduced a bill to transfer appellate jurisdiction in non-capital cases from the Supreme Court to the circuit courts of appeals. 27 CONG. REC. 2276. In the next Congress on Jan. 9, 1896, Vilas again introduced his bill which was reported from the Senate Judiciary Committee on Feb. 13, 1896. 28 *ibid.* 526, 1825; SEN. REP., No. 265, 54th Cong., 1st Sess., Ser. No. 3362. The bill will be found in full in 28 CONG. REC. 2386. It passed the Senate on Mar. 3, 1896, without debate. *Ibid.* 2690. It was reported out of the House Judiciary Committee on Mar. 6. *Ibid.* 2871; HOUSE REPORT, No. 666, 54th Cong., 1st Sess., Ser. No. 3459. It was debated in the House on Mar. 16, when Culberson, who, though a member of the Judiciary Committee had not been consulted on the bill, opposed it on the ground that the dockets of the circuit courts of appeals were in as congested a condition as that of the Supreme Court. On a motion to suspend the rules and pass the bill with an amendment, suggested by Connolly of Illinois, permitting direct review when a sentence of more than five years imprisonment was imposed, the bill failed to pass. 28 CONG. REC. 2850. In the next session on Jan. 13, 1897, the bill was again brought to the attention of the House. Culberson, after a study of the bill, now expressed himself satisfied with its provisions. The bill passed the House on the same day without division. 29 *ibid.* 765–766. Direct review by the Supreme Court from the district and circuit courts in capital cases was finally abolished by Section 238 of the Judicial Code.

construction of a statute arising under an indictment could be passed upon by the Supreme Court through a certificate of division of opinion from a circuit court.[56]   The Circuit Courts of Appeals Act put an end to this scheme of certification.[57]   To be sure, the Act of 1891 allowed direct review from the district and circuit courts in cases involving the constitutionality of a federal statute.   But shortly after the passage of the Act the Supreme Court ruled that in criminal cases, even though no double jeopardy arose, an appeal did not lie on behalf of the Government.[58]   The *Sanges* case disclosed a serious lacuna in the framework of the Circuit Courts of Appeals Act.   It left all federal criminal legislation at the mercy of single judges in the district and circuit courts.   This defect became all the more serious because it became operative just at the beginning of the movement for increasing social control through criminal machinery.

Attorney General Miller in his report for 1892 called attention to the situation that was thus created by the new Act:

" As the law now stands, therefore, it is in the power of a single district judge, by quashing an indictment, to defeat any criminal prosecution instituted by the Government, and to annul as against the Government any criminal statute enacted by Congress, and there is no possible remedy or way to right the wrong.   This is not a speculative suggestion, but is an actual experience which has occurred more than once since the enactment of the statute creating the circuit court of appeals, and is liable to occur at any term of the court in any district." [59]

---

[56] United States *v.* Curtis, 107 U. S. 671 (1882).   See *Ex parte* Gordon, 1 Black (U. S.) 503, 505 (1861).   *Cf.* United States *v.* Hall, 131 U. S. 50 (1889); United States *v.* Perrin, 131 U. S. 55 (1889).

[57] United States *v.* Rider, 163 U. S. 132 (1896).   So also as to the provisions of the Act of 1891 for *certiorari* from the circuit courts of appeals, United States *v.* Dickinson, 213 U. S. 92 (1909).

[58] United States *v.* Sanges, 144 U. S. 310 (1892).

[59] Rep. Atty. Gen. for 1892, xxiv.   Attorney General Miller's assertion that many prosecutions instituted by the Government were annulled is amply supported by a reference to the reported cases in the lower federal courts during the years 1891–1893.   In the following cases indictments were successfully demurred to or quashed or verdicts of acquittal were directed on the ground that the court had no jurisdiction of the offense, that a statute did not cover the facts, or that the particular indictment was insufficient.   United States *v.* Gibson, 47 Fed. 833 (N. D. Ill., 1891); United States *v.* Egan, 47 Fed. 112 (D. Minn., 1891); United States *v.* Thomas, 47 Fed. 488 (C. C. W. D. Wis., 1891); United

Richard Olney in his two reports to Congress repeated the recommendation of his predecessor,[60] which was renewed from time to time by succeeding Attorneys General. Griggs in 1899 and 1900,[61] Knox in 1903,[62] Moody in 1905 and 1906,[63] urged action upon Congress with increasing vehemence induced by repeated miscarriages of justice. Congress was heedless. As has happened so often in the history of federal judiciary acts, it required a case capable of popular dramatization to secure reform. This particular defect in the law of judicial review at last fell foul of Roosevelt's crusade against the abuses of " Big Business." Judge Humphrey of the Northern District of Illinois, in a decision which gave rise to one of the significant

---

States *v.* Sanges, 48 Fed. 78 (N. D. Ga., 1891); United States *v.* Trumbull, 48 Fed. 99 (S. D. Cal., 1891); United States *v.* Hom Hing, 48 Fed. 635 (N. D. N. Y., 1892); United States *v.* Baird, 48 Fed. 554 (N. D. Wash., 1891); United States *v.* Bedgood, 49 Fed. 54 (S. D. Ala., 1891); United States *v.* Durwood, 49 Fed. 446 (W. D. Wash., 1892); United States *v.* Ege, 49 Fed. 852 (E. D. Pa., 1892); United States *v.* Wardell, 49 Fed. 914 (E. D. N. Y., 1892); United States *v.* Greenhut, 50 Fed. 469 (D. Mass., 1892); United States *v.* Law, 50 Fed. 915 (W. D. Va., 1892); United States *v.* Rider, 50 Fed. 406 (C. C. S. D. Ohio, 1892); Harman *v.* United States, 50 Fed. 921 (C. C. D. Kan., 1892); United States *v.* Barnaby, 51 Fed. 20 (C. C. D. Mont., 1892); United States *v.* Elliott, 51 Fed. 807 (D. Ky., 1892); *In re* Corning, 51 Fed. 205 (N. D. Ohio, 1892); United States *v.* Males, 51 Fed. 41 (D. Ind., 1892); United States *v.* Chin Quong Look, 52 Fed. 203 (N. D. Wash., 1892); United States *v.* Nelson, 52 Fed. 646 (D. Minn., 1892); Tozer *v.* United States, 52 Fed. 917 (C. C. E. D. Mo., 1892); United States *v.* Bradford, 53 Fed. 542 (D. S. C., 1893); United States *v.* Hing Quong Chow, 53 Fed. 233 (E. D. La., 1892); United States *v.* Mellen, 53 Fed. 229 (D. Kan., 1892); United States *v.* Patrick, 53 Fed. 356 (C. C. M. D. Tenn., 1892); United States *v.* Burns, 54 Fed. 351 (D. W. Va., 1893); United States *v.* Singleton, 54 Fed. 488 (S. D. Ala., 1892); United States *v.* Patterson, 55 Fed. 605 (C. C. D. Mass., 1893); United States *v.* Ollinger, 55 Fed. 959 (S. D. Ala., 1893); United States *v.* Potter, 56 Fed. 83, 97 (C. C. D. Mass., 1892); United States *v.* Eno, 56 Fed. 218 (C. C. S. D. N. Y., 1893); United States *v.* Dwyer, 56 Fed. 464 (W. D. Tex., 1893); United States *v.* Wong Dep Ken, 57 Fed. 206 (S. D. Cal., 1893); United States *v.* Taylor, 57 Fed. 391 (C. C. E. D. Va., 1893); United States *v.* Bromiley, 58 Fed. 554 (E. D. Pa., 1893); United States *v.* McCabe, 58 Fed. 557 (C. C. S. D. N. Y., 1893); United States *v.* Brown, 58 Fed. 558 (C. C. S. D. N. Y., 1893); Grant *v.* United States, 58 Fed. 694 (9th Circ., 1893); United States *v.* Marthinson, 58 Fed. 765 (E. D. S. C., 1893); Woodruff *v.* United States, 58 Fed. 766 (C. C. D. Kan., 1893); United States *v.* Wilson, 58 Fed. 768 (N. D. Cal., 1893); United States *v.* Mitchell, 58 Fed. 993 (N. D. Ohio, 1893).

[60] REP. ATTY. GEN. FOR 1893, xxiv; *ibid.* FOR 1894, xxix.

[61] *Ibid.* FOR 1899, 34; *ibid.* FOR 1900, 40.

[62] *Ibid.* FOR 1903, vi.   [63] *Ibid.* FOR 1905, 10; *ibid.* FOR 1906, 4.

incidents of Roosevelt's administration, blocked the prosecution of the so-called Beef Trust.[64] The law officers of the Government and widespread public opinion were outraged by this decision and still more outraged that it lay in the power of a single judge thus to exercise final authority over the public will. " It is monstrous," wrote Attorney General Moody, himself soon to become a member of the Supreme Court, " that a law which has received the assent of the Senate, the House of Representatives, and the President can be nullified by the opinion of a single man, not subject to review by the court of appeals and the Supreme Court." [65] With characteristic vigor Roosevelt directed public attention to the importance of the issue that was raised by Judge Humphrey's decision, by putting it at the forefront of his annual message to Congress:

" It seems an absurdity to permit a single district judge, against what may be the judgment of the immense majority of his colleagues on the bench, to declare a law solemnly enacted by the Congress to be ' unconstitutional,' and then to deny to the Government the right to have the Supreme Court definitely decide the question.

" It is well to recollect that the real efficiency of the law often depends not upon the passage of acts as to which there is great public excitement, but upon the passage of acts of this nature as to which there is not much public excitement, because there is little public understanding of their importance, while the interested parties are keenly alive to the desirability of defeating them. The importance of enacting

---

[64] United States v. Armour & Co., 142 Fed. 808 (N. D. Ill., 1906). "I am quite willing to have it said, so far as I am concerned, that the decision of Judge Humphrey in the Chicago case led to the legislation that is now proposed." Patterson of Colorado in the Senate on Feb. 12, 1907, 41 CONG. REC. 2753.

[65] REP. ATTY. GEN. FOR 1906, 4. The case referred to by the Attorney General is United States v. Scott, 148 Fed. 431 (W. D. Ky., 1906), which, contrary to the unreported case of United States v. Hill decided in 1899 in the District Court of Massachusetts, held unconstitutional Section 10 of the Act of June 1, 1898, making it a misdemeanor for a carrier to threaten to dismiss an employee because of his membership in a labor organization. In the following year the District Court for the Eastern District of Kentucky reached the contrary result. United States v. Adair, 152 Fed. 737 (E. D. Ky., 1907). Attorney General Moody, later a member of the Supreme Court, did not sit when his brethren, against the dissent of Holmes and McKenna JJ., reversed the district court and invalidated the law. Adair v. United States, 208 U. S. 161 (1908). See Richard Olney, " Discrimination against Union Labor — Legal? " 42 AM. L. REV. 161, and President Roosevelt's Message to Congress, Dec. 8, 1908, 16 MESSAGES AND PAPERS OF THE PRESIDENTS, 7198, 7211.

into law the particular bill in question is further increased by the fact that the Government has now definitely begun a policy of resorting to the criminal law in those trust and interstate commerce cases where such a course offers a reasonable chance of success." [66]

Thus, a reform which had been urged by Attorneys General for fifteen years without evoking a ripple in Congress became a major political issue and forms part of the story of Roosevelt's conflict with the Senate in securing legislation to grapple with modern social-economic problems. The House promptly passed the bill, proposed by the Administration, to prevent the recurrence of a Humphrey decision by according the Government the right of appeal in criminal cases, where the defendant had not been put in jeopardy.[67] The Senate was recalcitrant.[68] Roosevelt encountered opposition from both sides of the chamber, similar to the opposition which his major legislative proposals had to meet at this time. Some Senators resisted outright, others sought to emasculate the measure by nullifying amendments.[69] Roosevelt countered by public appeals and the meas-

---

[66] 41 Cong. Rec. 22.

[67] The bill was introduced into the House by Jenkins on Feb. 22, 1906. 40 Cong. Rec. 2881. It was reported from committee on Mar. 7, 1906, by Nevin. *Ibid.* 3494. See House Report, No. 2119, 59th Cong., 1st Sess., Ser. No. 4906. The bill appears in full in 40 Cong. Rec. 5408. It provided that the United States should have the same right of review by writ of error in a criminal case as is accorded the defendant, providing, however, that even if there was error, a verdict for the defendant should not be set aside. The bill passed the House on April 17, 1906, without debate and division. *Ibid.* 5408.

[68] The bill was reported by Nelson from the Senate Judiciary Committee on May 29, 1906. 40 Cong. Rec. 7589. The report offered a substitute bill in lieu of the House bill. See Sen. Rep., No. 3922, 59th Cong., 1st Sess., Ser. No. 4905. The Senate bill permitted writs of error from the circuit and district courts to the Supreme Court or the circuit courts of appeals (according to the provisions of the Act of 1891) from a decision quashing an indictment, sustaining a demurrer to an indictment or any count thereof, from the arrest of a judgment of conviction on the ground of insufficiency of the indictment, and from a decision sustaining a special plea in bar when the defendant has not been put in jeopardy. On June 1, 1905, upon objection of Teller of Colorado, the bill was passed over. 40 Cong. Rec. 7684. On June 19 an amendment proposed by Nelson prohibiting a verdict for the defendant from being set aside even if there was error, was adopted. *Ibid.* 8695. On June 23 upon Spooner's suggestion, the amendment was reconsidered and disagreed to. *Ibid.* 9033. On the same day further consideration of the bill was prevented by objection. On June 25 upon Mallory's objection, the bill was again passed over, and the session closed without action by the Senate. *Ibid.* 9122.

[69] In the second session the bill, after being recommitted to the Judiciary

ure, not without confusing amendments,[70] finally prevailed.[71] One of the chief grounds of attack against the proposal in the Senate was the claim of unconstitutionality, a contention of which the Supreme Court made short shrift when the Act of

Committee, was reported out on Jan. 29, 1907. 41 CONG. REC. 1865; SEN. REP., No. 5650, 59th Cong., 2nd Sess., Ser. No. 5060. The bill was amended by a provision requiring that all objections to the sufficiency of the indictment in matters of form should be made and determined prior to the impaneling of the jury. 41 CONG. REC. 2190. The bill was debated by the Senate for three days. *Ibid.* 2190–2197, 2744–2763, 2818–2825. Hale of Maine and Whyte of Maryland resisted the bill outright and declared themselves in favor of the "traditional" provisions of the common law. Whyte's amendment to strike out all the provisions of the bill save that permitting an appeal from a judgment sustaining a demurrer to an indictment was defeated by a vote of 40–14. *Ibid.* 2195. Rayner of Maryland proposed an amendment providing that even if there was error, a verdict or judgment for the defendant should not be set aside. Senator Spooner curtly analyzed the proposal, saying: "If it means anything it means too much." *Ibid.* 2761. Consequently the phrase "or judgment" was withdrawn, and Rayner's amendment with the omission of these destructive words was adopted. *Ibid.* 2819. Carter of Montana succeeded in getting the adoption of an amendment requiring an appeal to be taken within thirty days and diligently prosecuted. *Ibid.* 2194. Newlands of Nevada offered an amendment permitting the defendant to be released on his own recognizance, which Piles of Washington further amended by adding "in the discretion of the presiding judge." *Ibid.* 2195. The Piles amendment was adopted by a vote of 29 to 23, and the Newlands amendment by 33 to 21. *Ibid.* 2196, 2197. Upon Spooner's suggestion Nelson secured a reconsideration of the Piles amendment and its rejection. *Ibid.* 2821. Clarke of Arkansas secured the adoption of an amendment restricting appeals from decisions quashing or sustaining a demurrer to an indictment or arresting a judgment of conviction for insufficiency of the indictment to cases involving the validity or construction of the statute upon which the indictment was founded. *Ibid.* 2822. The bill with these amendments is found in full in 41 CONG. REC. 2823. Culberson and Spooner suggested further amendments to the last clause of the bill, which was finally, however, struck out. *Ibid.* 2824, 2825.

[70] See, *e.g.*, Attorney General Moody's criticism of the Act and his request for its revision so as to force counsel for the defendant to argue and raise points of law before the moment of jeopardy is reached. REP. ATTY. GEN. FOR 1907, 4; *ibid.* FOR 1908, 4. In the House on Feb. 15, 1907, Jenkins of Wisconsin, the original proponent of the bill, attacked the Senate substitute saying: "I want to say here and now that if this Senate amendment had been drawn at the instance of any criminal in the United States, by the sharpest criminal lawyers in the United States, for the purpose of avoiding just exactly what the President of the United States and the Department of Justice sought, they could not have been more successful." 41 CONG. REC. 3044. The Act, however, has remained unchanged since its enactment and has not called forth professional criticism.

[71] The bill passed the Senate without division on Feb. 13, 1907, and was printed upon Spooner's motion. 41 CONG. REC. 2834. Its reception in the House brought an attack from its original sponsors, but a motion to refer it to the

March 2, 1907, familiarly known as the Criminal Appeals Act, came before it.[72]

The history of latter-day judiciary acts is largely the story of restricting the right of appeal to the Supreme Court. The Criminal Appeals Act is a striking exception to this trend. It enlarged the domain of the Court's business and as a matter of bookkeeping brought to the Court each term on the average ten additional cases.[73] But the steady pressure, particularly

Judiciary Committee was adopted. *Ibid.* 3044–3047. On Feb. 22, 1907, the House disagreed to the Senate bill, proposed a conference and named Jenkins, Birdsall, and De Armond as conferees. *Ibid.* 3647. The Senate named Nelson, Knox, Bacon. *Ibid.* 3623. The conference committee, aside from mere formal changes, revised the bill so as to divest the circuit courts of appeals of all review and invest this in the Supreme Court alone. Review was also to be only by writ of error. See HOUSE REPORT, No. 8113, 59th Cong., 2nd Sess., Ser. No. 5065. The report was agreed to by the Senate on Feb. 26 and by the House the following day. 41 CONG. REC. 3994, 4128.

[72] Taylor v. United States, 207 U. S. 120 (1907); United States v. Bitty, 208 U. S. 393 (1908). The Act applies where the lower court holds that the facts charged in an indictment do not bring the case within a statute; that is, an application of the statute involves its construction. United States v. Keitel, 211 U. S. 370 (1908); United States v. Biggs, 211 U. S. 507 (1909); United States v. Corbett, 215 U. S. 233 (1909); United States v. Sutton, 215 U. S. 291 (1909); United States v. Celestine, 215 U. S. 278 (1909).

[73] The following table, for which we are indebted to Mr. S. S. Isseks, tells the tale:

	Total	Constitutional Cases Reversed	Affirmed	Cases Decided on Construction Reversed	Affirmed	Dismissed on Motion
1907	3			2	1	
1908	10		1	4	5	
1909	8		1†	7		
1910	18	1		5	3	9
1911	11			7	2	2
1912	12*			6	4	1
1913	9°	1		5	1	
1914	7	1		4	2	
1915	8	1		4	3	
1916	6			3	2	1
1917	4			2	2	
1918	7	2		2	2	1
1919	4			3	1	
1920	14		2	4	2	6
1921	4			4		
1922	6	1		3		2
1923	1	1				
1924	5§				2	1
Totals	137	8	4	65	32	23

† Affirmed *per curiam,* and reversed on rehearing in the next term. It is counted as a constitutional case reversed in 1910 Term.

* One case was dismissed *per curiam* for lack of jurisdiction.

° Two cases were dismissed for lack of jurisdiction.

§ Two cases were dismissed for lack of jurisdiction.

since the Great War, to relieve the Supreme Court of business and to make the circuit courts of appeals to a large extent final appellate tribunals, has left this class of cases untouched.[74]   No serious proposal for cutting down the Supreme Court's business has attempted the elimination of this jurisdiction.   On the contrary, the latest enactment, with its radical limitation upon the Supreme Court's scope of appellate duty, has expressly saved writs of error direct from the district courts under the Criminal Appeals Act, and naturally so.   The reasons which impelled the enactment of the Act of 1907 remain.   They will continue to be controlling.   Congress is not apt to give the power of invalidating its legislation wholly to the inferior federal courts without an appeal as of right to the Supreme Court, and Congress is still less likely to do this with regard to criminal legislation.   The criminal law is increasingly resorted to, for the " achievement of some social betterment rather than the punishment of the crimes as in cases of *mala in se.*" [75]   The defeat of these purposes is not likely to be entrusted to any tribunal other than the Supreme Court.[76]

The Act of 1891 incontinently opened the door to appeals by the defendant in criminal cases; it unduly shut the door to criminal appeals by the government; and it negligently did not subject cases coming up from the District of Columbia to the restrictions which it imposed upon cases from the cognate courts of the United States.   Prior to the Act of 1891, for purposes of review by the Supreme Court of the United States, the District of Columbia was treated as a federal circuit.   The scope of review over cases from the Supreme Court of the District of Columbia was the same as that from the circuit courts of the United States.[77]   But while the Act of 1891 cut down the cases that could come to the Supreme Court for review from the inferior federal courts, it left untouched the wide latitude of review for cases from the District of Columbia.   The Act of 1891, therefore, begot the absurd result of giving access to the Supreme

---

[74] See Act of Feb. 13, 1925, § 1, amending Judicial Code, § 238.   43 STAT. 936.

[75] Taft, C. J., in United States *v.* Balint, 258 U. S. 250, 252 (1922).

[76] The proportion of reversals to affirmances, substantially two to one, under this Act illustrates the importance of permitting review by the Government in this class of cases.   See note 73, *supra.*

[77] See U. S. REV. STAT., § 705; 1875 DIST. COL. REV. STAT., § 846; 1894 DIST. COL. COMP. STAT., c. 35, § 43.

Court to litigants in the District of Columbia who, under the same circumstances in cases arising in any of the federal courts, were denied Supreme Court review. This anomaly was early emphasized by the Supreme Court.[78] Senator Hoar proposed to rectify it by putting District of Columbia litigation on a parity with that in the federal courts. His effort became entangled with the contemporary proposal for the establishment of a Court of Appeals for the District.[79] The Court of Appeals was established in 1893, unaccompanied however by the needed adjustment in the existing relation between the Supreme Court and the courts of the District. On the contrary, the Act creating the Court of Appeals for the District conferred the same power of review over decisions of the Court of Appeals of the District as theretofore governed the decisions of the Supreme Court of the District.[80] The upshot of the matter was that the Supreme Court was under a much broader duty of review of cases coming from the Court of Appeals of the District of Columbia than that which governed the decisions of the circuit courts of appeals.

With the growing congestion of the Supreme Court docket and the necessity to relieve it, the undue burden caused by District of Columbia litigation challenged attention. Thus, in 1907 out of a total docket of 471 cases 48 came from the courts of the District; in 1908 out of a total of 487 the District supplied 56; and 57 out of a total of 503 for the 1909 Term.[81] About a tenth of the business of the Supreme Court had its source in the District of Columbia courts. Even more striking is a comparison of the volume of business from the Court of Appeals of the District with that supplied by the nine circuit courts of appeals. For the 1907 Term 58 cases came to the Supreme Court from the nine circuit courts of appeals, while from the Court of Appeals of the District alone came 26 cases; for the 1908 Term 56 came from the circuit courts of appeals to 24 from the Court of Appeals of the District; for the 1909 Term 58 came from the cir-

---

[78] *In re* Heath, 144 U. S. 92 (1892). See also Chapman *v.* United States, 164 U. S. 436 (1896).

[79] See *supra*, p. 333.

[80] Act of Feb. 9, 1893, § 8, 27 STAT. 434, 436.

[81] See Statement of Jas. H. McKenney, Clerk of the Supreme Court, 35 AM. BAR ASSN. REP. 649.

cuit courts of appeals as against 28 from the Court of Appeals of the District.[82]

Attorney General Moody in his Report for 1906 asked Congress to remedy this situation:

"It seems anomalous that in the District of Columbia there should be a broader right of appeal to the Supreme Court than from the courts of the States or the inferior courts of the United States. I recommend that the law be amended so that the right of appeal from the Court of Appeals for the District of Columbia shall be substantially coextensive with the right of appeal from the several circuit courts of appeal." [83]

The Committee on Judicial Administration and Remedial Procedure of the American Bar Association in its report for 1909 urged the recommendation of the Attorney General.[84] The Association, however, rejected this recommendation at the insistence of members of the District of Columbia bar who betrayed the usual professional obstinacy in their adherence to a system in which they were trained.[85] No further help for this reform

---

[82] See REPORTS OF ATTORNEY GENERAL for the corresponding years.

[83] REP. ATTY. GEN. FOR 1906, 5. The only Congressional action this induced seems to have been a bill introduced by Henry of Texas (by request) in the House on Dec. 10, 1906, to enlarge the jurisdiction of the Supreme Court over the Court of Appeals of the District of Columbia. 41 CONG. REC. 230.

[84] 34 AM. BAR ASSN. REP. 491.

[85] Davis of the District of Columbia objected to the adoption of the Committee's report. It was consequently amended so as to eliminate the proposed changes in the appellate jurisdiction of the Supreme Court over the Court of Appeals of the District of Columbia. 34 *ibid.* 14–23. "Lawyers are essentially conservative. They do not take kindly to change. They are not naturally reformers. . . . The most successful lawyers are, as a rule, continually engrossed in their own cases and they have little time and little respect for the speculative and hypothetical. The lawyers who have authority as leaders of opinion are men, as a rule, who have succeeded in their profession, and men naturally tend to be satisfied with the conditions under which they are succeeding. . . . The measures which the committees of the Association have advocated have got a little farther each year, and they will ultimately arrive, but at every stage they have been blocked by opposition from lawyers. This has always come from lawyers who had succeeded and were content with things as they were; who did not want practice and proceedings changed from that with which they were familiar and who never had acquired the habit of responding to any public opinion of the Bar of the United States. If the administration of justice in the United States is to improve rather than to deteriorate, there must be such a public opinion of the Bar, and it must create standards of thought and of conduct which have their origin not in the interest of particular cases but in the broader considerations of those relations which the profession of the law bears to the adminis-

came from the Bar Association.[86] Attorney General Wickersham returned to Moody's recommendation in his Report for
1910.[87] Congress was now inattentive to this specific recommendation because the whole body of law affecting the judiciary
was in process of revision. In the winter of 1910 Congress was
debating the project of the Judicial Code submitted to it through
the labors of the Committee on the Revision of the Laws of the
United States.[88] That project, however, did not provide for a
rectification of the District of Columbia situation. The House
of Representatives, in passing the Code, also left untouched the
Supreme Court's review over District litigation. As a legislative measure the effort to assimilate the Court of Appeals of
the District of Columbia to the circuit courts of appeals first
appears as an amendment by Senator, now Mr. Justice, Sutherland to Section 237 of the bill to codify the laws relating to the
judiciary.[89] It passed the Senate without division, was accepted
by the House, and became Section 250 of the Judicial Code.[90]
Unfortunately Congress couched its purpose of restriction in
ambiguous terms. Section 250 allowed to be brought to the
Supreme Court from the District all cases in which " the construction of any law of the United States " was involved. A
literal construction would have opened wide the door to the Supreme Court, for every law concerning the District is a " law of
the United States " in that Congress passed it. But the Supreme
Court acted on the conviction " that Congress intended to effect
a substantial relief to this court from indiscriminate appeals "
and so confined Congressional language to acts of Congress of

---

tration of justice as a whole." Elihu Root, "The Layman's Criticism of the
Lawyer," 39 AM. BAR ASSN. REP. 386, 390–391. See also ROOT, ADDRESSES ON
CITIZENSHIP AND GOVERNMENT, 433.

[86] The Committee on Judicial Administration and Remedial Procedure made
no further suggestions, but in 1911 expressed itself as satisfied with the changes
effected by Section 250 of the Judicial Code. See 35 AM. BAR ASSN. REP. 617;
36 *ibid.* 456.

[87] REP. ATTY. GEN. FOR 1910, 81.

[88] See *infra*, p. 362.

[89] See 46 CONG. REC. 2134. A few days earlier the section that embodied
the existing law as to the appellate jurisdiction of the Supreme Court from the
District of Columbia had been passed over at the suggestion of Senator Root.

[90] The conference report made no significant changes in this section. See
ibid. 4000. Section 250 has now been repealed by the Act of Feb. 13, 1925,
§ 13, 43 STAT. 936, 941.

general application, thereby excluding " the purely local laws of the District." [91]   With the help of this interpretation the restriction upon District of Columbia appeals did bring prompt and substantial relief.   The cases from the Court of Appeals of the District fell to 12 during the 1911 Term, to 15 during the 1912 Term, and to 10 during the 1913 Term.[92]   Through the October Term, 1924, the appeals from the Court of Appeals of the District of Columbia average only 10 per term.

Two other defects of the Act of 1891, also due more to inadvertence than to design, were the failure to provide for appeal to the circuit courts of appeals from the denial of interlocutory injunctions and from the disposition of an application for a receiver.   The former was corrected without stirring much interest by the Act of Feb. 18, 1895.[93]   The receivership problem, however, involving as it did the uncontrolled authority of a single judge to appoint receivers, provoked fierce controversy. Around it centered all the prickly issues raised by the railroad receiverships in the nineties.   With one-fourth of the railroads of the country in the hands of federal receivers, old sectional passions were again aroused, intensified by deep economic differences between eastern creditors and southern and western communities.[94]   Here was an issue by which the federal courts were again swept into the vortex of politics and partisan strife. Even those who, like the then Circuit Judge Taft, vigorously upheld the exercise of judicial power in these receivership cases, recognized that there were " substantial reasons " for relieving the

[91] American Security & Trust Co. *v.* District of Columbia, 224 U. S. 491 (1912).

[92] See REPORTS OF ATTORNEY GENERAL for the corresponding years.

[93] A bill to this effect was introduced by Draper on Jan. 15, 1894, and reported from the House Judiciary Committee on Feb. 20, 1894. 26 CONG. REC. 847, 2327; HOUSE REPORT, No. 465, 53rd Cong., 2nd Sess., Ser. No. 3269. It passed the House without division on April 21. 26 CONG. REC. 3943. It was reported from the Senate Judiciary Committee on Jan. 28, 1895, by Senator Hoar with an amendment allowing the judge to require an additional bond as a condition of appeal. 27 *ibid.* 1441. It passed the Senate as amended on Feb. 12, and the amendment was concurred in by the House. *Ibid.* 2086, 2176. It became law on Feb. 18, 1895. 28 STAT. 666.

[94] A memorial of the legislature of South Carolina protesting against this aspect of federal jurisdiction was presented to the House on Jan. 22, 1894, and to the Senate on Jan. 24, 1894. See 26 CONG. REC. 1217, 1303, 2406.

federal courts of this task if it were feasible to do so.[95] The arduous burdens of railroad management involved in these receiverships interfered with the discharge of " regular judicial labors " and entailed " unpleasant public controversies " affecting the confidence of the public. The difficulties of this situation were intensified through the occasional practice of appointing receivers without granting injunctive relief in order to free the judge from the possibility of all review by an appellate court.[96] These circumstances, so familiar in the heated literature of the nineties concerning the Wabash and other receiverships, furnished the ammunition for the vigorous campaign by the American Bar Association to subject to review an interlocutory decree appointing a receiver.

As a matter of fact the earlier recommendations of the American Bar Association, which were the basis of the Evarts Act, contained such a provision. In the language of the American Bar Association Committee on Judicial Administration, the Act of 1891 " strangely omits " the right of appeal from such an interlocutory decree:

" The appeal from a final decree where there has been a previous interlocutory decree appointing a receiver, with intermediate orders for the sale of the res or receivers' certificates or, in any event, with the entire expenses of the receivership saddled on the estate, is like the justice that grants a new trial to the beheaded criminal." [97]

Three times the House passed a bill to correct this defect — in 1894,[98] 1896,[99] and 1899.[100] In the Senate Judiciary Committee

---

[95] See William H. Taft, " Recent Criticisms of the Federal Judiciary," 18 AM. BAR ASSN. REP. 237, 257.

[96] *Ibid.* 263.

[97] Report of Committee on Judicial Administration and Remedial Procedure for 1894, 17 AM. BAR ASSN. REP. 341.

[98] Turner of Georgia on May 31, 1894, introduced a bill to amend Section 7 of the Act of 1891, which was reported back favorably from the House Judiciary Committee on June 7, 1894. 26 CONG. REC. 5557, 5924; HOUSE REPORT, No. 1039, 53 Cong., 2nd Sess., Ser. No. 3271. The bill, set forth in full in 26 CONG. REC. 6062, was debated on June 9 and on June 13 passed without division. *Ibid.* 6062, 6233. On June 15 it was referred to the Senate Judiciary Committee, whence it never emerged. *Ibid.* 6319.

[99] Turner again introduced his bill in the House on Dec. 6, 1895. 28 CONG. REC. 52. On Jan. 21, 1896, Updegraff of Iowa from the Judiciary Committee reported out a substitute. *Ibid.* 952; HOUSE REPORT, No. 104, 54th Cong., 1st

three times it was buried. Despite the gradual termination of the provocative railroad receiverships in the federal courts, the American Bar Association continued to press its recommendation.[101] Possibly because of the reorganization of the railroads and their withdrawal from court supervision, following the McKinley " era of prosperity," the measure ceased to be immediately important and after a fourth passage by the House, the Senate allowed it to become law on June 6, 1900.[102] Unfortunately, however, the form of the Act was an amendment of the original Section 7 of the Act of 1891 rather than of that Section as amended by the Act of 1895 which permitted an appeal from an interlocutory order " refusing or dissolving " as well as granting an injunction. As a result the Act of 1900, either inadver-

---

Sess., Ser. No. 3457. The bill passed without debate on Mar. 24, 1896. 28 CONG. REC. 3146. On March 25 it was referred to the Senate Judiciary Committee and there buried. *Ibid.* 3166.

[100] On Feb. 17, 1898, Henderson in the House introduced a bill to amend Section 7 of the Act of 1891 so as to provide for appeals from interlocutory orders appointing receivers. 31 CONG. REC. 1865. It was reported out by Connolly of Illinois from the Judiciary Committee. 31 *ibid.* 4828; HOUSE REPORT, No. 1293, 54th Cong., 2nd Sess., Ser. No. 3721. This bill, which appears in 31 CONG. REC. 6203, was the bill drafted by a committee of the American Bar Association. See 21 AM. BAR ASSN. REP. 41. The attention of the American Bar Association had been directed to this defect in Section 7 of the Act of 1891 in 1894, 1895, and in 1897. See 17 *ibid.* 341; 18 *ibid.* 307; 20 *ibid* 347, 416. The bill passed the House without division on June 21, 1898. 31 CONG. REC. 6203. It was referred to the Senate Judiciary Committee and there buried. *Ibid.* 6229.

[101] See 22 AM. BAR ASSN. REP. 242. William Wirt Howe in his presidential address to the Association in 1898 urgently pressed the need for this legislation. See 21 *ibid.* 235, 243.

[102] A bill to this effect was introduced by Bartlett in the House on Dec. 20, 1899, and reported out of the Judiciary Committee on May 25, 1900. 33 CONG. REC. 608, 6509; HOUSE REPORT, No. 1758, 56 Cong., 1st Sess., Ser. No. 4027. The bill passed without debate on June 5, 1900, and on the next day was referred to the Senate Judiciary Committee. 33 CONG. REC. 7206, 7311. In the meantime Senator Thurston on Mar. 19, 1900, had introduced a similar bill in the Senate. *Ibid.* 3024. On April 9 he reported it from the Judiciary Committee asking unanimous consent for the present consideration of the bill, but this was denied. *Ibid.* 4164. On May 14 the bill again was passed over upon objection, despite Thurston's remarks that the American Bar Association urgently requested the passage of the bill. *Ibid.* 5933. On June 6 the Senate Judiciary Committee reported out the House bill urging its passage in the place of Thurston's measure. *Ibid.* 7335. It passed the Senate on the same day and became law as the Act of June 6, 1900. 31 STAT. 660.

tently or by design,[103] repealed the Act of 1895 through careless draftsmanship.[104] This defect in turn had to be remedied, an effort which required twelve years [105] and was finally accomplished by Section 129 of the Judicial Code.[106]

---

[103] It is generally assumed that the repeal was inadvertent; however, the fact that the House bill, as distinguished from Thurston's measure, omitted the provisions allowing an appeal from an interlocutory order refusing an injunction, leaves some doubt as to whether this was the intention of the Senate. See SEN. REP., No. 2206, 56th Cong., 2nd Sess., Ser. No. 4065.

[104] Columbia Wire Co. v. Boyce, 104 Fed. 172 (7th Circ., 1900); Rowan v. Ide, 107 Fed. 161 (5th Circ., 1901).

[105] Measures to correct this error were introduced immediately after it was discovered. On Jan. 24, 1901, Senator Fairbanks introduced a bill to amend Section 7 of the Act of 1891, as amended by the Act of Feb. 18, 1895, and the Act of June 6, 1900. 34 CONG. REC. 1502. The defect had been brought to the attention of the Senate through the action of the American Bar Association. See Thurston in the Senate on Feb. 19, 1901, *ibid.* 2931; 23 AM. BAR ASSN. REP. 37–40. The bill was debated on Feb. 19, 1901, but on objection was passed over. 34 CONG. REC. 2931. In the House on Jan. 26, 1901, Overstreet introduced a similar bill, which was reported out on Feb. 12, 1901. *Ibid.* 1657, 2566; HOUSE REPORT, No. 2849, 56th Cong., 2nd Sess., Ser. No. 4214. The bill was debated on Feb. 28, 1901, and was passed by a vote of 68 to 20. 34 CONG. REC. 3567–3569, 3574–3575. It was referred to the Senate Judiciary Committee who took no action upon it. *Ibid.* 3562. On Dec. 2, 1901, Overstreet again introduced his bill. 35 *ibid.* 13. It was reported out by the Judiciary Committee on Jan. 27, 1902, and passed the House on Feb. 13, 1902. *Ibid.* 1048, 1733; HOUSE REPORT, No. 186, 57th Cong., 1st Sess., Ser. No. 4399. The Senate Judiciary Committee, after holding the bill for over a year, reported it with amendments on Feb. 24, 1903. 36 CONG. REC. 2754. The Senate, however, took no action upon it. On Feb. 2, 1905, Powers of Massachusetts in the House introduced a bill for a like purpose. 39 *ibid.* 1811. It was reported without amendment on Feb. 4, 1905. *Ibid.* 1906; HOUSE REPORT, No. 4214, 58th Cong., 3rd Sess., Ser. No. 4762. The bill passed on Feb. 11 without division. 39 CONG. REC. 2413. It was referred to the Senate Judiciary Committee but never emerged. *Ibid.* 2453.

A further difficulty with appeals from interlocutory orders consisted in the fact that where such an appeal involved a constitutional question, an appeal on final decree lay directly to the Supreme Court. There being no provision for appeals from interlocutory decrees other than to the circuit courts of appeals, and the appeal to these courts under the existing legislation being available only where an appeal from a final decree would also lie to the circuit courts of appeals, the existence of a constitutional question would prevent all appeals from interlocutory orders. It thus became customary for the pleader to allege the existence of a constitutional question and thus seek to prevent all review from interlocutory decrees. See Bacon in the Senate on April 6, 1906, 40 CONG. REC. 4856. A bill to remedy this defect and provide for review of all interlocutory orders by the circuit courts of appeals was introduced in the House by Brantley on Jan. 22, 1906. *Ibid.* 1408. The text of the bill appears in 40 CONG. REC. 1723. It was reported out of the Judiciary Committee on Jan. 29, 1906, and

3.

Old political institutions like low forms of organism have tenacious vitality. The circuit court ceased to have justification by works when it ceased to function as a court of two judges, one of distinguished rank, in the disposition of important litigation. By 1869 the circuit courts were predominantly mere replicas of the district courts, more often than not presided over by the same district judge. Behind the elaborate machinery of two separate legal establishments were two sets of courts — on paper.[107] In practice the system spelt not only confusion and waste, but the inevitable abuse of power resulting from unlimited authority. And yet it took fifty years after the exposure of the perversion of an outworn system to eliminate its cluttering and costly forms. When finally the change did come to pass, it was over the protest of Joseph H. Choate and Elihu Root! [108]

The Judiciary Act of 1869 hoped to save the circuit court system by providing circuit judges. We have seen the failure of

---

on the same day passed the House without a division. *Ibid.* 1723; HOUSE REPORT, No. 542, 59th Cong., 1st Sess., Ser. No. 4906. The Senate Judiciary Committee reported it out with amendments on Mar. 29, 1906. 40 CONG. REC. 4429, SEN. REP., No. 2192, 59th Cong., 1st Sess., Ser. No. 4905. It was debated and passed by the Senate on April 6, 1906. 40 CONG. REC. 4857. The House concurred in the Senate amendments. *Ibid.* 5056. The bill became law by the Act of April 14, 1906, 34 STAT. 116.

[106] 36 STAT. 1087, 1134. See H. R. DOC., No. 127, 61st Cong., 2nd Sess., Ser. No. 5830, p. 57: "The act of 1900 amended the act of 1891, and overlooked the act of 1895. In view of this, the committee has restored the provisions of the act of 1895 permitting an appeal from an interlocutory order 'refusing or dissolving,' or 'refusing to dissolve an injunction.'"

[107] "From 1891 to the time of the adoption of the code, the Courts operated under a system the complicity [*sic*] of which demonstrated beyond question the need of reform in the direction of simplicity. . . . The jurisdiction of the two Courts was distinguished by no controlling principle. . . . Time and time again would the presiding judge have Court opened as a Circuit Court, and after the calling of the docket, have that Court closed with due solemnity. Immediately afterwards the crier would announce that the District Court was in session. There would be a switching of dockets, and the District Court would proceed to business." Robert W. Breckons, "The Judicial Code of United States with Some Incidental Observations on Its Application to Hawaii," 22 YALE L. J. 453, 457.

[108] Mr. Root, with customary acumen, has analyzed the psychology of leaders of the bar which prevents them from becoming leaders of reform. See Elihu Root, *supra*, note 85, 39 AM. BAR ASSN. REP. 386, 390–391.

the attempt. The new business which came to the courts exceeded the capacity of the new judges. Circuit judges could pay only sporadic visits to the different districts and for brief periods. Very soon the old conditions were revived in aggravated form. Circuit courts fell into the hands of single judges and, in the main, judges of the district courts did circuit court work. Therefore, beginning with the seventies, the abolition of the circuit courts and some form of intermediate appellate tribunal were the two chief planks in every program for judicial reform. The two proposals were interdependent. With a new system of appellate jurisdiction the old limited appellate power of the circuit courts became redundant. A weighty *nisi prius* court likewise became a needless safeguard if review became generally available through a new set of appellate courts. The Harris bill, the McCrary bill, the Davis bill, the Maury bill, all built on these assumptions. The Circuit Courts of Appeals Act, in the form in which it passed the House, likewise abolished the circuit courts. But we have already noted that a price had to be paid to overcome Evarts' original hostility to the creation of new appellate tribunals, wedded as he was to the traditional circuit court system. The chief concession which was made him was the retention of the circuit courts.

But the Act of 1891 in creating new comprehensive appellate courts had to eliminate at least the limited appellate power of the circuit courts.[109] Thus the new legislation only emphasized the growing " absurdity in the Federal judicial system "[110] of two courts substantially of concurrent jurisdiction, with no little uncertainty and confusion in determining the few instances in which their jurisdiction was not concurrent. The situation was aptly summarized by Reuben O. Moon, Chairman of the House Committee on the Revision of the Laws:

" The jurisdiction conferred by acts of Congress upon these courts is, in a large majority of cases, concurrent, and in a comparatively few cases is exclusive jurisdiction conferred upon them. This jurisdiction differs very little in character and is distinguished by no controlling principle. They both have jurisdiction of civil and criminal cases, the

---

[109] Act of Mar. 3, 1891, § 4, 26 STAT. 826, 827.

[110] Senator (now Mr. Justice) Sutherland, in the Senate on Feb. 8, 1911, 46 CONG. REC. 2137.

only distinction being that the circuit court has exclusive jurisdiction in capital cases. In some cases the line of demarcation is simply the amount involved in the litigation; in some cases there exists a mere arbitrary division, giving the admiralty and maritime jurisdiction ex- clusively to the district courts, and matters relating to revenue to the circuit courts; and during the past 25 years few, if any, acts of Con- gress have been passed that conferred jurisdiction upon courts in which the same jurisdiction has not been conferred upon both the circuit and the district courts." [111]

No wonder such a system was " perplexing and oftentimes con- fusing to litigants and attorneys." [112]

In 1894 the American Bar Association renewed its campaign for the elimination of this obsolete system.[113] The sluggish legis- lative story starts with the introduction of a bill by Senator Hoar on Feb. 1, 1897, not in the hope of its passage but to secure public attention.[114] At Senator Hoar's instance [115] a special com- mittee was appointed by the American Bar Association on the revision of the federal judicial system through consolidation of the district and circuit courts.[116] To this end a careful proposal was made and sponsored by Senator Hoar in a bill introduced on Feb. 27, 1899.[117] At this time, however, there was in existence the Commission, established by Congress on June 4, 1897,[118] for the revision and codification of the penal laws. The fusion of the circuit and district courts would entail minor revisions in a great mass of federal legislation. What was more natural and expedient than reference to this Commission of the proposal for

---

[111] 46 CONG. REC. 88.

[112] H. R. DOC., No. 127, 61st Cong., 2nd Sess., Ser. No. 5830, p. 5.

[113] Report of Committee on Judicial Administration and Remedial Procedure, 17 AM. BAR ASSN. REP. 336, 342.

[114] 29 CONG. REC. 1378.

[115] Senator Hoar in 1897 telegraphed the American Bar Association: " The Bar Association will confer a great benefit by appointing a committee to consider the present constitution of the U. S. Circuit and District Courts, whether they may not properly be consolidated or the present very singular distribution of jurisdiction otherwise improved." 20 AM. BAR ASSN. REP. 60.

[116] *Ibid.* 63. For the list of the special committee, see 21 *ibid.* 160.

[117] 32 CONG. REC. 2432. At the same time a letter from Edmund Wetmore, Chairman of the Special Committee on Federal Courts, advocating the adoption of the bill was printed as SEN. DOC., No. 142, 55th Cong., 3rd Sess., Ser. No. 3735. See also Report of the Committee on Federal Courts, 21 AM. BAR ASSN. REP. 485.   [118] 30 STAT. 58.

the revision of the judiciary acts!   The day after Hoar introduced the Bar Association bill he moved, in effect, to refer the
project for reorganizing the district and circuit courts to the
Commission on the Revision of the Laws.[119] By the Act of March
3, 1899, it became the duty of the Commission " to revise and
codify the laws concerning the jurisdiction and practice of the
courts of the United States, including the Judiciary Act. . . ." [120]

The specific proposal to abolish the circuit courts thus becomes
entangled in the larger project of the revision of the laws of the
United States.   A new incubating process of twelve years is
begun.   The circuit courts gain another and final lease of life,
because their death must await the adoption of a comprehensive
judicial code.   Independent legislative proposals cease.   No
further bills affecting the fate of the circuit courts appear.[121]
The drive against their retention is transferred from Congress
to the Commission.   Although this body was instructed to " revise and codify." the laws concerning the federal courts, it acted
as though it were given a mandate to frame the drastic change
involved in putting an end to the circuit courts.   The Commission
certainly was justified in assuming an overwhelming sentiment
for the reform, and fortified itself by further weighty opinion.[122]
Thus, the powerful Circuit Court of Appeals for the Sixth Circuit
fully concurred in the views of the Commissioners

---

[119] 32 CONG. REC. 2553.

[120] 30 STAT. 1116.

[121] Turner in the Senate on May 6, 1902, introduced a bill to abolish the
circuit courts and simplify appeals from the district courts to the Supreme Court.
35 CONG. REC. 5415. Just prior to the introduction of the bill that became the
Judicial Code, Moon of Pennsylvania, Chairman of the Committee on the
Revision of the Laws, introduced a bill to abolish the circuit courts. 45 *ibid.*
825. Neither of these bills was reported from committee.

[122] A statement for the year 1908 shows:

	Days
Circuit judges held circuit court	2,175
District judges held circuit court	15,771
In 9 districts circuit judges held circuit court	1,826
In 43 districts circuit judges held circuit court	349

In 25 districts circuit judges did not hold circuit court. See 46 CONG. REC. 1544.
The duplication of work under the system of circuit courts is illustrated by the
fact that in 1910 there were 77 circuit courts required by acts of Congress to be
held in 276 different places in the circuits, and also 77 district courts required to
be held in 276 different places. See *ibid.* 87.

" that there should be but one court of first instance and we think that you have taken the wisest course in reaching that end by transferring all the jurisdiction of the existing circuit courts to the district courts.

" The existence of the two courts of first instance has long been an anomaly, if not an absurdity, in the Federal judicial system, and their maintenance has been useful only as marking the unusual and in most respects praiseworthy conservatism which Congress has shown in dealing with proposed changes in the organization of the Federal courts." [123]

These were the views of three judges destined for membership on the Supreme Bench — Day, Lurton, and Taft.

Instead of disposing piecemeal of the different branches of federal legislation referred to, and to be drafted by, the Commission, Congress enlarged the scope of its assignment. By the Act of March 3, 1901,[124] the Commission was instructed to prepare a revision of all the permanent laws of the United States. The revision of the penal laws and of the judiciary acts were to form titles of the comprehensive project. The Commission reported the codification of the judiciary title to the Attorney General on November 15, 1901. Meanwhile, the revision of the other laws was proceeding, and by Resolution of March 3, 1905,[125] the Commission was ordered to incorporate in its final proposals any changes that had been made in the criminal and judiciary titles since its previous report. By Act of June 30, 1906,[126] completion of the work of the Commission was set for December 15, 1906. A resolution of March 2, 1907,[127] provided for a joint committee of Congress to consider the revision of the laws proposed by the Commission. After enacting the proposed codification of the penal laws into the Criminal Code of March 3, 1909,[128] the judiciary title, prepared by the Commission and considerably revised by the Joint Committee on the Revision of the Laws, was introduced in both Senate and House on March 9

---

[123] Letter of Nov. 3, 1899, from Taft, Lurton, and Day, Judges of the Circuit Court of Appeals for the Sixth Circuit, to Botkin, Watson, and Culberson, Commissioners on the Revision of Laws. 46 CONG. REC. 1544.

[124] 31 STAT. 1181.

[125] 33 STAT. 1285.

[126] 34 STAT. 697, 754.

[127] 34 STAT. 1423.

[128] 35 STAT. 1058.

and March 23, 1910, in the form of a Judicial Code.[129] For our
immediate purpose the significant feature of the Judicial Code
was the elimination of the circuit courts and the vesting of all
original jurisdiction in the district courts. The proposal had to
encounter final resistance in both houses. Apart from the place-
men whose clerical jobs were threatened,[130] some of the most
distinguished lawyers still opposed the change. The old circuit
court enlisted their loyalty, and the elimination of this ancient
institution went against the grain of their professional affections.
Senator Root, though in principle " inclining towards the measure of consolidation," [131] finally voted against it.[132] Congress
was memorialized by a protest of leading lawyers from all the
circuits, headed by Joseph H. Choate.[133] The American Bar
Association, which as we have seen, had taken the original lead
for this reform, had become quiescent while Commission and
Congressional committee were engaged upon revision. When
the reform was about to be realized, the American Bar Association not only failed to support its old measure; it actually
supported the forces of obstruction through a pusillanimous
resolution seeking further time for " investigation," meanwhile

---

[129] 45 CONG. REC. 2937, 3641.

[130] Reference is made in both Senate and House to the existence of "an
organization of the circuit court clerks of this country to defeat this legislation
simply because it deprives them of their positions." See Moon in the House on
Dec. 14, 1910, and Sherley in the Senate on Feb. 23, 1911. 46 CONG. REC. 301,
3219.

[131] 46 CONG. REC. 1544.

[132] "Mr. Root. I move to strike out section 274. I do that because I wish
to record a vote against the abolition and consolidation of the circuit and district
courts." 46 CONG. REC. 2136. The motion was defeated without a division.
Ibid. 2139.

[133] The signers of this memorial were Hollis R. Bailey of Boston, Mass.
(1st Circ.), Joseph H. Choate of New York, N. Y. (2nd Circ.), James Buchanon
of Trenton, N. J. (3rd Circ.), Charles D. Merrick of Parkersburg, West Va.
(4th Circ.), Alex. W. Smith of Atlanta, Ga. (5th Circ.), John B. Rouse of New
Orleans, La. (5th Circ.), George D. Lancaster of Chattanooga, Tenn. (6th
Circ.), James Quarles of Louisville, Ky. (6th Circ.), Otto Raymond Barnett of
Chicago, Ill. (7th Circ.), James H. Matheny of Springfield, Ill. (7th Circ.),
Ralph W. Breckenridge of Omaha, Neb. (8th Circ.), C. E. S. Wood of Portland,
Ore. (9th Circ.). The memorial is printed in 46 CONG. REC. 298, and 14 LAW
NOTES 225. Judge Pardee of the Fifth Circuit, the oldest circuit judge of the
day, joined the protest against the abolition of the circuit courts. His series of
spirited letters were placed before Congress and much use was made of them.
See 46 CONG. REC. 300.

requesting Congress to postpone action![134]   Two state bar associations, Connecticut[135] and Alabama,[136] had at least the courage
for out-and-out opposition.   But it was a lost fight.   The circuit
courts had outlived their adventitious existence.[137]   Their epitaph
was written by the Act of March 3, 1911,[138] and on January 1,
1912, the circuit courts had ceased to be.

The merger of circuit courts into district courts could not,
however, be accomplished merely by the mechanical transfer of
circuit court jurisdiction to district courts.   The difference between the territorial power of the district and circuit judges had
in action practical consequences.   Inasmuch as a circuit court
judge could sit in all districts within his circuit, in receivership
proceedings he was enabled to appoint the same individual as
receiver in all districts forming one circuit within which a single
enterprise, usually a railroad, was administering property.   But
a district judge was confined to his district, with the result that
each district judge might name a different receiver for different
portions of the same railroad in the same circuit.   As a matter
of practice district judges had left the disposition of this class
of litigation to their circuit judges.[139]   The mere elimination of
circuit courts would have put an end to such a practical adjustment.   The Choate memorial, speaking for " lawyers of large

---

[134] The resolution was offered by Walter George Smith of Pennsylvania and
referred to the Committee on Judicial Administration and Remedial Procedure.
See 35 Am. Bar Assn. Rep. 48.   The text of the resolution appears in 46 Cong.
Rec. 298.   The Committee " made strenuous efforts to obtain a postponement of
Congressional action on the bills covering the subject-matter of these resolutions,
but without avail."   See 36 Am. Bar Assn. Rep. 387.

[135] See 1911 Conn. State Bar Assn. Rep. 30, reprinted in 46 Cong. Rec.
2153.

[136] See Brantley of Georgia in the House on Dec. 14, 1910, 46 Cong. Rec.
298.

[137] An editorial in 1910 thus summarizes the situation: " The surprising thing
is that the Circuit Court of the United States has not long ago been abolished."
See 41 Nat. Corp. Rep. 625.

[138] § 289, 36 Stat. 1087, 1167.

[139] Thus Judge Pardee describes the practice in his circuit: " In this circuit,
the general understanding is that the circuit judges shall take care of the litigation brought in the several circuit courts which concerns property interests
(and needs ancillary bills) in more than one district.   In such litigation, the
circuit judge can secure uniformity in the rulings, and there is never a conflict as
to the management of the property or the appointment of receivers."   46 Cong.
Rec. 300.

practice on the equity side of the United States circuit courts," [140] seized upon this problem as one of the chief reasons for retaining the circuit courts. But legal ingenuity was not so barren as to be unable to meet an isolated difficulty, without retaining the whole barnacled system out of which it grew. The objection was easily met by the present Section 56 of the Judicial Code, whereby the action of a district judge in appointing a receiver covering property running across an entire circuit and including a number of districts, is rendered conclusive for purposes of preserving the *status quo,* but subjecting the appointment to confirmation, within thirty days, by a circuit judge or the circuit court of appeals.[141]

One other detail was seized upon as an excuse for preserving the old order. Under the Circuit Courts of Appeals Act circuit judges, particularly on the less busy courts of appeals, were available for *nisi prius* work on circuit courts. The existing situation to this extent permitted a flexible use of the judges. This advantage was retained by an amendment, now Section 18, authorizing circuit judges to hold district court.[142] For the rest, there were the usual prophecies that " the change will be unsettling and will substitute a judicial system not understood for one well-defined and known." [143] After a little over a decade, a new generation of lawyers has come to the bar hardly conscious that there had ever been circuit courts.

---

[140] *Ibid.* 299.

[141] This section was introduced as an amendment to the House bill by Chairman Moon and was adopted in substantially the same form as introduced. See 46 CONG. REC. 566–569, 3998.

[142] " Its purpose . . . is to permit circuit judges to try cases in the district courts, in order to prevent congestion of business in those courts, and to afford business for the circuit judges in circuits in which there is not sufficient business in the circuit courts of appeals to occupy the time of the judges." See H. R. Doc., No. 127, 61st Cong., 2nd Sess., Ser. No. 5830, p. 13. An amendment to Section 118 of the Judicial Code also permitted circuit judges to hold district court. Parker of New Jersey on the floor of the House sought to retain even more flexibility by an amendment to Section 13 intended to allow the Supreme Court Justices to be members of the district courts. 46 CONG. REC. 303. Under the Act of 1891 the Justices were still eligible to sit in the circuit courts, but they did not exercise this power. See *ibid.* 301. Parker's amendment — a last attempt in the long struggle to saddle the Justices of the Supreme Court with *nisi prius* work — was defeated without division. *Ibid.* 304.

[143] The Choate memorial, 46 CONG. REC. 299.

4

The continuous effort of twenty years to enable the federal courts to cope with mounting litigation by reforming their cumbersome and wasteful organization was paralleled by an equally vigorous movement to enable them to do their work by reducing the range of their business. For twenty years the *Congressional Record* registers this attempt to limit jurisdiction. The more moderate proposal was to increase the pecuniary amount necessary for resort to the federal courts. The more far-reaching remedy was the old attempt to remit litigation affecting foreign corporations to the state courts. It is the old strife between different sections of the country which, in Congress, is intensified by the clash between the popular House and the Senate.

It will be recalled that the House in 1887, by an overwhelming vote, for the fourth time sought to withdraw from the federal courts the growing volume of litigation drawn to them by the fiction of corporate citizenship. The Senate blocked this effort, yielding only an increase in the jurisdictional amount. The concession made by the Act of March 3, 1887,[144] did not allay the western sentiment behind Culberson's proposals. And so, after the efforts to relieve the Supreme Court were accomplished by the Act of 1891, Culberson returned to his chief interest. On January 7, 1892, he introduced his old measure adapting it to the changes wrought by the Acts of 1887 and 1891.[145] The bill proposed to keep out of the federal courts, under its jurisdiction based on diversity of citizenship, suits involving corporations doing business in a state but not chartered therein. The bill passed the House without debate and division.[146] It was reported adversely

---

[144] 24 STAT. 552, as amended by the Act of Aug. 13, 1888, 25 STAT. 433.

[145] 23 CONG. REC. 200.

[146] It was reported from the House Judiciary Committee on Feb. 11, 1892. 23 CONG. REC. 1070; HOUSE REPORT, No. 271, 52 Cong., 1st Sess., Ser. No. 3042. Buchanon of New Jersey submitted the views of the minority. The bill did not take away jurisdiction in this class of cases where suit was brought under the copyright or patent laws or where a federal question was involved. On Mar. 9 Culberson withdrew the bill, but he again brought it before the House during its second session on Dec. 19, 1892. 23 CONG. REC. 1877; 24 *ibid.* 217. The bill passed on the same day without division and was referred to the Senate Judiciary Committee. *Ibid.* 218.

by the Senate Judiciary Committee [147] with three favorable Southern votes [148] and never got beyond this stage.[149] Culberson in
the next Congress reintroduced his bill.[150] This time action
on it was suspended [151] to give the right of way to another measure [152] seeking the curtailment of federal jurisdiction over corporations, but restricted in its operation to railroads, the particular class of corporation at this time most fruitful in litigation.
A large number of railroads at this time, it will be remembered,
were operated under federal charter. As to them, the House
passed a measure providing that they were to be deemed citizens
of the states through which they passed and therefore could not
avail themselves of resort to the federal courts as a " federal
right " derived from federal incorporation.[153] The bill found its
way to the Senate morgue.[154] In the succeeding Congress
Culberson made a last futile attempt to secure action for his
measure.[155]

---

[147] *Ibid.* 1956 (Feb. 21, 1893).

[148] Pugh of Alabama, Coke of Texas, and George of Mississippi.

[149] On March 5, 1893, on the motion of Senator Harris, the bill was passed
over. *Ibid.* 2663.

[150] On Sept. 9, 1893. 25 CONG. REC. 1359.

[151] It was reported back from the Judiciary Committee on Dec. 12, 1893.
26 CONG. REC. 171; HOUSE REPORT, No. 207, 53rd Cong., 2nd Sess., Ser. No. 3269.
The bill was debated on Aug. 16, 1894, when Culberson adverted to the fact that
every circuit was clamoring for an additional judge and urged that the proper
method of relief was to restrict the scope of judicial business. 26 CONG. REC.
8593-8594. On Dec. 4, 1894, the bill was passed over without prejudice. 27
ibid. 18.

[152] On Sept. 9, 1893, Terry in the House introduced a bill making United
States railroad corporations citizens of states through which their railroad passed.
25 CONG. REC. 1360. The bill appears in full in 26 CONG. REC. 7603.

[153] Terry's bill was reported out of the Judiciary Committee on Feb. 9, 1894.
Ibid. 2050; HOUSE REPORT, No. 396, 53rd Cong., 2nd Sess., Ser. No. 3269. On
July 17, the bill was debated in the House, and Ray of New York moved to
strike out the provision which made them citizens of such states in which they
might carry on business. Boatner of Louisiana offered a substitute amendment to
limit the exclusive jurisdiction of the state courts to causes of action arising
within the state in which the suit was brought. Both amendments were rejected
by a vote of 136 to 44 and the bill passed by a vote of 158 to 12. 26 CONG.
REC. 7603-7609.

[154] The bill was referred to the Senate Judiciary Committee on Dec. 5, 1894,
from which it never emerged. 27 CONG. REC. 38.

[155] On Jan. 23, 1896, Culberson's bill was introduced in the House, but it
was not reported out of the House Judiciary Committee. 28 CONG. REC. 952.
In 1897 Culberson was appointed a member of the Commission to Revise the
Laws and left the House.

After 1896 Culberson's bill, sponsored by other members, was continuously introduced into Congress.[156] At one session it was proposed in the Senate by Senator Patterson of Colorado, with an elaborate supporting brief.[157] Resolutions appear for

---

[156] On April 2, 1894, Tucker, by request, had introduced a bill in the House to abrogate federal jurisdiction over state corporations. 26 CONG. REC. 3408. On Mar. 16, 1897, Allen introduced a bill in the House to restrict the jurisdiction of the federal courts. 30 *ibid*. 27. On Dec. 11, 1900, Burke of Texas introduced a bill in the House to limit the jurisdiction of the circuit and district courts. 33 *ibid* 210. McRae on April 21, 1902, introduced a bill in the House to limit the jurisdiction of the circuit and district courts in suits by and against corporations. 35 *ibid*. 4757. On Dec. 16, 1902, Senator Patterson introduced a bill to define the jurisdiction of the United States courts over corporations. 36 *ibid*. 343. On Nov. 9, 1903, Stephens of Texas in the House introduced a bill to limit the jurisdiction of the circuit and district courts. 37 *ibid*. 151. On Jan. 18, 1904, Senator Clay introduced a similar bill which was adversely reported by Hoar from the Judiciary Committee on Mar. 29, 1904, and indefinitely postponed. 38 *ibid*. 819, 3912. On Dec. 4, 1905, Stephens of Texas again introduced his former bill. 40 *ibid*. 54. On Jan. 29, 1905, Senator Patterson reintroduced his bill. *Ibid*. 1670. On Feb. 26, 1905, Garrett of Tennessee introduced two bills — to limit the jurisdiction of the circuit and district courts, and to amend the Act of 1887 so as to abrogate " federal jurisdiction over State corporations when the jurisdiction is founded only on the fact that the action or suit is brought between citizens of different States." *Ibid*. 3031. In the House on April 7, 1906, Parker introduced a bill to limit the jurisdiction of the United States courts. *Ibid*. 4921. On Dec. 13, 1906, Senator Carmack introduced a bill to limit the jurisdiction of the district and circuit courts, and a bill to abrogate jurisdiction over state corporations on the ground of diversity of citizenship. 41 *ibid*. 329. On Jan. 7, 1907, Senator Clay reintroduced his bill. *Ibid*. 669. On Dec. 3, 1907, Garrett in the House reintroduced his two bills. 42 *ibid*. 115. On Mar. 18, 1909, Kitchin in the House introduced a bill to prevent removal by non-resident corporations. 44 *ibid*. 101 On Mar. 19, 1909, Garrett reintroduced his two bills. *Ibid*. 114. On Dec. 14, 1909, in the House, Thomas of Kentucky introduced a bill to limit the jurisdiction of the circuit and district courts. 45 *ibid*. 140. On Dec. 15, 1909, Kitchin reintroduced his bill. *Ibid*. 180. On Feb. 21, 1910, Senator Clay reintroduced his bill. *Ibid*. 2150. On Mar. 15, 1910, Hughes of New Jersey introduced a bill to amend the Act of Aug. 13, 1888, and making certain changes in the procedure on removal. The bill was reported out on Mar. 25, 1910. *Ibid*. 3224, 3790; HOUSE REPORT, No. 832, 61st Cong., 2nd Sess., Ser. No. 5592. In the debate that occurred on April 4, 1910, Thomas of Kentucky offered an amendment increasing the jurisdictional amount necessary for removal from state to federal courts to $5,000. Garrett proposed an amendment to prevent jurisdiction by federal courts over state corporations on the ground of diversity of citizenship. The bill passed, with the Thomas amendment, by a vote of 123 to 117, and was referred to the Senate Judiciary Committee where it died. 45 CONG. REC. 4222–4227, 4259. On Dec. 21, 1910, Stephens of Texas reintroduced his bill. 46 *ibid*. 577.

[157] This brief, drawn by Henry Cohen and Jas. J. Sullivan of the Denver Bar, was printed as SEN. DOC., No. 46, 57th Cong., 2nd Sess., Ser. No. 4420.

constitutional amendments to accomplish the same purpose.[158] During this period proponents of curtailed jurisdiction also pushed a measure to raise the jurisdictional amount from $2,000 to $5,000.[159] But, as we have noted, while the judiciary title was in the hands of the Commission for the Revision of the Laws, legislative activity over judicial organization was, in the main, dormant in Congress.[160] The introduction of the bill embody-

---

[158] On Jan. 7, 1898, Senator Butler introduced a joint resolution for a constitutional amendment providing for the election of federal judges and doing away with federal jurisdiction in cases based on diversity of citizenship. 31 CONG. REC. 430. Again on Dec. 10, 1909, Russell in the House proposed a joint resolution for a constitutional amendment doing away with federal jurisdiction over corporations on the ground of diversity of citizenship. 45 CONG. REC. 91.

[159] On Dec. 7, 1897, Moon of Tennessee introduced a bill to increase the jurisdictional amount to $5,000. 31 *ibid.* 34. He reintroduced the bill on Dec. 5, 1899. 33 *ibid.* 57. He again introduced the bill on Dec. 2, 1901. 35 *ibid.* 16. On Jan. 17, 1908, the bill again appears in the House under the sponsorship of Moon. 42 *ibid.* 835. On May 13, 1909, Moon once more introduced his bill. 44 *ibid.* 2013.

[160] Among the minor attempts to secure legislation affecting the jurisdiction of the federal courts was a bill introduced by Henderson in the House on Dec. 6, 1897, providing that the party originally suing in a federal court or removing it to such court from a state court could not question the jurisdiction of the federal court; also, that neither party could question its jurisdiction if the case proceeded to trial on the merits, but the court on its motion could question either the non-existence of jurisdiction or could refuse to entertain jurisdiction on the ground that it had been obtained through collusion. 31 CONG. REC. 14, 3859. The bill was reported out of the Judiciary Committee on Feb. 25, 1898, and again on April 4, 1898. *Ibid.* 2213, 3536; HOUSE REPORTS, Nos. 546, 958, 55th Cong., 2nd Sess., Ser. Nos. 3719, 3720. The bill arose as a consequence of the decision of the Supreme Court in Walker *v.* Collins, 167 U. S. 57 (1897), where it was held that a case not depending on the citizenship of the parties nor otherwise specially provided for, cannot be removed from a state court into a United States court as one arising under the Constitution, laws, or treaties of the United States, unless that fact appears by the plaintiff's own statement; and if it does not appear, the want cannot be supplied by any statement in the subsequent pleadings or in the petition for removal. The House Report denounced the case as travesty upon justice. The minority report contended that the proposed legislation would practically extend federal jurisdiction over cases cognizable in the state courts alone. 31 CONG. REC. 3860. In the debate, although Connolly of the Judiciary Committee contended that the bill related only to jurisdiction over the person and could not be construed to extend further, Terry, looking only to the language of the bill, contended that it would confer jurisdiction by consent upon the federal courts. *Ibid.* 3860-3863. The bill passed the House on April 14, 1898, by a vote of 39 to 23. *Ibid.* 3863. It was referred to the Senate Judiciary Committee and there buried. *Ibid.* 3941.

From the year 1902 several attempts were made to broaden the right of removal from state to federal courts. These attempts took the form of per-ing the Judicial Code again precipitated the issue of lessening jurisdiction.   The various proponents of such legislation whose bills had heretofore been pigeon-holed, now found ample opportunity to propose amendments to the Judicial Code embodying their schemes.   In the debate that followed, the same ground was traversed with which we have become familiar in discussing the Culberson bill of the eighties.   In the House the advocates for limiting access to the federal courts prevailed.[161]   The jurisdic-

mitting removal in cases where a claim of right, privilege, or exemption under the Constitution, laws, or treaties of the United States was set up by the defendant prior to the trial.   Under the existing law such a claim had to be apparent in the plaintiff's own statement in order to permit the defendant to remove, and consequently cases where the defendant alone claimed such a right could only go to the United States Supreme Court from the state court of final appeal.   A bill of this nature was introduced in both houses concurrently. See 35 CONG. REC. 514, 564.   On April 11, 1902, in the Senate it was reported on adversely by Hoar of the Judiciary Committee.   *Ibid.* 4227; SEN. REP., No. 1077, 57th Cong., 1st Sess., Ser. No. 4261.   On June 3, 1902, Woods in the House introduced a similar bill.   35 CONG. REC. 6685.   The bill was reported from the Judiciary Committee on June 11, 1902.   *Ibid.* 7113; HOUSE REPORT, No. 2459, 57th Cong., 1st Sess., Ser. No. 4407.   This bill, like the earlier Senate bill, sought to restore the broad right of removal as it had existed under the Act of 1875, prior to its subsequent restriction under the Acts of Mar. 3, 1887, and of Aug. 13, 1888.   Clearly, legislation of this nature would not have affected the business of the Supreme Court inasmuch as that Court had jurisdiction of these cases on writ of error from the highest state court.   The House Report did not believe the bill would materially increase the litigation in the inferior federal courts and considered the measure as relieving the Supreme Court of " embarrassment " in reversing a state court.   On Jan. 6, 1903, consideration of the bill was objected to in the House and the bill was dropped. 36 CONG. REC. 558.   On Feb. 2, 1907, Senator Dick introduced a similar measure. 41 *ibid.* 2144.   It died in committee.

With the extensive use of the injunction by the inferior federal courts as a means of suspending state legislation and orders of state administrative agencies on the ground of unconstitutionality, measures to limit this interference are brought to the attention of Congress.   Bacon in the Senate on Feb. 6, 1908, introduced a bill to prevent the issuance of injunctions of this nature.   42 *ibid.* 1665.   On Feb. 10, 1908, Senator Patterson of Colorado introduced a bill to prevent any federal court inferior to the Supreme Court from issuing an injunction in any case wherein the validity of a state law or the act of any state official under it was called into question.   *Ibid.* 1795.   In the House on Aug. 3, 1909, Henry of Texas introduced a similar measure.   44 *ibid.* 4852.   The results of this movement belong to the history of the Commerce Court Act and of the Judicial Code, to be discussed later.

[161] On Dec. 14, 1910, Garrett offered an amendment to Section 24 of the bill embodying the Judicial Code making corporations citizens of every state where they had an office or an agent or in which they carried on their business. 46 *ibid.* 309.   On Jan. 11, 1911, he again brought the amendment to the atten-

tional amount was raised to $5,000,[162] and corporate litigation was restricted. Three serious qualifications were placed upon removal from state to federal courts by the Garrett amendment:

" no suit against a corporation or joint-stock company brought in a State court of the State in which the plaintiff resides or in which the cause of action arose, or within which the defendant has its place of business, or carries on its business, shall be removed to any court of the United States on the ground of diverse citizenship." [163]

In the Senate the attempt at restriction failed. The conflict between the two Houses on this important subject, among others, was transferred to the conference room. The House conferees were unyielding. The first conference report retained the Garrett amendment and compromised on the increase in the jurisdictional amount by raising it from $2,000 to $3,000 instead of $5,000.[164] But the Senate was immovable.[165] It stood out against the Garrett amendment and the House reluctantly yielded. In the second conference report to the Senate, the Garrett amendment disappeared.[166] The Judicial Code made no change in the ambit of jurisdiction except to increase by the slight lift of a thousand dollars the amount necessary to bring suit in the federal courts.

Other than these major changes this codification of the laws governing the federal judiciary achieved few significant reforms.

---

tion of the Committee of the Whole. Stephens of Texas offered a substitute amendment of a like nature. *Ibid.* 806–809. The amendment was debated on Jan. 18, 1911, and after several verbal changes adopted. *Ibid.* 1060–1073.

[162] Thomas of Kentucky on Jan. 18, 1911, moved an amendment raising the jurisdictional amount from $2,000 to $5,000, thus seeking by amendment to secure what Moon of Tennessee had pressed upon the House for many years previous by his various bills. See note 120, *supra*. The amendment was adopted by a vote of 95 to 14. 46 Cong. Rec. 1074–1077.

[163] *Ibid.* 1071.

[164] See the report made by the conference committee to the Senate on Mar. 1, 1911, which retained the Garrett amendment as a proviso to Section 28 of the Judicial Code. *Ibid.* 3760.

[165] The conference report was withdrawn on Mar. 2, 1911. *Ibid.* 3847.

[166] *Ibid.* 3853 (Mar. 2, 1911). This conference report was submitted to the House on the same day. Moon of the Conference Committee regretted the Senate's unyielding opposition to the Garrett amendment and, although mindful of the House's insistence upon the provision, deemed that it was best to yield. The House agreed to the conference report by a vote of 161 to 36. *Ibid.* 3998–4012.

On the floor of the House numerous attempts were made to
secure the passage of measures that for years had been vainly
sponsored in independent bills.[167]   Thus, proposals such as later
became the Clayton Act [168] failed of adoption in the House.[169]
On the other hand House amendments failed in the Senate or
finally went down in conference.[170]   We have seen the Senate's
successful resistance to the Garrett amendment seeking a drastic
curtailment of the jurisdiction of the federal courts, as well as

---

[167] Attempts to increase the salaries of the circuit judges were made by
Bennett of New York and Mann of Illinois. 46 CONG. REC. 810. Mann's
amendment seeking an increase to $8,500 was defeated by a vote of 152 to 125,
and Bennett's amendment raising this to $10,000 was lost by a vote of 217 to
50. *Ibid.* 1078, 1449–1451. An attempt to allow the Supreme Court Justices
to sit as members of the district court was twice made by Parker of New
Jersey. *Ibid.* 303, 1453. Parker thereby sought to retain the principle of the
old circuit system and reduce the number of appeals by having the best judges
sit at first instance.

[168] Act of Oct. 15, 1914, 38 STAT. 730.

[169] On Dec. 7, 1910, Wilson of Pennsylvania sought, by amendment, to
introduce a measure prohibiting the issuance of injunctions in disputes between
employers and employees unless such an injunction was necessary to prevent irreparable injury to property. Upon objection that the amendment was
not germane to the section under consideration, he consented to its being postponed until the House should deal with a later section of the bill. 46 CONG.
REC. 97. On Dec. 14, 1910, Stanley of Kentucky by amendment sought to
relieve agreements between employees from the provisions of the Sherman Act
and to prevent the issuance of any injunction in trade disputes save upon
reasonable notice to the defendants. By another amendment he sought to
divide contempts of court into categories of direct and indirect with a requirement for jury trial in the latter class of contempts. Both amendments went
over for consideration in connection with the Wilson amendment. *Ibid.* 318.
But the House did not thereafter consider these amendments.

[170] Besides the important Garrett, Thomas, and Madison amendments, Parsons
of New York, by a proviso to Section 116 of the bill, sought to give the circuit
judges throughout their circuits the powers and jurisdiction of a district judge.
Ibid. 1452. Parker of New Jersey sought to amend this amendment by giving
the Circuit Justices the same powers. *Ibid.* 2144. Hubbard of West Virginia
offered a substitute amendment allowing the district court to be held by the
circuit judge, the district judge, or both, and allowing cases to be heard by each
judge sitting apart at the direction of the circuit judge. In the event that both
sat together, the opinion of the circuit judge was to be controlling. *Ibid.* 1453.
Parker sponsored the amendment because it preserved the flexibility of the
circuit court system and permitted the court of original jurisdiction in important
cases to be presided over by two judges. Moon expressed the prevailing sentiment of the House in pressing its tendency to belittle the district judge. After
a two days' debate the House rejected the Hubbard and Parker amendments
and accepted the Parsons amendment. *Ibid.* 2155–2157. The Parsons amendment, however, failed to secure the approval of the Senate conferees. *Ibid.* 3998.

to the lesser amendment which sought to increase the jurisdictional amount to $5,000. One further effort by the House to make inroads on existing powers of the federal courts concerned a problem of continuing vitality. Madison of Kentucky prevailed on the House to adopt an amendment to Section 24 of the bill whereby district courts should be barred from taking jurisdiction of suits " to suspend, enjoin, or restrain the action of any officer of the State in the enforcement, operation, or execution of a statute of such State, upon the ground of the unconstitutionality of such a statute." [171]   The proposal was warmly espoused in the House, but the Senate was adamant. By way of " compromise," the Conference Committee reported a restatement of the existing law, contained in the Overman provision of the Mann-Elkins Act,[172] for a three-judge court in the form of a new Section, 266, of the Judicial Code.[173] Heyburn (who was in charge of the measure in the Senate) and Moon in the House wisely hesitated to imperil the success of the entire bill by loading it down with amendments embodying contentious proposals of wider import than questions of judicial organization. In piloting the Judicial Code through the House and Senate everything was subordinated to the attainment of its pivotal reform — the abolition of the circuit courts.

In minor changes the Code abounds. Some were the result

---

[171] *Ibid.* 313. Madison adverted to the existing situation as a " crying evil." *Ibid.* 314. Cullop of Indiana explained the purpose of the amendment as follows: " The amendment does not destroy the constitutional right of any citizen to have an investigation of his cause in a Federal court. . . . This simply gives the State courts the right to construe their own statutes before the Federal courts construe them in given cases, in order that the doctrine of the State court in the construction of a statute may be before the Federal court when it is called upon to review the statute." *Ibid.* 315. The amendment was agreed to without division. *Ibid.* 316. A short time previous Norris of Nebraska had proposed an amendment to prevent the issuance of injunctions against the collection of any state tax, but he withdrew it for future consideration under a later section of the bill. *Ibid.* 312.

[172] Act of June 18, 1910, § 17, 36 STAT. 557, subsequently amended by the Act of Mar. 4, 1913, 37 STAT. 1013.

[173] In the House Shirley especially protested against the acceptance of this compromise, asserting that the Overman Act was a step backward in that it permitted a restraining order still to be issued by a single judge and required three judges to set it aside, whereas it could formerly be set aside by one judge. Moon insisted that the restrictions of Section 266 were applicable to restraining orders as well as interlocutory injunctions. 46 CONG. REC. 4005.

of committee action prior to the introduction of the bill in Congress; others were the fruit of debate in the House or Senate; still others, of joint action in conference.[174] The significance of the Judicial Code, however, lies not in these. Since 1911 its three hundred and one sections have undergone much detailed revision; the process of amendment has greatly altered the face of the original act. But the long years of effort which culminated in the Judicial Code realized through it two durable results — the fusion of all *nisi prius* work in a single court of original jurisdiction through the eradication of an outworn system of circuit courts, and the substantial unification, in a comprehensive

---

[174] Among the more significant changes made by the committee were Section 18, providing for the designation of circuit judges to sit in district courts; Section 129, providing for appeals from interlocutory orders appointing a receiver; Sections 244, 245, and 247, assimilating review from the courts of Porto Rico, the territorial courts of Arizona and New Mexico, and the district court of Alaska, to review from the district courts; Section 254, dealing with the cost of printing the record; Section 256, clause 8, reënacting a provision that had mistakenly been repealed, giving the federal courts exclusive jurisdiction of suits against diplomatic and consular officials; Section 264, vesting in the district judge the power theretofore possessed by judges of circuit courts to issue injunctions; Section 287, increasing the number of peremptory challenges allowed the government. The main House amendments follow: (1) Section 20, which required a change of venue upon an affidavit filed by a party to a cause that the judge was disqualified by interest or bias. This was introduced by Cullop of Indiana and approved by the committee. It sought to make such a change of venue mandatory instead of discretionary. 46 CONG. REC. 320. It was debated at length before it was accepted. Upon the motion of Bennett of New York, it was further amended so that the same proceedings for a change of venue might be taken where the judge himself filed a certificate with the clerk that he deemed himself unable to proceed with absolute impartiality in the cause. *Ibid.* 2626–2630. In conference the Senate further amended it by requiring the party filing such affidavit to state that he did so in good faith. *Ibid.* 3998. See Berger *v.* United States, 255 U. S. 22 (1921). (2) Section 162, giving the Court of Claims jurisdiction to hear claims under the Act of Mar. 12, 1863, was proposed by Bartlett of Georgia and was adopted by a vote of 124 to 85. 46 CONG. REC. 2163–2167. (3) Section 218, increasing the salaries of the Supreme Court Justices was the contribution of Mann of Illinois. *Ibid.* 2617. (4) Sections 229 and 259, dealing with the distribution of reports and the travelling expenses of the judges, were also made on the floor of the House. In conference, at the instigation of the Senate conferees, the appellate jurisdiction of the circuit courts of appeals in copyright cases was made final; Section 240 was amended so as to leave no doubt of the Supreme Court's power to review by *certiorari* criminal cases in the circuit courts of appeals; and Section 182, giving the Supreme Court appellate jurisdiction of Indian litigation in the Court of Claims, was added as a new section. Other Senate and House amendments have already been noted.

code, of the scattered provisions relating to the business of the
federal courts. This was a creative achievement, although its
aims were limited and its details ephemeral. The Code is the
first attempt, since the general revision of 1874, to state in
ordered form the piecemeal changes wrought by forty years of
legislation affecting the power and procedure of the federal
courts.[175] It is the record of a successful endeavor to simplify
the maze of mysteries through which the practitioner in the federal courts had to guide his client's cause. Even more important, it is a systematic statement of the structural principles
defining the rôle of the federal courts in the American constitutional scheme. The shortcomings of this enterprise, combined
with the issues of a new decade, present the contemporary problems of federal judicial reform.

---

[175] The Judiciary Title (Title XIII of the Revised Statutes) embraces 563
sections as compared with the 301 sections of the Judicial Code. It includes
subjects such as fees, evidence, procedure, limitations, which are not dealt with
by the Judicial Code. An analysis of the various sections of the Code illustrates,
however, the extent to which it embodied legislation enacted since 1874. A
count, that considers the various clauses of Section 24 as separate sections, shows
the following summary: of sections drawn from the Revised Statutes or based
upon them, 156; of entirely new legislation since 1874, 96; of amendments made
to the bill during its passage through Congress, 20; of sections that drew from
various sources in summing up the existing law, 53.

Compare the remarks of the Attorney General, Sir Douglas Hogg, in piloting
through the Commons the 1925 revision of the laws of England relating to the
Supreme Court of Judicature (Act of July 31, 1925, c. 49, 15 & 16 Geo. V):

" The Statutes relating to the administration of justice in the English Court
of Judicature are spread over a series of years beginning as far back as Edward
III's reign and coming down to the present year, and for a long time past there
has been an increasing demand among those who practise in the Courts to have
the Statutes consolidated. Of course, that involves no alteration in the law, but
you would have it in one Statute, so that your law may be more easily and more
certainly ascertained. There are, it appears from the Schedule to the Bill, no
fewer than 105 Statutes which at present have to be consulted. In future, if
this becomes law, they will all be in one Statute." 186 Parl. Debates, 2632–2633.

CHAPTER IV
FEDERAL COURTS
OF
SPECIALIZED JURISDICTION

I

THE growing penetration of government into affairs, to counterbalance powerful economic forces, has called for increasing consideration of the means whereby governmental control may become effective. Perhaps the central juristic problem of our time is to harmonize " law in action " with " law in books." [1] The enormous legislative activity which began about a generation ago was concerned with intricate and technical issues. Old principles, like the common law of carriers, not only had to be adapted to new conditions, but new instruments had to be invented for the vindication of these old principles. The general doctrines governing public utilities were simple enough, but the subtlest difficulties were encountered in applying them. Problems of law became problems of administration. New instruments for expertness and precision were needed. Law had to meet the demands of an age of specialization.

To these requirements of a complex industrial society Congress had to respond in 1887, as soon as it began to exercise control over railroads. The Supreme Court itself recognized that without some such tribunal as the Interstate Commerce Commission, the public would be at the mercy of private enterprise.[2] When, a little later, the vast interests represented by

---

[1] See Pound, " Criminal Justice in the American City — A Summary," in CRIMINAL JUSTICE IN CLEVELAND, pt. VIII, 583–584. See Roscoe Pound, " The Limits of Effective Legal Action," 22 PA. BAR ASSN. REP. 221; " The Administrative Application of Legal Standards," 44 AM. BAR ASSN. REP. 445, 450 *et seq.*

[2] " An adjudication that Congress could not establish an administrative body with authority to investigate the subject of interstate commerce and with power to call witnesses before it, and to require the production of books, documents, and papers relating to that subject, would go far towards defeating the object for which the people of the United States placed commerce among the States under national control." Harlan, J., in Interstate Commerce Commission *v.* Brimson, 154 U. S. 447, 474 (1894).

claims to the public domain called for settlement by legal process, Congress again entrusted the task to a tribunal specially equipped to deal with this class of technical controversies.[3] These specialized tribunals, established to exercise control over successive fields of legislation entered by the Government, have in recent years multiplied to such an extent that the legal problems raised by them are in process of developing a distinct body of administrative law.[4]

But the same forces which have given rise to the new machinery and a new technique of administrative control have reacted upon the structure and scope of judicial control over these new tribunals. The very need for economy and expertness that led to the development of administrative agencies led to a demand for the same qualities on the part of courts sitting in judgment on these agencies. The American adaptation of the English judicial system, which in turn had its roots in the seventeenth century, was found inadequate for modern industrialized America. The momentum behind specialized administrative tribunals brought forth a demand for specialized courts. Thus, an important phase of the history of the federal judiciary deals with the movement for the establishment of tribunals whose business was to be limited to litigation arising from a restricted field of legislative control. As far back as the eighties, the special

---

[3] Act of Mar. 3, 1891, 26 STAT. 854, as amended by the Act of Feb. 21, 1893, 27 STAT. 470. " By article 8 of the treaty of Guadalupe-Hidalgo and article 5 of the Gadsden treaty, the property of Mexicans within the territory ceded by Mexico to the United States was to be 'inviolably respected,' and they and their heirs and grantees were to enjoy with respect to it 'guaranties equally ample as if the same belonged to citizens of the United States.' 9 Stat. 922, 929, 930; 10 Stat. 1031, 1035. While claimants under grants made by Mexico or the Spanish authorities prior to the cession had no right to a judicial determination of their claims, Congress, nevertheless, might provide therefor if it chose to do so. *Astiazaran* v. *Santa Rita Land and Mining Co.*, 148 U. S. 80. And it was for this purpose that the act of March 3, 1891, was passed, establishing the Court of Private Land Claims for the settlement of claims against the United States to lands 'derived by the United States from the Republic of Mexico, and now embraced within the Territories of New Mexico, Arizona, or Utah, or within the States of Nevada, Colorado, or Wyoming.' " United States *v.* Coe, 155 U. S. 76, 84 (1894). The Court's existence was continued until June 30, 1903, Act of April 28, 1902, 32 STAT. 120, 170.

[4] See Elihu Root, " Public Service by the Bar," 41 AM. BAR ASSN. REP. 355, 368; Review of Freund *et al.,* " Growth of American Administrative Law," by Felix Frankfurter, 37 HARV. L. REV. 638.

nature of patent litigation led to the sponsorship of a patent court.[5] From the nineties on we encounter similar proposals for an admiralty court,[6] a land court,[7] a pension court,[8] and other specialized courts.[9] Finally, strong influences led to the actual realization of the idea in the domain of customs and commerce.

2

The fact that the customs revenue for 1907 amounted to hundreds of millions of dollars [10] furnishes one of the clues to the movement culminating in the Court of Customs Appeals. For we are dealing with the collection of what was then the chief source of the Government's income. Undue delay, doubts and defeat in the collection of the country's revenue, due to inapt legal machinery, became a matter of first concern. But the significance of the administration of tariff laws is only meagerly told in terms of the huge amounts at stake. The whole fiscal system of the Government was involved because of the relation of other sources of taxation to income from imports.[11] Again,

---

[5] Bills to establish a patent court were introduced into Congress as early as Mar. 4, 1878, by Congressman Vance of North Carolina, and Mar. 11, 1878, by Senator Booth of California. 7 CONG. REC. 1457, 1627.

[6] See " The Supreme Court of the United States," 2 CENT. L. J. 2.

[7] On Dec. 5, 1906, Senator Hepburn introduced a bill to establish district land courts and an appellate land court. 41 CONG. REC. 51. He reintroduced the bill on Dec. 4, 1907. 42 *ibid.* 137. During the debate in the Senate on the Commerce Court provisions of the Mann-Elkins Act, Hepburn again offered his bill in the form of an amendment. 45 *ibid.* 2947.

[8] Congressman Miers of Indiana on Feb. 18, 1901, introduced a bill for a pension court. 34 CONG. REC. 2887. Similar bills were introduced in the House by Boernig on Dec. 17, 1901, and Feb. 1, 1902. 35 *ibid.* 370, 1219.

[9] Senator Clapp on Dec. 20, 1906, introduced a bill to establish a court for the settlement of claims by Indians against the United States. 41 *ibid.* 567.

[10] The customs receipts for 1907 were $332,233,362.70 out of a total of receipts from all sources (other than postal revenues) of $663,140,334.05; for 1908 customs receipts were $286,113,130.29 out of a total (other than postal revenues) of $601,126,118.53. REP. SEC. TREAS. FOR 1907, 1, 40; *ibid.* FOR 1908, 7. For 1925 customs receipts were only 14 per cent of the total. *Ibid.* FOR 1925, 8, 11.

[11] " In the making of a tariff bill the prime motive is taxation and the securing thereby of a revenue. Due largely to the business depression which followed the financial panic of 1907, the revenue from customs and other sources has decreased to such an extent that the expenditures for the current fiscal year will exceed the receipts by $100,000,000. It is imperative that such a deficit shall not continue, and the framers of the tariff bill must, of course, have in mind the total revenues likely to be produced by it and so arrange the duties as to secure an adequate income. Should it be impossible to do so by import

tariff legislation holds power of life and death over industries. In its repercussion the tariff vitally affects the balance between agricultural and industrial interests. But law means interpretation, and tariff laws especially present a confusing labyrinth. Tariff laws mean tariff law administration.[12]

Resort to an advanced type of administrative control in the enforcement of the tariff accompanied the overhauling of the tariff system by the McKinley Act. The Customs Administrative Act of 1890 [13] sought to add to ordinary judicial administration the sifting process of an administrative board specially suited to deal with the technical problems of classification of commodities and their valuation. While the Act allowed an appeal to the circuit courts, it was the expectation that the newly created Board of General Appraisers would largely divert from the courts litigation over tariff clauses. However, by allowing the introduction of new evidence before the circuit courts, the court proceedings turned into trials *de novo* and not reviews of the findings of the Board of Appraisers.[14] The new administrative machinery did not absorb the previous function of the courts; it served merely to provide another step in the chain of litigation. The Second Circuit, dealing with the vast imports through New York, was swamped with cases that were plain retrials of controversies before the Board.[15] It became common practice for

---

duties, new kinds of taxation must be adopted, and among these I recommend a graduated inheritance tax as correct in principle and as certain and easy of collection." Inaugural Address of President Taft, March 4, 1909, 16 MESSAGES AND PAPERS OF THE PRESIDENTS, 7370.

[12] " While with the country at large the Congress is popularly believed the determinative body of tariff rates and schedules, as a matter of fact the courts and the customs administrative officers finally, in a great number if not great majority of cases, determine these matters. The Dingley tariff law passed Congress in July, 1897. By reason of interpretation and construction of its provisions whole schedules and numerous rates have been greatly changed from the supposed, if not manifest, purpose of Congress. These changes frequently net 10 per cent, 15 per cent, and sometimes greater differences. . . . That administration and judicial construction of a tariff law determine its character has been the history of every such law." Report of the Board of Appraisers to the Subcommittee of the Senate Finance Committee, 44 CONG. REC. 4192.

[13] Act of June 10, 1890, § 12, 26 STAT. 131, 136.

[14] See Flint in the Senate on July 7, 1909, 44 CONG. REC. 4203.

[15] The Second Circuit absorbed 85 per cent of the customs litigation. 44 CONG. REC. 4194. From May 1, 1908, to April 30, 1909, 207 appeals were taken from the Board of General Appraisers to the Southern District of New York,

importers to withhold testimony until the case reached the courts.[16]   Resort to the administrative method brought, not relief through economical and expert disposition of technical litigation, but new delays, waste, and confusion.[17]   Under this system four and a half years were consumed while litigation travelled at a snail's pace towards a final decision.[18]   When the demand for relief became importunate in 1908, Congress passed palliative legislation, whereby cases in the circuit court were heard on the record of the proceedings before the Board of Appraisers and appeals to the circuit courts of appeals were restricted.[19] But a more drastic solution of the problem through the withdrawal of this whole field of litigation from the regular courts appears in Congress as early as 1906.   It was proposed at that time to take away all jurisdiction in customs cases from the regular federal courts and center it in a single court exclusively devoted to this subject matter.[20]   Two years later a sub-committee

---

330 appeals were disposed of, and 59 customs cases were carried to the Second Circuit Court of Appeals. *Ibid.* 4186.

16 " This case is another illustration of the faulty procedure in this class of cases in permitting the parties objecting to partially present their case before the Board of General Appraisers, and, after losing there, then wakening up to the necessity of properly presenting it, and producing the evidence before the court which could have as easily been submitted to the Board of General Appraisers." Holland, J., in United States *v.* Hempstead & Son, 159 Fed. 290, 291 (C. C. E. D. Pa., 1908). A collection of 26 cases where the Board of Appraisers was reversed by the court because of the introduction of additional testimony, can be found in 44 CONG. REC. 4203.

17 The following summary shows the amount of customs litigation in the federal courts:

	Circuit Courts		Circuit Courts of Appeals		Supreme Court
	Argued	Not Argued	Argued	Not Argued	
1905	154	131	36	12	1
1906	94	292	50	18	3
1907	121	161	44	15	5
1908	107	737	50	10	1

See 44 CONG. REC. 4216. That the movement for relief was directed primarily against the lower courts and not the Supreme Court is evidenced from the fact that from 1890 to 1908 the Supreme Court had passed upon only 15 appeals from the Board of General Appraisers. *Ibid.* 4196.

18 *Ibid.* 4193. The same estimate is made by Judge Somerville in a letter to Attorney General Wickersham on May 22, 1909. *Ibid.* 4200.

19 Act of May 27, 1908, § 2, 35 STAT. 403, 404, as to which see REP. SEC. TREAS. FOR 1908, 64.

20 On May 16, 1906, Congressman Needham introduced a bill to create a court of customs appeals. 40 CONG. REC. 6995. He reintroduced this bill on Dec. 2, 1907, and again on April 22, 1909. 42 *ibid.* 23; 44 *ibid.* 1480.

of the Senate Finance Committee made a thorough inquiry into tariff administration in anticipation of comprehensive tariff legislation made inevitable by the campaign of 1908.[21] Investigation disclosed great losses of revenue through the existing system of customs administration which permitted of extensive frauds, fatal delays, costly conflicts in the decisions of the circuit courts of appeals. The fiscal system of the Government was seriously affected by ill-adapted legal machinery. But the courts also suffered through a volume of business whose nature was outside of their usual province of experience, and which they did not effectively discharge. It became in fact a serious obstruction to the disposition of their traditional litigation. The courts needed relief as much as the Government.

A proposal which in 1906 never came out of committee became in 1909 part of the Payne-Aldrich Act.[22] Senator Aldrich sponsored the measure [23] and secured its adoption in the Senate over a strong opposition led by Senators Borah,[24] Cummins,[25] and Dolliver.[26] A specialized court in the federal judicial system encountered the fear of novelty. Such a court, it was urged, would acquire the vices of specialization — narrowness and partiality.[27] The inadequacy of the existing situation, contended Senator Borah, was due not a little to defects in legislation.[28]

---

[21] This sub-committee consisted of Taliaferro of Florida, Bailey of Texas, Money of Mississippi, Hopkins of Illinois, Platt of New York, Hansbrough of North Dakota, and Burrows of Michigan. 44 CONG. REC. 4192.

[22] Act of Aug. 5, 1909, § 29, 36 STAT. 11, 105. See JUDICIAL CODE, 188-199.

[23] He introduced it as an amendment to Section 5 of the bill. 44 CONG. REC. 1656.

[24] Borah's opposition to the measure led him, during the next session of the Senate, to introduce a bill on Mar. 1, 1910, to repeal the provision of the Payne-Aldrich Act establishing the Court of Customs Appeals. 45 *ibid.* 2541.

[25] 44 *ibid.* 4185. Senator Cummins' opposition to the Court has continued. See note 33, *infra.*

[26] 44 *ibid.* 4187.

[27] *Ibid.* 4185.

[28] " Mr. President, the fact is that for the last five or six years there has been growing up in this country a tendency to regard the federal court as a kind of emergency hospital for defective legislation. . . . There has been a tendency and a disposition upon the part of the Government to approach the federal courts by telegrams and letters and private communications, and try cases in that way. . . . If there has been an unfortunate use of language in our statutes, it can be remedied here; but it certainly ought not to be remedied by creating a court which will interpret the law, not as it is written, but as some one supposes it was written." 44 CONG. REC. 4191.

Vigorous objection also was taken to dealing with such an important change in the federal judicial system in the form of a tariff law rather than as an independent project.[29] But Senator Aldrich carried the day by a vote of 50 to 26.[30] The court also survived the conference committee,[31] which, however, changed its seat from New York to Washington.[32] In this form the Court of Customs Appeals came into being as part of the Act of August 5, 1909. The activities of this court divert from the general stream of professional interest. But if one may judge from the silent acquiescence in its performance and the absence of all attempts to alter what was wrought by the Act of 1909, the Customs Court has justified its creation.[33]

---

[29] See Dolliver in the Senate on July 7, 1909, 44 Cong. Rec. 4189.

[30] 44 Cong. Rec. 4225.

[31] The opposition on the part of the House conferees was apparently not strong. *Ibid.* 4630.

[32] Other changes were also effected. Instead of having its sessions at stated cities, sittings of the Court were to be held within the several judicial circuits at such places as the Court from time to time might designate. Provisos as to the disposition of pending cases were also added. The clerk's office was changed from New York to Washington. House Report, No. 20, 61st Cong., 1st Sess., Ser. No. 5591; Sen. Doc., Nos. 91 and 93, 61st Cong., 2nd Sess., Ser. No. 5576. The conference report was accepted, in the House by a vote of 195 to 183, and in the Senate by a vote of 47 to 31. 44 Cong. Rec. 4755, 4949. The Act of Aug. 5, 1909, contained no provision for appeals to the Supreme Court. Even *certiorari* would not lie to the Court of Customs Appeals. See Payne in the House on July 31, 1909, 44 Cong. Rec. 4698. A limited appellate jurisdiction was conferred upon the Supreme Court by the Act of Aug. 22, 1914, 38 Stat. 703. The bills that culminated in this Act were introduced by Webb in the House on June 9, 1914, and by Overman in the Senate on July 16, 1914. 51 Cong. Rec. 10125, 12198. The question of the 5 per cent discount or drawback on imports in American bottoms was then pending before the Court of Customs Appeals. The Attorney General had ruled that this provision was void because in violation of treaty obligations. Importers had protested against the failure to give this reduction, and claims totalling between ten and twelve million dollars had already accumulated against the Government. It was thus emergency legislation that desired to get a decision of this question from the Supreme Court. *Ibid.* 13986–7. See Five Per Cent Discount Cases, 243 U. S. 97 (1917). As a result of this Act an average of about two cases reaches the Supreme Court yearly from the Court of Customs Appeals.

[33] Senator Cummins, however, was of a different opinion. "Senator Cummins. We have nine judges sitting in various parts of the country with the Board of Appraisers, who ought to be regarded as a court, and I suppose are technically a court. I have never seen any use for the Court of Customs Appeals." Hearing before a Subcommittee of Senate Committee on Judiciary, 68th Cong., 1st Sess., on S. 2060 and S. 2061 (Feb. 2, 1924), p. 39.

3

The regulation of railways and the other great national utilities has always presented subtler complexities than tariff administration and has aroused correspondingly fiercer controversy. From the very beginning of federal railroad regulation the measure of control allotted to the courts has, perhaps, presented the most contentious issue. In the field of utility regulation not only the vast clash of interests behind railroad ownership, shippers, and the general public has to be resolved; unlike customs cases, interstate commerce litigation is also alive with prickly conflicts between state and national powers. The judiciary thus intervenes at highly sensitized regions in the economic and political life of the nation. Courts in this domain are the ultimate arbiters of what is one form of the taxing power of the country. By sanctioning or setting aside the rate determination of the Interstate Commerce Commission they may affect decisively the great agricultural territory of the Northwest, may mitigate or intensify New England's industrial dependence upon the coal-producing states, determine the competitive range between the intermountain country and the Pacific Coast. Litigation involving railroad valuation may affect generations of security holders and the social life of millions. Again, in adjusting the conflicting claims of the Federal Government and the states to control, the courts are involved in a perennial problem of American politics. The ultimate sources of judicial power in all these matters are the commerce and due process clauses of the Constitution, and the application of these clauses turns fundamentally not upon any settled and easily applied legal rules but upon judgments of policy resting on an understanding of economic and industrial facts.[34]

The establishment of the Commerce Court is part and parcel of the history of federal utility regulation beginning with Roosevelt's accession to the presidency. During the decade following 1901 enforcement of the Interstate Commerce Act is energized,

---

[34] See Henry W. Biklé, "Judicial Determination of Questions of Fact Affecting the Constitutional Validity of Legislative Action," 38 HARV. L. REV. 6; Felix Frankfurter and James M. Landis, "The Compact Clause of the Constitution," 34 YALE L. J. 685, 718; Walter F. Willcox, "Need of Social Statistics As an Aid to the Courts," 47 AM. L. REV. 259.

and the scope of federal control is greatly extended. The Government and the country were preoccupied with the so-called railroad problem. It is the constant subject of presidential utterances, gives rise to continuous debate in Congress, leads to major legislative enactments and litigations of the first order in the Supreme Court. This is the period of Attorneys General Knox, Moody, Bonaparte, and Wickersham, and their proceedings against railroads; of notable railway debates in the Senate participated in by Beveridge, Borah, Cummins, Dolliver, La Follette, Newlands, Spooner, and in the House by Adamson, Esch, Mann, and Townsend; of legislative accomplishments like the Elkins Act,[35] the Hepburn Act,[36] the Mann-Elkins Act;[37] of decisions like *Interstate Commerce Commission* v. *Baird*,[38] *New York, New Haven & Hartford R. R.* v. *Interstate Commerce Commission*,[39] *Texas & Pacific R. R.* v. *Abilene Cotton Oil Co.*,[40] the *Pipe Line Cases*.[41]

The relation of the Interstate Commerce Commission to the courts has been one of the most intractable problems since the Federal Government embarked upon utility regulation. Frequent reversals of the Commission's orders by the courts in the earlier days, the slow pace of customary court procedure in a domain of government where promptness is vital, conflicts in court decisions begetting territorial diversity where unified treatment of a problem is demanded, nullification by a single judge, even temporarily, of legislative or administrative action affecting whole sections of the country, these and like difficulties and irritations led to successive measures dealing with judicial review under the Interstate Commerce Acts. One aspect of this movement expressed itself vigorously in an effort to curb the courts; a totally different approach found the clue to the problem in the practical limitation of courts of general jurisdiction, with judges having only general experience, to deal with the peculiarly technical transportation issues which underlie this type of litigation. The solution for handling effectively a specialized class of controversies was sought in a specialized tribunal.

---

[35] Act of Feb. 19, 1903, 32 STAT. 847.
[36] Act of June 29, 1906, 34 STAT. 584.
[37] Act of June 18, 1910, 36 STAT. 539.
[38] 194 U. S. 25 (1904).

[39] 200 U. S. 361 (1906).
[40] 204 U. S. 426 (1907).
[41] 234 U. S. 548 (1914).

As early as 1893 organizations of shippers urged the creation of a special court of commerce for each judicial district.[42] In 1905 the proposal appeared in Congress as a procedural complement to a grant of rate-fixing powers upon the Interstate Commerce Commission. These general aims were embodied in two bills, radically different in details, sponsored in the House by Hearst of New York,[43] and Townsend of Michigan.[44] Save for its inclusion of suits for damages under the Interstate Commerce and Elkins Acts, the Townsend measure was essentially similar to the provision of the Mann-Elkins Act of 1910 which transferred the commerce jurisdiction of the circuit courts to a single court.[45] The Hearst bill aimed at extensive control of the whole field of interstate commerce.[46] It provided for a court of three judges with broad equity powers, with final jurisdiction save where the Supreme Court or the new court deemed a constitutional question was raised.[47] In effect the life of railroad legislation was to be entrusted to three judges. The whole subject was considered by the House Committee on Interstate and Foreign Commerce [48] which, on January 31, 1905, reported the Esch-Townsend bill embodying the Townsend proposal for a court of transportation.[49]

---

[42] Mann in the House on Sept. 8, 1913, 50 CONG. REC. 4541.

[43] On Mar. 11, 1904, Feb. 20, 1905, and Dec. 4, 1905, measures of this nature were introduced by Hearst. 38 CONG. REC. 3158; 39 *ibid.* 2960; 40 *ibid.* 55.

[44] 39 *ibid.* 952 (Jan. 16, 1905). The bill was again introduced by Townsend on Dec. 6, 1905. 40 *ibid.* 200. On Jan. 21, 1905, Hepburn had also introduced in the House a bill to create a commerce court. 39 *ibid.* 1215, 2198.

[45] *Ibid.* 2197.

[46] The bill appears in HOUSE REPORT, No. 4093, 58th Cong., 3rd Sess., Ser. No. 4762.

[47] Review in the Supreme Court was also limited to a determination of the constitutional question. The proposed court of transportation was given jurisdiction to review and enforce all orders of the Commission, including orders for the filing and publication of fares and charges, of suits brought by the Commission under Section 3 of the Elkins Act, and of proceedings to aid in the production of testimony before the Commission. It could suspend orders of the Commission pending review whenever it deemed them " clearly unjust, unreasonable, or unlawful."

[48] HOUSE REPORT, No. 4093, 58th Cong., 3rd Sess., Ser. No. 4762. The committee had under consideration 23 bills designed to give the Commission more power and to provide for expeditious determination upon its rulings.

[49] 39 CONG REC. 1662. This Act was largely drafted by Assistant Attorney General William A. Day under the direction of Attorney General Moody and at the suggestion of President Roosevelt. In committee it was combined with a measure introduced by Congressman Esch. See 48 CONG. REC. 7959.

Expedition in railroad litigation was deemed the chief objective.[50] Under the then Cannon rules amendments from the floor of the House were barred and cloture was strict. The opposition, therefore, had to choose between the Townsend bill and the Davey bill,[51] a Democratic substitute opposed to the principle of a special court. The Esch-Townsend bill passed the House,[52] but it never emerged from a Senate Committee. The effort for such concentrated jurisdiction was premature, as is evidenced by the limited scope of railroad legislation the following year. The Hepburn Act,[53] behind which was marshalled the full power of the Roosevelt Administration at its height, dropped the court provisions and confined " action to the recommendations of the President as contained in his annual messages of 1904 and 1905." [54] Still, in one form or another, the idea was kept alive in the House during succeeding years.[55] It was pushed to fruition by President Taft who, to a unique degree among Presidents, was interested in the effective working of the judicial machinery and conversant with the details of judicial administration. The Court of Customs Appeals was for him a controlling precedent in providing for court review under the Interstate Commerce Acts. In a special message to Congress he urged that " reasons precisely analogous to those which induced the Congress to create the Court of Customs Appeals " called for the establishment of a United States Commerce Court.[56]

President Taft's recommendation was promptly embodied in a number of separate bills,[57] and was finally incorporated in a

---

[50] Burke from the Committee on Feb. 8, 1905: " We believed, under all the circumstances and the testimony, that some separate tribunal must be created in order to expedite the findings of the Commission and to bring speedy relief. Looking at the experience which the Commission has had in the past under the existing interstate-commerce act, we found that its efforts were thwarted from year to year by processes and appeals in the existing Federal courts." 39 CONG. REC. 2083.

[51] This bill is fully set forth in 39 CONG. REC. 2191.

[52] The Davey bill was rejected by a vote of 187 to 151, and the Esch-Townsend bill was passed by a vote of 326 to 17. *Ibid.* 2205.

[53] 34 STAT. 584.

[54] HOUSE REPORT, No. 591, 59th Cong., 1st Sess., Ser. No. 4906, p. 3.

[55] Townsend and Hearst continued to bring their bills to the attention of Congress. See notes 43 and 44, *supra.*

[56] Message of Jan. 7, 1910, 45 CONG. REC. 378, 379.

[57] In the Senate by Elkins on Jan. 11, 1910, 45 CONG. REC. 501. In the

bill dealing comprehensively with other items of the Administration program on railway regulation. As such it was introduced in the Senate by Senator Stephen B. Elkins on February 25, 1910.[58] The commerce court proposal at once drew the fire of the then " insurgent "[59] group in the Senate. Senators Cummins, Clapp, and Newlands, representing this wing of the Republican majority, opposed it in a minority report of the Senate Committee on Interstate Commerce.[60] The gravamen of their objection furnishes the keynote of the opposition during the debate of the following five months and forecasts the fate of the court. It was feared that the bent of mind and the environment of the judges selected for such a court would incline them towards the railroads and against the public interest, in the dramatic conflict of " public " against " railroads," in terms of which the problem of railroad control was conceived. " We merely remind the Senate," reported the minority, " of the tremendous influences that will inevitably surround the selection of such a tribunal."[61]

Cummins led the fight on the floor of the Senate.[62] Through a variety of parliamentary manoeuvres, he sought the elimination of the clauses establishing a commerce court from the committee's bill.[63] He rang all the changes on his fear that such a court would fall under subversive influences.[64] His efforts to de-

House by Parker of New Jersey (by request) on Jan. 18, 1910; by Townsend of Michigan on Feb. 17, 1910, and Mar. 24, 1910. *Ibid.* 773, 2058, 3734.

[58] *Ibid.* 2379.

[59] See A. N. Holcombe, " Insurgents in Congress," 2 Cycl. of Am. Gov. 193.

[60] See 45 Cong. Rec. 2817; Sen. Rep., No. 355, 61st Cong., 2nd Sess., Ser. No. 5583.

[61] 45 Cong. Rec. 2821.

[62] On Mar. 15, 1910, Senator Cummins opened fire on the bill and continued through Mar. 16, 17, 18, and 19. *Ibid.* 3341–3386, 3463–3483.

[63] On May 16, 1910, Cummins, after the defeat of his amendment seeking to abolish the Court, proposed an amendment that the Court should consist of three judges appointed for three years, which was defeated by a vote of 35 to 25. *Ibid.* 6345–6346. On the following day he offered an amendment to make the Interstate Commerce Commission instead of the United States defendant in appeals from orders of the Commission. *Ibid.* 6389. Smith of Michigan amended the Cummins amendment by providing that the Commission upon its own motion might also appear as defendant. This was adopted by a vote of 40 to 23. *Ibid.* 6445–6462.

[64] " I do know that any judicial tribunal appointed or selected for the purpose only of adjusting or determining disputes between the great railway com-

feat the court failed by a vote of 37 to 28.[65] Senator Beveridge labored against the court by flank movements of obstruction.[66] Later La Follette unsuccessfully moved a number of restrictive amendments.[67] Borah and Hepburn of Idaho voiced the fears of shippers as well as the general objection to the innovating tendency towards specialized courts.[68] The Democrats under the

---

panies of the country and the people of the country will be subjected to that suspicion which naturally arises in the human heart. You can not subdue it; you can not overcome it." Cummins on Mar. 18, 1910, 45 CONG. REC. 3348. To like effect was Senator Shively: " A special court is apt to become the subject of special distrust, whatever may be the character of the judges. The wide variety of subject-matter passing through the court of general jurisdiction in itself assures public confidence in the court and tends to correct any possible special bias in the court itself. The mighty tide of human interests involved in railway interstate commerce should never be separated and set apart from other interstate interests and made the subject of special jurisdiction." *Ibid.* 7365. Clapp of Minnesota also objected to the centralizing nature of a specialized court for commerce and pointed out the inconvenience it would inflict upon shippers who, in order to intervene, would have to travel to Washington. *Ibid.* 6393.

[65] *Ibid.* 6342.

[66] Senator Beveridge's parliamentary skill was frequently utilized to help the " insurgent " attack.

[67] On June 1, 1910, La Follette's amendment for the physical valuation of the carriers' properties was defeated by a vote of 30 to 25. *Ibid.* 7196. On June 3 La Follette's amendment to prohibit any one holding official relation to a carrier or owning the stocks and bonds of a carrier or in any manner pecuniarily interested from becoming a judge of the Commerce Court was defeated by a vote of 32 to 29. *Ibid.* 7346–7347. La Follette also proposed an amendment providing that the designation of judges for the Commerce Court should be by the entire membership of the Supreme Court instead of, as provided in the bill, by the Chief Justice alone. *Ibid.* 7347. Senator Carter replied that John Jay, Marshall, and the other Chief Justices " might well turn in their graves in contemplation of this the first reflection proposed to be cast in the legislative halls of the United States upon the Chief Justices of this and succeeding times." *Ibid.* 7348. The future biographer of Marshall, Senator Beveridge, gleefully countered by saying that it had cast no reflection upon the President to transfer the designation of these judges from him to the Chief Justice and consequently La Follette's proposed transfer could be no reflection upon the Chief Justice. Senator Gore added: " This is a practical matter of government and should be dealt with in a practical way. . . . I agree with Thomas Jefferson when he said that judges are as honest as other men, and not more so. Sir, that is the beginning and the end of the true estimate of judges. . . . I apprehend that if a select court had been provided to try cases arising under the fugitive slave law, Senators here would have objected to the Chief Justice then presiding designating the judges to serve upon that court." La Follette's amendment was defeated by a vote of 39 to 18. *Ibid.* 7348–7351.

[68] Borah inveighed against a specialized court as " engrafting upon it [the judicial system] a principle in utter violation of the principles upon which the fathers built it." *Ibid.* 7364.

lead of Senator Bacon of Georgia supported the " insurgents." [69] The fate of this proposal would have been doubtful in the Senate had it been considered as an independent bill. As part of the Administration measure [70] on interstate commerce it was purposely tied up with legislation to which all parties were committed and its rejection would have jeopardized important amendments to the Interstate Commerce Act. On a final vote [71] of the

---

[69] On April 7, 1910, Bacon, by amendment, sought to vest the jurisdiction then possessed by the circuit courts over the Interstate Commerce Commission in the circuit courts of appeals. *Ibid.* 4366, 6342. It was defeated without division. *Ibid.* 6345. On June 3 Bacon moved to strike out the Commerce Court provisions from the bill, questioning the " constitutionality of an important and an essential feature of that court," and because of " the great injustice which is to be done in the disorganization and in the mutilation of our present judicial system." *Ibid.* 7359. Contending that the powers of a circuit judge were the powers of the circuit court, he claimed that the assignment of circuit judges to the Commerce Court for five years deprived them of their circuit powers and thus forced them to give up their offices for these five years and assume other offices. If Congress thus had the right to deprive a judge of his office for five years, they had the right to deprive him of it for all time. The motion was defeated by a vote of 38 to 25. *Ibid.* 7365. This objection to the constitutionality of the bill was renewed during the debate on the acceptance of the conference report. *Ibid.* 8380.

[70] The program of the Administration for interstate commerce legislation was formulated, under the President's immediate stimulus, by Attorney General Wickersham, Secretary Nagel, Solicitor General Bowers, Chairman Knapp and Commissioner Prouty of the Interstate Commerce Commission, and Congressman Townsend. They drafted a tentative bill which, upon report to and approval by the President, was introduced in Congress. See 48 Cong. Rec. 7959. " With the Committees of both Houses the Attorney General put himself in touch, and as a result of conferences, he rewrote many sections of the measure. When it was finally in satisfactory form, it was reported by the Senate Committee on March 28, without amendment, and without serious Committee consideration. The House Committee amended it radically before reporting it on March 24." Frank H. Dixon, " The Mann-Elkins Act," 24 Quart. J. Econ. 593, 594. " The commerce court is a mere incident to the bill, and finds a place in the bill because of the President's enthusiasm for speedy justice." Kennedy of Ohio in the House on April 19, 1910, 45 Cong. Rec. 5002.

[71] The changes that were effected by the Senate in the Commerce Court provisions of the bill are summarized by La Follette. As introduced the bill " created a new court, open to the railroads, to enjoin the orders of the Interstate Commerce Commission, and it denied the public admission to that court upon the same terms. 2. It attempted to create in the commerce court the broad power to review and set aside the findings of the commission upon grounds other than those involving jurisdiction and constitutional questions. 3. It provided that a judge of the court of commerce upon an *ex parte* showing, and without any notice whatever to the commission, could issue a temporary injunction restraining the enforcement of the commission's order reducing rates. 4. It pro-

entire bill only twelve Senators were recorded in the negative.[72]

The proposal went through the same fire in the House.[73] The debate, of course, was much more meager than in the Senate, but the grounds of opposition and the arguments in support paralleled those of the Senate. As in the Senate " insurgent " Republicans led by Lenroot of Wisconsin joined the Democrats [74] led

---

vided no appeal from an interlocutory order or decree by the court of commerce granting or continuing an injunction restraining the enforcement of orders of the Interstate Commerce Commission." The bill had been " amended by providing that the proposed law shall not be construed as enlarging the jurisdiction now possessed by the courts to review and set aside the orders of the commission. 2. It has been amended by a provision which permits appeals to the Supreme Court from interlocutory orders by the court of commerce. . . . 4. It has been amended by requiring five days' notice to the commission and opportunity for hearing before a temporary restraining order shall be issued in any case by the court of commerce." 45 CONG. REC. 7373. The importance of these amendments is revealed by the subsequent history of the Commerce Court.

[72] *Ibid.* 7375.

[73] The bill was introduced by Townsend of Michigan on Jan. 10, 1910, and reported from the Committee on Interstate and Foreign Commerce by Mann on April 1, 1910. *Ibid.* 497, 4146; HOUSE REPORT, No. 923, 61st Cong., 2nd Sess., Ser. No. 5712. It was given the privileged status of an appropriation bill and the debate was opened on April 12. 45 CONG. REC. 4240–4242, 4571. Mann adverted to the delay in the circuit courts and the injurious reaction of such delay upon shippers as the chief reason for establishing a Commerce Court. *Ibid.* 4573.

[74] *Ibid.* 4947. On April 26 Lenroot moved La Follette's proposal for the designation of the judges by the Supreme Court Justices. *Ibid.* 5424. Clark of Missouri had already objected to the designation of these judges by the Chief Justice in that the latter could only be held responsible through the cumbersome process of impeachment. *Ibid.* 5410. Lenroot proposed that the first designation of judges should be by the Supreme Court instead of by the President. Both amendments were adopted by votes of 143 to 118 and 135 to 131. *Ibid.* 5426. Lenroot also made a proposal to permit appeals from interlocutory orders granting or continuing an injunction restraining the enforcement of the orders of the Interstate Commerce Commission. Mann opposed it as being against the bill's expressed policy of expedition. Upon division the vote standing at 124 to 123, tellers were ordered and the amendment was rejected by a vote of 135 to 134. *Ibid.* 5428. Hubbard of Iowa also was a strong opponent of the Court. He objected to the increased control that it gave courts over the Interstate Commerce Commission. On his motion to strike out the entire section, the vote stood at 131 ayes to 130 noes when Chairman Scott voted in the negative and defeated it. Tellers being ordered the vote stood 140 ayes to 139 noes when the chair again voted in the negative. *Ibid.* 5427. Cary of Wisconsin then sought to transfer the jurisdiction of the circuit courts in commerce cases to the circuit courts of appeals, but this was defeated by a vote of 133 to 117. *Ibid.* 5427. Another energetic opponent was Lindbergh of Minnesota who considered the proposed Court "progressive, perhaps, in theory, but . . . reactionary in practice." *Ibid.* 5175. He continued: " The courts here in Washington do not,

by Adamson of Georgia.[75] The recurring argument in opposition was perhaps best put by Hardy of Texas:

" Environments affect us all. Our opinions gradually take a tinge from our association. I do not know that this amounts to very much, but when you get your court set aside for the trial of one class of cases only, with the representatives of the United States, far removed from the people, upon one side, and the representatives of the great railroads and other corporations immediately and vitally interested on the other, after a while your impartial judge begins to see things in a little different light from what he did before." [76]

In the House the. Administration prevailed by the narrowest margin, that is, the casting vote of the Chairman while the measure was in the Committee of the Whole.[77] On a final vote on the entire bill in the House as in the Senate the other provisions of the Mann-Elkins Act easily carried the court feature by a vote of 201 to 126.[78] When the bill got into conference,[79] on the many differences between Senate and House,[80] a vain effort

---

it seems to me, construe the laws and acts liberally in favor of the people, but more commonly resolve doubts in favor of the special interests. . . . When the court divides five to four on a great question like that involved in that decision [Pollock *v.* Farmers' Loan and Trust Co., 157 U. S. 429 (1895)], it is easy to understand that the life environments of the judges sitting practically determine results." *Ibid.* 5176.

[75] 45 CONG. REC. 4711–4725. Richardson of Alabama also denied that there was any necessity for relieving the circuit courts of this jurisdiction, and pointed to the additional expense that a Commerce Court would entail. *Ibid.* 4824–4852. Sims of Tennessee added his protest: " If we begin with this idea of creating special courts at the demand of every special interest, what is to become of our judicial system that has been built up under the Constitution and the laws of Congress. . . ? " *Ibid.* 4838. Among other Democratic opponents were Bartlett of Georgia, Hobson of Alabama, Macon of Georgia, and Sulzer of New York. The latter, however, proposed that the court be constituted by three instead of five judges and that its decisions should be final in all save constitutional questions. *Ibid.* 5418. Adamson, just before the final vote was taken, moved to recommit the bill with instructions to strike out the sections dealing with the Commerce Court. The motion was rejected by a vote of 176 to 157. *Ibid.* 6032.

[76] *Ibid.* 5162.

[77] See note 35, *supra*.

[78] 45 CONG. REC. 6033.

[79] The Senate conferees were Elkins, Aldrich, and Foster. Mann, Wanger, and Adamson represented the House. *Ibid.* 7564. Newlands was later named in place of Foster. *Ibid.* 8148.

[80] The bill as reported to the Senate, as passed by the Senate, as passed by

was once more made to eliminate the court provisions.[81]   But on June 18, 1910, the bill establishing the United States Commerce Court became law.[82]

4

The enterprise was launched in unfavorable winds.   It early encountered a heavy sea.   The creation of the Court was responsive neither to the eager desires of a majority opinion in Congress nor to the pressure of professional judgment.[83]   It thus started out without the powerful backing of widespread political or professional goodwill.   Moreover, it was ushered into existence at a time when the steady resort to the injunction in controversies of public concern was turned into an intense issue of party politics.   The aggressiveness of Roosevelt's policies partly derived from, and partly stimulated, new economic alignments, and the courts were inevitably called upon to act as arbiters between their conflicting demands.   The issues were bound to arouse the heat of politics.   Popular thought and feeling became impatient of what to them seemed the intrusion of the courts into political conflicts.   To the popular imagination the courts in these matters were obstructions to the tide of social progress.[84]

---

the House, is printed in three parallel columns in SEN. DOC., No. 606, 61st Cong., 2nd Sess., Ser. No. 5653, 45 CONG. REC. 7446.

[81] Newlands, who had been appointed to the conference committee in place of Foster, asserted that because of his dissentient views he had been excluded from participation in the proceedings.   See 45 CONG. REC. 8148.

[82] 36 STAT. 539.

[83] Borah in the Senate on Oct. 3, 1913, 50 CONG. REC. 5427.   Despite the fact that the proposal for a commerce court was for years pending in Congress, it evoked no comment from the legal profession.   Legal periodicals and bar association reports are barren, save for negligible descriptive articles.   Two contemporary articles by economists are however, to be noted.   See William Q. Rysley, " Present Problems in Railway Regulation," 27 POL. SCI. QUART. 428; Frank H. Dixon, " The Mann-Elkins Act, Amending the Act to Regulate Commerce," 24 QUART J. ECON. 593.   A complete bibliography appears in Hearing before Subcommittee of Senate Committee on Appropriations on H. R. 26680, Jan. 6, 1913, pp. 59–64.

[84] " . . . courts are less and less competent to formulate rules for new relations which require regulation.   They have the experience of the past.   But they do not have the facts of the present.   They have but one case before them, to be decided upon the principles of the past, the equities of the one situation, and the prejudices which the individualism of common law institutional writers, the dogmas learned in a college course in economics, and habitual association with

The railroad problem furnished a dominant economic issue. It cut across party lines. Demand for increasing governmental control was voiced by both party platforms in the campaign of 1904, although in each party there were varying shades of opinion concerning the proper relation of railroads and government. The legislation which eventuated had all the scars of compromise. What was achieved on the statute books had still to be given validity and meaning by the courts. The Hepburn Act of 1906, which first gave the Interstate Commerce Commission the power to make rates, triumphed none too easily in its passage through Congress over resourceful interests still nurtured in *laissez faire*. The Mann-Elkins Act of 1910 somewhat invigorated the Hepburn Act, but it took several years before the enlarged powers of the Interstate Commerce Commission, sought to be achieved by this legislation made themselves felt.[85]

---

the business and professional class, must inevitably produce. It is a sound instinct in the community that objects to the settlement of questions of the highest social import in private litigations between John Doe and Richard Doe. It is a sound instinct that objects to an agricultural view of industrial legislation. Judicial law-making for sheer lack of means to get at the real situation, operates unjustly and inequitably in a complex social organization. . . . Courts are fond of saying that they apply old principles to new situations. But at times they must apply new principles to situations both old and new. The new principles are in legislation. The old principles are in common law. The former are as much to be respected and made effective as the latter — probably more so as our legislation improves. The public cannot be relied upon permanently to tolerate judicial obstruction or nullification of the social policies to which more and more it is compelled to be committed." Roscoe Pound, " Common Law and Legislation," 21 HARV. L. REV. 383, 403–4, 406–7. " Courts continued to ignore newly arisen social needs. They applied complacently 18th century conceptions of the liberty of the individual and of the sacredness of private property. Early 19th century scientific half-truths, like ' The survival of the fittest,' which translated into practice meant ' The devil take the hindmost,' were erected by judicial sanction into a moral law. When statutes giving expression to the new social spirit were clearly constitutional, judges, imbued with the relentless spirit of individualism, often construed them away. . . . In the course of relatively few years hundreds of statutes which embodied attempts (often very crude) to adjust legal rights to the demands of social justice were nullified by the courts, on the grounds that the statutes violated the constitutional guaranties of liberty and property. Small wonder that there arose a clamor for the recall of judges and judicial decisions and that demand was made for amendment of the constitutions and even for their complete abolition. The assaults upon courts and constitutions culminated in 1912." Louis D. Brandeis, " The Living Law," 10 ILL. L. REV. 461, 464; BRANDEIS, BUSINESS — A PROFESSION, 349–350.

85 From the Hepburn Act of 1906 until the establishment of the Commerce Court only 57 suits had been instituted in the circuit courts, of which only 24

The powerful forces and tendencies which unsuccessfully opposed enactment transferred their interest to litigation. Invalidation and interpretation were invoked by suits in equity to nullify or at least mitigate in court what could not be averted in Congress. These were the turbulent waters upon which the Commerce Court embarked, and the impact of these forces, instead of being divided among the various circuit courts throughout the country, was now concentrated upon a single court which had been given exclusive jurisdiction over these contested issues. In addition, it had all the difficulties of a new court, including the task of working out the scope and nature of its jurisdiction. As was true of the Interstate Commerce Commission itself in earlier days,[86] the Commerce Court encountered numerous reversals by the Supreme Court on so-called questions of jurisdiction. What was merely a permissible resolution of doubt, largely inherent in the situation or in the ambiguities of legislation, with a corrective process available in the Supreme Court, was interpreted by popular feeling, ill-equipped fairly to judge these technical issues, as a conscious attempt on the part of the Commerce Court to usurp authority. To reversals on jurisdictional grounds were added reversals on substantive questions, and, unfortunately, questions full of dramatic interest around which clustered strong popular emotions. Everything combined to make the Court, and that very quickly, a battered bark.

The Commerce Court opened its session in Washington in February, 1911, with thirty-six cases transferred to it from the circuit courts. Probably no court has ever been called upon to adjudicate so large a volume of litigation of as far-reaching import in so brief a time. A succession of now classic cases promptly appeared on its docket. The *Intermountain Rate Cases*,[87] the *Pipe Line Cases*,[88] the *Shreveport Case*,[89] the *Tap Line Cases*,[90] *Louisville & Nashville R. R. Co.* v. *Interstate Commerce Com-*

---

had been determined. The remaining 33 were transferred to the Commerce Court. 48 Cong. Rec. 6144.

[86] The Commission was reversed in all but two of the first 23 cases in which the aid of the courts in enforcing its orders was sought. *Ibid.* 10945.

[87] 234 U. S. 495 (1914), reversing 191 Fed. 856 (1911).

[88] 234 U. S. 548 (1914), modifying 204 Fed. 798 (1913).

[89] 234 U. S. 342 (1914), affirming 205 Fed. 380, 391 (1913).

[90] 234 U. S. 1 (1914), affirming 209 Fed. 244 (1913).

mission,[91] *Procter & Gamble Co.* v. *United States,*[92] *Goodrich Transit Co.* v. *Interstate Commerce Commission,*[93] the *Los Angeles Switching Case,*[94] were but the more striking cases to come before it.[95] Ordinarily decisions of moment in the progress of the law are apt to pass unnoticed by Congress in the stress and strain of legislative life. But the work of the Commerce Court was involved in current political preoccupation with the whole question of government and the railroads.[96] The extension of the authority of the Interstate Commerce Commission was in part, at least, a way of meeting popular discontent with the courts in the movement to effectuate newer economic policies. Thus the Commerce Court entered an environment partial to the Commission and distrustful of courts. With undoubted courage and disinterestedness the Court, heedless of the public temper, promptly began to reverse the Commission and to curb its activity. But its legal wisdom was not equal to its indifference to popular sentiment. For the Commerce Court was itself promptly reversed and curbed by the Supreme Court.[97] For use

---

[91] 227 U. S. 88 (1913), reversing 195 Fed. 541 (1912).

[92] 225 U. S. 282 (1912), reversing 188 Fed. 221 (1911).

[93] 224 U. S. 194 (1912), reversing 190 Fed. 943 (1911).

[94] 234 U. S. 294 (1914), reversing 188 Fed. 229 (1911).

[95] 94 cases were docketed in the Commerce Court. 43 decisions were rendered, including one rehearing. Appeals were taken in 22 cases, of which 13 were reversed, 2 modified, and 7 affirmed. The following table gives an indication of the work of the Court:

Judges	Opinions Delivered	Concurring Opinions	Dissenting Opinions	Concurring in Dissents	Dissenting without Opinions
Knapp	7	1			
Archbald	6	2	2		2
Carland	13	1	1		
Hunt	5			1	1
Mack	10	1	4	1	3
Per Curiam	2				
Totals	43	5	7	2	6

[96] Memorials for the abolition of the Court were presented to Congress on Dec. 18, 1911, by the Railroad Commission of Nevada, and on May 23, 1912, by the Arizona Legislature. 48 Cong. Rec. 450, 6993.

[97] Five decisions were rendered by the Supreme Court during the October Term, 1911. The Commerce Court was reversed in Interstate Commerce Commission *v.* Goodrich Transit Co., 224 U. S. 194 (1912); Procter & Gamble Co. *v.* United States, 225 U. S. 282 (1912); Hooker *v.* Knapp, 225 U. S. 302 (1912); and Interstate Commerce Commission *v.* Baltimore & Ohio R. R., 225 U. S. 326 (1912). It was affirmed in United States *v.* Baltimore & Ohio R. R., 225 U. S. 306 (1912).

on the hustings, here was rich material for judicial critics. More important, however, the Court itself thus furnished apparent vindication of the foreboding prophecies of those who had bitterly contested its creation. The movement for its abolition, which was promptly under way, thus assumed the character of a revolt against the Administration and an insistence on the fulfillment of party pledges.

Sims of Tennessee led this movement. The Democrats were now in control of the House. On December 4, 1911, at the opening of the Second Session of the Sixty-second Congress, he introduced a bill transferring the jurisdiction of the Commerce Court to the district courts, providing for the return to the former practice of making the Interstate Commerce Commission and not the United States the defendant in suits involving its orders [98] and imposing added restrictions upon the issuance of temporary injunctions.[99] Hearings upon the Sims bill were held by the Committee on Interstate Commerce at which Attorney General Wickersham appeared in person to defend the Commerce Court.[100] Despite vigorous opposition and insistence that insufficient time had elapsed to make a just estimate of the worth of such a court, the bill was favorably reported.[101] But to evade the President's known opposition and to avert if possible his veto, the proposal for the Court's abolition was made part of one of the great appropriation bills of 1912.[102] When this section came before the House on May 1, 1912, it provoked sharp debate. The opponents of the Court urged bias of the judges,

---

[98] The provisions of the Mann-Elkins Act in entrusting the defense of suits involving orders of the Commission to the Department of Justice aroused severe criticism. The Commission could only appear as intervenor. According to a House Report the Attorney General was thereby empowered " to virtually overrule the orders of this commission." HOUSE REPORT, No. 472, 62nd Cong., 2nd Sess., Ser. No. 6131. But the transfer of the Commerce Court's jurisdiction to the district courts was accompanied by a retention of the procedure which theretofore prevailed in the Commerce Court. 38 STAT. 208, 220. The Interstate Commerce Commission must, however, be given five days' notice of applications to suspend, etc., its orders. *Ibid.*

[99] The bill is fully set forth in 48 CONG. REC. 5761.

[100] See *ibid.* 6151.

[101] HOUSE REPORT, No. 472, 62nd Cong., 2nd Sess., Ser. No. 6131.

[102] HOUSE REPORT, No. 633, 62nd Cong., 2nd Sess., Ser. No. 6131. Resort to an irrelevant rider — a standing reproach to our legislative methods — was naturally a large target for the opposition. Senator Borah on Oct. 3, 1913,

proved, to the satisfaction of those who pressed the argument, by the Court's attitude towards the Commission.[103] The uniformity which was hoped for from the Court, continued its enemies, was defeated by the persistent practice of appealing cases to the Supreme Court for want of confidence in the Commerce Court.[104] The Court's adherents countered with facts and figures and arguments,[105] but on final passage of this section only a small portion of the votes were recorded against it.[106]

---

exposed this procedure: " Mr. President, this entire legislation in regard to the Commerce Court illustrates how unsatisfactory it is to deal with these questions as we are dealing with this particular matter. The Commerce Court was created under the lash. It did not represent the judgment of the Senate or of Congress at the time it was created. It was created under the influence of the Executive authority and against the judgment of the Legislature which enacted the law. It has never been satisfactory because it did not receive the deliberate judgment and the deliberate affirmation of Congress in the first place. It was not asked for by the people. There was no public demand for it. Now, we are undertaking, in order to amend the situation, to abolish the court at a time when we are not prepared to consider it as such a measure ought to be considered." 50 CONG. REC. 5427.

[103] Sims pointed out that the jurisdiction of the Commerce Court was not invoked to enforce orders of the Commission but was always invoked against them, adding: " Is it possible for any five judges to remain unbiased under such conditions? " 48 CONG. REC. 5763. Shippers had only contested one-fifth of the orders of the Commission before the Court; the remaining four-fifths had been contested by the carriers. *Ibid.* 6147. Procter & Gamble Co. *v.* United States, 225 U. S. 282 (1912), was decided on June 7, 1912, and practically deprived the Court of all jurisdiction over appeals by the shippers. The Court's frequent resort to preliminary injunctions was also commented upon by the Commission. " In but three cases of any consequence where the Commission and the shippers have been opposed to the railroads, have the orders of the Commission been sustained even temporarily by the refusal to grant a temporary restraining order." 35 ANN. REP. I. C. C. 60 (1911).

[104] Good in the House on May 9, 1912, 48 CONG. REC. 6156.

[105] Attorney General Wickersham at the hearings insisted that the Commission had been reversed in 56% of the cases before the circuit courts, 45% before the Supreme Court, and only 41% before the Commerce Court. *Ibid.* 6152; Hearings before House Committee on Interstate Commerce on H. R. 19078, Mar. 14, 1912. Of 33 cases in the Supreme Court, the Commission had been reversed in 24; whereas of 22 cases in the Commerce Court, the Commission had been sustained in 12 and partly sustained in another. H. S. Drinker, Jr., in *Philadelphia Public Ledger*, Aug. 13, 1912, quoted in 48 CONG. REC. 10945. Stevens of Minnesota, the leader of the opposition in the House, pointed out that 7 of 13 applications for preliminary injunctions had been denied by the Court. *Ibid.* 6147. The figures, however, disclose little as to the relative importance of the cases.

[106] A motion to strike out the section abolishing the Court was defeated by a vote of 120 to 49. *Ibid.* 6162.

The Senate Committee on Interstate Commerce had reported in favor of the Court,[107] but on the floor of the Senate the attacks against the Court were even more bitter than in the House. Thus, savage charges of recklessness were leveled by Senator Overman at the expenditures of the judges for the furnishing of their court-rooms and even at their expense accounts while away from Washington.[108] But the prevailing themes in debate were the tendency of the Court unduly to extend its scope of review over the Commission and the Court's bias against the policies embodied in the Interstate Commerce Act and its amendments. By a vote of 36 to 24 the Senate declared itself in favor of putting an end to the Court.[109] It then turned its attention to a crucial question which the House had neglected: [110] What was to be done with the Commerce Court judges? Smith of Georgia proposed to abolish the judgeships as well as the Court.[111] Against this ready disposition were urged the usefulness of the judges to relieve congested circuits,[112] the injustice of terminating what everyone had assumed

---

[107] SEN. REP., No. 832, 62nd Cong., 2nd Sess., Ser. No. 6122.

[108] 48 CONG. REC. 7952–7954.

[109] *Ibid.* 7968. At Nelson's suggestion the provision was amended to provide specifically that the district courts should possess only the powers of the Commerce Court and that all appeals should lie direct to the Supreme Court. *Ibid.* 7966.

[110] The Sims bill had contemplated the retention of the Commerce Court judges as circuit judges in order to relieve the circuits. HOUSE REPORT, No. 472, 72nd Cong., 2nd Sess., Ser. No. 6131.

[111] 48 CONG. REC. 7992.

[112] Attorney General Wickersham writing on June 4, 1912, to Senator Warren of Wyoming thus described the situation: " This, in effect, creates a body of five circuit judges at large, who may be sent to places where there is a congestion of business or a shortage of judges; and but for the existence of this provision during the last year there would have been a much greater congestion of public business even than there is in many parts of the United States. For instance, Judge Carland was assigned to and sat in the circuit court of appeals in the eighth circuit during January of this year and came back with 20 cases in which he had been deputed to write the opinions of the court; and I have now a request from the senior circuit judge of that circuit asking that he be assigned to sit in the circuit court of appeals at the Denver term in September. Judge Hunt sat in the circuit and district courts in Montana from the middle of December until the end of January. He was then assigned to sit in the district court of Arizona during the month of April, and on May 1 he went to San Francisco to sit in the circuit court of appeals, to which he was assigned for May and June and where he is now sitting. Judge Mack sat in Chicago in all the Federal courts during the month of January and also during the month of March. On May 1 he went to Arizona, and has sat in the district court there during the

was to be life tenure,[113] and finally the constitutional inability of Congress to deprive a judge of his office save by impeachment. This last consideration led to an extended constitutional discussion but one less notable than the early debate of 1802 upon the abolition of the Federalist circuit judges. Those who urged the constitutional limitation upon Congressional power went far beyond the constitutional necessities. Thus, one of the leaders, Senator Sutherland of Utah, revived Story's doctrine of the duty and not merely the power of Congress to establish inferior tribunals and urged retention of the Commerce Court as a constitutional court.[114] Surely, this contention would not prevail with the Supreme Court. Only at a later stage of the debate, when the constitutionalists were reinforced by Senators Borah, Shields, and Walsh, was the constitutional argument brought into focus.[115] Nevertheless Smith's amendment passed the Senate without division,[116] but was surrendered to the House, in conference,[117] whereby the judges of the Commerce Court were retained as ambulatory circuit judges.[118] But the device of avoiding the presidential veto failed. On August 15, 1912, the doomed Court was given a further lease of life by President Taft. His message marshalled the arguments which in various forms had been put to Congress. It also mirrored a fear of the campaign for judicial recall which Roosevelt had launched in his startling speech at Ossawatamie: [119]

---

entire month of May. Presiding Judge Knapp has, as you doubtless know, been engaged for some weeks past in negotiation under the Erdman Act with Commissioner of Labor Neill in the negotiations for the settlement of one of the most serious labor troubles which has been impending over this country for a long time. This feature of the usefulness of this body of judges has not been brought very sharply to the attention of the public." 48 CONG. REC. 7972. This provision for the assignment of Commerce Court judges is still in force and vests in the Chief Justice full discretion to vest such a judge with authority to sit in the district or circuit courts of appeals of any circuit. Donegan *v.* Dyson, 269 U. S. 49 (1925).

[113] See 50 CONG. REC. 5414.

[114] 48 *ibid.* 7994–7998.

[115] A confused summary of this debate is to be found in CARPENTER, JUDICIAL TENURE IN THE UNITED STATES, 88–94.

[116] 48 CONG. REC. 8001.

[117] *Ibid.* 10057.

[118] *Ibid.* 10334, 10500.

[119] 2 CORRESPONDENCE OF THEODORE ROOSEVELT AND HENRY CABOT LODGE, 388–391; ROOSEVELT, PROGRESSIVE POLICIES, 84.

" I am utterly opposed to the abolition of a court because its decisions may not always meet the approval of a majority of the Legislature. It is introducing a recall of the judiciary, which, in its way, is
quite as objectionable as the ordinary popular method proposed." [120]

The President's veto acted merely as a stay of execution.
Even while Congress was moving against the Court, fresh causes
for dissatisfaction arose. In June, 1912, the Supreme Court announced its decision in *Procter & Gamble Co.* v. *United States* [121]
depriving the Commerce Court of jurisdiction in cases of dismissal of complaints by the Interstate Commerce Commission.[122]
The opponents of the Court saw in this decision merely the simple
terms of conflict between shippers and carriers, into which for
them the whole controversy resolved itself. By denying the
shipper any remedy where the Commission fell into error in refusing to grant him relief, the *Procter & Gamble* case served to
emphasize the character of the Court as a railroad tribunal.[123]
Efforts to remedy the procedural situation created by *Procter &
Gamble Co.* v. *United States* [124] merged into the larger movement for the abolition of the Court. But balked for the time by
the President's veto, the Sixty-second Congress turned its attention to a flank movement in effect against the Court, though ac-

---

[120] 48 CONG. REC. 11027. An attempt to pass the bill over the President's
veto failed in the House, by a vote of 147 to 107. *Ibid.* 11035.

[121] 225 U. S. 282 (1912), reversing 188 Fed. 221 (1911).

[122] As a result of this decision eleven cases, then pending, were dismissed by
the Commerce Court.

[123] The effect of this decision has too often been lost sight of in emphasizing
legal distinctions between negative and positive orders of the Commission. See,
e.g., CARPENTER, *op. cit.*, 83–87. Since the ordinary function undertaken by the
Commission in this class of cases is upon complaint by shippers against carriers,
its real effect, as Commissioner Prouty pointed out, "was to deny the shipper
relief against an error of law upon the part of the commission; while the carrier
has in such cases an adequate remedy." HOUSE REPORT, No. 1012, 62nd Cong.,
2nd Sess., Ser. No. 6133, p. 3.

[124] Immediately after the decision Borland of Missouri introduced a bill to
override it which was reported to the House on July 17, 1912. It gave the Commerce Court jurisdiction " over all cases brought to correct any error of law
made by the Interstate Commerce Commission in granting or refusing to grant
relief in any proceeding before said commission." HOUSE REPORT, No. 1012, 62nd
Cong., 2nd Sess., Ser. No. 6133. No action was taken upon the bill. A similar
bill was introduced by Broussard of Louisiana on June 6, 1913. 50 CONG. REC.
1926. Broussard also sought to accomplish this result by amendments to the bill
abolishing the Court. See note 130, *infra*.

tually involving grave charges of misconduct against only one of its members.[125] The impeachment of Judge Archbald justly cast no reflection against the Court as an institution nor any of its other members. Hence we find that during the final stage of the movement for the abolition of the Court, the Archbald impeachment does not figure in the debate. Yet the mere fact of the impeachment was a weighty, even if inarticulate, factor. For the conviction of one of the judges, although on conduct wholly peculiar to him and originating largely prior to his appointment as a Commerce Court judge, because it involved the use of his influence to secure favors from carriers litigating before him, confirmed the widespread claim of railroad bias and partisanship deemed inevitable in the very nature of so specialized and concentrated a tribunal as the Commerce Court.

When Democracy came to power on March 4, 1913, the Court's doom was sealed. On June 26, Chairman Adamson of the House Committee on Interstate Commerce began to set in motion the legislative machinery for its execution.[126] The proposal was again incorporated into an annual appropriation bill.[127] Although this provision, on submission to the Committee of the Whole, allowed amendments from the floor,[128] little opposition developed. Senator Lewis voiced the sentiment of the majority of both houses:

"It is my clear judgment — and in this I am so convinced that nothing could move me — that whenever the citizens of a free country

---

[125] In February 1912 charges of misconduct on the part of Judge Archbald were brought to the attention of President Taft. An investigation by the Department of Justice followed and the papers were transmitted to the House of Representatives. Thirteen articles upon which impeachment was sought were presented, charging that Judge Archbald had used his influence to secure from carriers litigating before him favorable contracts for the purchase of different properties by his business associates. Certain of the charges related to his conduct in the capacity of district judge prior to his appointment to the Commerce Court; those upon which he was convicted, concerned his actions as a Commerce Court judge. Finding him guilty on six of the articles, the Senate on Jan. 13, 1913, voted to remove him from office and disqualify him from holding any further office. 49 CONG. REC. 1439–1447.

[126] 50 *ibid.* 2216.

[127] On Sept. 2, 1913, Fitzgerald introduced a resolution making it in order to consider provisions for abolishing the Commerce Court in connection with the appropriation bill. *Ibid.* 4116.

[128] *Ibid.* 4310–4314.

lose their confidence in any established court, to maintain that court as an institution is a useless proceeding, because once that confidence is gone, all respect for its adjudications is ended and the court loses its usefulness either to itself as a court or as an agency of welfare to the community which it assumes to serve. Since this seems to be the view concerning the Commerce Court located at Washington, I affirm the opinion of the people as expressed by them in different branches that the Court should go. But it was not the character of all the judges which was aspersed; it was not the conduct of the men individually that was assailed; it was neither the want of capacity, as I understood, on the one hand nor their character on the other that called for this uniform condemnation; it was, rather, the assumption of jurisdiction and usurpation on the part of the Court — a thing which the public mind was not willing to accept or indorse." [129]

This time the House voted to abolish the judgeships together with the Court.[130] The issue sharply divided the Senate. How intense was the opposition is revealed by the close margin — 25

---

[129] *Ibid.* 5413.

Arguments based on the need for expertness in railroad litigation and support of the Commerce Court as the fulfillment of such need were met by the claim that the Supreme Court had to reverse the Commerce Court in 10 out of 12 cases. Sims in the House on Sept. 8, 1913, *ibid.* 4537. These figures refer to individual cases, several of which may have been disposed of by one decision. Besides the decisions referred to in note 97, *supra,* during the October Term, 1912, the Supreme Court reversed the Commerce Court in Interstate Commerce Commission v. Louisville & Nashville R. R., 227 U. S. 88 (1913), and Omaha & Council Bluffs Street Ry. v. Interstate Commerce Commission, 230 U. S. 324 (1913); partly reversed the Court in United States v. Union Stock Yard & Transit Co., 226 U. S. 286 (1912); affirmed the Court in United States v. Baltimore & Ohio Southwestern Ry., 226 U. S. 14 (1912).

[130] The amendment by Bartlett of Georgia to abolish the judgeships passed by a vote of 80 to 40. 50 CONG. REC. 4543. Broussard had offered an amendment to give the district courts jurisdiction "to correct any error of law made by the Interstate Commerce Commission in granting the rights and granting relief in any proceeding before said commission." Its purpose was to override the Procter & Gamble decision. Borland, its original sponsor, claimed that it had been indorsed by every traffic bureau and commercial body. *Ibid.* 4532–4533. On Sept. 15, 1913, Jones in the Senate presented a petition of the transportation bureau of the Seattle Chamber of Commerce supporting such a provision. *Ibid.* 4937. Broussard had also offered a second amendment, to be voted upon if the first failed, to make the orders of the Commission final on questions of law as well as of fact and forbidding courts to take jurisdiction of appeals from the Commission. Its purpose was to take away the right of appeal from railroads in that it was denied to the shippers. The amendments were defeated by votes of 67 to 8 and 70 to 3. *Ibid.* 4544.

to 23 — by which the Senate voted to retain the Commerce Court judges as circuit judges.[131] When the bill went to conference, the House conferees refused to concur in the retention of the judges,[132] but the Senate view finally prevailed in the House.[133] The bill thus passed, and on October 22, 1913, the Commerce Court, after less than three years of life, was legislated out of existence.[134]

Since then the idea of a Commerce Court has not been revived. The legal profession has not questioned the political judgment as to the value of such a tribunal. And yet there are doubts to be met. The experiment was too brief; the times were unpropitious; the problems involved too novel and complicated to evoke the mature judgment alike of Congress, Commission, and Court. But the puzzles of governmental control over railroads, its scope and nature, still remain. " Valuation " alone is a legal quagmire. Moreover, the field of governmental supervision has been immensely extended over all sorts of " public utilities," while we give little heed to the realization of the purposes behind these regulatory laws. The technique of administration, the qualifications of administrators, the scope of judicial review, in a word, the key issues in any fruitful system of utility regulation have hardly begun to emerge as pressing problems for scientific judgment. Until we have more disinterested wisdom, political action in regard to them necessarily is a game of blind man's buff, much confused by rank partisanship or undisciplined hopes and fears. Recently, too, the relation of government to utilities has been immensely complicated by the increasing body of judge-made requirements of " due process." Courts are less than ever technical expounders of technical provisions of the Constitution. They are arbiters of the economic and social life of vast regions and at times of the whole country.[135] In ends

---

[131] For the vote, see 50 CONG. REC. 5429.

On Oct. 3, 1913, Nelson moved to strike out the section abolishing the judges. *Ibid.* 5409. Borah, Shields, and Walsh came to his support while Bacon and Smith of Georgia supported the House amendment. Their arguments, too detailed for repetition in this connection, compare very favorably with any upon this subject.

[132] *Ibid.* 5551.

[133] By a vote of 82 to 42. *Ibid.* 5596.

[134] 38 STAT. 208, 219. The Court was to go out of existence on Dec. 31, 1913.

[135] *Cf., e.g.,* Intermountain Rate Cases, 234 U. S. 476 (1914); Railroad Com-

not different from those pursued by statesmen, courts determine the extent to which industries " clothed with a public interest " may exercise, through their rate structures, powers of taxation.[136] The wisdom of debatable policies, like the proper scope for competition or for monopoly,[137] policies never susceptible of quantitative judgments, is for their ultimate decision. Less than ever is it likely that Congress will entrust these issues to five men, even though invested with the authority of bench and woolsack and subject to the corrective scrutiny of the Supreme Court. But the adjustment of these conflicts, although social and economic in their essentials, lies largely within the control of the judicial power. And so, the manner of its exercise will continue to be of paramount public importance. For the issues reach beyond the specialized grasp of the legal profession, beyond the experience and insight of a single court, however well equipped.

5

The history of the movement to create a special court for patent litigation presents a striking contrast to the story of the Commerce Court. The problem of fashioning judicial machinery appropriate for railroad cases has been only one of the many tense political and economic issues in which " the railroad problem " is involved. Projects for a patent court have never been entangled with dominant political issues; they have not touched popular thought or feeling. The movement is professional in origin and largely so in interest. Its advocates, as well as its opponents, have been, for all practical purposes, members of that very restricted fraternity, the patent bar.

Patent law is not rooted in the ancient traditions of the common law, and its equitable remedies have a comparatively recent lineage. Equity was rarely invoked to protect patent rights[138]

---

mission of Wisconsin *v.* C. B. & Q. R. R., 257 U. S. 563 (1922) ; New England Divisions Case, 261 U. S. 184 (1923).

[136] *Cf.* New England Divisions Case, *supra,* at 196: " In other words, the additional revenues needed were raised partly by a direct, partly by an indirect tax."

[137] *Cf.* " Competition that Kills," in BRANDEIS, BUSINESS — A PROFESSION, 243.

[138] Early English and American cases are collected in CHAFEE, CASES ON EQUITABLE RELIEF AGAINST TORTS, 67.

before the Act of February 15, 1819 [139] specifically provided
injunctive relief. By the Patent Act of 1836 patent litigation
was in effect turned over to the United States courts.[140] The
stuff of this legal business is thus peculiarly federal in character.[141] The inventor's rights are determined by Congress; they
are interpreted and enforced through the federal judiciary.
Moreover, the content of patent law is extremely technical in
character. The layman knows little and cares less about patent
controversies. Juries are seldom brought in contact with its
issues.[142] The legal profession has generally abandoned patent
litigation to a specialized group of men whose legal equipment
is supplemented if not by scientific training and aptitude, at least
by understanding of the mechanical arts.[143] " The distinguishing
quality " in Lord Moulton's commanding position as a patent
lawyer, we are told by his son and biographer, was " his extraordinary capacity for scientific thought, even in fields wholly new
to him." [144] In fact the " law " of patent law is not its major
or most difficult part. The average patent case, according to a
judge extensively versed in patent litigation, requires " the careful study of intricate machinery, the manipulation of models, the
reading and re-reading of technical evidence, the elaborate comparison of documents couched in language which certainly is not
that of common speech, the close, hard thinking, sometimes pro-
longed for weeks. . . ." [145] Here is nothing to ignite popular
imagination. Devising judicial machinery and legal procedure
fitted for the enforcement of patent rights inevitably becomes
the specialized concern of those professionally engaged in this
most technical of the " federal specialties."

[139] 3 STAT. 481.

[140] Act of July 4, 1836, § 17, 5 STAT. 117, 124.

[141] For the statutory history of the jurisdiction of the federal courts in
patent controversies, see Root v. Railway Co., 105 U. S. 189, 191–194 (1881);
Bate Refrigerating Co. v. Sulzberger, 157 U. S. 1, 19–24 (1895).

[142] " During the 11 years the writer has sat on the circuit bench, there has
not been in this court a single jury trial in a patent cause." Lacombe, J., in
Wyckoff v. Wagner Typewriter Co., 88 Fed. 515, 516 (C. C. S. D. N. Y., 1898),
quoted in CHAFEE, *op. cit.* 70.

[143] See Hand, J., in Parke-Davis v. Mulford, 189 Fed. 95, 115 (C. C. S. D.
N. Y., 1911).

[144] MOULTON, LIFE OF LORD MOULTON, 38. His researches in electricity won
Moulton an F. R. S. *Ibid.* 105, 114.

[145] Lacombe, J., in Wyckoff v. Wagner Typewriter Co., *supra*, at 516.

The effective disposition of patent litigation thus presents its own special problems of personnel and procedure. The scope and method of proof, the element of time, the range of recoverable damages and the mode of their ascertainment have distinctive phases in patent litigation.[146]   Also, the most telling adjudications of patent controversies call for judges of special intellectual bent.[147]   Federal judges have not often had much experience at the patent bar. Their equipment for patent business must come through study of bewildering records in isolated cases, enlightened by the conflicts of partisan counsel and partisan experts. On the other hand, narrow technicalities must be corrected by applying in adjudication the broad considerations of policy underlying patent legislation; patent rights must be enforced as part of a general system of law, particularly of equitable doctrines invigorated elsewhere than in patent soil. In patent cases, as in others, a judge must have the philosophic insight which penetrates the particular to its general aspects.[148]

Dissatisfaction with processes of patent litigation fashioned in the primitive, agricultural days of the country was bound to manifest itself through the patent bar as soon as the increase of modern inventions began to reflect itself in the courts. The great economic impulses after the Civil War stimulated, and were intensified by, the powerful forces of invention beginning with the seventies. Up to the close of the year 1870 there had been taken out, since the United States began, 120,573 patents; from 1870 to 1911 there were issued 1,002,478 patents.[149]   We have seen the stark inadequacy of the federal judicial organization of the seventies to master the demands made upon it by the stupendous growth of the country's business. Programs for radical revision of the federal judiciary were in the air. What more natural than to propose a segregation of patent litigation in a

---

[146] Cf., e.g., George P. Dike, "The Trial of Patent Accountings in Open Court," 36 HARV. L. REV. 33.

[147] Cf. Hand, J., in Parke-Davis v. Mulford, supra.

[148] See, e.g., Motion Picture Patents Co. v. Universal Film Mfg. Co., 243 U. S. 502 (1917).

[149] Frederick P. Fish, "Letters Patent in Relation to Modern Industrial Conditions," 38 AM. BAR ASSN. REP. 805, 821. In 1925 there were 82,215 patent applications. 13 ANN. REP. SEC. COMM. 210.

patent court? Bills to this end begin to appear in 1878.[150] But while the evils of congestion in the courts at this period affected patent cases more seriously than others, because of the limited life of patent rights, demands for relief in patent litigation were lost in the general clamor for judicial reform. But the movement for a patent court persisted, and in 1888 bills embodying such a proposal came before Congress. The proposal was sidetracked in the Senate Judiciary Committee by Chairman Edmunds to make way for the more comprehensive program of intermediate appellate courts.[151]

The Act of 1891, however, while relieving the Supreme Court of the drain of patent litigation brought new difficulties for patent litigants. Prior to this Act appeals from infringement suits in the circuit courts lay directly to the Supreme Court. While the delay, in those days from three to four years, in reaching a Supreme Court decision was costly, at least a definitive decision, protecting a patent or denying its validity throughout the United States, was secured. But the Act of 1891 vested finality of patent jurisdiction in the circuit courts of appeals, subject only to certification and *certiorari* — methods of review only seldom to be invoked. Uniformity was thus replaced by the threatened diversity of nine appellate courts of coördinate jurisdiction. The danger showed itself to be a real one. Thus, the Seventh Circuit refused to follow a decision of the Eighth Circuit upholding the validity of a patent;[152] and on *certiorari* the Supreme Court sustained the freedom of circuit courts of appeals to disregard each other.[153] And so it came to pass that a patent which gave rise to rights and liabilities in Connecticut,

---

[150] On Mar. 4, 1878, Vance of North Carolina introduced a bill of this nature in the House; on Mar. 11, 1878, Booth of California introduced a similar bill in the Senate. 7 CONG. REC. 1457, 1627.

[151] See H. R. 9084, 19 CONG. REC. 8549, and HOUSE REPORT, No. 3426, 50th Cong., 1st Sess.; Report of the Committee on Patent, Trade-Mark and Copyright Law of the American Bar Association for 1919, 37 AM. BAR ASSN. REP. 472, 478.

[152] Mast, Foos & Co. *v.* Dempster Mill Mfg. Co., 82 Fed. 327 (8th Circ., 1897); Stover Mfg. Co. *v.* Mast, Foos & Co., 89 Fed. 333 (7th Circ., 1898).

[153] Mast, Foos & Co. *v.* Stover Mfg. Co., 177 U. S. 485 (1900). But where the validity of a patent had been sustained in one circuit, its validity is *res judicata* as between the same parties or their privies in another suit even though in another circuit. Kessler *v.* Eldred, 206 U. S. 285 (1907); Hart Steel Co. *v.* Railroad Supply Co., 244 U. S. 294 (1917).

Vermont, and New York was a nullity in Illinois, Indiana, and Wisconsin.[154] Thus, to the earlier justifications for the proposal of a patent court, namely, a desire for specialized judges and speed of disposition, was added the need for uniformity in decision and enforcement.

Relief through the Supreme Court was not to be hoped for. The condition of its docket and the general increase in federal litigation indicated that future legislation would curtail still more, and not enlarge, the obligatory appellate powers of the Supreme Court. To restore to the Supreme Court the right of appeal in patent cases was neither a likely nor a desirable event.[155] Certification to the Supreme Court was found an unwieldy instrument;[156] nor was *certiorari* an adequately sensitive response to the need for uniformity. Every motive of the Court, in view of its congested calendar, was enlisted against assuming jurisdiction where a particular case was, after all, only a particular case and that, too, involving, as patent cases are apt to, much time and labor.[157] To be sure, later cases indicated that diversity of decisions upon a single patent in different circuits was a basis for granting *certiorari*.[158] Even so, the validity of a particular patent must await conflicting litigation in two circuits, meanwhile leaving

---

[154] See, *e.g.*, Eldred *v.* Breitwieser, 132 Fed. 251 (C. C. W. D. N. Y., 1904); Rubber Tire Wheel Co. *v.* Goodyear Tire & Rubber Co., 232 U. S. 413, 415 (1914).

[155] "It is conceded on all hands that were conditions such as to make it practicable to restore the right of appeal in patent causes to the Supreme Court of the United States, that would be the best possible solution of the question. All familiar with the work of the Supreme Court realize, however, that that court has not the time to consider and decide patent appeals, and that to impose upon that court this duty would result in putting the court years behind its calendar." House Report, No. 1415, 60th Cong., 1st Sess., Ser. No. 5226, p. 2.

[156] *Cf.* Columbus Watch Co. *v.* Robbins, 148 U. S. 266 (1893).

[157] "So it has been that this court, while not doubting its power, has been chary of action in respect to certioraries." Forsyth *v.* Hammond, 166 U. S. 506, 513 (1897).

[158] Expanded Metal Co. *v.* Bradford, 214 U. S. 366 (1909); Diamond Rubber Co. *v.* Consolidated Tire Co., 220 U. S. 428 (1911); Abercrombie & Fitch Co. *v.* Baldwin, 245 U. S. 198 (1917); Grinnell Washing Machine Co. *v.* Johnson Co., 247 U. S. 426 (1918); Thomson Spot Welder Co. *v.* Ford Motor Co., 265 U. S. 445 (1924); Concrete Appliances Co. *v.* Gomery, 269 U. S. 177 (1925). But on an interlocutory appeal, even though conflict exists, the Court will not go into the merits. Leeds & Catlin Co. *v.* Victor Talking Machine Co., 213 U. S. 301 (1909); Meccano *v.* Wanamaker, 253 U. S. 136 (1920).

both inventor and public in doubt. The Government, it was urged, by conferring letters patent grants exclusive enjoyment in this species of property throughout the United States. The construction of this grant should be coextensive with the rights which it purports to confer. The patentee, on the one hand, is entitled to complete protection if he has been justly given a public grant. On the other hand, a patent " in a broad sense deals with and determines the rights of the public ";[159] if invalid, the public should have its invalidity recognized throughout the United States.[160] A decision of a circuit court of appeals, however, gives rise only to a limited right; nor does even such a limited adjudication dispose of incidental questions upon which the ultimate financial value of a patent may depend.[161]

And so, after the establishment of the circuit courts of appeals, the movement for a centralized patent tribunal grew apace. In 1894 the American Bar Association organized a Committee on Patent, Trade-mark and Copyright Law [162] which, for nearly twenty years, served as the spearhead for this judicial reform. Beginning with 1898 bills proposing such a court steadily appeared in Congress.[163] In 1900 a special committee of the American Bar Association submitted a plan " for the creation of a single court of last resort in patent causes " [164] which originated with Mr. Frederick P. Fish, the distinguished patent

---

[159] Electric Mfg. Co. *v.* Edison Electric Light Co., 61 Fed. 834, 837 (7th Circ., 1894).

[160] " The life of a patent is comparatively brief, and the inventor has a right to know as speedily as possible whether his patent is valid or not, and as a patent excludes all the people of the United States for a time from its use without the consent of the inventor, the public have a right to know as soon as possible whether or not they may use the article, and the decisions of the courts of last resort show that more than one-half of all the patents issued are invalid." HOUSE REPORT, No. 1415, 60th Cong., 1st Sess., Ser. No. 5226, p. 2.

[161] *Cf.* Rubber Tire Wheel Co. *v.* Goodyear Tire & Rubber Co., 232 U. S. 413 (1914) ; Seim *v.* Hurd, 232 U. S. 420 (1914).

[162] 17 AM. BAR ASSN. REP. 71.

[163] On Jan. 21, 1898, Hicks introduced in the House a bill to establish a patent court. 31 CONG. REC. 848. A bill to establish a court of appellate jurisdiction in patents, trade-marks, and copyrights was introduced in the Senate by Hansbrough on Mar. 28, 1898, and again on Dec. 19, 1899; by Sulzer in the House on Jan. 4, 1900. 31 CONG. REC. 3277; 33 *ibid.* 539, 686.

[164] Report of Committee of the Section of Patent, Trade-Mark and Copyright Law, 23 AM. BAR ASSN. REP. 543.

lawyer, then chairman of the Patent Committee.[165] The Patent
Section of the Bar Association approved the principles of the
report and requested the standing committee on patents to draft
an appropriate bill.[166] The plan thus sponsored called for a court
confined to patent litigation, " unless it should be thought best
to include also copyright and trade-mark cases," and to be final
in those cases on direct review from the trial courts, subject only
to certification to, or *certiorari* by, the Supreme Court.   Its
membership was to consist of a chief justice, to be appointed
from the circuit judges and associate judges (the Association's
bill later fixed the number at four) to be designated by the Chief
Justice of the Supreme Court from among the circuit judges, to
sit for six years.[167] By this device for the selection of the court's
personnel it was hoped to achieve at once expertness and range
of outlook in the judges. " Experience on the bench in the field
of general jurisprudence " would avoid the pitfalls of narrow
specialization and thus secure " a court of judges, and not of
mere patent lawyers." [168]

A bill embodying these proposals, varying only in minor details, was before Congress for the next ten years.[169] The Patent
Committee of the Bar Association year after year pressed for its
passage,[170] but the interest of Congress could not be aroused.

---

165 *Ibid.* 506, 507–510..

166 *Ibid.* 502–503.

167 *Ibid.* 547.

168 *Ibid.* 548.

169 Bills to establish a patent court were introduced in the House by Sherman
on Jan. 8, 1904 (38 CONG. REC. 588); by Currier on Jan. 21, 1904 (*ibid.* 1011);
by Otis on Feb. 26, 1904 (*ibid.* 2451); by Currier on Dec. 15, 1905 (40 *ibid.*
481); by Gilbert on Jan. 19, 1906 (*ibid.* 1300); by Needham on Dec. 2, 1907
(42 *ibid.* 23); by Overstreet on Jan. 16, 1908 (*ibid.* 811); by Harrison on Mar.
18, 1908 (*ibid.* 3548); by Chaney on April 6, 1908 (*ibid.* 4453); by Currier on
April 30, 1908 (*ibid.* 5509); by Currier on Dec. 14, 1909 (45 *ibid.* 141); by
Sulzer on May 18, 1911, and Aug. 14, 1912 (47 *ibid.* 1353; 48 *ibid.* 10955). In
the Senate they were introduced by Platt on Dec. 15, 1903, on Jan. 4, 1904, and
on Feb. 29, 1904 (38 CONG. REC. 237, 417, 2530); by Kittredge on Dec. 14,
1905 (40 *ibid.* 385); by Beveridge on Jan. 22, 1906, Jan. 7, 1908, and Jan. 10,
1910 (*ibid.* 1347; 42 *ibid.* 500; 45 *ibid.* 458).

170 See Reports of the Committee on Patent, Trade-Mark and Copyright
Laws for 1903, 1905, 1906, 1907, 1908, 1909, 26 AM. BAR ASSN. REP. 460; 28
ibid. 465; 29 *ibid.* 522; 31 *ibid.* 617; 33 *ibid.* 523; 34 *ibid.* 536. The Report for
1903 was printed on Jan. 12, 1904, as SEN. DOC., No. 81, 58th Cong., 2nd Sess.,
Ser. No. 4588. The draft bill of the Committee was by resolution approved by

The demand for the court came from too specialized a group; the larger implications of patent litigation could not be dramatized. Moreover, the circuit courts of appeals were too young to provoke corrective legislation; their conflicting decisions were attributed to inexperience rather than to defective scope of jurisdiction. Despite all the driving force of the Patent Committee of the Bar Association, until 1910 only two of the many bills came out of committee [171] and none reached passage in either House.

In 1910 the momentum of this effort was greatly reinforced through the success of the movements for specialized courts in customs and commerce cases. Senator Beveridge, long a vigorous advocate of the scheme, succeeded in getting his bill favorably reported from the Senate Committee on Patents on February 28, 1910.[172] But the legislative response to demands for specialized courts had spent itself. These demands, as we have seen, encountered powerful opposition. The energy and the interest behind the patent court was not equal to overcoming it. The Beveridge bill was referred to the Judiciary Committee of the Senate [173] and buried. The considerations which had enlisted the powerful support of President Taft for the Customs and Commerce Courts did not apply to a patent court. He was interested in the reform, but it did not have in it the ele-

---

the American Bar Association in 1906. 29 Am. Bar Assn. Rep. 30. Professional periodicals during this period are also alive with discussion. See Otto R. Barnett, " The Proposed Court of Patent Appeals," 6 Mich. L. Rev. 441; Edmund Wetmore, " Patent Law," 17 Yale L. J. 101, 106; " A New Federal Court," 20 Green Bag 203; " The Needed Reform of Patent Procedure," 22 Green Bag 408; " The Court of Patent Appeals," 12 Law Notes 21; 18 Harv. L. Rev. 217. Lay journals supported the measure. See, *e.g.*, William Macomber, " Patents and Industrial Progress," 191 N. Am. Rev. 895.

171 On April 9, 1908, Overstreet's bill was favorably reported from the Committee on Patents. House Report, No. 1415, 60th Cong., 1st Sess., Ser. No. 5226; 42 Cong. Rec. 4571. On Feb. 13, 1909, Currier's bill was favorably reported. House Report, No. 2145, 60th Cong., 2nd Sess., Ser. No. 5384; 43 Cong. Rec. 2336. It was favorably endorsed by the American Bar Association, the Bar Association of the City of New York, the Washington Patent Law Association, the Chicago Patent Bar Association, the Bar Associations of Oregon, of Colorado, of the City of Denver, and of the City of Los Angeles.

172 Sen. Rep., No. 296, 61st Cong., 2nd Sess., Ser. No. 5582.

173 It had been passed over on Mar. 9, and was referred to the Judiciary Committee on April 28, 1910. 45 Cong. Rec. 2951, 5482.

ments of a fighting issue. On the contrary, compromises were suggested which in the eyes of its proponents eviscerated the plan. One scheme, tentatively broached by President Taft before the American Bar Association in 1911,[174] and embodied in a bill then before the Senate,[175] proposed that the Commerce Court should be used as a patent court. A House bill sought to give patent jurisdiction to the Court of Appeals of the District of Columbia, increased, for the purpose, by two additional judges.[176] Both compromises brought forth sharp protest from the Patent Committee of the American Bar Association;[177] the latter even addressed a remonstrance to the President [178] and continued to press for a special patent court.[179]

But all for naught. Time made against the enterprise. The short-lived experience with the Commerce Court reinforced the opponents of specialization in judicial machinery. Legislative energy was increasingly diverted to more exigent issues by the Great War. The patent bar itself showed a change of mind. The death of Judge Robert S. Taylor, long chairman of its Patent Committee, eliminated the most persistent leader in the Bar Association's efforts for a patent court. A postponement of the measure, because of the circumstances engendered by the War, eventually ripened into hostility to the plan in the house of its friends. In 1918 the Patent Committee raised anew " the considerations which must be weighed against the advantages [of a court of patent appeals] which its advocates anticipate from its enactment " and urged that " discussion of their relative merit

---

[174] 36 AM. BAR ASSN. REP. 53, 55.

[175] Introduced by Bacon on May 18, 1911. 47 CONG. REC. 1299.

[176] *Ibid.* 1196.

[177] 36 AM. BAR. ASSN. REP. 417; 37 *ibid.* 472.

[178] 37 AM. BAR ASSN. REP. 473.

[179] In answer to the contention that a court devoted exclusively to patent cases would not be sufficiently occupied, the Patent Committee sought to demonstrate statistically that in view of the number of cases then pending " the time of the court will be very fully occupied with the business." 38 AM. BAR ASSN. REP. 515, 516. By 1919 the volume of business was urged as an objection to a single patent court: " The number and complexity of the patent cases which go to our nine circuit courts of appeals, and the demands which they make upon the time of the courts for their proper consideration has so increased that it would not be practicable for one court sitting in Washington to duly hear, consider and adjudicate all such cases from the nine circuits. Presumably this increase will continue." 5 AM. BAR ASSN. J. 440, 445.

. . . may properly be deferred until our legislators are less occupied by, and under the influence of war conditions."[180] The next year the Patent Committee urged disapproval of the bill then pending in Congress,[181] which failed, however, of adoption through the vigorous intervention of Mr. Frederick P. Fish. "It would be a most serious national misfortune," he urged, "if this Association should directly or indirectly disapprove this bill. More than that it would be a most serious stultification of the action of this Association of the past."[182] Mr. Fish's substitute prevailed, which referred the report back to the Committee "with instructions to report at the next annual meeting of the Association, what if any legislation is desirable in the direction of the establishment of a court of patent appeals, with the reasons for and against the establishment of such a court."[183] Accordingly, in 1920 the Committee reported that "no legislation is desirable in the direction of substituting a special court of patent appeals for the Appellate Jurisdiction now existing,"[184] and this conclusion triumphed.[185] After twenty years the movement for a specialized patent court was buried where it was born. Undoubtedly, however, time has resolved or softened earlier difficulties with the existing system. The Supreme Court has shown increasing liberality to review by *certiorari* conflicting patent decisions,[186] and delay in such dispositions has been measur-

---

[180] 4 AM. BAR ASSN. J. 471; 43 AM. BAR ASSN. REP. 57 *et seq.*

[181] 5 AM. BAR ASSN. J. 440; 44 AM. BAR ASSN. REP. 38 *et seq.* See also Thomas W. Shelton, "Why a Special Patent Court?" 92 CENT. L. J. 333.

[182] 44 AM. BAR ASSN. REP. 40.

[183] *Ibid.* 41–2.

[184] 6 AM. BAR ASSN. J. 505; 45 AM. BAR ASSN. REP. 398.

[185] On the other hand other professions have continued to question the competence of the general lawyer to determine scientific and technical issues. See C. A. P. Turner, "Need of a Special Patent Court — The Engineer's Point of View," 93 CENT. L. J. 96.

[186] From 1891 to 1907 *certiorari* was granted in only 10 patent cases. 31 AM. BAR ASSN. REP. 617–20. In its 1919 report the Patent Committee of the Bar Association stated, "The Supreme Court has adopted the practice of issuing writs of *certiorari* where such conflicts [between courts of different circuits] exist, and itself adjudicating them. This mitigates the objection to the present system so emphasized in former reports, without sacrificing what we regard as especially desirable incidents of this system, that of having the Supreme Court and the courts of appeal of the different circuits sufficiently in touch with this branch of litigation to understand and appreciate its significance." 5 AM. BAR. ASSN. J. 440, 445.

ably curtailed. Moreover, the circuit courts of appeals have acquired increasing skill in patent litigation and have consciously sought harmony in patent adjudications. Accord has been reached not so much by mechanical deference to one another's decisions as by common methods in reaching decisions. Thus, judicial administration has considerably obviated defects deemed inherent in judicial structure.

6

For the present, no vigorous impulse toward specialized federal courts is at work. But a vast congeries of administrative agencies is raising new juristic problems. This new form of legal control through law-administering agencies — new because of the impact of its incidence — must be adjusted to our traditional system of judicial justice. The development of a distinctive law is in process. " Administrative law " has ceased to be descriptive of an exotic.[187] Recognition of the part it is playing with us and in all English-speaking countries [188] has been voiced not merely by pioneering scholars, like President Goodnow and Profes-

---

[187] See FREUND, *et al.*, GROWTH OF AMERICAN ADMINISTRATIVE LAW; Warren H. Pillsbury, " Administrative Tribunals," 36 HARV. L. REV. 405, 583; Ray A. Brown, " The Functions of Courts and Commissions," 38 *ibid.* 141; Samuel C. Wiel, " Administrative Finality," 38 *ibid.* 447. *Cf.* DICEY, LAW OF THE CONSTITUTION, 8 ed., xxxvii *et seq.*, and c. IV, with Dicey, " Development of Administrative Law in England," 31 L. QUART. REV. 138. See also Harold J. Laski, " The Growth of Administrative Discretion," 1 J. OF PUB. ADM. 92; Sir Josiah Stamp, " Devolution of Legislative Function," 2 *ibid.* 23; Sir Lynden Macassey, " Law-Making by Government Departments," 2 J. OF SOC. COMP. LEG. (3rd Ser.) 73; LASKI, A GRAMMAR OF POLITICS, 387 *et seq.*; and, generally, Bankes, L. J., in *Ex parte* O'Brien, [1923] 2 K. B. 361, 381–2.

[188] See ANGLIN, CANADIAN ADMINISTRATIVE LAW (Ms. Thesis, Harvard Law School Library); A. Lourie, " Administrative Law in South Africa," 44 So. Afr. L. J. 10. For recent illustrative cases, see (a) as to Great Britain: Local Government Bd. *v.* Arlidge, [1915] A. C. 120; (b) as to Canada: Wilson *v.* Esquimault Ry., [1922] 1 A. C. 302; *Re* Carefoot & College of Physicians and Surgeons, [1926] 1 D. L. R. 237; (c) as to Australia: Architects' Registration Board *v.* Hutchinson, 35 Com. L. R. 404 (1925); British Imperial Oil Co. *v.* Federal Commissioner, 35 Com. L. R. 422 (1925); Federal Commissioner *v.* Australian Tesselated Tile Co., 36 Com. L. R. 119 (1926); (d) as to New Zealand: Park *v.* Minister of Education, [1922] N. Z. L. R. 1208; (e) as to South Africa: Shidinack *v.* Union Government, [1912] S. A. A. D. 642; Rex *v.* Padsha, [1923] S. A. A. D. 281.

sor Freund, but more recently by Mr. Root,[189] Mr. Justice
Hughes,[190] Mr. Justice (Mr. as he then was) Sutherland,[191]
and Mr. William D. Guthrie.[192] Its growth is particularly
luxuriant in the federal domain, exercised through a formidable
range and variety of federal administrative tribunals.[193] The

[189] See his presidential address before the American Bar Association in 1916:
"There is one special field of law development which has manifestly become
inevitable. We are entering upon the creation of a body of administrative law
quite different in its machinery, its remedies, and its necessary safeguards from
the old methods of regulation by specific statutes enforced by the courts.
. . . The Interstate Commerce Commission, the state public service commissions,
the Federal Trade Commission, the powers of the Federal Reserve Board, the
health departments of the states, and many other supervisory offices and agencies are familiar illustrations. Before these agencies the old doctrine prohibiting
the delegation of legislative power has virtually retired from the field and given
up the fight. There will be no withdrawal from these experiments. We shall
go on; we shall expand them, whether we approve theoretically or not, because such agencies furnish protection to rights and obstacles to wrong doing
which under our new social and industrial conditions cannot be practically
accomplished by the old and simple procedure of legislatures and courts as in
the last generation. Yet the powers that are committed to these regulating
agencies, and which they must have to do their work, carry with them great
and dangerous opportunities of oppression and wrong. If we are to continue a
government of limited powers these agencies of regulation must themselves be
regulated. The limits of their power over the citizen must be fixed and determined. The rights of the citizen against them must be made plain. A system
of administrative law must be developed, and that with us is still in its infancy,
crude and imperfect." 41 Am. Bar Assn. Rep. 355, 368-9.

[190] Charles E. Hughes, "Some Aspects of the Development of American
Law," 39 N. Y. St. Bar Assn. Rep. 266.

[191] Presidential address before the American Bar Association, 42 Am. Bar
Assn. Rep. 197, 206.

[192] William D. Guthrie, in his presidential address before New York State Bar
Association, 46 N. Y. St. Bar Assn. Rep. 169; Guthrie, League of Nations
and Miscellaneous Addresses, 352.

[193] Thus Mr. Justice Hughes in his address in 1916 before the New York
State Bar Association: "The content of the Federal authority over commerce has
not been enlarged since the beginning, and to understand its scope we recur to
the classic definition of Marshall; but there has been a profound change in the
disposition to use that authority. . . . Within a few years, plans of regulation
involving new exertions of Federal power have followed each other in swift
succession, reflecting convictions of recent origin with respect to national needs.
The Interstate Commerce Act, the Anti-Trust Act, the Safety Appliance Act, the
Hepburn Amendment and the Carmack Amendment to the Interstate Commerce
Act, the Food and Drugs Act, the Meat Inspection Act, the Hours of Service Act,
the Employers' Liability Act, the Clayton Act and the Trade Commission Act
have, to a considerable extent recast our law. . . . With this noteworthy change
in point of view, there have been constant manifestations of a deepening con-

body of administrative law thus fashioned may have its reflex in new forms of legal machinery. Appellate administrative tribunals have already evolved.[194] And the time may well come when pressure of judicial review over administrative decisions will lead to active consideration of the suggestion stirred by Mr. Guthrie for a special court of administrative reviews.[195] The need for a coherent system of administrative law, for uniformity and despatch in adjudication, for the subtle skill required in judges called upon to synthesize the public and private claims peculiarly involved in administrative litigation, these and kindred considerations will have to be balanced against the traditional hold of a single system of courts, giving a generalized professional aptitude to its judges and bringing to the review of administrative conduct a technique and a temperament trained in litigations between private individuals.

---

viction of the impotency of Legislatures with respect to some of the most important departments of law-making. Complaints must be heard, expert investigations conducted, complex situations deliberately and impartially analyzed and legislative rules intelligently adapted to a myriad of instances falling within a general class. It was not difficult to frame legislation establishing a general standard, but to translate an accepted principle into regulations wisely adapted to particular cases required an experienced body sitting continuously and removed so far as possible from the blandishments and intrigues of politics. This administrative type is not essentially new in itself, but the extension of its use in State and Nation constitutes a new departure." 39 N. Y. St. Bar Assn. Rep. 266, 268–70. Of course the phenomenon to which Mr. Justice Hughes thus called attention has had an enormous expansion during the decade since he spoke.

[194] See, *e.g.,* Edward C. Finney, Board of Appeals, Department of the Interior, 10 Am. Pol. Sci. Rev. 290, and Holmes and Brewster, Procedure and Practice before United States Board of Tax Appeals, dealing with an appellate administrative tribunal created by § 900 of the Revenue Act of 1924 (43 Stat. 253, 336). And as to British tendencies, see F. H. C. Wiltshire, " Appellate Jurisdiction of Central Government," 2 J. of Pub. Adm. 370; I. G. Gibbon, " Appellate Jurisdiction," *ibid.* 381.

[195] " I am not prepared to say that the time has yet come for the creation of special courts similar to the French administrative courts, although I am convinced that this will ultimately be found to be advisable." 46 N. Y. St. Bar Assn. Rep. 169, 187; Guthrie, League of Nations and Miscellaneous Addresses, 362, 377–8.

CHAPTER V
FROM THE JUDICIAL CODE
TO THE
POST–WAR JUDICIARY ACTS

I

PERHAPS the decisive factor in the history of the Supreme Court is its progressive contraction of jurisdiction. This tendency has been particularly significant since the Civil War. In contrast with the vast expansion of the bounds of the inferior federal courts, the scope of review by the Supreme Court has been steadily narrowed. Familiar devices for dealing with growth in business by adding to personnel have been eschewed. The serious proposals made from time to time to increase the membership of the Court, to add temporary judges, to break up an enlarged Court into divisions, did not prevail. There are intrinsic limits to the size of a court if it is to be a coherent instrument for the dispatch of business and at the same time to observe the needs of consultation and deliberation. The effective conditions for insuring the quality of judicial output of the Supreme Court have been maintained. Human limitations have been respected. Confidence in the competence of the Court has not been won by the presence of an occasional man of genius. The explanation lies rather in the capacity of the Court adequately to dispose of the tasks committed to it. Despite the country's phenomenal increase in population and wealth and the resulting extension of governmental activities, the duties of the Supreme Court have been kept within limits appropriate for nine judges who are not supermen. On the other hand, Congress, the executive departments, the commissions, and the lower federal courts have always had duties placed upon them which disregarded the limits of strength and capacity. As a result paper duties are neglected; incumbents of high position perform in name only; they are administrators without time to know what they are doing, or to think how to do it.

At times Congress has unduly delayed in narrowing the ambit of the Supreme Court's duties. In the end, however, legislation has been forthcoming to keep the Court sufficiently compact and the litigation within its compass. In a few instances, the Court, by the application of laws of doubtful meaning, has let down the bar to needless litigation. Against the views of Chief Justice Waite and Mr. Justice Miller it held in the *Pacific Railroad Removal Cases*,[1] that every case concerning a federal corporation was necessarily a case "arising under the Constitution or laws of the United States" within the meaning of the Removal Act of March 3, 1875, and thereby unduly burdened its own dockets as well as those of the lower federal courts.[2] Again, out of the doubtful provisions of the Circuit Courts of Appeals Act, the Court, over the protest of Chief Justice Fuller and Mr. Justice Brown, evolved a system of double appeals.[3] Finally — to anticipate the Act of September 6, 1916[4] — in considering when "is drawn in question the validity of a statute," the Court narrowly construed the relief intended by that Act, against the dissent of Mr. Justice Brandeis, concurred in by Mr. Justice Clarke.[5]

Very seldom, indeed, since the original Judiciary Act, has Congress broadened the base of resort to the Supreme Court. Judge Humphrey's decision in the *Beef Trust Case* led to the extension of jurisdiction involved in the Criminal Appeals Act of 1907.[6] Section 240 of the Judicial Code[7] further broadened the government's opportunity for appeal in criminal cases by allowing the United States to bring up criminal cases on writ of *certiorari* after reversal of a judgment of conviction in a circuit court of appeals.[8] The next enlargement of the Court's scope of

---

[1] 115 U. S. 1 (1885).

[2] See p. 69, *supra.*

[3] Spreckels Sugar Refining Co. *v.* McClain, 192 U. S. 397 (1904). See Charles W. Bunn, "Review in the Supreme Court," 35 HARV. L. REV. 902.

[4] 39 STAT. 726, c. 448, § 2.

[5] Dahnke-Walker Co. *v.* Bondurant, 257 U. S. 282 (1921).

[6] See pp. 115 *et seq., supra.*

[7] See United States *v.* Gulf Refining Co., 268 U. S. 542 (1925). For a more recent exercise of this jurisdiction, see United States *v.* Daugherty, 269 U. S. 360 (1926).

[8] This constituted a legislative modification of United States *v.* Dickinson, 213 U. S. 92 (1909), following the grounds taken in United States *v.* Sanges, 144 U. S.

review was again due to profound public concern over a particular case — *Ives* v. *South Buffalo Railway Company*,[9] this time a decision of the New York Court of Appeals. The outcome was a change in the policy of review of state courts by the Supreme Court as it had prevailed since the Union was established.

A vital chapter of American history derives from the famous twenty-fifth section of the Judiciary Act of 1789.[10] The story of its survival against legislative and judicial attacks is to no small degree a narrative of the conflict between national and state forces.[11] *Marbury* v. *Madison*[12] has unduly overshadowed *Cohens* v. *Virginia*.[13] For one hundred and twenty-five years this jurisdiction remained, in effect, as it was molded by the First Congress. Even the powerful centralizing impulses of the Civil War left it unchanged. A revision of the twenty-fifth section by the Judiciary Act of 1867,[14] however, furnished an opportunity for its expansion. From the omission in the Act of 1867 of the restrictive clause of the twenty-fifth section whereby, in reviews from the state courts, "no other error shall be assigned or regarded as a ground of reversal . . . than such as appears on the face of the record, and immediately respects the before mentioned questions of validity or construction of the said constitution, treaties, statutes, commissions, or authorities in dispute," it was urged[15] that the jurisdiction of the Supreme Court was no longer "limited to the correction of errors relating solely to Federal

---

310 (1892). The need for legislation to correct the restrictions against review by the Government of a reversal of conviction was first brought to the attention of Congress by Attorney General Bonaparte, REP. ATTY. GEN. FOR 1908, 4–5, renewed by Attorney General Wickersham the next year, REP. ATTY. GEN. FOR 1909, 20.

9 201 N. Y. 271 (1911).   10 1 STAT. 73, 85–7.

11 See Charles Warren, " Legislative and Judicial Attacks on the Supreme Court of the United States," 47 AMER. L. REV. 1.

12 1 Cranch (U. S.) 137 (1803).

13 6 Wheat. (U. S.) 264 (1821).

14 14 STAT. 385, c. 28, § 2. As amended by this Act it found its way as Section 709 into the Revised Statutes. A further amendment was made by the Act of Feb. 18, 1875, 18 STAT. 316, 318.

15 Particularly in a powerful brief submitted by Benjamin R. Curtis as *amicus curiae*. CURTIS, JURISDICTION OF THE UNITED STATES COURTS, 2 ed., 46 *et seq*. The brief is printed in full *ibid*. 59. Substantial extracts will be found in Murdock v. Memphis, 20 Wall. (U. S.) 590, 602 (1874).

law," [16] but extended to all questions in the record, even those of exclusive state concern. Three Justices acceded to the argument.[17] But the Court, in *Murdock* v. *Memphis*,[18] refused to impute to Congress such a "radical and hazardous change of a policy vital in its essential nature to the independence of the State courts." [19] It thereby also saved itself from a heavy increase in what is perhaps the most obscure field for its adjudications, namely, the interpretation of local statutes and local practices.

The twenty-fifth section of the Judiciary Act provided for writs of error to state courts only when a state court had denied a claim of federal right.[20] Fear of disobedience of national authority by state judiciaries determined this legislation. The framers of the Judiciary Act guarded against the danger of state

---

[16] Murdock *v.* Memphis, 20 Wall. (U. S.) 590, 630 (1874).

[17] Clifford, Swayne, and Bradley, JJ. Waite, C. J., having been appointed after the argument and re-argument of the case, took no part in the judgment.

[18] 20 Wall. (U. S.) 590 (1895).

[19] *Ibid.*, at 630.

[20] The material portion of the twenty-fifth section reads: "That a final judgment . . . in the highest court . . . of a State in which a decision in the suit could be had, where is drawn in question the validity of a treaty or statute of, or an authority exercised under the United States, and the decision is against their validity; or where is drawn in question the validity of a statute of, or an authority exercised under any State, on the ground of their being repugnant to the constitution, treaties or laws of the United States, and the decision is in favour of such their validity, or where is drawn in question the construction of any clause of the constitution, or of a treaty, or statute of, or commission held under the United States, and the decision is against the title, right, privilege or exemption specially set up or claimed by either party, under such clause of the said Constitution, treaty, statute or commission, may be re-examined and reversed or affirmed in the Supreme Court of the United States upon a writ of error. . . ." 1 STAT. 73, 85–6.

Cases in which the Supreme Court refused jurisdiction on the ground that the federal right had been upheld and not denied in the state courts are not numerous. See Gorden *v.* Caldcleugh, 3 Cranch (U. S.) 268 (1806); Montgomery *v.* Hernandez, 12 Wheat. (U. S.) 129 (1827); Commonwealth Bank of Kentucky *v.* Griffith, 14 Pet. (U. S.) 56 (1840); Fulton *v.* Morgan, 16 Pet. (U. S.) 149 (1842); Walker *v.* Taylor, 5 How. (U. S.) 64 (1847); Strader *v.* Baldwin, 9 How. (U. S.) 261 (1850); Linton *v.* Stanton, 12 How. (U. S.) 423 (1851); Burke *v.* Gaines, 19 How. (U. S.) 388 (1856); Reddall *v.* Bryan, 24 How. (U. S.) 420 (1860); Roosevelt *v.* Myer, 1 Wall. (U. S.) 512 (1863); Ryan *v.* Thomas, 4 Wall. (U. S.) 603 (1866); Missouri *v.* Andriano, 138 U. S. 496 (1891); Jersey City & Bergen R. R. *v.* Morgan, 160 U. S. 288 (1895); De Lamar's Gold Mining Co. *v.* Nesbitt, 177 U. S. 523 (1900); Kizer *v.* Texarkana & Ft. Smith Ry., 179 U. S. 199 (1900); Baker *v.* Baldwin, 187 U. S. 61 (1902).

judges whose inclination towards support of action by their
"sovereign states" would lead them to be unmindful of the national interest as expressed in the Constitution, laws and treaties
of the United States.[21] The constitutional litigation of the first
half of the nineteenth century does not prove these fears to have
been ill-founded.[22]

Though politically of great moment these cases prior to the
Civil War were not very numerous. After 1870, however, the
legislative momentum became accelerated. In turn the new
protection of the Fourteenth Amendment, with its "convenient
vagueness,"[23] was invoked against the various regulatory laws.
Judicial development of the Fourteenth Amendment put claims
of federal right within easy reach of astute counsel in the state
courts. Litigation was multiplied by the heavy legislative output,
concurring with the opportunities afforded by the Fourteenth
Amendment. The twenty-fifth section, in its modern phrasing,
became one of the most active sources of Supreme Court business.
With the twentieth century came the steady rise in the flood of
social legislation. But in 1905 it received a sharp check by
Lochner v. *New York*.[24] State courts added their force to the
ensuing ebb.[25] The broad language of Mr. Justice Peckham in
Allgeyer v. *Louisiana*[26] and later in the *Lochner* case was un-

---

[21] The historic consideration has thus been expressed by the Supreme Court:
"The object of the present judiciary act was not to give a right of review
wherever the validity of an act of Congress was drawn in question, but to prevent
courts of the several States from impairing or frittering away the authority of
the federal government, by giving a construction to its statutes adverse to such
authority." Missouri *v.* Andriano, 138 U. S. 496, 499 (1891).

[22] See, for instance, the fate of the Kentucky Court of Appeals which, against
the strong desires of the community, in Blair *v.* Williams, 4 Litt. (Ky.) 35 (1823),
held state laws staying the levy of executions and imposing restrictions upon
execution sales to be unconstitutional. Efforts at impeachment followed. See
McElroy, Kentucky in the Nation's History, 377, 387 *et seq.* This led to an
attempt to broaden the right of appeal to the Supreme Court. A bill was introduced by Senator Talbot, of Kentucky, permitting parties in suits involving a
federal question to remove them prior to trial to the federal courts. The bill,
however, was not pressed. See Charles Warren, "Legislative and Judicial Attacks
on the Supreme Court of the United States," 47 Amer. L. Rev. 1, 528.

[23] Charles M. Hough, "Due Process of Law — Today," 32 Harv. L. Rev. 218.

[24] 198 U. S. 45 (1905).

[25] For a summary of the trend of decision in the state courts at this period,
see Roscoe Pound. "Liberty of Contract," 18 Yale L. J. 454.

[26] 165 U. S. 578 (1897).

critically accepted, and constitutional adjudications drew heavily on loose dicta.[27]   Courts inculcated with the doctrine of *Matter of Jacobs*[28] found vindication in the *Lochner* case.   In 1908, however, application of a new technique[29] in constitutional arguments wherein an appreciation of facts is the decisive element,[30] brought forth *Muller* v. *Oregon*[31] and with it the hope of a restricted direction to the Fourteenth Amendment.   The philosophy behind the constitutional outlook of Mr. Justice Holmes, insofar as the generalities of due process were involved, appeared to be vindicated by demonstration in detail.   His warnings that " a constitution is not intended to embody a particular economic theory "[32] and that the " accident " of the Court " finding certain opinions natural and familiar or novel and even shocking ought not to conclude our judgment upon the question whether statutes embodying them conflict with the Constitution of the United States "[33] seemed at last to have been heeded, in the regard which was paid in *Muller* v. *Oregon* to the realities behind industrial legislation.[34]

---

[27] See Charles Warren, " The New Liberty under the Fourteenth Amendment," 39 HARV. L. REV. 431, 448, 449.

[28] 98 N. Y. 98 (1885).

[29] The application of the inductive method to constitutional cases, characterized later by Mr. Justice McKenna as an appeal to " a judgment from experience as against a judgment from speculation." Tanner *v.* Little, 240 U. S. 369, 386 (1916).   In the Muller case Mr. Justice Brewer thus indicated the significance of the new type of argument and brief first introduced by Mr. Brandeis appearing in this case for Oregon: " In patent cases counsel are apt to open the argument with a discussion of the state of the art.   It may not be amiss, in the present case, before examining the constitutional question, to notice the course of legislation as well as expressions of opinion from other than judicial sources.   In the brief filed by Mr. Louis D. Brandeis, for the defendant in error, is a very copious collection of all these matters, an epitome of which is found in the margin . . . when a question of fact is debated and debatable, and the extent to which a special constitutional limitation goes is affected by the truth in respect to that truth, a widespread and long continued belief concerning it is worthy of consideration.   We take judicial cognizance of all matters of general knowledge." 208 U. S. 412, 419, 420–21 (1908).

[30] See Felix Frankfurter, " Hours of Labor and Realism in Constitutional Law," 29 HARV. L. REV. 353, and Henry Wolf Biklé, " Judicial Determination of Questions of Fact Affecting the Constitutional Validity of Legislative Action," 38 HARV. L. REV. 6.

[31] 208 U. S. 412 (1908).

[32] Lochner *v.* New York, 198 U. S. 45, 75 (1905).   [33] *Ibid.*

[34] See, for instance, the significance which the present Chief Justice attaches to the basis which underlies Muller *v.* Oregon and the series of cases which followed

Into this atmosphere of expectancy workmen's compensation legislation was ushered. Its tried experience in other industrial countries, the long, careful investigations which preceded enactment, the thorough discrediting of common-law doctrines of master and servant when applied to modern industry, gave assurance to the belief that the broad outlines of the Constitution did not exclude the adaptation of legislation to modern industrial necessities. But the economic and social considerations which prevailed with the Supreme Court in 1908 were deemed irrelevant by the New York Court of Appeals in 1911.[35] In *Ives* v. *South Buffalo Railway Company* that court unanimously defeated the first American workmen's compensation law by finding it " a deprivation of liberty and property under the Federal and State Constitutions." [36]

The *Ives* decision aroused the fiercest criticism. Theodore

---

it " which may be said to have established a rule of decision." Adkins *v.* Children's Hospital, 261 U. S. 525, 563, 566 (1923). Both the Chief Justice and Mr. Justice Holmes in their dissenting opinions in the Adkins case assumed that this series of cases, ending with Bunting *v.* Oregon, 243 U. S. 426 (1917), had worn away the authority of the Lochner case. " I have always supposed," the Chief Justice put it, " that the *Lochner Case* was thus overruled *sub silentio.*" 261 U. S. at 564. And Mr. Justice Holmes " had supposed . . . that *Lochner* v. *New York*, 198 U. S. 45, would be allowed a deserved repose." *Ibid.*, at 570.

[35] " In arriving at this conclusion we do not overlook the cogent economic and sociological arguments which are urged in support of the statute. There can be no doubt as to the theory of this law. It is based upon the proposition that the inherent risks of an employment should in justice be placed upon the shoulders of the employer, who can protect himself against loss by insurance and by such an addition to the price of his wares as to cast the burden ultimately upon the consumer; that indemnity to an injured employee should be as much a charge upon the business as the cost of replacing or repairing disabled or defective machinery, appliances or tools; that, under our present system, the loss falls immediately upon the employee who is almost invariably unable to bear it, and ultimately upon the community which is taxed for the support of the indigent; and that our present system is uncertain, unscientific and wasteful, and fosters a spirit of antagonism between employer and employee which it is to the interests of the state to remove. . . . If such economic and sociologic arguments as are here advanced in support of this statute can be allowed to subvert the fundamental idea of property, then there is no private right entirely safe, because there is no limitation upon the absolute discretion of legislatures, and the guarantees of the Constitution are a mere waste of words." Ives *v.* South Buffalo Ry., 201 N. Y. 271, 294–95 (1911).

[36] 201 N. Y. 271, 294 (1911). For the further history of New York workmen's compensation legislation, see N. Y. Cent. R. R. *v.* White, 243 U. S. 188, 195–96 (1917).

Roosevelt led the critics in characteristic language,[37] but even such sober organs as the *New York Evening Post* and the *Springfield Republican* uttered vigorous speech.[38] Nor was the legal profession, on the whole, less outraged.[39] A notable protest of "teachers of Constitutional law in some of the principal law schools and universities of the country, who have devoted years of study to the principles of American Constitutions" included the names of Andrew A. Bruce, Ernst Freund, Frank J. Goodnow, James Parker Hall, and Roscoe Pound.[40]

The adverse New York decision came on the heels of the spacious conception of the scope of the due process clause announced by the Supreme Court in the famous case of *Noble*

---

[37] Theodore Roosevelt, "Workmen's Compensation," 98 OUTLOOK, 49, 53 (May 13, 1911). After quoting an "eminent jurist" to the effect that the decision was "another illustration that in many American courts property is more sacred than life," Roosevelt continued: " It is out of the question that the courts should be permitted permanently to shackle our hands as they would shackle them by such decisions as this, as the decision by the same Court many years ago in the tenement-house cigar factory cases, and the decision of the bakeshop cases shackled them. Such decisions are profoundly anti-social, are against the interests of humanity, and tell for the degradation of a very large proportion of our community; and, above all, they seek to establish as an immutable principle the doctrine that the rights of property are supreme over the rights of humanity, and that this free people, this American people, is not only forbidden to better the conditions of mankind, but cannot even strive to do the elementary justice that, among even the monarchies of the Old World, has already been done by other great industrial nations." For a reply to Roosevelt's criticism, see Charles C. Moore, " New York Workmen's Compensation Act," 15 LAW NOTES, 44.

[38] See press comments in 42 LITERARY DIGEST for Apr. 8, 1911.

[39] See, *e.g.*, the comment of Mr. Bernard Flexner: " The decision is a shock not only to the ' economist ' . . . ; it is quite as distinct a shock to a growing number of judges and lawyers who recognize that our employers' liability laws are barbarous. . . . A court which cites at this time *In re* Jacobs, as an illustration of the limitation of the exercise of police power, rightfully draws down upon itself the criticism not of laymen alone, but of lawyers who find in the economic, social, and ethical conditions that the New York court brushes aside with a few patronizing words the justification for a constantly widening exercise of the police power of the state." 26 SURVEY, 192 (Apr. 29, 1911). And see comments of other lawyers in the same issue of THE SURVEY. Also James P. Hall, " New York Workmen's Compensation Act Decision," 19 JOUR. POL. ECON. 694; Ernst Freund, " Constitutional Status of Workmen's Compensation," 6 ILL. L. REV. 432; A. A. Bruce, " The New York Employers' Liability Act," 9 MICH. L. REV. 684; Edward Q. Keasbey, " The Courts and the New Social Questions," 24 GREEN BAG, 114; Eugene Wambaugh, " Workmen's Compensation Acts," 25 HARV. L. REV. 129; and Notes in 11 COL. L. REV. 475 and 24 HARV. L. REV. 647.

[40] 98 OUTLOOK, 709, 710 (July 29, 1911).

State Bank v. *Haskell*.[41] Mr. Justice Holmes' opinion, speaking for a unanimous Court, gave solid hope that the justification which underlay workmen's compensation legislation would find ample shelter within the due process clause.[42] But the *Ives* case, so long as it stood, remained an obstacle if not a bar — short of constitutional amendment [43] — to workmen's compensation laws. For claims under the Federal Constitution had been asserted and sustained. Federal right had been vindicated, not denied. Under the existing appellate jurisdiction there was no way of reviewing the *Ives* result by the Supreme Court. When, shortly after, the Supreme Court of Washington upheld the constitutionality of a similar statute,[44] the demand for review by the Supreme Court was intensified by a wide-spread feeling that, in practice, constitutionality turned on geography.[45]

---

[41] 219 U. S. 104, 575 (1911).

[42] See, for instance, Professor Ernst Freund's prophecy "there is good reason to believe that the Supreme Court would sustain such a law," 26 SURVEY, 195, 196 (April 29, 1911), and Senator Root's remark: "There have been some cases in which the decisions of the courts of last resort in states have been in favor of the claim, giving to the provisions of the Federal Constitution an effect which many people think the Supreme Court would not give to those cases. The notable case in that connection is the Ives case in New York, regarding the workmen's compensation act." Address before the Judiciary Committee of the House of Representatives, February 27, 1914, printed in ROOT, ADDRESSES ON GOVERNMENT AND CITIZENSHIP, 466, 475.

[43] The inaptness of the suggestion of the New York court, to modify the conception of due process by constitutional amendment as a way of securing workmen's compensation legislation, was thus dealt with in the protest of the law teachers: "A court which condemns a rule of law as contrary to due process should not suggest a remedy by an appeal to the people; for such a suggestion creates the impression that the principle of due process is one susceptible of improvement." 98 OUTLOOK, 709, 711 (July 29, 1911).

[44] State v. Clausen, 65 Wash. 156, 117 Pac. 1101 (1911), vindicating the prophecy made shortly before this decision by Mr. Louis D. Brandeis in a letter to the editor of THE SURVEY: "I am inclined to think that we shall find legislatures of some of the other states undeterred by the decision of your Court of Appeals; and some other court will have the opportunity soon of making a more just decision." 26 SURVEY, 198 (Apr. 29, 1911). In a few years Mr. Justice Brandeis shared in decisions by the Supreme Court sustaining workmen's compensation laws more sweeping than the one temporarily defeated by the New York Court of Appeals. See Mountain Timber Co. v. Washington, 243 U. S. 219 (1917); Arizona Employers' Liability Cases, 250 U. S. 400 (1919); Ward & Gow v. Krinsky, 259 U. S. 503 (1922). For the steady extension of the workmen's compensation legislation movement, see Bulletins No. 272, 332 and 379 of United States Bureau of Labor Statistics.

[45] Anticipating that the Supreme Court of Washington would reach a result contrary to that reached by the New York Court of Appeals, the Committee of

Thus did the *Ives* case precipitate the movement to alter the appellate jurisdiction of the Supreme Court over state courts. The impetus given by that decision was sufficiently powerful to realize the desire for reform which it provoked. "Lawyers, as a class," wrote the lawyers of the House Judiciary Committee,

"are conservative and slow to change existing laws. Reforms in the law grow out of some concrete experience that so forcibly presents the necessity of change as to arouse public interest. The decision of the Ives Case in New York, which held the Workmen's Compensation Act passed by the Legislature of New York unconstitutional, on the grounds that it was in violation of the Fourteenth Amendment to the Federal Constitution served this purpose." [46]

Yet lawyers bore the heaviest testimony against the New York decision; and lawyers promptly exerted themselves to devise and promote legislation to effect the necessary change in the reviewing power whereby sterile applications of the Federal Constitution might be subjected to the livelier scrutiny of the Supreme Court. The lead was taken by a special committee of the American Bar Association.[47] In December, 1911, a bill drafted by it, extending writs of error to judgments of the highest court of the state upholding as well as denying a federal right, was introduced in both Houses of Congress.[48] Senator Root vigorously supported it in Congress.[49] The bill came out of the Senate Judiciary Committee with *certiorari* substituted for writ of error for the new class of cases.[50] This amendment met the occasion by furnishing a means of review and yet protecting the already over-loaded Court from further obligatory jurisdiction.[51] In this shape the bill encoun-

---

the Bar Association remarked: "We shall then be in the position of having the Constitution of the United States mean one thing in New York, and another in Washington." 36 Am. Bar Assn. Rep. 448, 464.

[46] House Report, No. 1222, 63rd Cong., 3rd Sess., Ser. No. 6766, 2.

[47] 36 Am. Bar Assn. Rep. 448, 462, 469.

[48] In the Senate on December 13, 1911, by Nelson (by request); and the House on Dec. 20, 1911, by Clayton. 48 Cong. Rec. 294, 580. Similar bills were introduced in the House by Lenroot on Jan. 4, 1912, and by French on Jan. 8, 1912. *Ibid.* 676, 736.

[49] See Root, *op. cit.* 467, 474.

[50] In this form it was reported out by Senator Root, Apr. 4, 1912. Sen. Rep., No. 560, 67th Cong., 2nd Sess., Ser. No. 6121; 48 Cong. Rec. 4274.

[51] "The idea of that modification was that the unlimited right would load down the calendar of the Supreme Court of the United States with a vast multi-

tered little opposition and passed the Senate without division.[52] Nevertheless the House adjourned without action.

The legislative effort was at once renewed in the new Congress. In various forms bills were introduced authorizing cases decided in favor of the claim of a federal right to be brought up to the Supreme Court.[53] But the legislative pace had slowed down as the spur of the *Ives* case weakened with time. Congress again had to be pushed from without. Thus, the Wisconsin Legislature memorialized Congress,[54] although a voluntary as distinguished from a compulsory compensation act, such as was involved in the *Ives* case, had already hurdled the constitutional barriers before the Wisconsin Supreme Court.[55] The American Bar Association continued to prod,[56] but the first Wilson Congress was preoccupied with more urgent demands for legislation, and not until January 20, 1914, was Senator Root's bill reported out of the Judiciary Committee.[57] The bill promptly passed the Senate,[58] but again encountered delay in the House, where it went over to the next session.[59] Meanwhile the New Jersey Supreme Court upheld a workmen's compensation statute [60] and thereby emphasized the geographic feature of constitutionality. As the House Judiciary Committee pithily reported: " The Fourteenth Amendment meant one thing on the east bank of the Hudson and the

---

tude of cases in which an appeal was taken for purposes of delay, and that in every case of public importance and concern involving a constitutional question the Supreme Court would exercise its jurisdiction." Root, ADDRESSES ON GOVERNMENT AND CITIZENSHIP, 467, 476.

[52] 48 CONG. REC. 6012.

[53] In the Senate by Root on Apr. 7, 1913; by Jones (for Clapp) on Apr. 21, 1913; by Nelson on May 5, 1913; by Gallinger on Dec. 1, 1913; by Smith of Georgia on Dec. 10, 1913; by Root on Jan. 14, 1914. 50 CONG. REC. 53, 239, 1094, 6051; 51 *ibid*. 593, 1622. In the House by Lenroot on Apr. 7, 1913; by French on Apr. 7, 1913; by Smith of Minnesota on Aug. 9. 1913. 50 *ibid*. 81, 90, 3202.

[54] *Ibid*. 1797.

[55] Borgnis v. Falk Co., 147 Wis. 327, 133 N. W. 209 (1911).

[56] 38 AM. BAR ASSN. REP. 45.

[57] Through Senator Root on Jan. 20, 1914, SEN. REP., No. 161, 63rd Cong., 2nd Sess., Ser. No. 6552; 51 CONG. REC. 2016.

[58] On Jan. 21, 1914, *ibid*. 2016.

[59] It was reported from the House Judiciary Committee on Dec. 14, 1914. See HOUSE REPORT, No. 1222, 63rd Cong., 3rd Sess., Ser. No. 6766; 52 CONG. REC. 199.

[60] Sexton v. Newark District Telegraph Co., 84 N. J. 85, 86 Atl. 451 (1913).

opposite thing on the west bank." [61]   When the bill finally reached the calendar of the House it moved easily.   The debate gave vent to feelings about the *Ives* case as well as about the general attitude of courts toward social legislation.   No one ventured to defend the *Ives* case,[62] and Lewis of Maryland took occasion to remark that the prevalent judicial mood had destroyed "some of the wisest state legislation enacted in this country on these difficult relations of capital and labor." [63]   The bill passed without division,[64] and on December 23, 1914, a new principle of appellate control over state courts became law.[65]

2

Since the Judicial Code, the Act of December 23, 1914, is the only instance of Congressional expansion of the jurisdiction of the Supreme Court.   But the story of a second attempt must be told, and for convenience it will be dealt with here, out of its chronological order.   The instance is important for its own sake, as well as for the legislative method which it discloses.   The history of federal judiciary acts is singularly free from a frequent tendency in state legislation whereby the special need of an individual in a particular litigation is written into a judicial code.[66]   Public interest and widely canvassed professional views have guided the laws by which the jurisdiction of the federal

---

[61] HOUSE REPORT, No. 1222, 63rd Cong., 3rd Sess., Ser. No. 6766, 2.

[62] 52 CONG. REC. 276.

[63] *Ibid.* 277.

[64] *Ibid.*

[65] 38 STAT. 790.

[66] See Senator Root's testimony, derived from special experience with the New York Code of Civil Procedure but reflecting a practice prevalent throughout the country:

"MR. McCOY.   Is it not true that a lawyer who has encountered something in his own particular practice is likely to go up to the legislature and get an amendment to the code?

"MR. ROOT.   Precisely.   And the prohibitions which are put in our constitutions against special legislation have contributed to that.   Somebody sees what seems to him an evil in his own practice, or he is disgruntled; something has been done that he does not like, and he becomes a member of the legislature, and he gets a change in the code of procedure.   That may be all very well for him, but it may be very bad, indeed, for ten thousand other people; and our system of practice has been built up in that way on special instances to answer the demands of the lawyer who thinks about his own case instead of considering the general interests of the public."   ROOT, *op. cit.* 467, 469–70.

courts is determined. The so-called Cummins Amendment of February 17, 1922,[67] furnishes a striking exception.

On May 17, 1921, Senator Cummins of Iowa introduced a bill [68] to amend Section 237 of the Judicial Code, which determines the scope of writs of error from judgments of state courts. The Senate Judiciary Committee reported the bill favorably but without comment.[69] A perfunctory debate followed, a short colloquy between Senator King and Senator Nelson, who had charge of the measure, revealing very clearly that neither was aware of the purpose or effect of the proposal.[70] In this atmosphere of indifference and senatorial courtesy it passed the Senate without division.[71] In the House the measure received more serious consideration. The report of the House Judiciary Committee, supplemented by the remarks [72] of Congressman

---

[67] 42 STAT. 366. The Act amended Section 237 of the Judicial Code by the following addition: " In any suit involving the validity of a contract wherein it is claimed that a change in the rule of law or construction of statutes by the highest court of a state applicable to such contract would be repugnant to the Constitution of the United States, the Supreme Court shall, upon writ of error, re-examine, reverse, or affirm the final judgment of the highest court of a state in which a decision in the suit could be had, if said claim is made in said court at any time before said final judgment is entered and if the decision is against the claim so made."

[68] 61 CONG. REC. 1497.

[69] *Ibid.* 348.

[70] *Ibid.* 5011. Senator Nelson, in the absence of Senator Cummins and at his request, pressed the bill: " MR. NELSON. Mr. President, I ask unanimous consent to go back to Senate bill 1831, to amend section 237 of the Judicial Code. That bill was introduced by the senior Senator from Iowa [MR. CUMMINS], who is ill, and he is very anxious to have it passed." That Senator Nelson misconceived the implication of the bill is plain from his reply to a question from Senator King: " This [bill] does not enlarge the jurisdiction [of the Supreme Court] at all, in any shape or manner." *Ibid.*

[71] *Ibid.*

[72] " When a person contracts in keeping with the law then in force, as declared by the supreme court of the State, he thus acquires a property interest that can not be taken away by a subsequent reversal by the supreme court of that State of its former holding. However, the supreme court of a State does sometimes reverse its former holdings without declaring the fact, and in such case, where vested property rights are affected adversely, the Supreme Court of the United States will right the wrong, if the question is properly presented. In order to have review by the Supreme Court of the United States the question must have been first claimed or the right asserted in the State court. This bill affords the remedy, and by making claim in a petition for rehearing in the State supreme court the Supreme Court of the United States will entertain a writ of error and correct any errors of the State court." 62 CONG. REC. 2188.

Boies of Iowa, the House proponent, leaves no doubt as to the actual intent of Congress:

" The purpose of this amendment is to provide a litigant the opportunity to amend his pleadings before final judgment in a case where the Supreme Court of a State in reversing its previous holdings thereby renders a contract valid at the time of execution invalid by reason of the new holding, in such a manner as to preserve the right to carry the case on writ of error to the Supreme Court of the United States, in order to have the opinion of the Supreme Court upon the right of the party complaining to have his contract construed and upheld under and according to the law as proclaimed by the Supreme Court of a State at the time of the due execution of the contract." [73]

Members of the House were more inquisitive about the origin and objects of the bill than was the Senate, even though Mr. Boies claimed for the bill the support of the Chief Justice and the Attorney General.[74] Discussion did not remove doubts, and the bill went over to a later date. When next considered, Mr. Mann of Illinois allayed suspicion by denying that the bill was in the nature of private legislation for a particular litigant:

" I am informed there was a case in the Supreme Court of the State of Iowa where this provision might have been desirable under certain circumstances. That case was disposed of and this will not apply to it; but one of the judges of the Supreme Court of Iowa who took part in the decision of that case considered it important enough afterwards, when he was no longer a judge of the supreme court, to call attention to it, so it is not intended to apply to any particular case." [75]

With these assurances the bill passed the House and was allowed to become law on February 17, 1922.

Mr. Mann was misinformed. There was a case then pending in the Supreme Court of Iowa to which the Act did apply, and it was this case to which Mr. Mann undoubtedly referred.[76]

---

[73] HOUSE REPORT, No. 534, 67th Cong., 2nd Sess., Ser. No. 7955.

[74] 62 CONG. REC. 1227. This claim seems extraordinary in view of the opinion of the Chief Justice in Tidal Oil Co. *v.* Flanagan, 263 U. S. 444 (1924).

[75] 62 CONG. REC. 2188.

[76] Fleming *v.* Fleming, 194 Iowa 71 (1922). The original decision in this case was rendered on Dec. 16, 1919. A petition for rehearing was filed on Feb. 5, 1920, resulting in a supplemental decision on Dec. 20, 1920. A second petition for rehearing was filed on Feb. 17, 1921, leading to a third decision on Sept. 28,

The Iowa judge indicated by Mr. Mann had been a dissenting judge in *Fleming* v. *Fleming*[77] and after he left the Supreme Court of Iowa he joined Senator Cummins, who had been acting as counsel in the case.[78] In their brief[79] they relied upon the Act of February 17, 1922, to support the Supreme Court's jurisdiction.

But to no avail. The Act encountered "the long line of decisions"[80] establishing the settled constitutional doctrine that a change by the state court of a rule of law governing a contract is not equivalent to a "law" impairing the obligation of contracts. When the Cummins Amendment came before it, the Supreme Court reinterpreted the "intent" of Congress and completely defeated the aim of Senator Cummins, which certainly his senatorial colleagues did not apprehend. By a familiar canon of constitutional construction the Supreme Court was constrained to disregard the actual but unconstitutional intent of the promoters of this legislation if thereby it could save the Act, however restricted in its scope.[81] Chief Justice Taft him-

1921, in which the Iowa Supreme Court specifically denied that a federal question was involved. A third petition for rehearing was filed on Nov. 5, 1921, which the Iowa supreme court overruled without opinion on Apr. 23, 1922. See Transcript of Record, Supreme Court of the United States, Fleming *v.* Fleming, Oct. Term, 1923, No. 175, 85, 131. The writ of error from the Supreme Court was not allowed until Dec. 16, 1922. *Ibid.* 139. The record discloses no evidence of any effort to secure such a writ prior to the passage of the Act of February 17, 1922.

[77] See dissenting opinions of Salinger, J., in Fleming *v.* Fleming, 194 Iowa at 89, 109.

[78] See Fleming *v.* Fleming, 194 Ia. 71, 73, 174 N. W. 946, 947, 180 N. W. 206, 184 N. W. 296 (1920–21–22); s. c. 264 U. S. 29, 30 (1924).

[79] See Brief for Appellant, in Fleming *v.* Fleming, in the Supreme Court of the United States, 10.

[80] See Tidal Oil Co. *v.* Flanagan, 263 U. S. 444, 451 (1924).

[81] A month prior to the argument in Fleming *v.* Fleming, *supra,* note 78, the case of Tidal Oil Co. *v.* Flanagan, *supra,* note 80, was decided, involving an exactly similar situation. Following the decision in Tidal Oil Co. *v.* Flanagan, *supra,* on Jan. 7, 1924, Senator Cummins and Judge Salinger, as counsel for plaintiffs in error in the Fleming case, filed a reply brief contending that in the Flanagan case the court fell into "error as to what said act affects." Roughly speaking, it provides that where there is a suit involving the validity of a contract and it is claimed therein that the highest court of the state has made a change in the rule of law or construction of statutes applicable to such contract which it is asserted is repugnant to the Constitution of the United States, the Supreme Court shall upon writ of error re-examine, etc., provided that said claim is made by a stated time." Reply brief, Fleming *v.* Fleming, 10–11.

self wrote the opinion of the Court demonstrating the futility of the purpose avowed by Mr. Boies:

" The intention of Congress was not, we think, to add to the general appellate jurisdiction of this Court existing under prior legislation, but rather to permit a review on writ of error in a particular class of cases in which the defeated party claims that his federal constitutional rights have been violated by the judgment of the state court itself, and further to permit the raising of the objection after the handing down of the opinion. This Court has always held it a prerequisite to the consideration here of a federal question in a case coming from a state court that the question should have been raised in that court before decision, or that it should have been actually entertained and considered upon petition to rehear. A mere denial of the petition by the state court without opinion, is not enough. . . .

" It was the purpose of the Act of 1922 to change the rule established by this formidable array of authorities as to the class of cases therein described. . . .

" We can not assume that Congress attempted to give to this Court appellate jurisdiction beyond the judicial power accorded to the United States by the Constitution." [82]

Tidal Oil Co. v. *Flanagan* [83] and *Fleming* v. *Fleming* [84] thus accomplished a practical nullification of the Amendment.[85] Its elimination in the revised enactment of Section 237 in the Act of February 13, 1925,[86] leaves the abortive measure an interesting episode in the history of federal judicature, and a striking warning against such legislative methods.

---

[82] Tidal Oil Co. *v.* Flanagan, 263 U. S. at 454, 455.

[83] *Supra,* note 80.

[84] *Supra,* note 78.

[85] Senator Cummins, in the petition for rehearing filed in Fleming *v.* Fleming, thus characterizes the decision: " It is true that the special act intended a new time limit as to such cases as the one at bar is, but that was not all that was intended. For if a matter may not be reviewed at all, it is idle to make time provisions as to it. In a word, the opinion holds Congress intended nothing by the Act it passed and which it expected the President to sign." Petition for Rehearing, 3.

[86] 43 STAT. 936. It is interesting to note that Judge Salinger, Senator Cummins' associate in Fleming *v.* Fleming, opposed the legislation which eventuated in the Judiciary Act of 1925, partly because it would repeal the Act of Feb. 17, 1922, *supra.* We quote the following from his testimony before the House Judiciary Committee on Apr. 18, 1922:

" Judge Salinger. . . . The ink is hardly dry on a measure that passed the

3

The rest of our story concerns the period ushered in by the World War and the sharp stimulus to the growth of the business of the federal courts which followed in its wake. We shall briefly record the efforts which resulted in an increase in the number of federal judges, in a steady decrease of the obligatory jurisdiction of the Supreme Court and in firmer articulation of the federal judicial system.

When the Act of December 23, 1914,[87] was going through the House, Mr. Mann of Illinois noted its tendency further to increase the work of the Supreme Court, and prophesied that the next Congressional action would have to be directed towards lessening its burden.[88] His discernment was soon vindicated. In fact, while the Act of 1914 was in the legislative mill, measures for relief were before the House. On October 2, 1914, Beall of Texas sponsored a bill,[89] the principal object of which was to shut off reviews as of right by the Supreme Court in bankruptcy litigation. The House Judiciary Committee stated conclusive reasons for this curtailment of an overburdened docket:

" The bankruptcy law has now been so thoroughly construed that there is not much doubt about any of its provisions, and cases now coming to the Supreme Court under it involve complicated questions of fact rather than law. Besides all of this many of these matters now have four hearings — one before the referee, one in the district court, one in the circuit courts of appeals and one in the Supreme Court.

House on February 6, last, with expressed approval of the Chief Justice and of the Department of Justice. Same is now a law and provides that if the objection is raised before the court of last resort enters final judgment there shall be review by writ of error where a contract that was, when made, approved by the decisions of said State court of last resort, and that court now overrules such decisions. Under the bill before you that law will be repealed and it will become matter of discretion whether the Supreme Court will interfere. . . .

" Mr. Walsh. That was passed to cover an exceptional case, and such change-of-front cases would probably be very few.

" Judge Salinger. It was passed to cover cases that are in a class by themselves. But they are not few. . . ." Hearing before the Committee on the Judiciary, House of Representatives, 67 Cong., 2nd Sess., on H. R. 10479, Ser. 33, Pt. 2, Apr. 18 and 27, 1922, p. 2.

[87] 38 STAT. 790.
[88] 52 CONG. REC. 277.
[89] 51 CONG. REC. 16097.

Certainly all litigants ought to be satisfied with a hearing before the referee, a trial in the district court, an appeal to the circuit court of appeals, with a right of review in the Supreme Court of the United States by a writ of *certiorari* upon a sufficient showing." [90]

The bill also gave the circuit courts of appeals finality in cases under the trademark laws; [91] and by attaching Porto Rico to the first circuit withdrew from the Supreme Court review of the District Court of Porto Rico, save in cases where appeal lay from the federal district courts.[92]   After a smooth and unevent-

---

[90] HOUSE REPORT, No. 1182, 63rd Cong., 2d Sess., reprinted in 52 CONG. REC. 435.

[91] Under the Act of Feb. 20, 1905, § 18, 33 STAT. 724, the right of appeal in trademark cases arising under that Act was assimilated to the prevailing right of appeal in patent causes, thereby making circuit courts of appeals the final tribunal, subject only to review by *certiorari*. Hutchinson, Pierce & Co. *v.* Lowey, 217 U. S. 457 (1910). The Judicial Code left this situation unchanged. Street & Smith *v.* Atlas Mfg. Co., 231 U. S. 348 (1913). Since few cases involving trademarks arose save under the Act of 1905, the change affected was more formal than substantial.

[92] The consideration which led Congress to attach Porto Rico to the First Circuit rather than the Second was thus put by Senator Root: "the disposition made in the bill by the House, and which was anticipated by the Judiciary Committee of the Senate, would facilitate the disposal of business coming from Porto Rico much better than to send it to the second circuit. The second circuit appears to be overburdened, and the effect of sending it there would be probable delay in the disposition of causes that come up. The opportunity to get a swift decision in the first circuit, I think, is very much better." 52 CONG. REC. 1545–6. Senator Root then proceeded to state the reasons which led to the withdrawal of this jurisdiction from the obligatory duties of the Supreme Court: "The transaction of business in Porto Rico and Hawaii and different outlying possessions has been gradually shaping down to a fixed course of procedure and a common understanding of the relations of the judicial proceedings in those islands to the general administration of justice in the United States. There was a period during which everything was chaotic; there were great misunderstandings and differences of understanding, and it was probably desirable at that time that the Supreme Court of the United States should supervise the settling of the law. I think that time has passed. I think they are getting down to an ordinary regular course of procedure in the administration of justice, which makes it appropriate to apply to them the same principle with respect of appeals and with respect of the review of decisions which we apply to our own States. Inasmuch as it is quite certain that as we go on we must progressively relieve the Supreme Court, it seems to me that this step which puts Porto Rico on the same basis with Connecticut and Rhode Island and Vermont and the other New England states is timely and is called for. The enormous growth of this country and the still greater growth of national business as compared with local state business and the great extension of the field over which national authority is asserted are creating an enormous number of new questions and increasing the burden upon the

ful passage in both houses,[93] the bill became law on January 28, 1915.[94]

The Act of 1915 was a feeble palliative. The number of cases on the Supreme Court's docket steadily mounted and the delay in their disposition lengthened. From 509 cases docketed in

---

Supreme Court, and as the process of extension goes on that increase of burden will go on. The judges of our Supreme Court now are driven to the very limit of their human power to do their work, and if you drive them too hard, if you impose too great a body of duty upon them, you do not get good work; you do not get the operation of fresh and active minds, and thus we are going to have the great and all-important function for the whole country which is performed by the Supreme Court done in an inferior way." 52 CONG. REC. 1546.

For an illuminating instance of the corrective review still exercised by the Supreme Court on *certiorari* over decisions of the Circuit Court of Appeals involving Porto Rican law see Diaz v. Gonzalez, 261 U. S. 102 (1923). Mr. Justice Holmes, for the Court, uttered admonitions of humility, applicable to every tribunal when called upon to administer an unfamiliar body of law: "This Court has stated many times the deference due to the understanding of the local courts upon matters of purely local concern. . . . This is especially true in dealing with the decisions of a Court inheriting and brought up in a different system from that which prevails here. When we contemplate such a system from the outside it seems like a wall of stone, every part even with all the others, except so far as our own local education may lead us to see subordinations to which we are accustomed. But to one brought up within it, varying emphasis, tacit assumptions, unwritten practices, a thousand influences gained only from life, may give to the different parts wholly new values that logic and grammar never could have got from the books." 261 U. S. at 105–6.

[93] It was reported to the House (HOUSE REPORT 1182, 63rd Cong., 2nd Sess.) on Oct. 8, 1914 (51 CONG. REC. 16345) and passed on Dec. 16, (52 *ibid.* 282–3). It passed the Senate with minor amendments on Jan. 14, 1915 (*ibid.* 1542–6), in which the House concurred on Jan. 22 (*ibid.* 2137).

[94] 38 STAT. 803. The Act also took out of the federal courts the litigation, at one time heavy, which the Pacific Railroad Removal Cases, 115 U. S. 1 (1885) had brought there, by providing in § 5 that "no court of the United States shall have jurisdiction of any action or suit by or against any railroad company upon the ground that said railroad company was incorporated under an Act of Congress." In the House Mr. Sherley of Kentucky vainly sought to extend this section by renewing the effort to restrict the scope of jurisdiction based on diversity of citizenship. "You have a bill here," he said, "undertaking to change the jurisdiction of the Federal courts as to railroads that are incorporated by the United States. You are dealing with one little evil. All the railroads of the country exercise the right to transfer actions from a State court to the Federal court on the ground of diverse citizenship, although at the time that the provision was put into the law originally there were not a hundred corporations in the country to be affected by it." 52 CONG. REC. 283. At the time of its passage the Texas and Pacific Ry. Co. was the only road still operating under federal law.

1910, the number increased to 528 in 1914 and 647 in 1916.[95] Under the pressure of this increase the Court disposed of 637 cases in 1916 as compared with 539 in 1914 and 455 in 1910.[96] The addition to the docket through the 1914 Amendment was negligible.[97] The source of the new business was elsewhere.

As a result of the *First Employers' Liability Cases* [98] national legislation for the protection of railroad employees had in theory to be limited to injuries suffered at the time of employment in interstate commerce.[99] The theory was based on an illusory differentiation between interstate and intrastate commerce. Railroad men were engaged in transportation; neither they nor their employers, in the practical conduct of life, allocated their duties to interstate or intrastate commerce. But this unreal line determined whether relief was to be had under the Federal Employers' Liability Act or whether the plaintiff was to be relegated to state remedies. Judicial astuteness had to decide, as a solemn problem of constitutional law, whether a particular employee at a particular moment was acting in his interstate or intrastate capacity. An erroneous guess on the part of counsel, a confused ruling by the trial court, subjected the plaintiff to all the waste and tribulation of delay and frequently of defeat. The many opinions by the Supreme Court, to say nothing of the dissents, revealed an obstinate problem and sterility

---

[95] See REP. ATTY. GEN. FOR 1911, 1915, and 1917.   [96] *Ibid.*

[97] Until the Act of 1916 only three petitions for *certiorari* were filed under the 1914 Amendment. All were refused. See 33 HARV. L. REV. 102, 104 (1919). For a recent resort to this jurisdiction where a state court found, and not unnaturally, narrower limits upon state power than the Supreme Court subsequently recognized, see Red Cross Line v. Atlantic Fruit Co., 264 U. S. 109 (1924).

[98] 207 U. S. 463 (1908). The effect of this decision upon the practical administration of justice by the courts has been neglected by commentators. See, for instance, Mr. Warren's comment upon the decision: " This was later cured by an amendment of the Act confining its operation to interstate transactions, so that this decision had no permanent effect." WARREN, CONGRESS, THE CONSTITUTION AND THE SUPREME COURT, 239. Thus, even Mr. Warren, comprehensive student that he is of the functioning of the federal judiciary, is too intent upon the abstract constitutional line drawn by the First Employers' Liability Cases to concern himself with the practical problems of application raised by them.

[99] The second Federal Employers' Liability Act of Apr. 22, 1908, 35 STAT. 65, drawn to conform to the decision in the First Employers' Liability Cases, *supra,* note 98, was sustained in the Second Employers' Liability Cases, 223 U. S. 1 (1912).

of solution. Such standards as were evolved [100] proved elusive in application. The differences of opinion among the judges stimulated appeal. From both state and lower federal courts the volume of this litigation steadily increased.[101] A reading of

---

[100] See, *e.g.,* Shanks *v.* D., L. & W. R. R., 239 U. S. 556 (1916). Summing up the distinctions applied in prior cases the Shanks case formulated this test: " Was the employee at the time of the injury engaged in interstate transportation or in work so closely related to it as to be practically a part of it? " *Ibid.* at 558. This test left open a wide door for differences in judgment and litigation was encouraged to enter this door.

[101] Of the 554 cases remaining undisposed of on June 21, 46 arose under the Employers' Liability Act. James D. Maher, Clerk of the Court, estimated that each year brought an average of 30 more of these cases to the docket. See SEN. REP., No. 775, 64th Cong., 1st Sess., Ser. No. 6899, 3. An enumeration of the cases involving the Act that reached the Supreme Court as of right can alone give an adequate conception of the volume of this litigation, and the facts of the cases will disclose their inappropriateness as business for the Supreme Bench. Second Employers' Liability Cases, 223 U. S. 1 (1912); American R. R. *v.* Birch, 224 U. S. 547 (1912); Phila., Balt. & Wash. R. R. *v.* Schubert, 224 U. S. 603 (1912); Seaboard Air Line *v.* Duvall, 225 U. S. 477 (1912); M., K. & T. Ry. *v.* Wulf, 226 U. S. 570 (1913); Mich. Cent. R. R. *v.* Vreeland, 227 U. S. 59 (1913); Winfree *v.* Northern Pac. Ry., 227 U. S. 296 (1913); Troxell *v.* D., L. & W. R. R., 227 U. S. 434 (1913); Gulf, Colo. & S. F. Ry. *v.* McGinnis, 228 U. S. 173 (1913); Seaboard Air Line Ry. *v.* Moore, 228 U. S. 433 (1913); St. L., Iron Mountain & So. Ry. *v.* Hesterly, 228 U. S. 702 (1913); Norfolk & West. Ry. *v.* Earnest, 229 U. S. 114 (1913); Pedersen *v.* D., L. & W. R. R., 229 U. S. 146 (1913); St. L., S. F. & T. Ry. *v.* Searle, 229 U. S. 146 (1913); St. L. & Iron Mountain Ry. *v.* McWhister, 229 U. S. 265 (1913); Pennell *v.* Phila. & Reading Ry., 231 U. S. 675 (1914); North Carolina R. R. *v.* Zachary, 232 U. S. 248 (1914); Taylor *v.* Taylor, 232 U. S. 363 (1914); Young *v.* Cent. R. R. of N. J., 232 U. S. 602 (1914); M., K. & T. Ry. *v.* West, 232 U. S. 682 (1914); Grand Trunk Ry. *v.* Lindsay, 233 U. S. 42 (1914); So. Ry. — Carolina Division *v.* Bennett, 233 U. S. 80 (1914); Ill. Cent. R. R. *v.* Behrens, 233 U. S. 473 (1914); Seaboard Air Line Ry. *v.* Horton, 233 U. S. 492 (1914); So. Ry. *v.* Gadd, 233 U. S. 572 (1914); *Ex parte* Roe, 234 U. S. 70 (1914); Wabash R. R. *v.* Hayes, 234 U. S. 86 (1914); So. Ry. *v.* Crockett, 234 U. S. 725 (1914); Garrett *v.* L. & N. R. R., 235 U. S. 308 (1914); Yazoo & Miss. Valley R. R. *v.* Wright, 235 U. S. 376 (1914); McGovern *v.* Phila. & Reading Ry., 235 U. S. 389 (1914); T., St. L. & W. R. R. *v.* Slavin, 235 U. S. 454 (1915); Norfolk & West. Ry. *v.* Holbrook, 235 U. S. 625 (1915); Seaboard Air Line Ry. *v.* Padgett, 235 U. S. 668 (1915); Ariz. & N. M. Ry. *v.* Clark, 235 U. S. 669 (1915); Robinson *v.* B. & O. R. R., 237 U. S. 84 (1915); Seaboard Air Line Ry. *v.* Tilghman, 237 U. S. 499 (1915); St. L., Iron Mountain & So. Ry. *v.* Craft, 237 U. S. 648 (1915); St. L. & S. F. R. R. *v.* Conarty, 238 U. S. 243 (1915); N. Y. C. & H. R. R. R. *v.* Carr, 238 U. S. 260 (1915); Norfolk So. R. R. *v.* Ferebee, 238 U. S. 269 (1915); D., L. & W. R. R. *v.* Yurkonis, 238 U. S. 439 (1915); Cent. Vt. Ry. *v.* White, 238 U. S. 507 (1915); Kan. City So. Ry. *v.* Leslie, 238 U. S. 599 (1915); Pa. Co. *v.* Donat, 239 U. S. 50 (1915); C., R. I. & P. Ry. *v.* Devine, 239 U. S. 52 (1915); Atl. Coast Line R. R. *v.* Burnette, 239 U. S. 199 (1915); A. T. & S. F. Ry. *v.* Swearingen, 239 U. S.

the opinions constrains one to believe that these federal employers' liability cases constitute the most copious and futile waste
of the Supreme Court's efforts.

---

339 (1915); Great Northern Ry. v. Otis, 239 U. S. 349 (1915); Seaboard Air Line
Ry. v. Koennecke, 239 U. S. 352 (1915); Chicago & Alton R. R. v. Wagner, 239
U. S. 452 (1915); Reese v. Phila. & Reading Ry., 239 U. S. 463 (1916); Southern
Ry. v. Lloyd, 239 U. S. 496 (1916); C., R. I. & P. Ry. v. Wright, 239 U. S. 548
(1916); Shanks v. D., L. & W. R. R., 239 U. S. 556 (1916); Kanawha & Mich.
Ry. v. Kerse, 239 U. S. 576 (1916); Seaboard Air Line Ry. v. Horton, 239 U. S.
595 (1916); Kan. City Western Ry. v. McAdow, 240 U. S. 51 (1916); Ill. Cent.
R. R. v. Skaggs, 240 U. S. 66 (1916); Pecos & Northern Texas Ry. v. Rosenbloom,
240 U. S. 439 (1916); Great Northern Ry. v. Wiles, 240 U. S. 444 (1916); C., R. I.
& P. Ry. v. Bond, 240 U. S. 499 (1916); Great Northern Ry. v. Knapp, 240 U. S.
464 (1916); Seaboard Air Line Ry. v. Kenney, 240 U. S. 489 (1916); Osborne v.
Gray, 241 U. S. 16 (1916); C., B. & Q. R. R. v. Harrington, 241 U. S. 177 (1916);
Kan. City So. Ry. v. Jones, 241 U. S. 181 (1916); M. & S. L. R. R. v. Bom-
bolis, 241 U. S. 211 (1916); S. L. & S. F. R. R. v. Brown, 241 U. S. 223 (1916);
Jacobs v. So. Ry., 241 U. S. 229 (1916); Baugham v. N. Y., P. & N. R. R.,
241 U. S. 237 (1916); C. & O. Ry. v. Carnahan, 241 U. S. 241 (1916); Louisville &
Nashville R. R. v. Stewart, 241 U. S. 261 (1916); Seaboard Air Line Ry. v. Renn,
241 U. S. 290 (1916); Chesapeake & Ohio Ry. v. De Altey, 241 U. S. 310 (1916);
Chesapeake & Ohio Ry. v. Proffitt, 241 U. S. 462 (1916); San Antonio & Arkansas
Pass. Ry. v. Wagner, 241 U. S. 476 (1916); Chesapeake & Ohio Ry. v. Kelly, 241
U. S. 485 (1916); Spokane & Inland Empire R. R. v. Campbell, 241 U. S. 497
(1916); Louisville & Nashville R. R. v. Parker, 242 U. S. 13 (1916); Atl. City R. R.
v. Parker, 242 U. S. 56 (1916); Great Northern Ry. v. Capital Trust Co., 242 U. S.
144 (1916); B. & O. R. R. v. Whitacre, 242 U. S. 169 (1916); Ill. Cent. R. R. v.
Peery, 242 U. S. 292 (1916); B. & O. R. R. v. Wilson, 242 U. S. 295 (1916); Erie
R. R. v. Welsh, 242 U. S. 303 (1916); M. & S. L. R. R. v. Winters, 242 U. S. 353
(1917); Atl. Coast Line R. R. v. Mims, 242 U. S. 532 (1917); McCluskey v.
Marysville & Northern Ry., 243 U. S. 36 (1917); Bay v. Merrill & Ring Logging
Co., 243 U. S. 40 (1917); Raymond v. C., M. & St. P. Ry., 243 U. S. 43 (1917);
N. Y. C. R. R. v. White, 243 U. S. 188 (1917); St. Joseph & G. I. Ry. v. Moore,
243 U. S. 311 (1917); Seaboard Air Line Ry. v. Lorick, 243 U. S. 572 (1917);
M. & St. L. R. R. v. Gotschall, 244 U. S. 66 (1917); N. Y. C. R. R. v. Winfield,
244 U. S. 147 (1917); Erie R. R. v. Winfield, 244 U. S. 170 (1917); Lehigh Valley
R. R. v. Barlow, 244 U. S. 183 (1917); Mo. Pac. Ry. v. Taber, 244 U. S. 200
(1917); Erie R. R. v. Purucker, 244 U. S. 320 (1917); N. Y. C. R. R. v. Tonsel-
lito, 244 U. S. 360 (1917); Southern Ry. v. Packett, 244 U. S. 571 (1917); Washington Ry. & Elec. Co. v. Scala, 244 U. S. 630 (1917); Boldt v. Pa. R. R.,
245 U. S. 441 (1918); U. P. R. R. v. Huxoll, 245 U. S. 535 (1918); G. N. Ry. v.
Donaldson, 246 U. S. 121 (1918); Nelson v. Southern Ry., 246 U. S. 253 (1918);
Great Northern Ry. v. Alexander, 246 U. S. 276 (1918); U. P. R. R. v. Hadley,
246 U. S. 330 (1918); Louisville & Nashville R. R. v. Holloway, 246 U. S. 525
(1918); Dickinson v. Stiles, 246 U. S. 631 (1918); New Orleans & Northeastern
R. R. v. Harris, 247 U. S. 367 (1918); N. Y. C. R. R. v. Porter, 249 U. S. 168
(1919); New Orleans & Northeastern R. R. v. Scarlet, 249 U. S. 528 (1919);
Yazoo & Miss. Valley R. R. v. Mullins, 249 U. S. 531 (1919); Gillis v. N. Y., N. H.
& H. R. R., 249 U. S. 515 (1919). The Federal Employers' Liability Act of June

Here was a source of jurisdiction both prodigal of the Court's time [102] and indifferent to the Court's significance. For it is almost grotesque that the ultimate voice of the Constitution should be invoked to determine whether " the requisite employment in interstate commerce exists " [103] where a car repairer is replacing a drawbar in a car then in use in such commerce,[104] as contrasted with a worker in a railroad machine shop who alters the location of a fixture communicating power to machinery used in repairing engines hauling both intrastate and interstate trains! [105] The elimination of the duty to review cases of this nature became the main objective of relief measures for the Court.[106] If finality of decision could not normally be left in such cases to the state courts and the circuit courts of appeals, then no litigation involving federal legislation could safely be entrusted to those tribunals. The principle on which the Circuit Courts of Appeals Act was founded — the division of federal questions according to their intrinsic public importance, and the immunity of the obligatory jurisdiction of the Supreme Court from cases significant only to the litigants — obviously invited extension of the principle to curb the mischief revealed by the downpour of employers' liability litigation. To be sure, the renewed necessity for enabling the Supreme Court to dispose of its business revived the old panaceas [107] of an

---

11, 1906, 34 STAT. 232, being held valid as to carriers in the District of Columbia and the territories, El Paso etc., Ry. v. Gutierrez, 215 U. S. 87 (1909), during this period gave rise to the following cases: Chicago, I. & L. Ry. v. Hackett, 228 U. S. 559 (1913); Santa Fe Cent. Ry. v. Friday, 232 U. S. 694 (1914); Wash. & Mt. Vernon Ry. v. Downey, 236 U. S. 190 (1915).

102 " Many of these cases ought not to be reviewed; the delays are unfortunate and the time that should be devoted to important subjects is trenched upon." HOUSE REPORT, No. 794, 64th Cong., 1st Sess., Ser. No. 6905, 2.

103 Shanks v. D., L. & W. R. R., 239 U. S. 556, 558 (1916).

104 See Shanks v. D., L. & W. R. R., 239 U. S. 556, 558 (1916), referring to Walsh v. N. Y., N. H. & H. R. R., 223 U. S. 1 (1912).

105 Shanks v. D., L. & W. R. R., *supra*, note 103.

106 " . . . it was preëminently the decision of questions like these from which Congress sought to relieve this court by the Act of September 6, 1916. . . . Of the cases on the docket for the preceding term of this court 37 presented the question whether the employee was engaged in interstate or intrastate commerce." Brandeis, J., (dissenting) in Dahnke-Walker Co. v. Bondurant, 257 U. S. 282, 299, n. 1 (1921).

107 See pp. 70 *et seq., supra.*

enlarged Court with divisional sittings.[108]   The Court itself
quietly rejected a form of relief which would beget more evils
than it cured.[109]   The main source of the Court's embarrassment
was too obvious to sustain much vitality this time for a scheme
which would change the whole character of the Court and impair
its processes of deliberation.

On April 28, 1916, Chairman Webb of the House Judiciary
Committee introduced the measure [110] which brought the needed
relief.   Elimination of cases due to the Federal Employers'
Liability Act was its chief aim.[111]   Similar litigation arising
under the Hours of Service and Safety Appliance Acts, but
much less voluminous, was also relegated to final disposition
by the circuit courts of appeals.   These restrictions upon the
obligatory jurisdiction of the Supreme Court, in cases coming
from the circuit courts of appeals, involved the simple device of
eliminating review of litigation arising under specific statutes.
At the same time reviews from the Supreme Court of the Philippine Islands were restricted to *certiorari.*[112]   The period for

---

[108] In 1916, the Committee of the American Bar Association, to Suggest
Remedies and Formulate Proposed Laws to Prevent Delay and Unnecessary Cost
in Litigation, in considering legislation then pending before Congress, called attention to the old Evarts plan looking to the division of the Supreme Court into three
departments as well as to the divisional schemes in the House of Lords and
the Judicial Committee of the Privy Council.   The Committee suggested an
increase in the membership of the Court " with the proviso that the whole number shall not sit at the same time, and that the concurrence of less than a
majority of the whole number shall be sufficient to make a decision. . . . This
would enable the Court to transact business through the whole term without re-
cess." 2 Am. Bar. Assn. Jour. 603, 612, 613.

[109] The Court's attitude, elicited at a conference between the Bar Association
Committee and the Chief Justice, is thus indicated in the Committee's report for
the following year: " We learned that the court is not unmindful of the danger of
delay caused by the increased number of cases brought before it under existing
legislation, but the court is of opinion that it will be able to cope with this increase in the number of cases brought before it by delivering fewer opinions and
by making the opinions more concise in most cases.   It was very obvious that the
delay caused by the increased number of cases brought before it under existing
conditions.   We therefore felt it our duty to proceed no further in this particular
matter." 42 Am. Bar Assn. Rep. 334, 335.   See also, Alexander W. Smith, " Relief of the Supreme Court of the United States," 4 Law and Bank, 128.

[110] 53 Cong. Rec. 7014.   It was reported from the Judiciary Committee on
June 1, 1916. House Report, No. 794, 64th Cong., 1st Sess., Ser. No. 6905.

[111] See House Report, No. 794, 64th Cong., 1st Sess.

[112] Under Section 248 of the Judicial Code review could be had by writ of
error or appeal in Philippine cases involving " The Constitution, or any statute,

perfecting appeals was cut down,[113] and, at the Court's suggestion, the length of its term was extended.[114]

The occasion was also utilized to restrict the scope of the appellate jurisdiction over state courts which had prevailed since 1789. The principle of review under Section 25 of the Judiciary Act, as later embodied in Section 237 of the Judicial Code, was simple in statement and easy of application. Prior to 1914, the denial of a federal right by the highest court of a state in which a decision upon the question could be had, was reviewable upon writ of error. The Act of 1914 permitted review by *certiorari* in the same class of cases, when the state court upheld instead of denied the federal right. The Webb bill of 1916, however, altered the provinces of writ of error and *certiorari*. It drastically narrowed the area of review as of right by the Supreme Court of state decisions denying federal claims. Writ of error was left available for only two types of state court decisions: (1) where the validity of a treaty or statute of, or an authority exercised under, the United States was drawn in question and the decision was against its validity; and (2) where the validity of a statute of, or an authority exercised under, any state on the ground of its repugnance to the Constitution, treaties or laws of the United States was drawn in question and the decision was in favor of its validity. All other cases were left

---

treaty, title right or privilege of the United States, . . . or in causes in which the value in controversy exceeds twenty-five thousand dollars, or in which the title or possession of real estate exceeding in value the sum of twenty-five thousand dollars, . . . is involved. . . ." See Cariño *v.* Insular Government, 212 U. S. 449, 456 (1909); Harty *v.* Victoria, 226 U. S. 12 (1912).

113 Under Section 22 of the Act of Sept. 24, 1789, 1 STAT. 73, 85, writs of error could be "brought" within five years after rendering the judgment or decree complained of. The provision was later limited to two years. U. S. REV. STAT., § 1008. The time within which a writ of error was "brought" was calculated from the date when the writ was filed in the court to which it issued. Brooks *v.* Norris, 11 How. (U. S.) 204 (1850); Scarborough *v.* Pargoud, 108 U. S. 567 (1883); Polleys *v.* Black River Improvement Co., 113 U. S. 81 (1885). The Act of 1916 reduced the period to three months and only required that the writ of error, appeal, or writ of *certiorari* shall be "duly applied for" within that period. The date of application thus becomes relevant. See Citizens Bank *v.* Opperman, 249 U. S. 448, 449, (1919); Puget Sound Co. *v.* King County, 264 U. S. 22, 24 (1924). See Charles C. Moore, "Appellate Review by United States Supreme Court Limited to Three Months," 21 LAW NOTES, 5.

114 "They want a little shorter vacation and more time to do work when the weather is better." Webb, in the House, on June 10, 1916, 53 CONG. REC. 9442.

to the judicial grace of *certiorari*.[115]   Thus, in addition to the cases where the state court sustained a federal claim when its denial would have given rise to writ of error, *certiorari* was now extended, as the only means of securing review, to cases where any title, right, privilege or immunity was claimed under the Constitution, or under any treaty or statute of, or commission or authority derived from, the United States, and the decision was either for or against the title, right, privilege or immunity so claimed.   Cases arising in the state courts under the Federal Employers' Liability Act came, of course, within this qualifica-

---

[115] In his address before the American Bar Association in 1922, Chief Justice Taft gave this explanation for the change: " The general power of *certiorari* in such constitutional questions was conferred in the Act of 1916, and has been exercised ever since.   It was granted because Congress found that counsel were often astute in framing pleadings in state courts to create an unsubstantial issue of Federal constitutional law and so obtain an unwarranted writ of error to the supreme court." 47 REP. AM. BAR ASSN. 250–56. In Dahnke-Walker Co. *v.* Bondurant, 257 U. S. 282, 294 (1921), Mr. Justice Brandeis, in a dissenting opinion, attributed to the legislation a more far-reaching purpose: " But the Act of 1916 made the nature of the constitutional question raised in applying the statute a matter of importance. If the question is a denial of the power of the legislature to enact the statute as construed, a review may be had as of right. If the question concerns merely the propriety of the particular use of the statute or of the manner of applying or administering it, the review may be had only in this court's discretion.   The classification thus introduced rests upon broad considerations of policy. The steady increase of the business of this court had made it necessary to limit the appellate jurisdiction in cases arising under § 237. To this end Congress determined in 1916 that even cases involving constitutional questions should be reviewed here only where the public interest appeared to demand it. Congress left parties a review as of right where the validity of a state statute had been drawn in question; because the decision of such a question is usually a matter of general interest. But whether a valid state statute has in a particular case been so used as to violate a constitutional guaranty is ordinarily a matter of merely private interest. Hence, Congress provided that where the validity of the statute is not assailed, the denial of a claim that in applying it a right, privilege or immunity had been violated, should not be reviewed, unless this court, in its discretion to be exercised upon petition for a writ of certiorari, should direct the review. That is, Congress treated a right, privilege or immunity claimed to have been violated by the courts' erroneously applying a confessedly valid statute to the particular facts of a case, just as it treated a claim that the right, privilege or immunity had been violated by a decision erroneous in some other respect."

Senator Walsh has criticised the inconsistency of the Act of 1916: " The Act left, however, illogically subject to review by writ of error or appeal just such questions [coming from the state courts and subject to review only by *certiorari*] if they came to the Supreme Court from the Circuit Court of Appeals." Thomas J. Walsh, " The Overburdened Supreme Court," 1922 REP. VA. BAR ASSN. 216, 223, reprinted in 62 CONG. REC. 8545.

tion. A sharp line was thus drawn between the validity of legislation and the application of legislation. Where a case concerned
the power of the state to enact laws or exercise authority in
alleged defiance of a federal bar, the issue obviously partakes
of that public interest upon which the Supreme Court sits in
judgment. Where, however, a claim relates to the assertion of
a federal right apart from the conflict of such right with the
power of a state, the matter is apt to be of restricted private
concern, and the national interest is sufficiently safeguarded
through appeal to the Court's discretionary jurisdiction.[116]

Here was a marked change of policy, albeit in form merely
an extension of the principle of discretionary jurisdiction through
certiorari derived from the Circuit Courts of Appeals Act. But
the chief aim of this measure — to save the Supreme Court from
the voluminous futilities of employers' liability litigation — was
so compelling, that the important innovation of the Act went
through Congress without serious consideration, certainly without
debate.[117] Since then, one of the most powerful lawyers of the
Senate, Thomas J. Walsh of Montana, has vigorously depre-
cated its enactment.[118] But at the time, the bill passed both
Houses as though it were a perfunctory measure,[119] and became
law on September 6, 1916.[120] The authorship of this measure

---

[116] See Brandeis, J., dissenting, in Dahnke-Walker Co. *v.* Bondurant, *supra,*
quoted in note 115. Senator Walsh has questioned the validity of the distinction.
See Thomas J. Walsh, *supra,* 1922 REP. VA. BAR ASSN. 216, 224.

[117] Upon an explanatory statement from Webb, the bill passed the House on
June 10. 53 CONG. REC. 9441. It was reported from the Senate Judiciary Committee on Aug. 11 with an amendment, eliminating the House provision restricting
appeals in *habeas corpus* proceedings. SEN. REP., No. 775, 64th Cong., 1st Sess.,
Ser. No. 6899. The purpose of the House provision was to avoid delays, and assimilate all appeals on *habeas corpus* to appeals in those cases where the petitioner
complained of detention by state authority in violation of a federal right. See
Act of March 10, 1908. 35 STAT. 40. The Bill as amended passed the Senate
without debate on Aug. 26. 53 CONG. REC. 12478, 13279. On Sept. 1, the House
concurred in the Senate amendment. *Ibid.* 13579.

[118] See Thomas J. Walsh, *supra,* 1922 REP. VA. BAR ASSN. 216; also Senator
Walsh's remarks in the Senate on Feb. 3, 1925, 66 CONG. REC. 2925.

[119] See note 117, *supra.*

[120] 39 STAT. 726. The same session of Congress, strangely enough, saw an attempt to enlarge the appellate jurisdiction of the Supreme Court. Senator Nelson,
by request, on Dec. 10, 1915, introduced a bill imposing on the Supreme Court
review of all decisions by circuit courts of appeals reversing the judgment or
decree of a district court in all cases where review could be had as of right from

is generally attributed to Mr. Justice McReynolds, whose experience, as former Attorney General, with the members of the Judiciary Committees of both the House and the Senate greatly promoted its enactment.

The Act brought prompt relief.[121] Employers' liability cases ceased to drain the Court's time, though they still evoke needless *certiorari*.[122] But the Act of 1916 in its new classification of review over state courts led to perplexing distinctions, puzzling alike to court and counsel. The Court's refusal to extend the

a final decision of a circuit court of appeals in such a suit. The bill, which is printed in 53 CONG REC. 9233, aimed at securing review of decisions of circuit courts of appeals upon interlocutory orders and judgments lacking the customary quality of finality. It was reported from the Judiciary Committee by Senator Sutherland on Apr. 19, 1916, SEN. REP., No. 363, 64th Cong., 1st Sess., Ser. No. 6898, and passed the Senate, without debate, on June 3. 53 CONG. REC. 9233. In the House the bill went quietly to sleep.

[121] The effect of the Act of 1916 in reducing cases reaching the Supreme Court as of right from state courts and the circuit courts of appeals is illustrated by the following statistics covering the Terms of the Court during which that Act was making itself progressively felt. The figures relate to the cases disposed of during each Term of Court.

Term	On error to state courts	On appeal from or error to circuit courts of appeals
1916	157	36
1917	150	48
1918	132	48
1919	101	25
1920	69	38
1921	65	29

See also 33 HAR. L. REV. 102.

[122] See Yazoo & M. R. R. v. Mullins, 249 U. S. 531 (1919); N. Y. C. R. R. v. Porter, 249 U. S. 168 (1919); Kinzell v. C., M. & St. P. Ry., 250 U. S. 130 (1919); Phila., B. & W. R. R. v. Smith, 250 U. S. 101 (1919); So. Pac. Co. v. Industrial Accident Comm., 251 U. S. 259 (1920); Lee v. Central of Ga. Ry., 252 U. S. 109 (1920); C., R. I. & P. Ry. v. Ward, 252 U. S. 18 (1920); Hull v. Phila. & Read. Ry., 252 U. S. 475 (1920); Phila. & Read. Ry. v. Hancock, 253 U. S. 284 (1920); Erie R. R. v. Szary, 253 U. S. 86 (1920); Erie R. R. v. Collins, 253 U. S. 77 (1920); Southern Pac. Co. v. Berkshire, 254 U. S. 415 (1921); Wells Fargo & Co. v. Taylor, 254 U. S. 175 (1920); Troy Union R. R. v. Mealy, 254 U. S. 47 (1920); Phila. & Read. Ry. v. Polk, 256 U. S. 332 (1921); Phila. & Read. Ry. v. Di Donato, 256 U. S. 327 (1921); Reed v. Director General, 258 U. S. 92 (1922); Ind. Comm. v. Davis, 259 U. S. 182 (1922); Davis v. Green, 260 U. S. 349 (1922); N. Y. C. R. R. v. Kinney, 260 U. S. 340 (1922); B. & O. S. W. R. R. v. Burtch, 263 U. S. 540 (1924); Frese v. C., B. & Q. R. R., 263 U. S. 1 (1923); B. & O. R. R. v. Groeger, 266 U. S. 521 (1925); Chicago, R. I. & P. Ry. v. Schendel, 270 U. S. 611 (1926); C. & O. Ry. v. Nixon, 271 U. S. 218 (1926); St. Louis-San Francisco Ry. v. Mills, 271 U. S. 344 (1926).

interpretation of " the exercise of an authority under a state " [123] to include constitutional objections to the exercise of an authority under a state statute whose validity had not been attacked,[124] has resulted in diminution of review as of right.[125] On the other hand, in *Dahnke-Walker Co.* v. *Bondurant*,[126] the Court needlessly burdened its docket by entertaining a writ of error where the validity of a statute was not in issue but merely its particular unconstitutional application, put in terms of *ad hoc* invalidity.[127] Unexpected difficulties disclosed themselves in practice, as is generally true of new procedural measures. But the *Dahnke-Walker* decision added to the confusion of counsel by increasing the uncertainties to which the Act gave rise. With surprising frequency counsel mistook the proper method for seeking re-

---

[123] See Baltimore & Potomac R. R. *v.* Hopkins, 130 U. S. 210 (1889).

[124] Jett Bros. Distilling Co. *v.* City of Carrollton, 252 U. S. 1 (1920).

[125] Shepard's Citations of Jett Bros. Distilling Co. *v.* City of Carrollton, *supra*, note 124, indicates the frequency with which its doctrine has led to the dismissal of cases from state courts.

[126] 257 U. S. 282 (1921), commented on in 35 HARV. L. REV. 618 (1922). See Eureka Pipe Line Co. *v.* Hallanan, 257 U. S. 265 (1921); United Fuel Gas Co. *v.* Hallanan, 257 U. S. 277 (1921).

[127] The embarrassments created by this decision were thus put by Mr. Justice Brandeis in his dissent: " If jurisdiction upon writ of error can be obtained by the mere claim in words that a state statute is invalid, if so construed as to ' apply ' to a given state of facts, the right to a review will depend, in large classes of cases, not upon the nature of the constitutional question involved but upon the skill of counsel. The result would be particularly regrettable, because the decision of such cases often depends not upon the determination of important questions of law (which should in the main engage the attention of this court), but upon the appreciation of evidence frequently voluminous." 257 U. S. at 298. The case has since been followed in Gillespie *v.* Oklahoma, 257 U. S. 501 (1922); Cudahy Packing Co. *v.* Parramore, 263 U. S. 418 (1923); Kansas City Structural Steel Co. *v.* Arkansas, 269 U. S. 148 (1925). *Cf.* Phila. & Reading C. & I. Co. *v.* Gilbert, 245 U. S. 162 (1917); Dana *v.* Dana, 250 U. S. 220 (1919). The principle of the Dahnke-Walker case has, however, not been extended to a situation where the application of a confessedly valid state statute is claimed to be in conflict with a federal law. Although the basis of review in such a case would seem to be the same, cases of this nature have been reviewed by *certiorari. Cf.* Mo. Pac. R. R. *v.* Boone, 270 U. S. 466 (1926); Harrigan *v.* Bergdoll, 270 U. S. 560 (1926). But *cf.* Davis *v.* Cohen & Co., 268 U. S. 638 (1925). The applicability of the principle of the Dahnke-Walker case to suits in state courts involving maritime law, and its tendency thereby to increase the Court's obligatory jurisdiction in such cases, has been adverted to by Brandeis, J., in Washington *v.* Dawson & Co., 264 U. S. 219, 237, note 19 (1924). *Cf.* Miller's Indemnity Underwriters *v.* Braud, 270 U. S. 59 (1926).

view.[128]   The extent of dismissals for want of jurisdiction by the
Court led the Chief Justice to speak of the situation thus created,
or at least intensified, by the Act of 1916, as " more or less a
trap." [129]   Certainly, however, this Act shunted from the Supreme
Court cases which are not within its function and released its
energies for those problems which are its proper concern.   The
wisdom of the reform is perhaps best gauged by the enormous
extension of the principle of *certiorari* introduced by the Act of
February 13, 1925,[130] which brings us, finally, to the post-war
judiciary acts and the accession to the Chief Justiceship of William Howard Taft, whose influence largely shaped the legislation.

---

[128] *Cf., e.g.*, Rust Land and Lumber Co. *v.* Jackson, 250 U. S. 71, 76 (1919).

[129] William H. Taft " Reforms in the Administration of Justice in the Federal
Courts " 47 REP. AM. BAR ASSN. 250, 258, (1922).

[130] 43 STAT. 936.

CHAPTER VI

CONFERENCE

OF

SENIOR CIRCUIT JUDGES

I

IN framing the judiciary acts thus far considered, Congress was preëminently concerned with features peculiar to the federal judicial system rather than with more general principles of the effective administration of justice. Two great factors, in various aspects and with shifting intensities, underlie all the controversies and compromises which produced the federal judiciary acts: first, that we are a federation; second, that we are a continent. How to distribute judicial power between state and national courts, how to make a system of national courts workable over so vast and diversified a country, have been far-reaching political issues since 1789. They presented problems on the whole so unique that outside currents of judicial reform did not touch them. In consequence, neither Congress nor the profession thought much about those elements of organization and administration called for by all modern judicial systems.

Legislation after the Great War marks a change. A long-matured critique of judicial administration had by this time subjected all courts, both federal and state, to scrutiny, and ample experiments had provided guidance for the wise conduct of judicial business. The federal courts no longer appear outside the orbit of general judicial experience. The story of the Act of 1922 is thus part of the recent history of judicial reform in the United States, and must be placed in its setting.

Efficiency in government is not merely a new slogan; it is a new insistence. Especially true is it of the United States that alertness to administration is a very late stage in the art of government. A new nation of limited powers, moving in an atmosphere fearful of centralized authority and composed of states jealous of their vague " sovereignty," naturally would not be preoccupied with the effectiveness of its administrative organization. The novelty of the federal experiment, the growing democratic temper, the use of patronage in the development of political parties, combined against scientific standards of government. Irrespective of the tenets of the party in power, deep forces made for a rule that was easy-going, loose-jointed and unprofessional. Undoubtedly the system bred waste and inefficiency; but these were regarded as minor exuberances of the forms of democratic government. The Civil War, however, abated local ascendancies, stimulated habits of centralization, and greatly extended the area as well as the scope of federal authority. Above all, it accelerated the rise of industrialism with all its repercussions upon organization in government. The democratic philosophy of a small-scale national economy was engulfed by powerful industrial forces. Business and government interacted more and more, and the aims and slogans of business were carried over to the conduct of government. As though business and government had the same ends, the promise of a " business administration " not infrequently summed up a political program.

The tendencies thus hastily sketched are reflected in judicial organization and administration. The root conceptions of our federal judicial system were independence and localism. Life tenure for United States judges grew out of the doctrine of the separation of powers.[1] An independent judiciary was part of the scheme of counterpoises in government. But not only were the judges rendered independent of the President and Congress; they were rendered independent of each other. Congress created a hierarchical system of courts, not of judges. Moreover, in establishing United States courts Congress was mindful of state loyalties. With a negligible exception,[2] federal judicial districts did

---

[1] THE FEDERALIST, No. 78; CARPENTER, JUDICIAL TENURE IN THE UNITED STATES, 29.

[2] By the Act of Feb. 13, 1801, § 21, 2 STAT. 89, 96, the District of Potomac was created, embracing the territory of Columbia and portions of the territory of Virginia and Maryland. A district court therein was to be held by the district judge of Maryland. Prior to the repeal of the Act of 1801, by the Act of Mar. 8, 1802, 2 STAT. 132, a circuit court had been established for the District of Columbia, the chief judge of which was authorized to preside over the District Court of the United States for the District of Potomac. See Act of Feb. 27, 1801, § 3, 2 STAT. 103, 105; Act of Mar. 3, 1801, § 7, 2 STAT. 123, 124.

not cross state lines, and district judges were confined to the districts in which they were resident.[3] Only in strictly limited emergencies could a district judge be drawn upon for litigation outside of his circuit, however small the local demands upon him and however overburdened another circuit might be.[4] The riding circuit Justice was also a manifestation of localism. His circuit limited his powers and his activity.[5] Mobility of judicial personnel ran counter to all the traditional conceptions of American judicial organization.

---

[3] Under the First Judiciary Act no provision was made for the assignability of a district judge from one district to another. The inability of the judge to act resulted in the adjournment of the court. Act of Sept. 24, 1789, § 6, 1 STAT. 73, 76.

[4] Since 1850 the accumulation or urgency of business in a district court, or the inability of the district judge to hold court, permitted the circuit judge or Justice of that circuit to designate another district judge in the same circuit to perform or help perform the duties of the district judge. U. S. REV. STAT., §§ 591–96. If the circuit judge or justice was absent or unable to make such a designation, the Chief Justice of the United States was permitted to make the designation, and also to appoint a district judge from the circuit next contiguous. U. S. REV. STAT., § 593. In 1911 this provision was amended to permit such designation by the Chief Justice from any other circuit. JUDICIAL CODE, § 15. The effect of such a designation is to add another district to the territory within which the judge may perform judicial duties. Apgar *v.* United States, 255 Fed. 16 (5th Circ., 1919); *In re* American Home Furnishers' Corp., 296 Fed. 605 (4th Circ., 1924). With the abolition of the circuit courts in 1912, circuit judges upon designation by a senior circuit judge, a circuit justice, or the Chief Justice, could hold district court. JUDICIAL CODE, § 18. This permitted the designation of a circuit judge upon disqualification of a district judge. United States *ex rel.* Fehsenfeld *v.* Gill, 292 Fed. 136 (4th Circ., 1923). It also permitted a circuit judge who had been sitting in a circuit court to continue to deal with the same suit when transferred to the district court after the abolition of the circuit court. See Pennsylvania Steel Co. *v.* New York City Ry., 221 Fed. 440, 442 (S. D. N. Y., 1915). Orders of a circuit judge sitting without designation are treated as if made by a *de facto* judge. Luhrig Collieries Co. *v.* Interstate Coal & Dock Co., 287 Fed. 711 (2nd Circ., 1923).

[5] Under the First Judiciary Act and prior to the Act of Mar. 2, 1793, 1 STAT. 333, the Justices of the Supreme Court were confined to fixed circuits. That Act enabled them to take the circuits in turn. See 1 WARREN, THE SUPREME COURT IN UNITED STATES HISTORY, 89. By the Act of Apr. 29, 1802, 2 STAT. 156, the Justices of the Supreme Court were specifically allotted to the various circuits. With every new appointment to that Court a new allotment was to be made by the judges, and such allotment was to be binding until another allotment could be made. Not until Mar. 3, 1863, was provision made for the justice of one circuit to take the place of the justice of another circuit. U. S. REV. STAT., § 617. For the present allotment of Justices, see 268 U. S. iv.

2

The constant increase in the volume of litigation had hitherto merely led to continuous resort to the devices of more judges and new courts. New territory did require new judges and new courts, and the vast distances made for localism in judicial organization. Professional thinking and Congressional action had concerned themselves from time to time with different parts of the federal judicial organization, but without regard to the fact that they were parts of a system. With the transformation of the country into a predominantly industrial nation, the demands of localism could not be pursued to the exclusion of pertinent national considerations. Inevitable disparities and fluctuations in the volume of judicial business in different districts exposed the futility of merely establishing new judgeships as a solution. But not until 1922 did the inadequacies of a system based on the needs, the geography and the temper of 1789 provoke reëxamination in the light of new conditions and the experience of other nations.

The system was without direction and without responsibility. Each judge was left to himself, guided in the administration of his business by his conscience and his temperament. The bases for informed public judgment and self-criticism were wanting, since adequate judicial statistics were unknown.[6] The types and volume of litigation, the character of issues, the duration of trials, the speed of disposition, the delay of appeals, — these and kindred data must be known in order to determine competence or laxity in judicial administration. Such information is particularly indispensable for any fruitful scrutiny of the workings of a single system of courts extending over so vast an area as that of the United States.[7] Without it, the demands of different districts for more

---

[6] Judicial statistics for federal courts were totally lacking until 1875. Only scattered reports, mainly estimates to which we have referred in the course of this study, were prepared for occasional use by Congressional committees. Since 1875 the annual reports of the Attorney General purport to classify, and to give the volume of, litigation; but no analysis, except in broad terms, has been attempted. See p. 52, n. 174, *supra*.

[7] " Ours is the only modern nation without data concerning the work of its

judges have to be decided in the dark. Nor will statistics gotten up for the occasion serve the purpose.[8] There must be recognized standards of interpretation and continuity of observation. Thus only can the system be subjected to scientific accountability.

The defects and inadequacies of the federal judicial organization had their counterpart in the states. The states, like the United States, vested their judicial power in a multitude of independent and local judges with over-lapping and ambiguous jurisdictions. Administration was the weakest spot in the enforcement of law, whether through the courts or the executive. The United States persisted in eighteenth-century habits and institutions long after England had completely modernized the system in which our own was rooted.[9] Popular dissatisfaction with the workings of

---

courts. It would be difficult to exaggerate the extent of our loss in this respect. Precise criticism is impossible, but vague and sketchy accusations are encouraged. It prevents agreement as to the causes for alleged defects. It prevents a common understanding and acceptance among judges of their responsibility. It leaves us without data greatly needed for social, criminal and procedural legislation." " The Unified State Court," 1 J. Am. Jud. Soc. 5.

[8] " I now come to what I consider a very significant statement made by Judge [Chief Justice] Taft before our committee. He continues: ' You gentlemen are all familiar with the fact that dockets are quite misleading in the number of cases that they seem to show. There is a lot of stuffing in the dockets. Many of the cases ought to be dismissed.' The point I make is . . . that the Judiciary Committee by its investigation has never determined where those districts are, or the proportion of cases pending there that represent stuffed dockets or cases that ought to be dismissed." Sumners of Texas, in the House on Dec. 9, 1921, 62 Cong. Rec. 154. " The number of cases pending tells mighty little. They may be cases that have been on the calendar for a long while. They may be, as in the case of part of the criminal cases in my own State, a lot of draft cases, 10,000 of them, that may never come to trial. They may be little customs cases that go through very quickly; they may be small cases at law." Parker of New Jersey, in the House on Dec. 9, 1921, *ibid.* 155–56.

[9] " The first step towards meeting and surmounting the evils complained of will be the consolidation of all the Superior Courts of Law and Equity, together with the Courts of Probate, Divorce, and Admiralty, into one Court, to be called ' Her Majesty's Supreme Court,' in which Court shall be vested all the jurisdiction which is now exercisable by each and all the Courts so consolidated. . . . From the consolidation of all the present Superior Courts into one Supreme Court, it follows, that all the Judges of those Courts will become Judges of the Supreme Court; and . . . will be competent to sit in any other Division of the Court, whenever it may be found convenient for the administration of justice." First Report of the Judicature Commission (1869), 9. The late Albert M. Kales summarized the English judicial reforms as " The application of the principle of placing in an administrative head and a governing committee the power to direct the energies of the judges to the work of the court, thereby fixing upon known individuals respon-

English courts had led to the solid labors of the Royal Commission from 1869 to 1873,[10] enlisted the powerful talents of Cairns, Selborne and Westbury,[11] and culminated in the Judicature Act of 1873, with its noble achievement of the Supreme Court of Judicature.[12] With the turn of the century popular dissatisfaction with the workings of American courts also made itself felt. Unfortunately, neither in the states nor in the nation have we any functionary comparable to the Lord Chancellor, who, to a large degree, is charged with the duties, or, at least, with the opportunities, of a Ministry of Justice.[13] Thus in America, the leadership for reform was largely unofficial.

---

sibility for the due administration of justice and the keeping of the judges on the bench subject to supervision and discipline." " The English Judicature Acts," 1913 ILL. BAR ASSN. REP. 325; 4 J. AM. JUD. SOC. 133. See William E. Higgins, " English Courts and Procedure," 7 *ibid.* 185; " The Supreme Court of Judicature Act, and Law Reform," 8 AM. L. REV. 256. The flexibility of the English system is illustrated by the recent example of Lord Chancellor Birkenhead acting as a judge in the Probate, Admiralty and Divorce Division, when after the World War the divorce lists had reached a stage of unprecedented congestion. 65 SOL. J. 620. Further flexibility in making the judges of the House of Lords and the Judicial Committee of the Privy Council available for work in the Supreme Court of Judicature, has been advocated. See Thomas Snow, " The Waste of Judicial Power," 7 LAW QUART. REV. 256.

[10] The first and second reports of the English Judicature Commission, the most important of the reports, were reprinted in 5 MASS. L. QUART. 254, 295.

[11] Lord Cairns was chairman of the Commission at the time of the first report, Lord Hatherly was chairman at the time of the second. The leader in the preparation of these reports and in the acts following them was Sir Roundell Palmer (Lord Selborne), who was Lord Chancellor in 1873, when the Supreme Court of Judicature Act was passed. See 1 SELBORNE, MEMOIRS, c. 14; HOLLAMS, JOTTINGS OF AN OLD SOLICITOR, *passim.* Lord Westbury's work was pioneer in its character, acting as the foundation for the efforts of the later Lord Chancellors. See 2 NASH, LIFE OF LORD WESTBURY, c. 4; Roscoe Pound, " Anachronisms in Law," 3 J. AM. JUD. SOC. 142, 146.

[12] See BRYCE, JUDICATURE ACT OF 1873; FINLASON, OUR JUDICIAL SYSTEM, c. 1. The judicial system in Ontario, modelled upon the English system in its principles of unification, has also been brought to the attention of the American legal profession. See Herbert Harley, " The Courts of Ontario," 1913 ILL. BAR ASSN. REP. 307; and " Ontario Courts and Procedure," 12 MICH. L. REV. 339, 447; William R. Riddell, " The Judiciary and the Administration of Justice in the Province of Ontario," 6 J. AM. JUD. SOC. 6; and " The Courts of Ontario," 5 *ibid.* 144.

[13] See, *e.g.*, 1 BIRKENHEAD, POINTS OF VIEW, c. 4, " A Ministry of Justice." The need for a ministry of justice was voiced in England in the Report of Lord Haldane's Committee on the Machinery of Government (1918); in America by Benjamin N. Cardozo, " A Ministry of Justice," 35 HARV. L. REV. 113; and by Roscoe Pound, " Juristic Problems of National Progress," 22 AM. J. SOC. 721, and " Anachronisms in Law," 3 J. AM. JUD. SOC. 142.

In 1906 Roscoe Pound roused the attention of the profession to the relation between our antiquated judicial organization and popular dissatisfaction with the administration of justice.[14] The English experience furnished him the text for his criticisms as well as the principles of reform. His paper, delivered before the American Bar Association, led to the creation of a committee charged with proposals for legislation.[15] Its report for 1909 [16] has given the lead to all contemporary movements for judicial reform.[17] To its principles [18] we owe the momentum for a unified judiciary and a judicial council.

The agitation begun before the American Bar Association was echoed before state and local bar associations and voiced by civic

[14] " The Causes of Popular Dissatisfaction with the Administration of Justice," 29 AM. BAR ASSN. REP. 395.

[15] At the conclusion of Mr. Pound's address, Everett P. Wheeler moved that four thousand copies of the paper be printed and that its subject matter be referred to the Committee on Judicial Administration and Remedial Procedure. The motion as adopted was amended so as merely to refer the subject matter to the committee. 29 AM. BAR ASSN. REP. 12, 55–65. As a consequence of that reference, the Committee on Judicial Administration and Procedure in the following year reported in favor of the creation of a special committee to prevent delay and unnecessary costs in litigation.

[16] Report of the Special Committee to Suggest Remedies and Formulate Proposed Laws to Prevent Delay and Unnecessary Cost in Litigation, 34 *ibid*. 578. See Roscoe Pound, " Organization of Courts," BULL. AM. JUD. SOC., No. 6.

[17] See the references to legislation enacted as a result of the Committee's activities, as set forth in its reports during the period of its existence.

[18] Four principles were enunciated, of which the first embodies the basis for the unification of the judiciary:

" I. The whole judicial power of each state, at least for civil causes, should be vested in one great court, of which all tribunals should be branches, departments or divisions. The business as well as the judicial administration of this court should be thoroughly organized so as to prevent not merely waste of judicial power, but all needless clerical work, duplication of papers and records, and the like, thus obviating expense to litigants and cost to the public.

" II. Whenever in the future practice acts or codes of procedure are drawn up or revised, the statutes should deal only with the general features of procedure, and prescribe the general lines to be followed, leaving details to be fixed by rules of court, which the courts may change from time to time, as actual experience of their application and operation dictates.

" III. Wherever the error complained of is defect of proof of some matter capable of proof by record or other incontrovertible evidence; defective certification or failure to lay the proper foundation for evidence which can, in fact, without involving substantial controversy, be shown to be competent, the court of review should be given power to take additional evidence for the purpose of sustaining a judgment.

" IV. All clerks and other employees of courts and all persons having perma-

bodies throughout the country.[19]   The movement was launched in
an atmosphere of general hopefulness for reform, and stimulated
by faith, so active in the days of Roosevelt, in the efficacy of

nently to do in any way with the administration of justice should be compensated
by fixed salaries and all fees collected should be paid into the public treasury."   34
AM. BAR ASSN. REP. 589, 595, 598, 600.

[19] The program for a unified judiciary and a judicial council has been steadily
urged before State Bar Associations and considerable legislative activity has been
stirred. *California:* In 1917 Orrin K. McMurray addressed the State Bar Association
in behalf of a unified judiciary. " Unified Courts," 1 J. AM. JUD. SOC. 119. In
1925 the California legislature proposed a constitutional amendment to establish a
judicial council. See 8 *ibid.* 173; Charles H. Paul, " The Growth of the Judicial
Council Movement," 10 MINN. L. REV. 85, 93. It was ratified by the people in
November, 1926, and a Judicial Council has been organized. *Colorado:* In 1912
Henry C. Hall advocated the unification of the courts in the annual presidential
address before the bar association. See 15 COLO. BAR ASSN. REP. 97, 111. *Illinois:*
In 1917 Herbert Harley advocated unification before the Judicial Section of the
Illinois State Bar Association. See " Reorganizing Illinois Courts," 1 J. AM. JUD.
SOC. 83. The idea had already been advocated in detail by Albert M. Kales and
William E. Higgins. See " Judicial Reorganization," 7 ILL. L. REV. 119; " Procedural Reform and the Bar," 1913 ILL. BAR. ASSN. REP. 291. In 1922 the constitutional
convention drafted an article for consolidating the courts of Cook County, which
met opposition from the Municipal Court of Chicago in that it violated the principles
of a unified judiciary. See " Chicago Demands Unified Court," 5 J. AM. JUD. SOC.
173. The article was changed in accordance with these demands, but, despite its
warm advocacy, it was rejected by the people. See " Consolidate Chicago Courts,"
6 *ibid.* 3; " Illinois' Great Opportunity," *ibid.* 81; Harry Olson, " The New Constitution and the Administration of Justice," *ibid.* 108; " Illinois Rejects Proposed
Constitution," *ibid.* 158. *Iowa:* In 1922 unification of the judiciary was urged before
the State Bar Association by its president. See Jesse A. Miller, " Would Improve
Iowa Courts," 7 *ibid.* 17. *Louisiana:* In 1915 Herbert Harley had advocated unification before the Bar Association. See " Administration of Justice," 16 LA. BAR ASSN.
REP. 132. In 1921 the Bar Association drafted a scheme for boards of judicial administration which, however, the constitutional convention refused to adopt. See
" Louisiana Bar Association Performs Notable Service in Formulating Judicial
System," 5 J. AM. JUD. SOC. 19. *Massachusetts:* A judicature commission was
created in 1919 by the state legislature. See 1919 MASS. ACTS, c. 223. Its second
report in 1921 advocated the adoption of the principle of unification as far as the
ideal could be approached, and specifically recommended and drafted legislation for
a judicial council. See 6 MASS. L. QUART., No. 2. The council movement received
the support of the State Bar Association before the legislature, and legislation to that
end was enacted in 1924. See 1924 MASS. ACTS, c. 244; 5 J. AM. JUD. SOC. 107;
" Judicial Council in Massachusetts," 7 *ibid.* 245; " Massachusetts Judicial Council
Appointed," 8 *ibid.* 84. The council, under the guidance of former Justice Loring,
has already established itself as a powerful influence. See First Report in 11 MASS.
L. QUART., No. 1; Second Report in 12 MASS. L. QUART., No. 2. On the practical
workings of the council, see Robert G. Dodge, 12 AM. BAR. ASSN. J. 579, 657.
Michigan: Unification was urged by William W. Potter before the State Bar
Association in 1922. See " Give Judiciary Greater Power," 6 J. AM. JUD. SOC.

political effort.   American politics had, perhaps, reached its lowest level in city governments, and the municipal courts of the great cities presented the most dramatic illustration of the mischief due

---

164. *Minnesota:* In 1914 unification was urged before the State Bar Association by Roscoe Pound. See " Organization of Courts," 1914 MINN. BAR ASSN. REP. 169. *Mississippi:* In 1915 Chief Justice Sydney Smith, President of the Mississippi State Bar Association, advocated the unified court in his annual address before that Association. BULL. AM. JUD. SOC., No. 9.   In 1917 the Bar Association by committee reported a plan for unification and a judicial council. See " A Unified Court for Mississippi," 1 J. AM. JUD. SOC., No. 1, 15. *Missouri:* A committee of the St. Louis Bar Association in 1921 reported in favor of unification, and in 1922 the Committee on the Judiciary of the constitutional convention presented an article creating a judicial council. See " Judicial Council in Missouri Constitution," 6 *ibid.* 87.   Despite warm advocacy the judiciary article was defeated at the polls in 1924. See " Missouri Judicial System Unified in Revised Constitution," 7 *ibid.* 117; " What a Judicial Council Can Do," *ibid.* 159; " Missouri Rejects Judicial Reform," *ibid.* 183. *Nebraska:* In 1914 Herbert Harley advocated unification before the State Bar Association. See " A Unified State Court System," 1914 NEB. BAR. ASSN. PROC. 108. *North Carolina:* In 1925 a " judicial conference " was created. See Charles H. Paul, *supra,* 10 MINN. L. REV. at 91; 4 N. C. L. REV. 40; 9 J. AM. JUD. SOC. 15. *North Dakota:* In 1925 a committee headed by Judge A. G. Burr reported to the State Bar Association in favor of a judicial council. See *ibid.* 103. *New York:* In 1915 drafts of plans for unification of the judiciary and creation of judicial boards of assignment and control were presented by the Phi Delta Fraternity and the Phi Delta Phi Club of New York City. See " Two Model Judiciary Articles," 1 *ibid.,* No. 2, 3; " To Unify New York State Courts," *ibid.* 68.   In 1921 the City Club of New York City through its Committee on Courts submitted a brief to the constitutional convention advocating a unified judiciary. See " Unified Court Proposed to New York Constitutional Convention," 5 *ibid.* 121; Austin W. Scott, Felix Frankfurter and Roscoe Pound, " Organization of the Courts," 3 NEW REPUBLIC, 60 (May 22, 1915).   The convention in its report, however, made no fundamental changes. See " New York Convention Reports," 5 J. AM. JUD. SOC. 142.   In 1923, upon the recommendation of Governor Smith, the legislature created a special commission to investigate defects in the law and its administration.   This commission recommended the creation of a " Law Revision Committee," which was to constitute a permanent body for the study of defects in procedural and substantive law and judicial organization.   The report was approved by the New York City Bar Association but has so far failed to stimulate legislative action. See Charles H. Paul, *supra,* 10 *ibid.* at 78, 82. *Ohio:* In 1923 Ohio created a judicial council.   See Clarence D. Laylin, " Judicial Council in Ohio," 17 AM. POL. SCI. REV. 608; " Ohio Adopts Judicial Council," 8 MASS. L. QUART., No. 5, 52; " New Judicial Council," 21 OHIO L. REP. 240. *Oklahoma:* In 1919 the State Bar Association by committee studied the unified court plan and drafted legislation to secure its adoption.   See " Oklahoma Bar Studies Unified Court," 3 J. AM. JUD. SOC. 126; " To Unify Oklahoma Courts," *ibid.* 179. *Oregon:* In 1918 the Oregon legislature authorized the Supreme Court to appoint a commission on judicature. See 2 *ibid.* 145.   As a consequence of its report, legislation creating a judicial council was enacted. See William G. Hale, " The Oregon Judicial Council," 3 ORE. L. REV. 60; James D. Barnett,

to an archaic system of judicial organization.[20] The reorganization of the local courts of Chicago into a unified municipal court
was a concrete demonstration of the part to be played by organization and administration in securing competence, dispatch and
economy from courts.[21] The success of this Chicago experiment
gave the impetus of concrete achievement to the new movement.[22]
Though the ways of law and of courts are frequently too mysterious to arouse the laity to anything except fruitless criticism or
uncritical reverence, this program for judicial reorganization was
within the layman's ken and enlisted the support of his interest

---

"Judicial Council in Oregon," 17 Am. Pol. Sci. Rev. 611; 4 Ore. L. Rev. 257.
Pennsylvania: In 1920 a plan for a unified judiciary was presented to the constitutional convention by the Constitutional Club of Philadelphia. See "Two Schools
Clash," 4 J. Am. Jud. Soc. 48. The proposal was rejected by the convention, but in
1925 the Bar Association by committee reported in favor of a similar plan, and pro-
posed the introduction of legislation to that effect in 1927. See 31 Pa. Bar Assn.
Rep. 159; 9 J. Am. Jud. Soc. 47. Opposition from the judges of the appellate di-
vision has caused the Bar Association to withdraw its recommendations. See Robert
G. Dodge, "Judicial Councils," 12 Am. Bar Assn. J. 579, 580. *South Carolina:*
The judicial council was sponsored before the State Bar Association in 1913 by Judge
Robert W. Winston. See Sen. Doc., No. 377, 63rd Cong., 2nd Sess., Ser. No. 6593.
Tennessee: In 1914 unification was urged before the Bar Association. See Nathan
W. MacChesney, "A Plan for Modern Unified Courts," 1914 Tenn. Bar Assn.
Rep. 103. *Texas:* In 1918 the Bar Association drafted a plan for a unified judiciary
which was submitted to the legislature, but which met defeat in the lower house.
See "Court Reorganization in Texas," 2 J. Am. Jud. Soc. 133; "Texas Bar
Thwarted," 3 *ibid.* 21. *Washington:* In 1925 legislation creating a judicial council
was enacted. See Charles H. Paul, "The Growth of the Judicial Council Move-
ment," 10 Minn. L. Rev. 85; "Washington Creates Judicial Council," 9 J. Am. Jud.
Soc. 102.

[20] See 2 Munro, Municipal Government and Administration, 211.

[21] Chief Justice Harry Olson made this claim for his court: "The Municipal
Court of Chicago is near the end of its sixteenth year. During that entire period it
has never permitted its criminal cases to fall into arrears." See "The New Constitution and the Administration of Justice," 6 J. Am. Jud. Soc. 108, 111. See also
Herbert Harley, "Administration of Justice," 1915 La. Bar Assn. Rep. 132; Olson,
Municipal Court of Chicago; Carter, Early Courts of Chicago and Cook
County. The Municipal Courts of Chicago, Cleveland and Philadelphia publish
annual statistical reports of their work, which furnish the best source for a study
of their achievements.

[22] To the success of the Chicago experiment must be attributed the general
municipal court movement of the larger American cities. The Municipal Courts of
Cleveland, Detroit, and Philadelphia were the immediate outgrowth of the Chicago
court. See Brown, Municipal Court of Philadelphia; Herbert Harley, "The
Small Claims Branch of the Municipal Court of Chicago," Bull. Am. Jud. Soc.,
No. 8; Herbert Harley, "The Model Municipal Court," 3 Nat. Mun. Rev. 57;
3 J. Am. Jud. Soc. 5; 4 *ibid.* 38, 189; 5 *ibid.* 83, 133, 165; 6 *ibid.* 18; 9 *ibid.* 36.

and experience.[23]   Thus, a business man made possible the establishment of the American Judicature Society and its intensive efforts towards modernizing judicial machinery.[24]   The first state to take action was, characteristically enough, Wisconsin.   In 1913 it established the first judicial council.[25]   Its duties, in brief, were to serve as a clearing-house for information in regard to the judicial business of the state, and to distribute the judges of the state according to the needs of the various districts.   In varying form, the mechanism of a judicial council has been adopted in a number of states and the idea is being vigorously pushed ·in others.[26]

With all the weight of his authority and experience, ex-President Taft directed this general movement for judicial reform into federal channels.   In an address before the Cincinnati Law School in 1914 he diagnosed the inadequacies of the federal judicial organization and the burdens thereby entailed upon the country.[27]   The key for his recommendations he found in an analysis of the essential features of the English judicature:

---

[23] Proposals for the unification of the judiciary and for administrative supervision were put forward by organizations not primarily composed of lawyers but interested in problems of civic reform.   In 1914 the " Preliminary Report on Efficiency in the Administration of Justice," made for the National Economic League by Charles W. Eliot, Louis D. Brandeis, Roscoe Pound, Adolph J. Rodenbeck, and Moorfield Storey, advocated as its basic remedy the vesting of the whole judicial power in one organization, with an administrative head who should be responsible for a failure to use the judicial power effectively.   In 1919 the National Municipal League drafted a model judiciary article embodying therein a judicial council.   See 6 J. AM. JUD. SOC. 48.   In 1921 the City Club of New York submitted a brief in behalf of a unified judiciary to the New York Constitutional Convention.   See 5 *ibid*. 121.   The movement for the judicial council in California originated with the Commonwealth Club of San Francisco.   See S. C. Fay, " The Judicial Council," 1 OHIO ST. BAR J. 35, 39; 8 J. AM. JUD. SOC. 173.

[24] See " In Recognition of the Public Services of Charles F. Ruggles," 9 J. AM. JUD. SOC. 132; Herbert Harley, " The American Judicature Society; An Interpretation," 62 U. OF PA. L. REV. 340.   In 1914 the Society published model acts to unify the courts of a large city and of a state.   They had been drafted by Albert M. Kales, whose wide forensic experience in Chicago enabled him to adapt English principles of unification to the conditions of American life.   BULL. AM. JUD. SOC., Nos. 7, 7a.

[25] See Chester A. Fowler, " Wisconsin's Board of Circuit Judges," 4 *ibid*. 101; C. S. Potts, " Unification of the Judiciary; A Record of Progress," 2 TEX. L. REV. 445.

[26] See note 19, *supra*.   See Robert G. Dodge, " Judicial Councils," 12 AM. BAR ASSN. J. 579.

[27] William H. Taft, " Attacks on the Courts and Legal Procedure," 5 KY. L. J., No. 2, 3.

" When the system is studied, the two great features of it are the simplicity of its procedure and the elasticity with which that procedure and
the use of the judicial force provided by Parliament can be adapted to
the disposition of business. The success of the system rests on the
executive control vested in a council of judges to direct business and
economize judicial force, to mould their own rules of procedure, and also
on the learning, ability and experience of the individual judges and the
consequent ease and quickness with which they dispose of cases coming
before them, so that in the great majority of cases the judgment of the
court is pronounced at the close of the argument." [28]

The lines of Mr. Taft's remedies converged with those along which
the American Bar Association and the American Judicature Society had been working. He made six proposals which have been
the basis of the judiciary acts introduced in, and enacted by, Congress since 1914.[29] Our present concern is with his insistence on
a mobile federal judicial force and a judicial council as the instrument for its effective direction. He deemed essential

" the adjustment of our judicial force to the disposition of the increasing
business by introducing into the administration of justice the ordinary
business principles in successful executive work, of a head charged with
the responsibility of the use of the judicial force at places and under
conditions where the judicial force is needed. We have in the entire
United States say 120 Federal judges in courts of first instance, thirty
judges of the intermediate appellate courts, with power to sit in the
courts of first instance, and nine supreme judges, with power to sit
either in the intermediate appellate courts or in courts of first instance.
Now either through the Chief Justice, and if he is to have the duty and
responsibility he should have an adequate force of subordinates to enable
him to discharge it, or through a judicial committee of the judges, the

---

[28] *Ibid.* 13.

[29] Among six proposals there submitted were the following: " Fourth — Authority and duty should be conferred upon the head of the Federal judicial system, either
the Chief Justice, or a council of judges appointed by him, or by the Supreme
Court, to consider each year the pending Federal judicial business of the country
and to distribute the Federal judicial force of the country through the various
districts and intermediate appellate courts, so that the existing arrears may be attacked and disposed of.

" Fifth — There should be a reduction of the appeals to the Supreme Court, by
cutting down to cases of constitutional construction only the review as of right, and
by leaving to the discretion of that court, by writ of certiorari, the power to hear
such cases from the lower courts as it deems in the public interest." *Ibid.* 14–15.

business of the United States Courts throughout the Union should be considered each year, and assignments made of the judicial force to various districts and circuits, with a view to the most economic use of each judge for the disposition of the greatest amount of business by him. In this way tab could, and would be, kept on individual efficiency by the Supreme Court, and nothing would so stimulate effective work of each judge in the reduction of arrears. Then if the judicial force seems inadequate, then if business is not disposed of, it will be entirely easy to know how many judges should be added and in what districts and circuits they should be appointed. Now they are increased in a most haphazard way, and other considerations than the public too frequently enter into such legislation. Of course, the judges, district and circuit, must be appointed primarily in particular districts and circuits; but already there has been introduced in a limited way the practice of using judges from one circuit and one district in another, and there is no reason why this principle should not be extended so that the whole Federal judicial force of the country would be strategically employed, against the arrears of business, existing or probable. Then with the simplicity of procedure, then with the giving adequate sufficient force to the places where needed, we could have the dispatch of business that is essential to justice and that reduces much the cost of litigation.

" The plan of executive management of the judicial force and making the head of the court responsible for the disposition of all judicial business is vindicated by the example of the Municipal Court of Chicago, where under the direction of a Chief Justice in a court of limited jurisdiction, but in a court of the people with a great mass of judicial business of all sorts, the associate justices are massed at one point or another in respect of the litigation pending so that the increased speed in the disposition of cases is shown by the statistics to be marked and most satisfactory." [30]

These views expressed abiding convictions, and the great prestige of the Chief Justiceship later enabled their author to persuade Congress to translate them into action.[31]

---

[30] *Ibid.* 16.

[31] Chief Justice Taft advocated the passage of the Act of 1922 during its pendency in Congress in speeches before the American Bar Association, the Canadian Bar Association, and the Chicago Bar Association. 46 AM. BAR ASSN. REP. 561; 9 PROC. CAN. BAR ASSN. 138; " Three Needed Steps of Progress," 8 AM. BAR ASSN. J. 34; " Possible and Needed Reforms in the Administration of Civil Justice in the Federal Courts," 47 AM. BAR ASSN. REP. 250, 8 AM. BAR ASSN. J. 601, 57 AM. L. REV. 1, 6 J. AM. JUD. SOC. 36.

3

The World War sidetracked efforts for judicial reform. But its aftermath overwhelmingly accentuated its need. After the armistice, the factors which had made for a similar increase in federal court business following the Civil War became operative over a wider area and with greater intensity.[32] Two sources of litigation particularly swamped the courts. The extensive cancellation of wartime contracts crowded the civil dockets, and prohibition brought a flood of petty criminal cases. This enormous increase in the volume of business [33] found the federal judiciary in

---

[32] " This congestion is due to the natural growth of the country, but is temporarily aggravated by legislation of Congress increasing the jurisdiction of the Federal courts, by war legislation, shipping and railroad operations on the civil docket, and prohibition, selective service, and the narcotic law on the criminal docket. It is thought that the generally congested condition throughout the United States, due to these new laws and temporary war conditions, will show a decrease after a few years. Hence, an elastic method of relieving this congestion would be the most efficient and least expensive one. . . . For the above reasons and because of the necessity for economy we confined our recommendations to an elastic method of handling the generally congested condition of the United States courts. We believed that immediate temporary relief was necessary. In those districts where congestion is permanent and due to normal growth of business, there should be additional judges, but in many districts the congestion is but temporary and can be relieved by the use of a judge at large who will assist in clearing the docket and then proceed to another district." REP. ATTY. GEN. FOR 1921, 3–4.

[33] The following statistics were submitted to Congress as to the condition of the dockets in 1921. The figures relate to cases pending on June 30, 1921. There are obvious errors in these figures, but we give them as we find them in the Congressional Record (62 CONG. REC. 2584–86):

Circuit	Judges	Civil	Criminal (including Prohibition)	Admiralty	All other Civil	Total	Bankruptcy	Draft	Prohibition	Population
1	5	297	733	265	1,405	3,670	1,993	3,990	277	6,965,622
2	11	3,358	12,605	4,926	4,278	16,096	6,194	9,071	3,139	12,117,150
3	9	790	1,825	701	4,574	7,890	4,159	11,751	980	12,093,536
4	10	471	2,912	415	1,199	4,977	2,133	78	1,318	9,459,729
5	16	1,559	6,511	564	2,441	11,075	8,829	836	1,837	14,453,483
6	10	742	2,509	44	2,251	5,546	3,428	669	1,046	14,179,792
7	7	565	2,613	27	1,683	4,888	2,733	102	1,024	12,047,481
8	19	1,367	3,514	35	4,493	9,409	4,313	618	1,206	18,258,896
9	20	621	2,544	892	4,489	8,596	3,460	553	908	7,267,187
Total	105	9,770	26,686	7,869	26,813	71,138	37,242	27,677	11,735	106,840,878
D. C.	6	75	2,732	5	3,544	6,622	46	8	266	437,571

The wide-spread congestion of business led Graham of Pennsylvania on Apr. 14, 1921, to submit to the House a concurrent resolution for the appointment of a committee of five Senators and seven Congressmen to consider legislation in regard to the organization and procedure of the United States courts. A similar resolution was introduced by Sterling in the Senate on June 6, 1921. See 61 CONG. REC. 2127.

different districts undermanned. For a number of years the two houses of Congress had not agreed on bills providing for additional judges, and thus interrupted the traditional policy of appointing new judges to meet increases in judicial business.[34] Being of different political complexion, the Senate and House were deadlocked over the division of the spoils.[35] An exigent situation confronted the federal courts. In some of the large centers, and particularly in New York, the enforcement of criminal law suffered wholesale neglect and the interest of private litigants was sacrificed to an extent which disregarded the elementary requirements of justice.[36]

---

[34] " During the entire eight years of the Democratic administration, during the period of the enactment of many of the additional Federal statutes to which the Senator from Ohio (Mr. POMERENE) has referred, during the period when the war in Europe brought about an enormous increase in business in the Federal courts, during the period of the war while we were engaged in it, when that volume had swelled, there was just one additional Federal judgeship created — a Federal judge for the district of New Jersey. . . . Half a dozen different bills for that purpose [the creation of additional judgeships] passed the Senate of the United States, went to the other branch of Congress, and were turned down over there or allowed to die, without any bones being made of it; it was openly declared and expressed in the corridors and in the committees that Republican Members over there did not intend to allow any more Democratic judges to be appointed." Walsh of Montana, in the Senate on Apr. 7, 1922, 62 CONG. REC. 5152. " There can be no question, Mr. President, that the House of Representatives refused to pass the bills proposing to create new judgeships which had been acted upon favorably by the Senate because, even though they were necessary, they would have involved the appointment of Democratic judges. Now, however, although we could not secure the appointment of Democratic judges who were needed, we have before us a bill proposing to provide 22 additional Republican judges. Is such a bill as that a logrolling measure? Is it a pork-barrel bill? It is a pork-barrel judges bill." Overman of North Carolina, in the Senate on Apr. 6, 1922, *ibid.* 5097.

[35] Senator Walsh in *ibid.* 5152, lists 12 bills providing for additional judges which, between 1915 and 1921, passed the Senate but died in the House.

[36] " When we contemplate a situation in which thousands and thousands of persons accused of crime must lie in jail for a year or two years, if they are unable to discharge themselves by giving bond, awaiting trial, and when we reflect upon the fact that in many parts of the United States it is utterly impossible to secure the trial of a civil case within a year or two years, where both attorneys and parties are ready to proceed with the trial, it is to me a source of great humiliation. . . . There were pending on the 30th of June, 1921, in all of the district courts of the United States 26,802 criminal cases, not including what are ordinarily known as draft cases, of which there were 27,582." Cummins of Iowa, in the Senate on March 10, 1922, *ibid.* 4840, 4841. Mr. Mills, testifying before a subcommittee of the House Committee on Judiciary on conditions in the southern district of New York, said: " On the admiralty calendar there were 1,000 cases and it will take on an average a year and a half for a case to be reached; there are 764 civil jury cases and it will take from 9 to 12 months; 224 equity cases and it will take a year; 8,958 criminal cases, and

Here was a tempting opportunity for wholesale judicial appointments, especially since the election of 1920 vested the control of the Executive and both houses of Congress in the same party. It was inevitable that a goodly number of new judgeships would be created. Equally inevitable was the pressure to satisfy local interests in their appointment. Partly to avoid conflicting political claims, partly in response to the agitation for better judicial organization, the Attorney General appointed a committee of judges and United States attorneys to report on the needs of the lower federal courts and the manner of meeting them.[37]   This committee was primarily concerned with a detailed inquiry into the state of judicial business of the different districts and the number of new judges required for the relief of what was widely assumed to be a permanent condition. But these committee members did not deem themselves assessors of patronage. Any disinterested inquiry into relief was bound to go beyond the antiquated practice of treating the federal courts as independent units.

Congress had already made two significant inroads on this practice. The abnormal load of business in the Southern District of New York, compared with the rest of the country, led Congress in 1913 to vary the settled habit of providing new judges for new business by making judges of districts not having much business available for assignment to the Second Circuit.[38]   A particular situation — the uniqueness of New York City — led to a reconsideration of the traditional system. The disparities between New York and Arkansas or Ohio and Montana induced inquiry into the possibility of the freest transfer of federal judges to any dis-

---

there is a note in connection with the number of criminal cases to the effect that the United States Attorney's office estimates that the trial of mail-fraud cases now pending would occupy the time of one judge for over a year, and that the other criminal business pending and coming in is sufficient to keep two judges busy continuously." Hearings before the Committee on Judiciary, House of Representatives, 67th Cong., 1st Sess., on S. 395, H. R. 264, S. 259, H. R. 2261, H. R. 2873, and S. 1288, June 17 and 22, 1921, at 33.

[37] The committee consisted of Judge Sater, Judge Pollock, Judge Grubb, and United States Attorneys William H. Hayward, of New York, and Charles F. Clyne, of Chicago. Their report, submitted to the Attorney General on July 21, 1921, appears in Hearings on S. 2432, 2433, 2523, before the Committee on the Judiciary, U. S. Senate, 67th Cong., 1st Sess., Oct. 5 and 11, 1921.

[38] Act of Oct. 3, 1913, 38 STAT. 203. The validity of the act was upheld in Lamar *v.* United States, 241 U. S. 103 (1916).

trict where congestion needed relief, instead of treating the different circuits as watertight compartments. To generalize the New York situation, it was proposed in the Senate to allow the district judges to be assigned wherever the needs of judicial business might require their assistance.[39] Even this proposal conditioned service outside of his circuit upon the consent of the visiting judge as well as of the circuit judge of his circuit.[40] But this was too far-reaching an innovation; it crossed the deep grain of sectional prejudice. While New York attracts distant judges as it does other visitors,[41] totally different feelings were aroused by the thought of eastern judges holding court in southern or southwestern districts. Congress, therefore, restricted the principle of deploying the judicial force wherever business demanded by applying it exclusively to the Second Circuit.[42] Again, the abolition of the Commerce Court created for Congress, as we have

---

[39] A bill to this end was introduced by Senator O'Gorman of New York on May 19, 1913, and passed the Senate on June 23. 50 CONG. REC. 1630, 1839, 2132. The bill was vigorously sponsored by Judge Lacombe, the senior Circuit Judge of the Second Circuit, and H. Snowden Marshall, United States Attorney for the Southern District of New York. See *ibid.* 5211–12.

[40] An objection raised in the House to the proviso requiring the consent of the district judge in order to permit of his assignment to another circuit, gave rise to the following colloquy: " Mr. Clayton . . . because if that provision were left out, the practical working of it would be that the judge would be consulted before he was designated. Having been a district attorney myself, I know that the practice is to confer with the judges before they are designated. Mr. Payne. The gentleman never knew of a judge going to another circuit to hold court unless he was willing to go, did he? Mr. Clayton. I never knew of it. Mr. Payne. It practically depends upon the will of the judge who is to go there. Mr. Clayton. Certainly; that is practically the way in which it is done now." *Ibid.* 5209.

[41] " From time to time I have met judges from other districts in the United States who have come to this city for their own personal enjoyment of a vacation, their present work all done, no new work for them apparent for many weeks to come. Some of them have told me how pleased they would be if when the work within their own jurisdiction was temporarily disposed of they could come here for a month or six weeks and hold a term of court. Experiences like that are helpful to a judge." Judge Lacombe to Congressman Clayton, *ibid.* 5211.

[42] After the bill had passed the Senate, on June 26 Clarke of Arkansas having given notice of a motion to reconsider, O'Gorman moved to limit the powers of the assigned judge to the trial of causes. Objection being raised by Sutherland to this limitation it was recommitted to the Judiciary Committee, and on June 27 reported out limited to the second circuit. In this form it passed the Senate without division. *Ibid.* 2182–83, 2229, 2237–38. Clayton in the House gave this explanation of the Senate's action: " The bill as originally introduced in the Senate was of general application, but it was amended in the Senate. It seemed that it could not pass

seen,[43] the necessity of devising some expedient for the continued utilization of the Commerce Court judges. By making them judges at large, subject to assignment by the Chief Justice to any circuit, Congress again departed from the traditional practice of territorial fixity.[44]

Here then were two applications of the principle of a flexible judiciary. Both, to be sure, were hit upon in dealing with what were deemed to be exceptional problems. The two instances, however, evoked considerations nation-wide in their applicability. The precedent of the Commerce Court judges was urged to secure the full utilization of the judges of the Court of Customs Appeals whenever the business of that court did not fully engage the time of its judges.[45] It was inevitable that a comprehensive and disinterested scrutiny of the tasks and the needs of the federal judiciary should explore the implications of the New York [46] and

---

without this amendment making it applicable alone to the second circuit, and that is the history of it." *Ibid.* 5209. It was reported favorably from the House Judiciary Committee on Sept. 22, 1913, and passed that body with little debate on Sept. 27. *Ibid.* 5210.

[43] See p. 168, n. 112, *supra.*

[44] The Commerce Court judges prior to the abolition of the Court had been available for assignment to the different circuits. In such a capacity they were much in demand. *Ibid.*

[45] In 1917 and 1918 the Attorney General had recommended legislation for the assignment of the judges of the Court of Customs Appeals to work in the circuits. REP. ATTY. GEN. FOR 1917, 15; *ibid.* FOR 1918, 8. Bills to that effect were introduced by Webb of North Carolina in the House on March 12, 1918, and by King of Utah, in the Senate on Apr. 25, 1918. 56 CONG. REC. 3412, 5591. On Nov. 19, 1919, a similar bill was introduced by Volstead of Minnesota in the House, reported out favorably from committee, and on Jan. 19, 1920, passed that body. 58 *ibid.* 8822; 59 *ibid.* 1206, 1742; HOUSE REPORT, No. 532, 66th Cong., 2nd Sess., Ser. No. 7652. It was ignored by the Senate Judiciary Committee. On Nov. 16, 1921, the bill was reintroduced in the House by Volstead. 61 CONG. REC. 7833.

[46] Chairman Walsh of Massachusetts, of the House Judiciary Committee, in introducing the bill before the House adverted to the New York experiment: " New York City, which is in the southern district of New York, has four judges, with a population of 3,801,364. They are also assisted at times by judges from one or more other districts. That is the only district to which judges under the existing law can now be sent from other districts or circuits without their consent. They even sent one of the judges from the Florida district, and I think Judge Mack, one of the commerce judges, has been sitting in New York quite frequently and has been there until a short time ago. In the last three or four years, I am informed by the gentleman from New York (Mr. SNELL), the records show that there have been from 30 to 33 outside judges helping out there." 62 *ibid.* 150.

Commerce Court precedents. And so, the Attorney General's committee did not limit itself to an ascertainment of the number of judges required by the congested dockets on the basis of the old principle of restricting district judges to fixed districts. The new theory of a mobile judicial force was drawn upon:

" The existing condition can be relieved only by increasing the number of district judges and by providing a method of mobilizing the judicial forces so as effectively to reach and relieve congested districts." [47]

The committee generalized the New York and the Commerce Court instances by recommending the appointment of eighteen district judges at large and the assignability of new and old judges to any part of the country.[48]

These recommendations were submitted to Congress in the Attorney General's report,[49] and legislation formulating them was promptly introduced in the Senate.[50] But the most important feature of the enactment which resulted from this bill, a federal judicial council, was added to the suggestions submitted by the Attorney General. Undoubtedly this proposal owed its immediate inspiration to Chief Justice Taft.[51] For the first time since 1911 the whole structure of the federal judicial establishment was opened up in debate. And this time new theories of judicial organ-

---

[47] See Hearings on S. 2432, 2433, 2523, before the Committee on the Judiciary, U. S. Senate, 67th Cong., 1st Sess., Oct. 5 and 11, 1921, at 9.

[48] For the committee's report, see note 46, *supra*. In 1919 and 1920 the Attorney General had recommended the enactment of legislation making district judges freely assignable to the various circuits. See REP. ATTY. GEN. FOR 1919, 3; *ibid.* FOR 1920, 4.

[49] *Ibid.* FOR 1921, 3.

[50] By Nelson of Minnesota, on Aug. 20, 1921. 61 CONG. REC. 5316. The bill, introduced by Joseph Walsh in the House on Nov. 14, 1921, which finally became the Act of Sept. 14, 1922, substituted additional district judges for judges at large. *Ibid.* 7689. On Feb. 4, 1921, and June 13, 1921, Senator Nelson had introduced bills providing for the ready assignability of district judges. 60 *ibid.* 2553; 61 *ibid.* 2474.

[51] " This proposal was made by the Chief Justice of the United States and was submitted by him to the Senate Judiciary Committee and also to the House Judiciary Committee, and necessarily it was felt that the proposition should be concluded in rather general terms, because it would hardly seem necessary for the Congress to lay down any narrow, restricted limits within which this conference should operate." Joseph Walsh in the House on Dec. 10, 1921, 62 CONG. REC. 202. Other bills for the creation of a judicial council were introduced in the House by Volstead on June 13, 1921; by Boies on Oct. 7, 1921; by Walsh on Oct. 26, 1921. 61 *ibid.* 2548, 6117, 6827. See REP. ATTY. GEN. FOR 1921, 4.

ization and administration challenged discussion. Four features came before Congress. The creation of new judgeships involved the time-honored motives of politics and patronage. But new ideas were stirred by the suggestions of a " flying squadron of judges," [52] by the assignability of district judges throughout the country, and the creation of a judicial council as the promoter and instrument of a coördinated national judicial system.

The proposal for judges at large did not survive the committee stage.[53] Regard for local representation is one of the most obstinate characteristics of American politics. The sectional diversities and traditions of a continent explain its persistence as something more intelligible than the parochial partisanship of politicians. Of course, personal and political motives also asserted themselves. The theory of judges at large without local responsibilities and attachments was decisively rejected,[54] while a heavy increase in

---

[52] " Federal judges at large will permit elasticity in the Federal judicial system and economy in the handling of temporarily congested dockets. It will encourage uniformity in judicial procedure and prompt expedition of business, for as these judges render services when necessary in any district where assigned, they will receive and carry with them the beneficial practices of each district and thereby become familiar with reforms and improvements in practices." *Ibid.*

[53] " The suggestion of a flying squadron of judges did not meet with approval in the House, and their Judiciary Committee preferred to add local district judges for the congested districts." William H. Taft, " Possible and Needed Reforms in the Administration of Civil Justice in the Federal Courts," 47 Am. Bar Assn. Rep. 250, 251.

[54] "He [Judge Grubb] recommended that these other judges — 18 roving, carpetbag judges, as they are sometimes called — and the Chief Justice should have a meeting here in Washington, like the head of an army, a chief of staff, and have the circuit judges here constitute the general staff to assign these judges, to send a man from Maine to California, or from North Carolina to Wisconsin, to hold court. What does he know about the law in Wisconsin? What does he know about your people? What does he know about the conditions existing there? It is wrong in principle, and the Judiciary Committee turned it down. We would not pass any such bill as that, although these judges, who came here and recommended it, are good men, able men, but impractical. We would not stand for that bill at all, and I do not think that any man in the Senate would stand for such a bill as that — to have 18 roving judges to be sent around at the will of the Chief Justice and his staff here in Washington, coming here once a year to send them around all over the country. It is fundamentally wrong." Overman of North Carolina, in the Senate on Apr. 6, 1922, 62 Cong. Rec. 5097, 5098. " In conclusion let me say that I am heartily pleased that the Committee on the Judiciary had the courage to utterly reject the proposed plan for the appointment of 18 district judges with roving commissions . . . it is unfortunately true that there are some Federal judges who, through the long-continued exercise of power, have become inconsiderate and arbi-

the judiciary stimulated Congressional appetites. It was not difficult to justify the desires of different districts for additional judges, and the habit of log-rolling prevailed.[55] The House of Representatives disregarded the moderation of the Attorney General's experts and voted for twenty-two new judges.[56] The testimony before Congressional committees,[57] the insistence of localities and

trary. Almost the only restraining influence upon them is that, by reason of their selection from the bar of the State in which they continue to reside, old friends can address them with frankness respecting their official conduct. Judges with no fixed assignment would be without even this slight check upon their actions on the bench, with the result that they would soon be looked upon as judicial despots whose coming was to be dreaded. The entire proposal was wrong in its conception and it is well that it has been definitely abandoned." Hayden of Arizona, in the House on Dec. 10, 1921, *ibid.* 206–07.

[55] See charges made by Senator Overman of North Carolina and Senator Fletcher of Florida, *ibid.* 4975, 5097. Senator Walsh of Montana, after charging that the Department of Justice was handling the judgeships in the Territory of Hawaii " to promote the election of a Republican Delegate from that jurisdiction," added: " I do not assent to the charge made that this is a pork barrel bill, but I do assert that it is a log rolling bill and a vicious form of legislation. I can find no justification whatever for the other branch of Congress absolutely refusing to pass the single bills we have presented to them from time to time and then passing what might be regarded as an omnibus bill. The temptation to get into a bill of this kind a provision for the appointment of judges in places where they should not be appointed, in order to secure the number of votes necessary to pass the bill, is too great to be resisted. It should not pass without protest. . . . The vicious tendency of legislation of this character must be recognized by everyone, and it ought not to pass without just criticism." *Ibid.* 5153, 5154.

[56] The bill, as introduced, provided for an additional judge for the district of Colorado, making 23 in all. This provision was eliminated in committee. *Ibid.* 150. It is of interest to note that Attorney General Daugherty estimated that, in the event that judges at large would not be created, at least 30 new district judges would be required. REP. ATTY. GEN. FOR 1921, 3.

[57] That the criteria were not necessarily based on public welfare is revealed by the testimony of Mr. Sears of Florida before the House Committee on Judiciary: " Now, I want simply to bring out this point and fact: It is immaterial whether there are 2,000 cases pending or 70,000 cases pending . . . it is the work that the judge is doing, and the number of cases that he has disposed of, and whether he can keep up with his work or not, that should be considered. If my district has a thousand cases undisposed of and that judge has worked night and day trying to dispose of them and the cases are accumulating, perhaps in another district where the judge has not worked so hard and there are 4,000 cases pending, that would not entitle that district to an extra judge and Florida to none." Hearings before the Committee on Judiciary, House of Representatives, 67th Cong., 1st Sess., on H. R. 8875, Nov. 7, 1921, at 15. See also Hearings before the Committee on Judiciary, House of Representatives, 67th Cong., 1st Sess., on S. 78, S. 694, and H. R. 5754, May 3, 17, and 23, 1921; *ibid.* on S. 395, H. R. 264, S. 259, H. R. 2261, H. R. 2873, and S. 1288, June 17 and 22, 1921; *ibid.* on H. R. 6114, and H. R. 6873, July 15 and 22, 1921; *ibid.* on S. 1960, Oct. 22, 1921.

the debates in House and Senate,[58] show how easy it was to prove
the need of particular districts and how unreliable were the statistics upon which the claims were based.[59]   The whole course of this
legislation demonstrates that without a scientific system of judicial
statistics judgment on the functioning of courts is playing at blind
man's buff.[60]   The Senate had its own interests in patronage; it re-
distributed some of the new district judges provided for by the
House bill.[61] The conflicting claims of the two houses were resolved
in conference out of which came twenty-four new judges — six
more than the Attorney General's committee had recommended.[62]

The other two features of the bill — the assignability of judges
and the judicial council — met objections of constitutional policy
and the opposition of challenged tradition.   For they both ran
counter to the principles of localism and independence.   To subject the district judges to the direction of the Chief Justice, however safeguarded, aroused strange visions of autocracy [63] and far-

---

[58] 62 CONG. REC. 146–210, 4840–65, 4913–23, 4972–78, 5055–66, 5095–5116, 5147–
75.

[59] " Mr. Goodykoontz. The number of cases on the docket in a given district
is not a conclusive test as to the requirements of that district with respect to the
number of judges?

" Mr. Daugherty. No; but it is about as good as any one test.

" Mr. Goodykoontz. Has your department, or any other department of the
Government, any agency that inquires into the question as to whether or not the
Federal judges work as much as they should?

" Mr. Daugherty. We know pretty generally about how they work. . . . There
is quite a difference in the manner in which Federal judges expedite their business.
You can take the number of cases pending and that will be a better guide than any
other particular test but it is not by any means a safe thing to depend upon finally."
Hearings before the Committee on the Judiciary, House of Representatives, 67th
Cong., 1st Sess., on H. R. 8875, Nov. 7, 1921, at 9.

[60] An interesting comparison is afforded by the situation resulting in England
where, as a result of the World War, two additional judges for the King's Bench
Division were deemed necessary for the dispatch of the increased business. The
rigorous scrutiny with which Parliament examined the plea of the Lord Chancellor
and the Attorney General for additional judges and the control retained by Parliament over future vacancies in the judgeships illustrate the standards of efficiency
imposed upon the English judicial force. 130 PARL. DEBATES, 5th series, June 16,
1920 (Commons) 136 et seq.; 40 ibid. (Lords) 642 et seq.

[61] The Senate dropped the House provisions for judges for the eastern district
of Virginia, the middle district of Tennessee, and the eastern district of Illinois, and
substituted therefor judges for the districts of New Jersey and New Mexico, and
one judge for the northern and southern districts of Georgia.

[62] SEN. DOC., No. 241, 67th Cong., 2nd Sess., Ser. No. 7988.

[63] Shields of Tennessee contended in the Senate that the effect of granting such

fetched fears of using partisan judges against the sentiments of a locality.[64] There was a more well-founded concern that distant judges would be unfamiliar with the pertinent diversities of local experience and local law.[65] The New York admiralty bar would welcome as little a Montana judge sitting in admiralty as Montana lawyers would like to try a mining case before a New York judge. But in addition, a more uncritical attachment to locality asserted itself in the debate. The ardent John Sharp Williams of Mississippi thus expressed this feeling:

" I am frankly opposed to a perambulatory judiciary, to carpet-bagging Nebraska with a Louisianian, certainly to carpetbagging Mississippi or Louisiana with somebody north of Mason and Dixon's line, which will almost certainly happen if this bill passes." [66]

To soothe these perturbations, the New York precedent was urged, as well as the safeguards which hedged about the new proposals. The Chief Justice was not given uncontrolled power. He could not move judges autocratically over the chess-board of the United States. His authority was conditioned upon a certificate of need by the senior circuit judge or circuit Justice of the demanding district and a certificate of dispensability from the circuit judge of

---

powers to the Chief Justice was to make him, like the Lord Chancellor of England, the political as well as the judicial head of the judiciary. He characterized the legislation as " provisions for the mobilization of the Federal judiciary with the Chief Justice as commander in chief." 62 Cong. Rec. 4853, 4855.

[64] " Even now, before this bill has become a law, selfish interests are contriving and conspiring to take advantage of it to control the courts and judicial decisions by securing the designation to try their cases of judges who are in sympathy with them or who have fixed convictions upon the law and the facts. I am reliably informed that the Anti-Saloon League, through its paid lobbyists, has attempted to influence Senators to vote for the provisions of this bill giving the Chief Justice the power to assign judges in his discretion to courts, and, of course, to try certain cases pending in those courts. . . . If this bill becomes a law the Chief Justice may be assailed with applications from all sorts of interests and all sorts of influence in the designation of judges. The Anti-Saloon League and the whiskey interest may contend before him. The coal operators may ask for judges to try striking miners and the miners will want a judge who will favor them. Capital and corporations may ask for judges favoring their views upon public questions, and various interests — labor, farmers, and others — may also clamor for representation upon the bench." Shields of Tennessee, in the Senate on March 31, 1922, *ibid.* 4861, 4862.

[65] This was the basis of the objections raised in the House by Stevenson of South Carolina. *Ibid.* 204.

[66] *Ibid.* 5107.

the releasing circuit.[67]   The proposal weathered the opposition in both Houses and achieved enactment.[68]

The idea of a judicial council aroused constitutional fulminations.   The doctrine of the separation of powers was voluminously invoked.[69]   To create an annual conference with the Chief Justice at its head was interpreted as a political device involving the exercise of authority in no wise judicial.   It was the function of judges, so ran the sterile logic, to judge — not to watch the workings of the judicial system, to explore its defects and devise remedies.[70] " In making a survey," protested Lea of California, " they will perform a legislative function that belongs to a committee of Congress and not to a judicial body." [71]   To these empty constitutional objections were added prophecies of futility.   The same Congress that log-rolled judicial appointments, feared that the proposed judicial council would entail an expense resulting in an unproductive annual junket.[72]

---

[67] Act of Sept. 14, 1922, § 3, 42 STAT. 837, 839, amending JUDICIAL CODE, § 13.

[68] On Dec. 9, 1921, Volstead proposed an amendment making the judges of the Court of Customs Appeals available for work as district judges.   62 CONG. REC. 190.   The amendment was agreed to by a vote of 56 to 44.   *Ibid.* 209.   It survived the conference and appears as § 5 of the Act of Sept. 14, 1922, 42 STAT. 837, 839.

[69] See, *e.g.,* Lea of California, in the House on Dec. 9, 1921, Shields in the Senate on Apr. 5, 1922, 62 CONG. REC. 202, 4863.

[70] " Judges should never be authorized to exercise powers not strictly judicial. . . .   They should be wholly judges, always judges, and nothing but judges." Shields in the Senate on Apr. 5, 1922, *ibid.* 4863.   " I am opposed to this section for four reasons.   In the first place, it places the judiciary of the country in a self-seeking position.   In the second place, it assigns to the judges legislative and political functions, and throws the judiciary of the country into the fields of destroying controversies.   In the third place, the conference proposed would easily deteriorate into a publicity-seeking propaganda effort.   And, in the fourth place, it is cheapening to the judiciary for its judges to desert court work, to assemble annually at public expense in what would be regarded by the public as more or less a junket or annual vacation."   Lea in the House on Dec. 9, 1921, *ibid.* 202.

[71] *Ibid.* 203.

[72] " When these judges come to Washington at the expense of the taxpayers, I was about to say, what will they do?   They will meet with the Chief Justice. They will be dined every evening somewhere.   They will be run to death with social activities.   I would like to pause right here to say, Mr. President, that I do not believe there is any man who can stick his legs under the tables of the idle rich every night and be fit the next day to sit in judgment upon those who toil.   Honest though he may be, he can not get away from the atmosphere that will surround him, and ninety-nine times out of one hundred it will affect him and get him in the end."   Norris of Nebraska, in the Senate on Apr. 6,

The course of the debate showed how unreal were the constitutional doubts which the measure had aroused and how groundless the fears of political perversion. The case for the judicial council was clear,[73] but it is doubtful whether it would have prevailed had it not had behind it the powerful support of the new Chief Justice.[74] The House passed this feature of the bill without a division; [75] in the Senate the opposition was more powerful, but it passed by a vote of 36 to 29,[76] and the bill containing it became law on September 14, 1922.[77]

More new judgeships were provided for by this Act than were established by the First Judiciary Act founding the federal judicial system.[78] But the importance of the Act of September 14, 1922,

---

1922, *ibid.* 5113–14. " I fully agree with the statement made by the Senator from Nebraska that it means absolutely nothing on earth except a junket and a dinner. If the annual conference in Washington with the Chief Justice shall be held, the senior circuit judge of each of the nine circuits in the country, all estimable gentlemen, will come here; the Chief Justice will give them a dinner and the Representatives from their various States will give them a dinner; they will have a good time and then go home. There is not any business, so far as I can see, which they can transact; there is no information which they can give which, to my mind, can not as well be conveyed by a letter written by the judges annually to the Chief Justice for his guidance and information in the discharge of the duties which he is to perform." Walsh of Montana, in the Senate on Apr. 6, 1922, *ibid.* 5156.

[73] " It is to find out the condition of the various districts and, as far as possible, make provision in advance for the transfer and designation of judges from one district to the other, to take care of business for the year ensuing, and also to arrange, if possible, for uniformity of procedure, and to get the benefit of the knowledge and experience of the various judges as to how cases in particular districts are disposed of relating to particular classes and perhaps to have some uniformity in the matter of sentences." J. Walsh from the House Judiciary Committee on Dec. 9, 1921, *ibid.* 202. See also HOUSE REPORT, No. 482, 67th Cong., 1st Sess., Ser. No. 7921. The American Judicature Society appealed to its members in behalf of the bill. 5 J. AM. JUD. SOC. 121. President Severance of the American Bar Association also asked support for the plan before the Chicago Bar Association in October, 1921, before the Kansas Bar Association in 1921, and before the meeting of the American Bar Association in Cincinnati in the summer of 1921. See 54 CHIC. LEG. NEWS, 152; 39 KAN. BAR ASSN. REP. 48.

[74] Chief Justice Taft had appeared before the Senate Judiciary Committee in behalf of the bill. See Hearings on S. 2432, 2433, 2523, before the Committee on the Judiciary, U. S. Senate, 67th Cong., 1st Sess., Oct. 5 and 11, 1921, at 11. He had advocated the plan before the Chicago Bar Association in 1921 and before the American Bar Association in 1922. See note 31, *supra*.

[75] 62 CONG. REC. 203.

[76] *Ibid.* 5170.

[77] 42 STAT. 837.

[78] The First Judiciary Act provided for 6 Supreme Court Justices and 13 dis-

lies elsewhere. It marks the beginning of a new chapter in the administration of the federal courts.[79] It is the first recognition by Congressional legislation that effective and economic adjudication is to no small measure dependent upon the ways in which the federal courts transact business. Hundreds of judges holding court in as many or more districts scattered over a continent must be subjected to oversight and responsibility as parts of an articulated system of courts. The judiciary, like other political institutions, must be directed.[80] But it must be self-directed. An executive committee of the judges, with the Chief Justice of the United States at its head, is a fit and potent instrument for the task.

4

The Conference of Senior Circuit Judges thus launched by the Act of 1922 made no structural changes, involved no increase in personnel, and led to no heavy expenditure. But the impulses and specific reforms which have already issued from the five annual conferences [81] signify the presence of a powerful new ferment

---

trict judges; the Act of Feb. 13, 1801, created 15 new circuit judgeships, shortly thereafter abolished; the Act of Apr. 10, 1869, created 9 new circuit judgeships; the Act of Mar. 3, 1891, created 9 new circuit judgeships.

[79] See "New Law Unifies Federal Judiciary," 6 J. AM. JUD. SOC. 69.

[80] " . . . These provisions allow team work. They throw upon the council of judges, which is to meet annually, the responsibility of making the judicial force in the courts of first instance as effective as may be. They make possible the executive application of an available force to do a work which is distributed unevenly throughout the entire country. It ends the absurd condition, which has heretofore prevailed, under which each district judge has had to paddle his own canoe and has done as much business as he thought proper." William H. Taft, *supra,* 47 AM. BAR ASSN. REP. at 252.

[81] Beginning with the report of the conference for 1924, its recommendations have been published in the annual reports of the Attorney General to Congress. The earlier recommendations of the Conference appeared in scattered legal periodicals, *viz.,* the reports for 1922 and 1923 in C. S. Potts, " Unification of the Judiciary, A Record of Progress," 2 TEX. L. REV. 445, 448; 8 J. AM. JUD. SOC. 85, 92; the reports of the conference for 1924, 1925, and 1926 may be found, respectively, in 10 AM. BAR ASSN. J. 875; 98 CENT. L. JOUR. 13, 31; 12 AM. BAR ASSN. J. 687.

The reports of the Attorney General are practically inaccessible to the profession at large and the results of the Conference ought to be made readily known to the bar. Until the Conference has reached a development calling for an independent series of annual reports, it might be well to have its annual reports published both in the Supreme Court Reporter and in the Federal Reporter, in the volumes immediately following the meeting of the Conference.

in the federal judicial system. The Conference represents the infusion of intelligence in the use of existing instruments. What was long delayed through the sheer force of inertia and finally resisted by prejudice and fear has quickly established itself as a permanent feature of the federal judicature.

The activities of the Conference cluster around two functions. Congress it serves as an authoritative advisor on legislation governing the judiciary; the lower federal courts as the promoter of effective standards of judicial administration. Of course, it is not expected that Congress should abdicate its responsibility for independent judgment upon proposals affecting the judiciary. But questions of federal jurisdiction and procedure are largely matters of a technical and non-partisan nature. In legislating upon them Congress will, it may be confidently hoped, rely upon the Conference more and more as the authoritative voice of the needs and experience of the federal bench. In speaking to the lower federal courts the Conference speaks with immediate authority; and this not merely because the Conference represents the Chief Justice and the circuit judges who, presumably, exert the strongest influence in the deliberations of their respective appellate tribunals when reviewing the conduct of lower courts. The recommendations and suggestions of the Chief Justice of the United States and the nine senior circuit judges carry intrinsic weight. The interchange of experience among the senior circuit judges means a pooling of problems and solutions. It helps to invigorate the presiding judge of each circuit, and this, in turn, through the contact of each senior circuit judge with the judges of his circuit, makes for alertness and dispatch in the conduct of judicial business. An annual survey of the results of judicial labors reveals defects and stimulates their correction. Comparative study of the conditions and work of the different circuits enlists a proper pride in sectional achievements. Moreover, an individual judge of vigor and initiative no longer has to meet professional conservatism and prejudice singlehanded, but is encouraged and supported by the weight of the judicial system.

At the annual conference each senior circuit judge renders a detailed report on the state of the business of his circuit. This scrutiny searches the condition of the calendar district by district, reveals the localities that are over-burdened, those that keep abreast of their work, and those that have a surplus of judicial time. Critical analysis differentiates merely temporary congestions from permanent accretions of business, calling for permanent relief. This assures searching inquiry into methods of relief — the possibility of improvement in procedure, curtailment of jurisdiction either through increase in the necessary *per damnum* or through transfer of litigation to the state courts, better utilization of available judges, or, finally, additional judges. Upon the basis of such data, the Conference has been making its recommendations to Congress for new judgeships.[82] Congress has yielded only in small measure to them.[83] Of course, every issue of patronage arouses

---

[82] Additional district judges recommended by the Conference included one each for the districts of Maryland and Connecticut, the northern district of Georgia, the western district of New York, the eastern district of Pennsylvania, the northern district of California, the southern district of Iowa, the eastern district of Michigan, the western district of North Carolina, the eastern district of New York, and two (increased to three in the fourth report) for the southern district of New York. Two circuit judges for the Eighth Circuit and one for the Second Circuit were also recommended.

[83] The two circuit judges for the Eighth Circuit, recommended by the Conference, were provided for by the Act of Mar. 3, 1925, 43 STAT. 1116. The recommendation for an additional judge for the northern district of Georgia was taken care of by the Act of May 28, 1926, 44 STAT. 670, providing for an additional district with an additional judge. An additional judge for Indiana was provided for by the Act of Jan. 16, 1925, 43 STAT. 751. Additional district judges were also created by the Acts of Feb. 17 and Mar. 2, 1925, 43 STAT. 949, 1098, for the western district of Michigan and the district of Minnesota but these were emergency measures to take care of the death or sudden incapacity of the existing judge. During the sixty-eighth and sixty-ninth Congresses numerous bills for additional judges were introduced, but failed of passage. A bill providing for two district judges for the southern district of New York was defeated in the House by a vote of 160 to 150. 65 CONG. REC. 8843. During the first session of the sixty-ninth Congress bills for additional judges for Connecticut, Georgia, Iowa, Maryland, the western district of New York, North Carolina, and the eastern district of Pennsylvania, passed the Senate but, with the exception of Georgia, have as yet failed to secure action by the House. 67 CONG. REC. 4886, 7265, 7268, 7952, 8605. In the House an omnibus bill introduced by Graham on March 29, 1926, providing for one additional judge each for the northern district of New York, the western district of New York, the district of Connecticut, the eastern district of Pennsylvania, the district of Maryland, the eastern district of South Carolina, the eastern district of Michigan, the southern district of California, the district of South Dakota, and three judges for the southern district of New York, was reported from the Committee on the Judiciary on Apr. 13, and succeeded in passing the House on June 8 by a vote of 215 to 97 with amendments for two additional district judges. *Ibid.* 6545, 7392, 10959. It was reported from the Senate Judiciary Committee but no action was taken by the Senate before the session expired. *Ibid.* 11797. Out of the twelve additional judges provided for by this omnibus bill, it will be noticed that only seven were recommended by the Conference. That a particular judge was recommended by the Conference has

the most sensitive interest of Congress. It requires a continuous process of education to wean both parties from past appetites. Nor must it be forgotten that federal judges are called upon to deal with issues of the liveliest political and social implications. Inevitably Senate and House are watchful of the sensibilities and interests, as they conceive them, of different sections of the country. Moreover, the statistical data on which recommendations for more judges now have to be based are still extremely unscientific.[84] In course of time the information by which the Conference will be guided will be more precise and more dependable for purposes of comparing the work in different districts, and will undoubtedly result in securing greater persuasiveness for its recommendations to Congress.

More effective coördination of the existing personnel was one of the chief hopes underlying the passage of the Act of 1922. That hope has been fulfilled. Instead of the wholly unsatisfactory method of long distance correspondence, entreaties and accommodations in securing relief for congested districts through the release of unoccupied judges elsewhere, the Conference supplies a systematic examination of business and personnel, and an adjustment of personnel to business throughout the country. The mobilization of the judicial force cannot be achieved merely by an adequate system of judicial statistics, though their lack is bound to be supplied by guesswork. A knowledge of the adaptabilities, of special equipment, even of the idiosyncrasies of judges is essential. These relevant personal factors are canvassed in their bearing upon the needs of different districts revealed by objective judicial bookkeeping.[85] The federal courts are thus enabled to

often been referred to in debate, and also embodied in the reports of the judiciary committees. See, *e.g.*, House Report, No. 10821; Sen. Rep., Nos. 2762, 3418, 69th Cong., 1st Sess.

[84] During a debate on the proposal for additional judges for the Southern District of New York, Representative Celler of New York maintained that dead cases were used to inflate the dockets in order to give the appearance of urgency for additional judges. 67 Cong. Rec. 10946 (June 8, 1926). With an established and authoritative system of judicial statistics like the English, a like argument in the House of Commons seems unthinkable.

[85] At the first conference a committee was created on " the need and possibility of transfer of judges." They reported the following year " that information on the subject could be best obtained from the reports submitted by the various senior circuit judges at the conference meetings as to the condition of business within their respective circuits." See C. S. Potts, *supra*, 2 Tex. L. Rev. at 460. This procedure

articulate as a system while, at the same time, the individual factors due to differences in communities and in types of litigation are given proper emphasis.[86]

The Conference has found rich opportunities for improving judicial administration without the need of further legislation through resources now available to courts. The rule-making power of courts, their control over the docket and over those details of procedure called practice, are being explored by the Conference to effect a tightening of the judicial machinery. Through recommendations which have been enforced by appropriate changes in rules of court and rules of practice governing the docket and the trial of causes, the Conference has already stimulated important improvements affecting both civil and criminal litigation.

Abuses in bankruptcy administration have long awaited correction. When the business community and the bar sought relief partly by changes in rules of court, the Conference furnished an apt organ for working out the reforms.[87] A joint committee

---

has since obtained. During the year commencing on July 1, 1924, some 12 judges were assigned from the various other circuits to sit in the southern district of New York. See REP. ATTY. GEN. FOR 1925, 5. As to the impossibility of fulfilling the needs of this district by resort to outside judges, United States Attorney Buckner said: " We have never been able to secure sufficient out-of-town judges to carry on our work." 67 CONG. REC. 10944. Of the practice the Bar Association of the City of New York reported: " Without the assistance of judges from other districts, sitting by assignment in the southern district, congestion of the calendar would be much greater. Judges coming by assignment have done a great deal of excellent and helpful work. Nevertheless, it is impracticable for visiting judges to dispose satisfactorily of a volume of work equivalent to that which could be disposed of by an equal number of resident judges in like periods. The time of arrival of the visitors is uncertain, the length of their stay is likewise uncertain, and frequently they are unfamiliar with local peculiarities." *Ibid.* 10943.

[86] The Conference at its first meeting recommended that Congress grant an additional appropriation for clerks and attorneys to serve the needs of visiting judges, which was done by the Act of Mar. 4, 1923, 42 STAT. 1527, 1542. Of late the Conference has also concerned itself with securing necessary equipment for the adequate functioning of judges, particularly sufficient library facilities for the circuit courts of appeals. The last three reports of the Conference have requested additional appropriations for these purposes, together with suggestions as to the expenditure of existing appropriations. See also " An Unfortunate Federal Economy," 10 MASS. L. QUART., No. 3, 70.

[87] In response to a request for coöperation from the Bankruptcy Law Executive Committee of the National Association of Credit Men, the first conference appointed Judge Buffington of the Third Circuit a committee on recommendations as to bankruptcy rules. The Credit Men's Committee thereupon made a survey of conditions

representing the Conference, the American Bar Association, the National Association of Credit Men and the Commercial Law League of America formulated detailed changes in the bankruptcy rules to cope with the evils of dishonest bankruptcies.[88] These proposals were subjected to changes when submitted to the Conference in 1924 [89] and in their amended form were promulgated by the Supreme Court.[90] Similarly, the Conference in 1924 reported the desirability of changes in the equity rules,[91] and drafted the proposed amendment which the Supreme Court duly promulgated.[92] Finally, the complicated new problems of appellate procedure, raised by review of the decisions of the Board of Tax Appeals by the circuit courts of appeals,[93] led to the formulation of separate rules governing these appeals for adoption by the nine circuit courts of appeals.[94]

As soon as the Conference began to study the condition of the federal dockets it found a great deal of dormant and dead litigation. With a callous disregard of the essentials of a civilized system of adjudication, a large volume of cases, it was found, had been allowed needlessly to encumber the calendars. Failure to

---

in the larger commercial centers, which was presented to Judge Buffington and by him laid before the second conference. That conference authorized a copy of the report to be sent to the various district judges to invite their criticisms of the proposed changes. See George W. Carr, " The Federal Judicial Council and the Movement for Better Bankruptcy Administration," 7 J. AM. JUD. SOC. 180. At the suggestion of Chief Justice Taft, speaking on the report of the Committee on Professional Ethics and Grievances before the meeting of the American Bar Association in 1923, it was resolved that the Bar Association's Committee on Practice in Bankruptcy Matters should confer with the committee of the Judicial Conference, the National Credit Men's Association Committee and the committee of any other organization of like character upon the problem of reform in bankruptcy administration. See 48 AM. BAR ASSN. REP. 49–51.

[88] This conference was held in Philadelphia in January, 1924. For the report, see 49 AM. BAR ASSN. REP. 461; 3 DOCKET, 2795.

[89] 10 AM. BAR ASSN. J. 875.

[90] 267 U. S. 613 (1925).

[91] 10 AM. BAR ASSN. J. 875, 876.

[92] 268 U. S. 709 (1925).

[93] Act of Feb. 26, 1926, § 1001 (b), 44 STAT. 9, 109.

[94] The Conference conceived it to be " its duty to refrain from framing any rule that seems to declare any opinion in respect of the scope of the jurisdiction of the Circuit Courts of Appeals," and limited itself to prescribing rules " wholly procedural " and " not covered by the existing rules of the several circuits, or rules of practice prescribed by the Supreme Court." 12 AM. BAR ASSN. J. 687, 689; REP. ATTY. GEN. FOR 1926, 9. The Second, Third, Fourth and Sixth Circuits have already adopted these rules.

bring cases to an issue and an absurd indulgence in the allowance of continuances, so characteristic of American litigation, made for an extravagant waste of judicial energies. The Conference, by a very simple device, proposed an end to these evil practices. District judges were urged not to allow continuances on frivolous grounds,[95] and to strike from the docket cases which had not been pressed to issue after a year.[96] Statistics giving the time history of federal litigation are as yet unknown,[97] but there can be no doubt that a vigorous adherence by district judges to the recommendations of the Conference will make justice less leaden-footed in the federal courts. Even more important becomes the observance of rules for the prompt dispatch of business in criminal cases; laxity in the disposition of criminal cases has subtle consequences on the moral sway of law over the community. The last Conference was especially emphatic in urging the district judges to exercise their powers for the dispatch of criminal business.[98]

---

[95] This suggestion, made in 1923 and repeated in the following reports, provided: " Continuance to another term by agreement of counsel shall not be allowed. Other engagements of counsel should not be accepted as a ground for continuance. No continuance should be allowed except for good cause shown by affidavits, such as sickness of a party or unavoidable absence of an important witness." 10 AM. BAR ASSN. J. 875.

[96] " In any case which might have been brought to trial, in which no action has been taken by the parties for one year, it shall be the duty of the clerk to mail notice thereof to counsel of record and to the parties thereto, if their postoffice addresses are known, thirty days before the opening of the term of court following the first of January in each year. If such notice has been given and no action has been taken in the case in the meantime, an order of dismissal shall be entered as of course at the opening of such term of court." *Ibid.*

[97] For examples of the kind of information that ought to be systematically obtained, see Arthur E. Sutherland, Jr., " Federal Police Courts — A Comparative Study of the Criminal Business in the United States Court for the District of Massachusetts in 1913 and 1924," 11 MASS. L. QUART., No. 5, p. 43 ; Sam B. Warner, " Procedural Delay in California," 8 CALIF. L. REV. 369.

[98] The further suggestion was embodied that " Criminal cases should be forced to trial within what the Court deems a reasonable time. To that end indictments and informations should be placed by the Clerk on the trial docket calendar or list at the term following issue joined, if trial can not be justly held at the term wherein plea is entered. Criminal cases are subject to the same control by the Court as are civil cases, and indictments and informations should be ordered for trial, and tried or dismissed for delay substantially as has been above recommended in respect of pending causes generally." 12 AM. BAR ASSN. J. 687; REP. ATTY. GEN. FOR 1926, 7. The Supreme Court of the United States has set an example in ordering the advancement of criminal appeals on its docket and setting them for hearing at the earliest opportunity. See Orders of Dec. 6, *U. S. Daily,* Dec. 7, 1926.

The Conference has also addressed itself to the removal of other familiar abuses in American criminal procedure. The foolish practice of long-drawn-out examination of jurors on the *voir dire* makes not only for a waste of precious time but for an atmosphere of pettifoggery in which the healthy administration of criminal justice cannot thrive.[99] By suggesting the assumption by the trial court of a brief but searching inquiry, which ought to disclose a man's fitness for jury service, instead of leaving these preliminaries to serve as a Roman holiday for counsel, the Conference has led to a considerable saving of time and to the infusion of appropriate austerity in criminal trials.[100] Again, so ingrained had become the habit of granting bail after conviction that it was widely treated as almost an unwritten part of the Constitution. This practice has undoubtedly been a contributing factor in the debilitating delays of American criminal procedure.[101] The power to grant or deny bail after conviction rests within the discretion of federal judges. The Conference has urged that this discretion should be exercised " to discourage review sought, not with hope of new trial, but on frivolous grounds merely for delay." [102] Ca-

---

[99] See, *e.g.*, STOREY, THE REFORM OF LEGAL PROCEDURE, 210.

[100] " Examination of prospective jurors shall be by the judge alone. If counsel on either side desires that additional matter be inquired into, he shall state the matter to the judge, and the judge, if the matter is proper, shall conduct the examination." 10 AM. BAR ASSN. J. 875. This recommendation of the Conference was specifically approved by the Circuit Court of Appeals for the Sixth Circuit in Kurczak v. United States, 14 F. (2d) 109 (6th Circ., 1926). See also Carroll v. United States, 16 F. (2d) 951 (2nd Circ., 1927).

[101] The bearing of bail on the expedition of criminal appeals is illustrated by a comparison of Morse v. United States, 174 Fed. 539 (2nd Circ., 1909) with Walsh v. United States, 174 Fed. 615 (7th Circ., 1909). Both were cases arising out of misconduct in connection with the administration of national banks; both cases involved similar issues of fact and law. Morse was denied bail after conviction; Walsh was admitted to bail; the verdict in the Walsh case was reached on Jan. 18, 1908, and the Circuit Court of Appeals did not finally dispose of the case on review until Dec. 3, 1909 (see record in Walsh v. United States, 215 U. S. 609 (1910)). Morse was found guilty on Nov. 5, 1908, and his conviction was sustained in the Circuit Court of Appeals on Oct. 11, 1909 (see record in Morse v. United States, 215 U. S. 605 (1909)). In other words, nearly two years intervened between verdict and affirmance on appeal in the Walsh case and less than a year in the Morse case.

[102] REP. ATTY. GEN. FOR 1925, 6. This standard was applied and interpreted by Mr. Justice Butler sitting as Circuit Justice in the Circuit Court of Appeals in United States v. Motlow, 10 F. (2d) 657 (7th Circ., 1926). For the prior practice, *cf.* Walsh v. United States, 174 Fed. 621 (7th Circ., 1909).

pricious difference in sentences for the same offense due to varying views of different judges is another familiar evil of American criminal justice which has claimed the attention of the Conference. Individualization in punishment has been accepted as a guiding consideration of modern criminal science.[103]   But individualization resting upon the idiosyncracies of individual judges makes for a sporting theory of justice, and, by leaving the accused to jockey for trial before favoring judges, is destructive of the necessary confidence that reason guides the judicial judgment.[104]   Prohibition cases presented a field of glaring inequality in the imposition of sentences and the Conference has sought to secure some common standards of action.[105]   With one system of criminal law operating over so vast a territory as that administered by the federal courts, the effort to secure appropriate uniformity in criminal sentences is beset by serious factors of legitimate diversity.   But alertness by an organ of national superintendence, like the Conference, will tend to check an undue exuberance of such diversities.

The Conference has been alive to the abuses of prosecutors as well as those due to the dilatory tactics of accused.   The misuses to which the conspiracy statute may be put by reckless or incompetent prosecutors have been the occasion of criticism.   The statute has drag-net potentialities in allowing prosecutions of defendants at distant places [106] and subjecting them to all the hazards of the wide scope of admissible evidence peculiar to conspiracy cases. Moreover, conspiracy trials, because of the multiplicity of defendants and the range of the testimony, tend to be long drawn out, consuming weeks and even months of available court time.   Other criminal business, let alone civil litigation, is bound to suffer.   All these considerations have led the Conference to speak sharply

---

[103] See SALEILLES, THE INDIVIDUALIZATION OF PUNISHMENT, with introduction by Roscoe Pound.

[104] See CLEVELAND SURVEY OF CRIMINAL JUSTICE, *passim*, particularly 308 *et seq.*

[105] The Attorney General, in reporting to the second conference, called attention to the want of uniformity of sentences in prohibition cases between different judges and different districts.   The conference resolved to submit a series of questions upon the subject, together with questions as to the performance by United States commissioners of their duties under the prohibition act, to the Attorney General and send copies of his replies to the various district judges. See C. S. Potts, *supra*, 2 TEX. L. REV. at 460.

[106] See, *e.g.*, Hyde *v.* United States, 225 U. S. 347 (1912), and Brown *v.* Elliott, 225 U. S. 392 (1912), particularly the dissenting opinions of Mr. Justice Holmes.

against abuses of conspiracy charges. In a recommendation addressed to the district judges " with the request that they present it to the district attorneys," it was urged " that this form of indictment be hereafter not adopted hastily but only after a careful conclusion that the public interest so requires." [107]   The Conference also suggested that it would consider the advisability of seeking legislative alteration of the conspiracy statute in order to prevent such use of the statute as permitted the transformation of a misdemeanor into a felony merely because joint action by the defendants involved concert of action.[108]

The great increase in prosecutions for petty offenses in the federal courts, for which prohibition is largely but not exclusively responsible, has cast burdens upon federal courts that to no small degree transform their traditional place in our federal system.[109] A transfer to them of fields of social control which heretofore have been in the keeping of the states not only involves important political changes; it affects their capacity to deal adequately with those professional problems which have always been their special concern. The Conference has added its authority to the widely-felt conviction that, in some way or other, the district courts must be relieved of the mass of petty prosecutions which now come before them. Not only does this mean an inordinate drain of time on the elaborate machinery of jury trials; if unchanged, it is bound to exert considerable influence on the quality of future federal judges. For men of large scope and intellectual distinction — the kind of lawyers who alone ought to be put on the district courts — will refuse to be drawn into police court work. The Conference proposed that petty prosecutions should be brought, at least in the first instance, before United States commissioners with limited review by the district courts.[110]   This proposal, of

---

[107] REP. ATTY. GEN. FOR 1925, 5–6.

[108] *Ibid.*

[109] See Report of Special Committee on Congested Calendars, 1926 YEAR BOOK OF ASSOCIATION OF THE BAR OF THE CITY OF NEW YORK, 330.

[110] At the second conference, following the report of the Committee on Recommendations to District Judges of Changes in Local Procedure to Expedite Disposition of Pending Cases and to Rid Dockets of Dead Litigation, the conference resolved: " That the chairman of the committee be authorized to prepare a bill, for the approval of the council, upon the subject matter of the following recommendations made by the committee: In prohibition and other misdemeanor cases, authorize the United States commissioners, in all cases in which the defendants do not file

course, involves the power of Congress under the Constitution to adopt summary procedure, in view of the safeguards for jury trial in Article III and Amendment VI.[111]   But one may confidently assert that the Constitution allows no small relief from the present situation, apart from the lessening of prosecutions in the federal courts by a curtailment of federal jurisdiction.[112]

The Conference has been going along empirically, seeking to check the most glaring defects in judicial administration, proposing improvements which had behind them the experience of modern practice of both English and American courts.   But in almost every phase of its concerns, the Conference has been handicapped by the absence of authoritative judicial statistics:

> " Everyone who has attempted to deal with the question of delays in the administration of justice has found his path obstructed by a mass of unintelligible statistics in respect to the exact condition of the dockets and the real business of the courts." [113]

Particularly important are adequate statistics [114] in the administration of a judicial system spread over a continent, broken up into over a hundred districts and nine circuits.   Only by a thorough system of judicial statistics will the executive direction of the judiciary have a dependable basis for the mobile use of its personnel, and Congress secure disinterested data on which to determine the extent to which the " judicial power " of the Constitution may wisely be employed and effectively distributed.   The

---

written demands for jury trial, to take and file written pleas of guilty and to hear the evidence on pleas of not guilty and to file in court their reports of the cases and their recommendations of what judgment should be entered.   That the conference now express its opinion that such a bill as is referred to in the preceding paragraph would be expedient, provided the machinery proposed is within constitutional limits." See C. S. Potts, *supra,* 2 TEX. L. REV. 461. The following conferences disclose no further action taken along these lines.

111 See Felix Frankfurter and Thomas G. Corcoran, " Petty Federal Offenses and the Constitutional Guaranty of Trial by Jury," 39 HARV. L. REV. 917.

112 See *ibid.*; and Charles Warren, " Federal Criminal Laws and the State Courts," 38 HARV. L. REV. 545.

113 Report of the Fifth Conference, 12 AM. BAR ASSN. J. 687, 688; REP. ATTY. GEN. FOR 1926, 5, 7.

114 Of existing judicial statistics, the Conference said: " The statistics as they are now rendered need investigation and analysis to distinguish between real cases which should be tried, and those which merely lumber the docket and should be dismissed." *Ibid.* See also note 6, *supra.*

last Conference, therefore, appointed a committee of two of its members, Judge Hough and Judge Denison, to devise a plan for the improvement of judicial statistics concerning the United States courts.[115]

Doubtless the excellent system of judicial statistics for England and Wales which, ever since 1859, has rendered an annual accounting of the work of their courts [116] will furnish some aid to the committee of the Conference in planning a system for the United States courts. But, of course, the problems presented by a federal system of judicature are also for the statistician different from those presented by a unitary country. A great mass of the information contained in the English reports, which sheds light upon the social life of England, can be looked for only in adequate systems of judicial statistics for the separate states. Federal judicial statistics can furnish us only a knowledge of the limited volume of private litigation with which the federal courts have been entrusted as well as of the prosecutions of federal offenses. But this knowledge in its appropriate details is indispensable. We ought to know how the different districts and different judges dispose of their business, the demands of different classes of litigation upon court time, the expedition or delay in adjudications, the part

---

[115] " If the result of what the Conference is able to do in this matter is encouraging, it may well lead to a recommendation for the establishment, perhaps under the auspices of the Conference, of a small bureau of judicial statistics, engaged during the whole year in ascertaining the exact facts." 12 AM. BAR ASSN. J. 687, 688.

[116] Section 14 of the Police Counties & Boroughs Act of July 21, 1856, 19 & 20 VICT., c. 59, required the justices of every county and watch committee of every borough to transmit to the Principal Secretary of State an annual statement of crimes committed within their jurisdiction, and required that a classified abstract of these reports be annually laid before Parliament. The first report of criminal statistics was thus issued in 1856. A bill for more complete returns was introduced during the same year by Lord Brougham but failed of passage. In 1857 action was taken by the Home Secretary looking forward to collecting civil statistics and in 1859 complete returns from all courts were purported to be rendered. Following the Police Returns Act, 1892, 55 & 56 VICT., c. 38, a revision in the collection of statistics was introduced. Since then exhaustive annual reports on both civil and judicial statistics have been rendered. See for illuminating reports on the English system the Criminal Statistics Report for 1893 and Civil Statistics Report for 1894. Massachusetts has devised a system of criminal court statistics which has been in existence for over thirty years. See Annual Reports of Mass. Commissioner of Correction. See also 1899 IND. ACTS, c. 227; 1919 *ibid.*, c. 181; 1923 WIS. STAT. 68, 13; 1924 IOWA CODE, §§ 3808, 3811; 1910 OHIO CODE, §§ 173, 174; 1895 WASH. LAWS, c. 85.

played by jury trials, the administration of extraordinary remedies, the relation between federal courts and state courts, and the work of the federal courts in regard to litigation involving no peculiar federal questions. Similarly, appropriate annual statistics of the circuit courts of appeals — now happily free from arrears — will give us an authoritative knowledge of courts which, since the Act of 1925,[117] are in so large a measure ultimate courts of appeal. Such an adequate system of judicial statistics, improved and amplified by experience, will, through the critical interpretation of the figures,[118] steadily make for a more vigorous and scientific approach to the problems of the administration of justice.

---

[117] Act of Feb. 13, 1925, 43 STAT. 936.

[118] As to the functions of " the statistical method of dealing with social problems " see comments of Dean (now Mr. Justice) Stone, quoted on p. 53, n. 174, *supra.*

CHAPTER VII
THE JUDICIARY ACT OF 1925

I

IN securing legislation for the more effective administration of the inferior federal courts, Chief Justice Taft accomplished one half of his program of judicial reform. The other half sought to improve the Supreme Court's disposition of litigation by curtailing its jurisdiction. The aim of the Act of September 6, 1916,[1] it will be recalled, was to enable the Court to keep more nearly abreast of its docket by shutting off cases of minor importance. This was accomplished by giving finality to the decisions of state courts and circuit courts of appeals in certain types of litigation, leaving the protection of whatever national interest might be involved to a discretionary review by the Supreme Court. The effect of this upon appeals from, and writs of error to, the circuit courts of appeals was negligible. On the other hand, the number of writs of error to state courts was appreciably diminished. From 157 cases on error to the state courts decided during the 1916 Term there is a steady decline, until the low point is reached with 75 cases in the 1920 Term.[2] But the general post-war increase in all judicial business soon augmented the litigation from the state

---

[1] 39 Stat. 726.

[2] See Table I, *infra*, p. 295. In that the Table includes only cases disposed of after consideration by the Court and does not include " cases disposed of without consideration by the Court " (see, *e.g.*, 269 U. S. 588 *et seq.*) differences will occur between the figures there set forth and others, *e.g.*, the figures of Mr. Justice Van Devanter in Hearing before the Committee on the Judiciary, House of Representatives, 68th Cong., 2nd Sess., on H. R. 8206, Dec. 18, 1924, at 10; and Hearing before a Subcommittee of the Committee on the Judiciary, Senate, 68th Cong., 1st Sess., on S. 2060 and S. 2061, Feb. 2, 1924, at 44. Three cases, Smith *v.* Interstate Commerce Comm., 245 U. S. 33 (1917); Smith *v.* Interstate Commerce Comm., 245 U. S. 47 (1917); Jones *v.* Interstate Commerce Comm., 245 U. S. 48 (1917), on direct appeal from the Supreme Court of the District of Columbia, have been omitted from the tabulation.

courts and increased the volume of cases coming to the Supreme Court from sources uncontrolled by the 1916 legislation. Moreover, petitions for *certiorari* steadily multiplied, making a heavy drain upon the Court's time. These petitions increased from 270 in the 1916 Term to 429 in the 1922 Term, and reached 456 in the 1924 Term.

Furthermore, the Act of 1916 left untouched a number of feeders of Supreme Court jurisdiction. Cases coming from the district courts, the Court of Claims and the Court of Appeals of the District of Columbia were unaffected. These sources of the Supreme Court's business [3] had been swelled by the war's aftermath. Especially was this true of cases coming from the Court of Claims, offering for review predominantly problems of contract law.[4] In the 1916 Term the Supreme Court disposed of five cases coming from the Court of Claims; in the 1924 Term there were 34 such decisions.

After the 1916 Act had begun to make itself felt in cutting down cases on error to the state courts, the most prolific source of the Court's business became direct review of district court decisions. Under pressure the Supreme Court disposed of more cases as more cases came to it.[5] Dispatch was partly facilitated by establishing a " summary docket " in which argument was limited to half an hour for a side.[6] Despite this device and the increased

---

[3] See Table I, *infra*, p. 295.

[4] Out of 29 cases from the Court of Claims disposed of with opinions during the 1924 Term, 11 involved only questions of contract law. Of the same character were 18 cases out of 46 during the 1925 Term. In Sun Ship Building Co. *v.* United States, 271 U. S. 96, 99 (1926), the Chief Justice, after disposing of three such cases from the Court of Claims, added: "Valuable time was taken in hearing these cases. After arguments on behalf of the claimants, we declined to hear the other side because the correctness of the judgments of the Court of Claims was clear. It is fortunate for all that under the Act of February 13, 1925, judgments of the Court of Claims entered after May 13, 1925, can only be reviewed here after a showing of merits." *Cf.* Louisville Bedding Co. *v.* United States, 269 U. S. 533 (1925).

[5] The following figures as to the appellate docket of the Court are taken from REP. ATTY. GEN. FOR 1926, 11:

	1916	1917	1918	1919	1920	1921	1922	1923	1924	1925
Total number on docket ...	1169	1114	1077	988	941	1012	1128	1093	1291	1282
Disposed of during term ...	637	619	669	602	598	595	760	655	758	844
Remaining at end of term..	532	495	408	386	343	417	368	438	533	438

[6] The summary docket was created by paragraph 6 of Rule 6 of the Rules of 1911. See 222 U. S., Appendix. During the 1922 Term 10 cases were transferred to

labors of the Court, it became clear by 1921 that the Court would inevitably go further into arrears. To be sure, cases heard in their order and not advanced because of an exigent public consideration were reached for argument in considerably less than two years after docketing.[7] The Supreme Court practitioner of the eighties would have found satisfaction instead of grievance in such a condition. Preceding the Circuit Courts of Appeals Act of 1891 [8] it had taken a case three years to be heard.[9] But the standards for judicial administration had decidedly improved since the eighties, and the abuses of delay to which the profession and the public then submitted would now be deemed intolerable.

Experience with the Act of 1916 had shown the potentialities of discretionary jurisdiction, first made available to the Supreme Court by the Circuit Courts of Appeals Act. To resolve conflicts among coördinate appellate tribunals and to determine matters of national concern are the essential functions of the Supreme Court.[10] But such issues appear in myriad forms and no general classification of cases can hope to forecast the specific instances deserving the Court's ultimate judgment. On the whole, the bar affords little help in the selection of cases appropriate for the Supreme Court's attention. Clients are prone to attach to their cases an exaggerated public significance, and the absence of a

---

the summary docket, 39 during the 1923 Term, 22 during the 1924 Term, and 16 during the 1925 Term. The scope of cases transferable to the summary docket was increased by the 1925 Rules. See Rule 6, paragraph 6, Rule 26, paragraphs 3 and 6, 266 U. S. 657, 673, 674.

[7] Different estimates as to the length of time between the docketing of the case and its hearing have been made. According to Mr. Justice Van Devanter, the time was 12 to 13 months. See Hearing on S. 2060, *supra* note 2, at 42. The Chief Justice's estimate was 18 to 24 months. See Hearing before the Committee on the Judiciary, House of Representatives, 68th Cong., 2nd Sess., on H. R. 10479, Mar. 30, 1922, at 12. See also William G. Rice, Jr., " How the Supreme Court Mill is Working," 56 AM. L. REV. 763. See also Plates I and II, *infra*, pp. 296, 297.

[8] Act of Mar. 3, 1891, 26 STAT. 826.

[9] See p. 86, *supra*.

[10] " The Supreme Court's function is for the purpose of expounding and stabilizing principles of law for the benefit of the people of the country, passing upon constitutional questions and other important questions of law for the public benefit. It is to preserve uniformity of decision among the intermediate courts of appeal." Chief Justice Taft in Hearing before the Committee on the Judiciary, House of Representatives, 67th Cong., 2nd Sess., on H. R. 10479, Mar. 30, 1922, at 2. See also note 13, *infra*.

cohesive Supreme Court bar, with a high professional *esprit de corps,* makes lawyers see cases through their clients' eyes.[11]   In marking the boundaries of the Court's jurisdiction its broad categories must be supplemented by ample discretion, permitting review by the Supreme Court in the individual case which reveals a claim fit for decision by the tribunal of last resort.

The establishment in 1891 of intermediate appellate tribunals had to overcome a deep professional feeling against taking away from litigants the right to resort to the Supreme Court for vindication of their federal claims.   The long resistance to circuit courts of appeals as the courts of last resort in the ordinary instances, even in cases where diversity of citizenship or federal statutory claims alone were involved, proves how unquestioned was the assumption that the Supreme Court was, as a matter of course, the guardian of all constitutional claims.   The circuit courts of appeals could not have been established if a fair share of appellate review over claims of a federal character had not been reserved to the Supreme Court directly from the district courts.   It was then only natural that distrust should be felt towards conferring on new and untried courts power over cases theretofore traditionally within the competence of the Supreme Court.   Thirty years of active and efficient functioning on the part of the circuit courts of appeal had resulted in a different temper.[12]   These courts were now taken for granted as courts of great authority.   The prestige they enjoyed invited greater reliance upon them in the general burden of appellate review.   Very different considerations could thus guide the framers of new judiciary acts from those that confronted the authors of the Judiciary Act of 1891.

The burdensome increase in the Court's business and the grow-

---

[11] See William H. Taft, " Possible and Needed Reforms in the Administration of Justice in the Federal Courts," 47 AM. BAR ASSN. REP. 250, 256; John H. Clarke, " Practice Before the Supreme Court," 8 VA. L. REG. (N. S.) 241, 242–43; John H. Clarke, " Methods of Work of the United States Supreme Court Judges," 20 OHIO L. REP. 398, 402.   *Cf.* Salinger *v.* United States, 272 U. S. 54 (1926).

[12] See Plate III, *infra,* p. 298.   " The Circuit Courts of Appeals worked well. Speaking generally, they were always abreast of their dockets, and their activity soon removed the ' hump ' in the docket of the Supreme Court."   William H. Taft, " The Jurisdiction of the Supreme Court under the Act of February 13, 1925," 35 YALE L. J. 1, 2.   See also Martin T. Manton, " Organization and Work of the United States Circuit Court of Appeals," 12 AM. BAR ASSN. J. 41.

ing recognition of the availability of the circuit courts of appeals as fit means for deflecting litigation from the Supreme Court coincided with William H. Taft's appointment to the Court. The new Chief Justice had for some time sponsored further limitation upon the Supreme Court's business.[13] In 1914 he had urged that the Court be saved from the burden of improvident appeals and the public inconveniences of undue congestion by cutting down its obligatory jurisdiction and extending the scope of discretionary review.[14] Furthermore, unlike some of his predecessors, Chief Justice Taft deemed it the prerogative and even the duty of his office to take the lead in promoting judicial reform and to wait

---

[13] As early as his first annual message to Congress, President Taft wrote: " It is not impossible to cut down still more than it is cut down, the jurisdiction of the Supreme Court so as to confine it almost wholly to statutory and constitutional questions." See 16 Richardson, Messages and Papers of the Presidents, 7431. These views he expanded in his second annual message of Dec. 6, 1910: " No man ought to have, as a matter of right, a review of his case by the Supreme Court. He should be satisfied by one hearing before a court of first instance and one review by a court of appeals. The proper and chief usefulness of a Supreme Court, and especially of the Supreme Court of the United States, is, in the cases which come before it, so to expound the law, and especially the fundamental law — the Constitution — as to furnish precedents for the inferior courts in future litigation and for the executive officers in the construction of statutes and the performance of their legal duties. Therefore, any provisions for review of cases by the Supreme Court that cast upon that Court the duty of passing on questions of evidence and the construction of particular forms of instruments, like indictments, or wills, or contracts, decisions not of general application or importance, merely clog and burden the Court and render more difficult its higher function, which makes it so important a part of the framework of our Government. The Supreme Court is now carrying an unnecessary burden of appeals of this kind, and I earnestly urge that it be removed." See *ibid.* 7523-24.

[14] " The Supreme Court has great difficulty in keeping up with its docket. The most important function of the court is the construction and application of the constitution of the United States. It has other valuable duties to perform in the construction of statutes and in the shaping and declaration of general law, but if its docket is to increase with the growth of the country, it will be swamped with its burden, the work which it does will, because of haste, not be of the high quality that it ought to have, and the litigants of the court will suffer injustice because of delay. For these reasons the only jurisdiction that it should be obliged to exercise, and which a litigant may, as a matter of course, bring to the court, should be questions of constitutional construction. By giving an opportunity to litigants in all other cases to apply for a writ of certiorari to bring any case from a lower court to the Supreme Court, so that it may exercise absolute and arbitrary discretion with respect to all business but constitutional business, will enable the court so to restrict its docket that it can do all its work, and do it well." William H. Taft, " The Attacks on the Courts and Legal Procedure," 5 Ky. L. J., No. 2, 3, 18.

neither upon legislative initiation in Congress nor upon professional opinion.[15]   He sponsored energetically the work of a committee of his colleagues engaged in formulating in detail the principle of a wider discretionary review.   This committee consisted of Justices Day, Van Devanter and McReynolds; Mr. Justice Day was succeeded on his retirement by Mr. Justice Sutherland, a former member of the Judiciary Committee of the Senate.[16]   The task of draftsmanship fell chiefly to Mr. Justice Van Devanter, who submitted the committee's labors to the whole Court late in 1921.   After full consideration a revised draft became the Court's proposal to Congress, where it became known as the Judges' Bill.[17]

2

At the heart of the proposal was the conservation of the Supreme Court as the arbiter of legal issues of national significance. But this object could hardly be attained so long as there persisted the obstinate conception [18] that the Court was to be the vindica-

---

[15] See the remarks of the Chief Justice [then Mr. Taft] before the Judicial Section of the American Bar Association, 41 Am. Bar Assn. Rep. 743; also the remarks of Mr. Justice McReynolds, the draftsman of the Act of 1916, before the same body, 39 *ibid.* 967.

[16] " Before I came into the court a committee had been appointed for its preparation, consisting of Justice Day, Justice McReynolds, and, I suppose, ex officio, the Chief Justice. It was taken up again and a very careful and very much extended examination of it made by the committee, to which Justice Van Devanter was added."   Chief Justice Taft, in Hearing before the Committee on the Judiciary, House of Representatives, 67th Cong., 2nd Sess., on H. R. 10479, Mar. 30, 1922, at 1. " The members of the Court, afraid that the docket might become more congested, brought the matter to the attention of the Judiciary Committees of both Houses of Congress, and it was there suggested that the Court prepare a bill to help matters. A committee of the Court was appointed, of which Mr. Justice Day was Chairman, Mr. Justice Van Devanter and Mr. Justice McReynolds were members, and the Chief Justice acted ex officio. Upon the retirement of Mr. Justice Day, Mr. Justice Van Devanter became the Chairman of the Committee."   William H. Taft, *supra,* 35 Yale L. J. at 2.   See also William H. Taft, " Possible and Needed Reforms in the Administration of Justice in the Federal Courts," 47 Am. Bar Assn. Rep. 250, 254.

[17] It was introduced by Senator Cummins and Congressman Walsh on Feb. 17, 1922. 62 Cong. Rec. 2686, 2737.

[18] This notion was reinforced by the nineteenth-century American habit of double appeals. See Roscoe Pound, " The Causes of Popular Dissatisfaction with the Administration of Justice," 40 Am. L. Rev. 729, 746; Roscoe Pound, " A Practical Program of Procedural Reform," 22 Green Bag, 438, 442; William H. Taft, " The Administration of the Criminal Law," 15 Yale L. J. 1, 14; Edson R. Sunderland, " The Problem of Appellate Procedure," 5 Tex. L. Rev. 126.

tor of all federal rights.[19] This conception the Judges' Bill completely overrode.[20] Litigation which did not represent a wide public interest was left to state courts of last resort and to the circuit courts of appeals, always reserving to the Supreme Court power to determine that some national interest justified invoking its jurisdiction.

The Act of 1891, as interpreted by *Spreckels Sugar Refining Co.* v. *McClain*,[21] afforded wide opportunity of review by the Supreme Court of decisions of courts of first instance which had already been reviewed by the circuit courts of appeals. Thus, from the 1916 Term to the 1925 Term, the Supreme Court had to entertain an average of 40 cases which had already gone through the circuit courts of appeals.[22] The Chief Justice has listed the following large classes of cases in which a second review as a matter of right could be had in the Supreme Court after prior appeal to the circuit courts of appeals:

" . . . civil suits —

(1) Brought by the United States, or by any officer thereof authorized by law to sue.

(2) Between citizens of the same State claiming lands under grants from different States.

---

[19] Senator Heflin of Alabama was by no means alone in entertaining the following views: " I understand that out of some 115 cases that came here the Supreme Court decided that a mistake was made in appealing eighty-odd cases. I submit that if one man's rights were preserved and safeguarded the court in that action served a just purpose and it could well afford to consider 100 to 200 cases if necessary, in order to do justice by even one American citizen. The Bible tells us that it were better that 99 guilty persons go free than that 1 innocent man should suffer. . . . I am not ready to surrender the average citizen's right to appeal and accept in its stead discretionary power given to the judges of the Supreme Court." 66 Cong. Rec. 2928 (Feb. 3, 1925).

[20] The form in which the Judges' Bill was introduced into the two houses of Congress is printed in Hearing before a Subcommittee of the Committee on the Judiciary, Senate, 68th Cong., 1st Sess., on S. 2060 and S. 2061, Feb. 2, 1924, at 1–6, and in 66 Cong. Rec. 2750.

[21] 192 U. S. 397 (1904). In MacFadden v. United States, 213 U. S. 288 (1909), the doctrine of the Spreckels case permitting an appeal from a decision of the circuit court of appeals to the Supreme Court where the case involved a further question besides one directly appealable to the Supreme Court under § 5 of the Act of Mar. 3, 1891, 26 Stat. 826, 827, was explained to deny such an appeal unless the ground upon which federal jurisdiction was invoked included a question directly appealable from the district or circuit courts to the Supreme Court. See also Lemke v. Farmers Grain Co., 258 U. S. 50 (1922).

[22] See Table I, *infra*, p. 295.

(3) Where more than $3,000 is involved and the suit arises under the Constitution or laws or treaties of the United States.

(4) Seizures on land or waters not within admiralty or maritime jurisdiction.

(5) Cases arising under the postal laws.

(6) Suits and proceedings under any law regulating commerce, except such as may be covered by special statutes already mentioned.

(7) Civil suits and proceedings for enforcement of penalties and forfeitures and incurred under any law of the United States.

(8) Suits for damages by officers and persons for injury done him in protection or collection of United States revenue or to enforce right of citizens to vote.

(9) Suits for damages by citizens injured in their Federal constitutional rights.

(10) Suits against consuls and vice consuls.

(11) Suits under immigration and contract labor laws.

(12) Private suits under the antitrust act.

(13) Suits by Indians or part blood Indians for allotment under any law or treaty.

(14) Suits by tenant in common or joint tenant for partition of land in which the United States is also tenant in common or joint tenant." [23]

The Judges' Bill put an end to two appeals as of right.[24] All cases disposed of in the circuit courts of appeals were by the new plan made reviewable only by the discretionary writ of *certiorari*.

Not only were the circuit courts of appeals made final appellate tribunals as to business that had previously come to them; the Judges' Bill sought also to make them, in effect, the courts of review of decisions by the district courts. Even after the Circuit Courts of Appeals Act, cases which entirely involved the " construction or application of the Constitution of the United States," " the constitutionality of any law of the United States or the validity or construction of any treaty made under its authority,"

---

[23] Hearing before a Subcommittee of the Committee on the Judiciary, Senate, 68th Cong., 1st Sess., on S. 2060 and S. 2061, Feb. 2, 1924, at 23.

[24] Judges' Bill, § 1, amending JUDICIAL CODE, § 240. The section also permits the issuance of *certiorari* " either before or after a judgment or decree by such lower court." Though the writ theretofore had issued prior to the rendering of a decision in a circuit court of appeals (The Three Friends, 166 U. S. 1 (1897)), the recent decision in White v. Mechanics Securities Corp., 269 U. S. 283 (1925), foreshadows more frequent exercise of this power.

or the jurisdiction of the district court as a federal court, and cases in which a state constitution or law was " claimed to be in contravention of the Constitution of the United States," together with prize cases, went directly from the district courts to the Supreme Court.[25] The Judges' Bill abolished this bifurcated system of appeals, with four important exceptions: (1) suits under the anti-trust and interstate commerce laws; (2) writs of error by the United States in criminal cases; (3) suits to enjoin the enforcement of state statutes or action by administrative officers of the states; (4) suits to enjoin orders of the Interstate Commerce Commission.[26] The cases included under these four excepted categories ordinarily raise issues transcending in importance the immediate interests of litigants and involve those national concerns which are in the keeping of the Supreme Court. It is to be noted that in the last two classes, judicial review is in the first instance by a district court of three judges sitting in judgment upon the prior action of administrative tribunals; [27] that cases under the anti-trust and interstate commerce laws normally involve vast economic interests extending over great areas; and, finally, that the prompt and uniform administration of criminal justice requires the validity and construction of provisions of the Federal Penal Code to be authoritatively declared by the highest court.[28]

The empirical nature of judiciary legislation is strikingly illustrated by the anomalous condition of appellate jurisdiction over cases arising in the District of Columbia. We have already referred to the effort to narrow review over cases from the Court of Appeals of the District of Columbia to the limits prescribed for those from the circuit courts of appeals.[29] The Judicial Code of 1911, as interpreted by *American Security & Trust Co.* v. *District*

---

[25] JUDICIAL CODE, § 238, reënacting Act of Mar. 3, 1891, § 5, 26 STAT. 826, 827.

[26] Judges' Bill, § 1, amending JUDICIAL CODE, § 238. Direct review by the Supreme Court of interlocutory or final judgments in these four classes of cases had been provided for by the Act of Feb. 11, 1903, § 2, 32 STAT. 823; Act of Mar. 2, 1907, 34 STAT. 1246; Act of Mar. 4, 1913, 37 STAT. 1013; Act of Oct. 22, 1913, 38 STAT. 208, 220.

[27] Act of Mar. 4, 1913, 37 STAT. 1013; Act of Oct. 22, 1913, 38 STAT. 208, 220.

[28] See p. 120, *supra.*

[29] See p. 122, *supra.*

of Columbia,[30] left District of Columbia litigants an unwarranted freedom of appeal to the Supreme Court. This the Judges' Bill corrected by putting the Court of Appeals on a level with the circuit courts of appeals.[31] Again, great saving of time for the more compelling problems that come before the Supreme Court was proposed by eliminating the obligatory review over Court of Claims decisions.[32] To be sure, the Court of Claims is a court of first instance and thus litigants were to be deprived of the customary opportunity for revision by an appellate court. However, the *nisi prius* court for these causes is a court of five judges, and there remains the corrective safeguard of *certiorari*. Claims against the government under the Tucker Act[33] (involving less than

---

[30] 224 U. S. 491 (1912).

[31] Judges' Bill, § 1, amending JUDICIAL CODE, § 240. Sections 250 and 251 of the Judicial Code were also repealed by § 13 of the Bill.

[32] Judges' Bill, § 3, and § 13, repealing JUDICIAL CODE, §§ 242, 243.

[33] Act of Mar. 3, 1887, § 2, 24 STAT. 505. Direct appeals from the district courts to the Supreme Court could be had from a judgment against the United States without regard to the pecuniary amount of the judgment, and the right of appeal reserved to both claimant and to the United States was the right of appeal reserved in the statutes relating to the Court of Claims. United States v. Davis, 131 U. S. 36 (1889). The Act of Mar. 3, 1891, 26 STAT. 826, in redistributing the appellate jurisdiction of the Supreme Court between it and the newly established circuit courts of appeals, omitted to make any reference to the Tucker Act and its provisions allowing direct review of the decisions of the district and circuit courts by the Supreme Court. Confusion resulted, which subsequent decisions of the Supreme Court only increased. In Ogden v. United States, 148 U. S. 390 (1893), the Court held that the Act of 1891 had diverted review in cases under the Tucker Act to the circuit courts of appeals. But in Chase v. United States, 155 U. S. 489 (1894), despite its oft-asserted warning that the appellate jurisdiction of the Supreme Court is always open to scrutiny, the Court without examination, took jurisdiction on writ of error from a judgment of a circuit court under the Tucker Act. In Reid v. United States, 211 U. S. 529 (1909), the Court held that the direct review of decisions of the district and circuit courts by the Supreme Court was not abrogated by the Act of 1891, but made no mention of the Ogden case. That case was not overruled until ten years later in J. Homer Fritch, Inc. v. United States, 248 U. S. 458 (1919). The same confusion prevailed concerning the power of circuit courts of appeals over decisions by the district and circuit courts under the Tucker Act. Subsequent to the Reid case the Court entertained jurisdiction of an appeal from a circuit court of appeals which reviewed the action of a district court under the Tucker Act, thus impliedly recognizing a power of review in the circuit court of appeals. United States v. Buffalo Pitts Co., 234 U. S. 228 (1914). In J. Homer Fritch, Inc. v. United States, *supra*, at 462, 463, direct review by the Supreme Court of such decisions was held to exclude any review by the circuit courts of appeals, and this puzzling chapter in the attempts of the Supreme Court to determine its own jurisdiction was brought to a close by the comment of Chief Justice White that " the effect of the ruling in *Reid* v. *United States* was to overrule the

$10,000) brought not in Washington but before district courts which, upon the analogy of the jurisdiction of the Supreme Court over the Court of Claims, were appealable direct to that Court, were by the Judges' Bill transferred to the circuit courts of appeals.

The proposed bill explicitly confined to two classes cases which could as a matter of course be taken from the state courts to the Supreme Court: (1) where the validity of a state statute was challenged under the Federal Constitution and its validity sustained; (2) where a federal statute or treaty was invoked and its validity denied.[34] This partially removed a difficulty which the Act of 1916 had introduced into the Judicial Code. Ever since the First Judiciary Act, the Supreme Court had been able to review the judgment of a state court which denied an attack, based on the Federal Constitution, on " an authority exercised under any State." [35] The Act of 1916 eliminated review upon an assailed exercise of authority; the " validity " of authority, not an illegitimate exercise of it, alone furnished warrant for a writ of error from the Supreme Court.[36] Subtle distinctions were thereby invited,[37] which were happily dispensed with by the Judges'

Ogden Case," and that " the action of this court in the *Buffalo Pitts Case* must be regarded as a mere inadvertent assumption of jurisdiction rather than as a decision that such jurisdiction existed."

[34] Judges' Bill, § 1, amending JUDICIAL CODE, § 237.

[35] Act of Sept. 24, 1789, § 25, 1 STAT. 73, 85.

[36] Jett Bros. Distilling Co. *v.* City of Carrollton, 252 U. S. 1 (1920). See also Philadelphia & Reading Coal & Iron Co. *v.* Gilbert, 245 U. S. 162 (1917); Ireland *v.* Woods, 246 U. S. 323 (1918); Stadelman *v.* Miner, 246 U. S. 544 (1918); Arkansas *v.* St. Louis-San Francisco Ry., 269 U. S. 172 (1925). See Raymond W. Clifford, " Appellate Procedure through State and Federal Courts," 1924 WASH. BAR ASSN. REP. 187, 193.

[37] The following cases have been dismissed on the basis of Jett Bros. Distilling Co. *v.* City of Carrollton, *supra* note 36: Fitch, Connell & Co. *v.* Atchison, T. & S. F. Ry., 254 U. S. 618 (1921); Denee *v.* Morrison, 254 U. S. 618 (1921); Nagel *v.* Iowa, 254 U. S. 620 (1921); Great Northern Ry. *v.* Minneapolis, 254 U. S. 620 (1921); Sanger Bros. *v.* Hunsucker, 254 U. S. 621 (1921); Supreme Lodge *v.* Overton, 255 U. S. 559 (1921); Rennie *v.* Gibson, 257 U. S. 611 (1921); Watts *v.* Arizona, 257 U. S. 617 (1921); Jones *v.* Seifert, 257 U. S. 618 (1921); Kansas City Motion Picture Machine Operators *v.* Hughes, 257 U. S. 621 (1922); Missouri Pacific R. R. *v.* Izard County Highway Imp. Dist. No. 1, 257 U. S. 623 (1922); Schaff *v.* Famechon Co., 258 U. S. 76 (1922); Bank of Sturgeon *v.* Palmer, 258 U. S. 603 (1922); Abo Land Co. *v.* Tenorio, 258 U. S. 604 (1922); Corbett *v.* South Carolina, 258 U. S. 606 (1922); Collins *v.* Byrnes, 258 U. S. 607 (1922); Denson *v.* Georgia, 258 U. S. 608 (1922); Bailey *v.* Oregon-Washington R. R. &

Bill.[38] This proposal probably did not effect a reduction of cases; it did avoid waste in litigation.

Review of cases coming from the dependencies of the United

Nav. Co., 258 U. S. 611 (1922); Keokuk & Hamilton Bridge Co. *v.* Illinois, 258 U. S. 613 (1922); Stevens *v.* Southern Pac. Land Co., 259 U. S. 578 (1922); McIntosh *v.* Dill, 260 U. S. 694 (1922); Mittle *v.* South Carolina, 260 U. S. 705 (1922); Reed *v.* Village of Hibbing, 260 U. S. 709 (1923); American Trust Co. *v.* McNinch, 261 U. S. 606 (1923); Huey *v.* Brock, 261 U. S. 609 (1923); Union Stock Yards Co. *v.* Mayhall & Neible, 262 U. S. 731 (1923); Swartwood *v.* Lehigh Valley R. R., 263 U. S. 674 (1923); American Ry. Express Co. *v.* Kentucky, 263 U. S. 674 (1923); Wear *v.* Johnston, 263 U. S. 675 (1923); Webb & Co. *v.* Pingree Cattle Loan Co., 264 U. S. 570 (1924); LaChapelle *v.* Union Pacific Coal Co., 264 U. S. 575 (1924); Neil *v.* Utah Wholesale Grocery Co., 265 U. S. 572 (1924); Missouri Pacific R. R. *v.* Burnett, 265 U. S. 572 (1924); Pluto Oil & Gas Co. *v.* Miller, 265 U. S. 573 (1924); Clinton *v.* Gypsy Oil Co., 265 U. S. 574 (1924); Patterson *v.* Patterson, 266 U. S. 594 (1925); Van Auken *v.* Smith, 266 U. S. 595 (1925); Crisp *v.* Davis, 267 U. S. 572 (1925); Hurr *v.* Davis, 267 U. S. 572 (1925); Cowokochee *v.* Chapman, 267 U. S. 572 (1925); Clay *v.* District Court, 267 U. S. 574 (1925); Corby Estate *v.* City of St. Joseph, 267 U. S. 578 (1925); Canard *v.* Snell, 267 U. S. 578 (1925); Tiger *v.* Drumright, 267 U. S. 578 (1925); Singleton *v.* Georgia, 267 U. S. 579 (1925); Crowson *v.* Cody, 267 U. S. 579 (1925); Hallenborg *v.* Green Consolidated Copper Co., 267 U. S. 582 (1925); Durand *v.* First State Bank, 267 U. S. 582 (1925); Northern Pacific S. S. Co. *v.* Soley, 267 U. S. 583 (1925); Gilseth *v.* Risty, 267 U. S. 584 (1925); Brambini *v.* United States, 267 U. S. 584 (1925); County of Tuolumne *v.* Railroad Comm. of California, 267 U. S. 584 (1925); McCalla Co. *v.* California, 267 U. S. 585 (1925); Sala *v.* Crane, 267 U. S. 585 (1925); Hiawassee River Power Co. *v.* Carolina Tennessee Power Co., 267 U. S. 586 (1925); Crew Levick Co. *v.* Philadelphia, 268 U. S. 676 (1925); Cox *v.* Florida, 268 U. S. 680 (1925); First Nat. Bank *v.* Jackson, 268 U. S. 681 (1925); St. Louis & Hannibal R. R. *v.* Jackman, 268 U. S. 682 (1925); Bowling *v.* Beaver, 269 U. S. 527 (1925); Chicago, R. I. & P. Ry. *v.* Janney, 269 U. S. 528 (1925); Tyner *v.* Buffington, 269 U. S. 529 (1925); Apalachicola Land, etc. Co. *v.* McRae, 269 U. S. 531 (1925); Showalter *v.* Hampton, 269 U. S. 533 (1925); Meier *v.* Florida, 269 U. S. 533 (1925); Rowe *v.* Sartain, 269 U. S. 537 (1925); Weston *v.* Tulsa, 269 U. S. 540 (1926); Chesapeake & Ohio Ry. *v.* Williams Slate Co., 269 U. S. 540 (1926); Lancaster *v.* Smith, 269 U. S. 541 (1926); Lancaster *v.* Graham, 269 U. S. 541 (1926); Chicago & Eastern Illinois Ry. *v.* Chicago Heights Terminal Transfer R. R., 270 U. S. 626 (1926); Patterson *v.* Virginia, 270 U. S. 632 (1926); Lynch *v.* Nashville, Chattanooga & St. L. Ry., 271 U. S. 641 (1926); Marsino *v.* Massachusetts, 271 U. S. 642 (1926); Chicago, R. I. & P. Ry. *v.* Murphy, 271 U. S. 642 (1926); Samuels *v.* Childers, 271 U. S. 644 (1926); Scott *v.* Morris Nat. Bank, 271 U. S. 646 (1926); Ross *v.* South Dakota, 271 U. S. 646 (1926); Tiger *v.* Fewell, 271 U. S. 649 (1926); Fisher *v.* Crider, 47 Sup. Ct. Rep. 342 (1927).

38 The Act of 1916 in amending JUDICIAL CODE, § 237, provided: " A final judgment or decree in any suit in the highest court of a State in which a decision in the suit could be had, where . . . is drawn in question the validity of a statute of, or an authority exercised under any State, on the ground of their being repugnant to the Constitution, treaties, or laws of the United States, and the decision is in favor

States had been provided for *ad hoc*. Successive laws affecting Hawaii,[39] Alaska,[40] Porto Rico,[41] the Philippines,[42] the Canal

---

of their validity, may be re-examined and reversed or affirmed in the Supreme Court upon a writ of error." *Certiorari* was permitted in cases " where any title, right, privilege, or immunity is claimed under the Constitution, or any treaty or statute of, or commission held or authority exercised under the United States." 39 STAT. 726, 727. The words, " the validity of . . . an authority exercised under any State," that gave rise to the numerous dismissals collected in note 37, *supra*, were eliminated by the Judges' Bill from the revision of § 237 of the Judicial Code. Claims of that character can now be reviewed only by *certiorari* and then only if they fall within the scope of a " title, right, privilege, or immunity . . . specially set up or claimed by either party under the Constitution, or any treaty or statute of, or commission held or authority exercised under, the United States." The Judges' Bill also omitted from cases subject to review by writ of error under the Act of 1916 those in which the validity of " an authority exercised under the United States " was drawn into question and the decision was against the validity. Cases of this nature were also subject to serious uncertainties. Prior to the Act of 1916, cases only raised the problem of whether a claim concerned the construction of the state statute by the state court or whether the claim involved its validity. *Cf.* Commercial Bank of Cincinnati *v.* Buckingham's Ex'rs, 5 How. (U. S.) 317 (1847); Bridge Proprietors *v.* Hoboken Co., 1 Wall. (U. S.) 116 (1863). The Act of Mar. 3, 1885, 23 STAT. 443, regulating appeals from the Supreme Court of Columbia and the supreme courts of the territories, first introduced the distinction between a claim of right or title under an authority exercised under the United States and a question involving the validity of the authority itself. The draftsman of the Act of 1916 embodied this principle as one of distinction between writs of error and of *certiorari*, evidently convinced by Chief Justice Fuller's remark that " the distinction is palpable between a denial of the validity of the authority and a denial of a title, right, privilege or immunity claimed under it." See Baltimore & Potomac R. R. *v.* Hopkins, 130 U. S. 210, 223 (1889). The numerous dismissals heretofore referred to make it evident that the distinction is far from palpable, at least to the bar, and bear out the wisdom of Chief Justice Chase's remark: " In many cases the question of the existence of an authority is so closely connected with the question of its validity that the court will not undertake to separate them. . . ." Millingar *v.* Hartupee, 6 Wall. (U. S.) 258, 262 (1867). *Cf.* Gill *v.* Oliver's Ex'rs, 11 How. (U. S.) 529 (1850).

[39] By the Act of Apr. 30, 1900, § 86, 31 STAT. 141, 158, the Ninth Circuit Court of Appeals was given appellate jurisdiction in all cases in the District Court of Hawaii similar to cases in which appeals would lie from the district courts to the circuit courts of appeals. By the Act of Mar. 3, 1905, § 3, 33 STAT. 1035, the Supreme Court was given appellate jurisdiction over the Supreme Court of Hawaii in all cases where the amount exceeded $5,000. By the Act of Mar. 3, 1909, § 1, 35 STAT. 838, 839, appeals and writs of error could be taken from the District Court of Hawaii to the Supreme Court of the United States in all cases where such appeals would lie from the district courts to the Supreme Court. The Ninth Circuit Court of Appeals was given appellate jurisdiction over all other cases. These provisions were substantially reënacted in the Judicial Code, § 128. By § 246 of the Judicial Code the Supreme Court of the United States was given appellate jurisdiction over the Supreme Court of the Territory of Hawaii in the same class of

cases in which the final judgment of state courts could be reviewed; also in all cases where the sum involved exceeded $5,000. By the Act of Jan. 28, 1915, § 2, 38 STAT. 803, the provisions with respect to direct appeals from the District Court of Hawaii to the Supreme Court were reënacted, but cases involving $5,000 in the Supreme Court of Hawaii theretofore appealable to the Supreme Court of the United States were now made appealable to the circuit courts of appeals. By the Act of July 9, 1921, § 313, 42 STAT. 108, 119, 120, the provisions with respect to the appellate jurisdiction of the Supreme Court and of the circuit courts of appeals over the District Court of Hawaii were reënacted.

⁴⁰ By the Act of Mar. 3, 1899, § 202, 30 STAT. 1253, 1307, appeals and writs of error in criminal actions in the District Court of Alaska could be taken to the Supreme Court or the Ninth Circuit Court of Appeals in the same manner as from the circuit and district courts. By the Act of June 6, 1900, § 504, 31 STAT. 321, 414, the Supreme Court of the United States was given appellate jurisdiction over the District Court of Alaska in prize cases and in all cases involving the construction or application of the Constitution, constitutionality of any law, the validity or construction of a treaty, or the constitutionality of a state constitution or law. All other cases where the amount exceeded $500 were reviewable by the Circuit Court of Appeals. By § 505 of the same Act the decisions of the Circuit Court of Appeals were made final, but the Circuit Court of Appeals could certify questions to the Supreme Court in these cases. The only review of the decisions of the Circuit Court of Appeals was thus by certification. Alaska Pacific Fisheries *v.* Alaska, 249 U. S. 53 (1919); Alaska Salmon Co. *v.* Alaska, 249 U. S. 62 (1919). There was no direct review to the Supreme Court in capital cases. Itow *v.* United States, 233 U. S. 581 (1914). The provisions with respect to review by the Circuit Courts of Appeals were reënacted in Judicial Code, § 134, and the provisions for direct review by the Supreme Court in Judicial Code, § 247.

⁴¹ By the Act of Apr. 12, 1900, § 35, 31 STAT. 77, 85, the Supreme Court of the United States was given appellate jurisdiction over the Supreme Court and District Court of Porto Rico in the same cases in which it had appellate jurisdiction over the supreme courts of the territories. By the Judicial Code, § 244, appellate jurisdiction over these courts was given to the Supreme Court in cases involving the validity of a copyright, and in cases involving the validity of a treaty or statute of or authority exercised under the United States, or wherein the Constitution of the United States or a treaty or statute thereof was brought in question, and the right claimed thereunder denied, and in all other cases involving $5,000. By the Act of Jan. 28, 1915, § 1, 38 STAT. 803, § 128 of the Judicial Code was amended to give the First Circuit Court of Appeals appellate jurisdiction of all cases in the District Court of Porto Rico, unless such cases were appealable direct to the Supreme Court; § 238 of the Judicial Code was amended to give the Supreme Court appellate jurisdiction of all cases in the District Court of Porto Rico similar to the cases in which it was given direct appellate jurisdiction from the district courts; § 246 of the Judicial Code was amended to give the Supreme Court appellate jurisdiction over the Supreme Court of Porto Rico in the same classes of cases in which it had appellate jurisdiction over the state courts and in all other cases it was competent for the Supreme Court to review the decisions of the Supreme Court of Porto Rico by *certiorari;* all cases wherein the amount involved exceeded $5,000 could be prosecuted in the circuit courts of appeals. By the Act of Mar. 2, 1917, §§ 42, 43, 39 STAT. 951, 966, these provisions were reaffirmed.

⁴² By the Act of July 1, 1902, § 10, 32 STAT. 691, 695, the Supreme Court of the United States was given appellate jurisdiction over the Supreme Court of the

Zone,[43] the Virgin Islands,[44] as well as American rights in China,[45] had dealt unrelatedly with appeals from their courts.[46] As judiciary acts addressed themselves to the need of relieving the Supreme Court of business, there was a piecemeal transfer of this appellate jurisdiction from the Supreme Court to the circuit courts of appeals.[47] The Judges' Bill proposed a complete withdrawal of these miscellaneous reviews by the Supreme Court, distributing authority over the dependencies (except the Philippines) to appropriate circuit courts of appeals.[48] The bill thus provided a

---

Philippine Islands in all cases involving the Constitution or any statute, treaty, title, right, or privilege of the United States, or cases in which the value in controversy or the title or possession of real estate exceeded $25,000. Judicial Code, § 248, reënacted this provision. The Act of Aug. 29, 1916, § 27, 39 STAT. 545, 555, again reënacted these provisions. By the Act of Sept. 6, 1916, § 5, 39 STAT. 726, 727, no review could be had of any judgment of the Supreme Court of the Philippine Islands except by *certiorari* which under § 5 of the Act had to be applied for within three months after the entry of the judgment.

[43] By the Act of Aug. 24, 1912, § 9, 37 STAT. 560, 566, the Fifth Circuit Court of Appeals was given appellate jurisdiction over the District Court for the Canal Zone of cases involving the Constitution, a statute, treaty, title, right, or privilege of the United States, or cases involving more than $1,000, or criminal cases where the crime charged was punishable as a felony. The decisions of the Fifth Circuit Court of Appeals were subject to review by the Supreme Court " as in other cases authorized by law." By the Act of Sept. 21, 1922, § 3, 42 STAT. 1004, 1006, this section was reënacted with an additional clause giving the Fifth Circuit Court of Appeals jurisdiction of cases in which the jurisdiction of the trial court was in issue.

[44] By the Act of Mar. 3, 1917, § 2, 39 STAT. 1132, the Third Circuit Court of Appeals was given appellate jurisdiction of all cases in the courts of the Virgin Islands theretofore reviewable by the courts of Denmark, and the decisions of the Court of Appeals were to be final except as provided in §§ 239, 240 of the Judicial Code.

[45] By the Act of June 30, 1906, § 3, 34 STAT. 814, 815, the Ninth Circuit Court of Appeals was given appellate jurisdiction of all cases in the United States Court for China. The decisions from the Circuit Court of Appeals were reviewable by the Supreme Court in these cases as in cases in the circuit courts of appeals from the district and circuit courts. Judicial Code, § 131, reënacted this provision.

[46] " As illustrating the present lack of uniformity in this regard, section 134, Judicial Code, authorizes the Circuit Court of Appeals for the Ninth Circuit, in cases pending in that court from the District Court for Alaska, to certify questions to the Supreme Court, but no power is conferred upon the Supreme Court to order up the whole record and decide the whole controversy, or to issue a writ of certiorari upon the petition of a party to the cause. . . ." Hearing before a Subcommittee of the Committee on the Judiciary, Senate, 68th Cong., 1st Sess., on S. 2060 and S. 2061, Feb. 2, 1924, at 7.

[47] See notes 39–45, *supra*.

[48] The bill gave the circuit courts of appeals appellate jurisdiction over all cases in the district courts of Hawaii and Porto Rico, and the United States Court for

certain uniformity of treatment as to procedure and subject-matter of review in these territorial cases.

The episodic enactments affecting review from the dependencies were not the only instances of disjointed legislation governing the federal judiciary. The Judicial Code was an incomplete codification, and since 1911 it was overlaid with patches here and there, which made a crazy-quilt of the laws affecting the jurisdiction and procedure of the federal courts. In the language of Mr. Justice Van Devanter the statutes were " widely scattered, fragmentary, and not harmonious." [49] Courts and counsel were confused, and litigants were the victims of mysterious refinements. In addition to its main purpose of reducing litigation before the Supreme Court, the Judges' Bill was an effort at " a revision and restatement — a bringing together in a harmonious whole — of the statutes relating to the appellate jurisdiction of the circuit courts of appeals and the Supreme Court." [50]

China. The circuit courts of appeals were given appellate jurisdiction over the district courts of Alaska, the Virgin Islands and the Canal Zone in: (1) all cases involving the Constitution, a statute or treaty of, or authority exercised under the United States; (2) all civil cases involving more than $1,000; (3) all criminal cases where the offense was punishable by imprisonment for more than one year or by death; (4) in all *habeas corpus* proceedings. The circuit courts of appeals were given appellate jurisdiction over the Supreme Court of Hawaii and Porto Rico in: (1) all cases involving the Constitution, a statute or treaty of, or authority exercised under the United States; (2) all civil cases involving more than $5,000; (3) all *habeas corpus* proceedings. Judges' Bill, § 1, amending JUDICIAL CODE, § 128. Section 7 of the Judges' Bill retained the existing provisions permitting *certiorari* from the Philippine Supreme Court to the Supreme Court of the United States. See note 42, *supra*.

[49] Hearing before a Subcommittee of the Committee on the Judiciary, Senate, 68th Cong., 1st Sess., on S. 2060 and S. 2061, Feb. 2, 1924, at 26. Mr. Justice Van Devanter again added: " You will have noted that several sections that are not changed at all are brought into this bill. The purpose in this is to bring into one compact, correlated body all of the statutes defining and regulating the appellate jurisdiction of the courts of the United States and the modes of invoking that jurisdiction." *Ibid.* 41.

[50] *Ibid.* 26. " This bill has another object, and that is to state succinctly the jurisdiction of the court in one statute where it can be found by any lawyer, and, I might say, by any judge. I am very much troubled in coming into the court to find a wilderness of statutes to be consulted in determining what the jurisdiction of the Supreme Court is. The purpose of the framers of this bill is to enable any lawyer, judge, or layman to look to one statute and be sure that it contains all there is on the appellate jurisdiction of the Supreme Court. Another object of the statute is to determine what the appellate jurisdiction of the Circuit Court of Appeals is, because, that, too, is involved in doubt and needs clarification." Chief

Further, a series of minor procedural reforms were proposed, all of them seeking to promote the essentials of litigation and to eliminate needless cost and delay. Thus, the time for taking appeals was reduced; [51] the substance of cases was dealt with, regardless of the technical form in which review was sought; [52] the injustice by which claims against the public are defeated because of the retirement or demise of an officeholder, who was the nominal defendant, was corrected by allowing the substitution of his successor in office as party defendant.[53]

Justice Taft in Hearing before the Committee on the Judiciary, House of Representatives, 67th Cong., 2nd Sess., on H. R. 10479, Mar. 30, 1922, at 3–4.

[51] Under the First Judiciary Act of Sept. 24, 1789, § 22, 1 STAT. 73, 85, all writs of error had to be " brought " within five years after the rendition of the decree complained of. The time within which the writ of error had to be brought was calculated from the date when the writ was filed in the court to which it had issued. Brooks v. Norris, 11 How. (U. S.) 204 (1850). By §§ 1003 and 1008 of the Revised Statutes, reënacting Act of June 1, 1872, § 2, 17 STAT. 196, the time limit was reduced to two years, and the calculation made in the same way. Scarborough v. Pargoud, 108 U. S. 567 (1883) ; Polleys v. Black River Imp. Co., 113 U. S. 81 (1885). Under the Act of Sept. 6, 1916, § 6, 39 STAT. 726, 727, the time limit was reduced to three months, and under that Act the date of application for the writ, not the date of its issuance or of filing, is significant. Citizens Bank v. Opperman, 249 U. S. 448, 449 (1919) ; Puget Sound Power & Light Co. v. County of King, 264 U. S. 22, 24 (1924). Section 8 of Judges' Bill reënacted the provisions of the Act of 1916 with a proviso allowing an extension of the time for 60 days upon a showing of good cause.

[52] This reënacted the provisions of Act of Sept. 6, 1916, § 4, 39 STAT. 726, 727. For the application of the provision, see Elkhart Carriage & Motor Car Co. v. Partin, 9 F. (2d) 393 (6th Circ., 1925) ; Monroe Body Co. v. Herzog, 13 F. (2d) 705 (6th Circ., 1926).

[53] Judges' Bill, § 11. The doctrine of the abatement of the proceeding by the death of the official against whom the action was brought, was taken over by the Supreme Court from prior English practice. The Secretary v. McGarrahan, 9 Wall. (U. S.) 298 (1869) ; United States v. Boutwell, 17 Wall. (U. S.) 604 (1873). Cf. The Sapphire, 11 Wall. (U. S.) 164, 168 (1870). The principle was consistently followed. United States v. Chandler, 122 U. S. 643 (1887) ; Warner Valley Stock Co. v. Smith, 165 U. S. 28 (1897) ; United States v. Lochren, 164 U. S. 701 (1896) ; United States v. Butterworth, 169 U. S. 600 (1898). On the other hand there is no abatement of the suit where the action lies against a governmental corporate entity represented by an elective official or officials who may have ceased to hold office prior to the pendency of the suit. Commissioners v. Sellew, 99 U. S. 624 (1878) ; Thompson v. United States, 103 U. S. 480 (1880) ; Hemingway v. Stansell, 106 U. S. 399 (1882) ; In re Hollon Parker, 131 U. S. 221 (1889) ; Murphy v. Utter, 186 U. S. 95 (1902) ; Marshall v. Dye, 231 U. S. 250 (1913) ; Irwin v. Wright, 258 U. S. 219 (1922). Cf. Boston v. Jackson, 260 U. S. 309 (1922) ; Gorham Mfg. Co. v. Wendell, 261 U. S. 1 (1923). By the Act of Feb. 8, 1899, 30 STAT. 822, suits against officers of the United States were not to be abated

The bill was essentially a bill to relieve the Supreme Court, not by any reëxamination of the existing sources of federal jurisdiction, but by a drastic transfer of existing Supreme Court business to the circuit courts of appeals. The wisdom of the present distribution of judicial power as between state and federal courts was taken for granted. The growing volume of business coming before the district courts, with its inevitable reflex upon the burdens of the circuit courts of appeals and the Supreme Court, was also left unchecked, with a single minor exception. The Act of 1915, it will be recalled, withdrew resort to the federal courts by railway corporations on the mere excuse of a federal charter.[54] This restriction was enlarged to apply to all corporations chartered by Congress which sought the federal courts on that ground.[55]   By this proposal the Court now invoked the help of

---

by their ceasing to hold such office prior to the determination of the action, but the court could substitute the successor in office at any time within twelve months. After the expiration of the twelve months there could, however, be no substitution and the suit abated. LeCrone v. McAdoo, 253 U. S. 217 (1920); Hoy v. Lane, 255 U. S. 566 (1921); Payne v. Ind. Board of Illinois, 258 U. S. 613 (1922); Payne v. Stevens, 260 U. S. 705 (1923). The Act, however, did not permit substitution in suits against state officials. The decision in Payne v. Stevens, *supra,* involving the abatement of suits against the Director General of Railroads came as a shock to the bar. Four different Directors General had succeeded each other and suits had been brought against all of them in which lawyers had not thought it necessary to institute a revival of the action upon the retirement of each successive Director General. Following the decision Senator Cummins immediately introduced a bill to amend § 206 of the Transportation Act of 1920 so as to prevent abatement in suits brought under that Act against the Director General. See 64 CONG. REC. 5077; HOUSE REPORT, No. 1598, 67th Cong., 4th Sess., Ser. No. 8158. Cummins' bill passed without any opposition. See Act of Mar. 3, 1923, 42 STAT. 1443. The fact that the substitution under the existing legislation did not cover suits against territorial, insular, state or county officers caused the dismissal of numerous suits. See Mr. Justice Van Devanter in Hearing before a Subcommittee of the Committee on Judiciary, Senate, 68th Cong., 1st Sess., on S. 2060 and S. 2061, Feb. 22, 1924, at 41–42. Under the new Act the court of its own motion will order the required substitution in order to prevent abatement. See Miller v. Poe, Sup. Ct. J. (1925 Term) 74.

[54] Act of Jan. 28, 1915, § 5, 38 STAT. 803. See also p. 205, n. 94, *supra.*

[55] Judges' Bill, § 12. "Mr. Justice VAN DEVANTER. It extends the railroad section so as to cover any kind of Federal corporation. If there happens to be some other ground for taking the case into a Federal court, it can go there. But Federal incorporation alone is not enough. If one were to sue a reserve bank on a check, the question involved being whether the check was a forgery or not, the

Congress to nullify its own decision in the *Pacific Railroad Removal Cases.*[56]

3

The legislative history of the measure proposed by the Court is quickly told. The draft as it came from the Justices was introduced into the House and Senate in 1922, and in hearings held by the House Judiciary Committee the Chief Justice sponsored the legislation.[57] In the meantime, through direct appeal by the Chief Justice, the influence of the American Bar Association was enlisted in the cause.[58] But not until 1924 did the Judges' Bill attain real momentum. Beginning with the hearing before a subcommittee of the Judiciary Committee of the Senate on February 2, 1924,[59] Congress responded with unusual speed and deference

---

fact that the bank was a Federal corporation would not be a ground for suing in a court of the United States or removing the case into such a court.

"Mr. Justice McReynolds. Whereas, as the law now stands, it could be removed into the Federal court.

"Mr. Justice Van Devanter. Yes."

See Hearing before a Subcommittee of the Committee on the Judiciary, Senate, 68th Cong., 1st Sess., on S. 2060 and S. 2061, Feb. 2, 1924, at 41. The section has been sufficient to destroy the jurisdiction of a district court over a pending cause brought against a Federal Land Bank. Federal Land Bank of Omaha *v.* U. S. Nat. Bank, 13 F. (2d) 36 (8th Circ., 1926).

[56] 115 U. S. 1 (1885).

[57] Hearing before the Committee on Judiciary, House of Representatives, 68th Cong., 2nd Sess., on H. R. 10479, Mar. 30, 1922.

[58] The Committee on Jurisprudence and Law Reform in 1921 in reporting on Graham's resolution in the House for a joint committee " to consider what legislation in relation to United States courts, procedure therein and judgments thereof, would tend to improve the administration of justice," declared that the existing burden upon the Supreme Court demanded either limitations upon the right of review or else an increase in the number of Justices to eleven. 46 AM. BAR ASSN. REP. 384, 391. This latter revival of an old proposal met with the Court's opposition and was never pressed. After Chief Justice Taft, in an address before the Association in 1922, advocated resort to an extension of the principle of discretionary jurisdiction, the Committee on Jurisprudence and Law Reform reported in favor of the Judges' Bill which was then pending before both Houses. 47 *ibid.* 72, 356, 362; William H. Taft, " Possible and Needed Reforms in the Administration of Justice in the Federal Courts," *ibid.* 250, reprinted in 57 AM. L. REV. 1. In its 1923 report the Committee again advocated the passage of the bill. 48 AM. BAR ASSN. REP. 325, 334. In 1924 President Saner sponsored the bill in his annual address. See R. E. L. Saner, " Governmental Review," 49 *ibid.* 127, 142–46. In 1925 the Committee reported the passage of the bill. 50 *ibid.* 406, 414.

[59] Hearing before a Subcommittee of the Committee on the Judiciary, Senate, 68th Cong., 1st Sess., on S. 2060 and S. 2061, Feb. 2, 1924.

to the energetic arguments of the Court. The drafting committee, Justices Van Devanter, McReynolds and Sutherland, spoke for the Court and analyzed at length the state of the Supreme Court's business and its tendencies, and the hope of relief which underlay the proposed distribution of appellate jurisdiction. A favorable report from the Judiciary Committee to the Senate followed, but too late for action at the then session of Congress.[60] Early in the Second Session of the new Congress, the House Judiciary Committee held hearings upon the bill, which afforded another opportunity for a statement of the Court's views by the Chief Justice and the three Justices having charge of the measure.[61]

The House quickly ratified the favorable report of its Committee,[62] practically without debate.[63] The questions raised from the floor were slight and singularly unenlightened. Thus, members got into a snarl over the minor issue of appeals from the Canal Zone. In answer to a question by Denison of Illinois, Chairman Graham of the Judiciary Committee replied that the bill made no change in appeals from the Canal Zone. The assurance failed to allay Denison's fears to the contrary. He moved for reconsideration of the bill after its passage. The motion was not pressed, upon a promise from Graham to secure the adoption of an amendment in the Senate striking out the provisions that were applicable to the Canal Zone.[64] Accordingly, an amendment was later adopted by the Senate eliminating reference to the Canal Zone, without inquiry as to whether the appellate jurisdiction of the Canal Zone was affected, whether any change in that phase of jurisdiction was proposed, and, if so, whether such change was desirable.[65] In fact, Denison's concern

---

[60] SEN. REP., No. 362, 68th Cong., 1st Sess., Ser. No. 8220. The bill had been introduced into the Senate by Cummins on Jan. 17, 1924, and by Graham into the House on Mar. 25, 1924. 65 CONG. REC. 1074, 4992.

[61] Hearing before the Committee on the Judiciary, House of Representatives, 68th Cong., 2nd Sess., on H. R. 8206, Dec. 18, 1924.

[62] HOUSE REPORT, No. 1075, 68th Cong., 2nd Sess., Ser. No. 8390.

[63] The bill passed without a roll-call on Feb. 2, 1925. The House rejected an amendment proposed by McKeown giving to Indians holding allotted lands under acts of Congress or treaty stipulations the right to go to the Supreme Court by writ of error where their claims were denied by the highest state court. 66 CONG. REC. 2879-80.

[64] Ibid. 2880, 2902.

[65] Ibid. 2917.

was groundless, for the bill was practically declaratory of the existing law so far as it affected review over cases from the Canal Zone.[66] But the Senate amendments may have accomplished a result different from what either Denison or the Senate desired. The amendment struck out the provisions of the bill dealing with review by the Fifth Circuit Court of Appeals over the Canal Zone but inadvertently omitted to strike out the clause in the bill repealing the basic provisions under which such appellate jurisdiction is exercised, so that the act as passed leaves doubt whether any court possesses any appellate jurisdiction over the district courts for the Canal Zone.[67]

The House behaved like an uninformed and indifferent ratifying body, manifesting no awareness that it was passing a bill involving really great changes in the disposition of federal litigation. As is usually the case, the Senate showed more responsibility. The measure was in charge of Senator Cummins, as Chairman of the Judiciary Committee, who opened the debate on January 31, 1925.[68] He relied heavily on the judicial authorship of the bill, but at the same time was eager to exclude the inference that the Judiciary Committee of the Senate had surrendered its legislative responsibility to the Court. In the course of his advocacy he appears both as the author of the bill [69] and the proponent of a measure drafted by a committee of the Justices.[70] The de-

---

[66] The new bill explained felony as a crime punishable by imprisonment for a term of one year. For the provision of the Act of Sept. 21, 1922, § 3, 42 STAT. 1004, 1006, permitting review where the jurisdiction of the trial court was in issue, it substituted review in all *habeas corpus* proceedings. See note 43, *supra*. Otherwise the existing jurisdiction was left unchanged.

[67] The Act of Feb. 13, 1925, § 13, 43 STAT. 936, 941, retained the provisions of the Judges' Bill repealing § 9 of the Act of Aug. 24, 1912, 37 STAT. 560, 565. This section as amended by § 3 of the Act of Sept. 21, 1922, 42 STAT. 1004, 1006, stated the existing appellate jurisdiction over the Canal Zone. Since the later Act merely amended the former, the repeal of the former threatens to carry with it the repeal of the amending provisions of the Act of Sept. 21, 1922, even though they are specifically referred to in § 1 of the Act of Feb. 13, 1925. See the result of the Act of June 6, 1900, 31 STAT. 660, in repealing the Act of Feb. 18, 1895, 28 STAT. 666, set forth on pp. 126–7, *supra*.

[68] It was debated in the Senate on Jan. 31, and Feb. 3, 1925. 66 CONG. REC. 2750, 2917.

[69] " The PRESIDENT pro tempore [Senator Cummins]. The Chair is somewhat embarrassed, because he is the author of the bill. . . ." *Ibid.* 980.

[70] " The bill was prepared by a committee of the members of the Supreme Court

bate as a whole, however, leaves no doubt that the Senate clearly understood that the bill emanated from the Supreme Court. This, in fact, was the impulse behind its passage. Little opposition developed to its crucial features. If lawyers in the Senate had doubts about the measure, they were singularly reticent about uttering them. Only Senator Walsh of Montana expressed serious disagreement. He was opposed to making the circuit courts of appeals final arbiters of constitutional questions. " I find it difficult," he said, " to yield to the idea that the Supreme Court of the United States ought to have the right in every case to say whether their jurisdiction shall be appealed to or not." [71] He distrusted the principle which underlay the bill, namely, the extension of the discretionary jurisdiction of the Supreme Court. Resort to *certiorari* appeared to him too precarious for litigants because too capricious in its actual operation. But, finding himself isolated in his position, he abstained from thwarting the wishes of the Court by exercising his power of opposition. Instead, he proposed corrective amendments. Thus, Senator Walsh adverted to the failure of the Judges' Bill to clear up the difficulties introduced by the Act of 1916 whereby the dividing line between writ of error and *certiorari* became so shadowy that it was a not uncommon practice for counsel to seek review by both methods.[72] To clear up the old confusion and to avert further complication an amendment was adopted, permitting, in cases of overlapping jurisdiction under writs of error and *certiorari,* review by either method.[73] This eliminated the possibility that the new features defining review as a matter of right would override provisions for review by *certiorari.*

Senator Copeland [74] became the conduit of arguments of New

---

after a long and careful study of the subject, at the suggestion of the American Bar Association, and has the approval of every member of that Court." Cummins in SEN. REP., No. 362, 68th Cong., 1st Sess., Ser. No. 8220, at 1.

[71] 66 CONG. REC. 2756.

[72] *Ibid.* See also Thomas J. Walsh, "The Overburdened Supreme Court," 1922 VA. BAR ASSN. REP. 216, 223.

[73] 66 CONG. REC. 2919. This amendment to the Act of Feb. 13, 1925, appears as § 237b of the Judicial Code.

[74] The inaptness of a physician being called upon to present extremely technical legal arguments was evident to the Senator, who avowed that he was " not competent, of course, to discuss the question." 66 CONG. REC. 2754.

York lawyers [75] against the elimination of review as of right of decisions by the circuit courts of appeals upon questions of constitutionality. Attention was drawn to the disparity between the want of obligatory review over such decisions and the existence of obligatory jurisdiction over a similar class of cases in the state courts. Senator Copeland rehearsed before the Senate correspondence he had had on this point with the Chief Justice,[76] who had urged that if it was desirable to put the circuit courts of appeals on the same level with the state courts, it would be better to withdraw review as of right from the state courts and subject the decisions of both the state courts and the circuit courts solely to a discretionary review by the Supreme Court, rather than to allow obligatory review over all constitutional cases from both courts.[77] The Chief Justice, however, justified the proposed discrimination on the ground that a circuit court of appeals in deciding a federal constitutional question " would be more likely to preserve the Federal view of the issue than the State court, at least to an extent to justify making a review of its decision by our court conditional upon our approval." [78] However, an amendment prevailed which met this discrimination by allowing writ of error to the circuit courts of appeals in cases sustaining a constitutional claim against a state statute.[79] The argument advanced by the Chief Justice thus became the basis for a new development of the principle which since 1789 had been the basis of Supreme Court review of the highest courts of the states. Due to the belief that the state courts would be more jealous of local rights than of federal claims, review had lain as of right where the constitutional claim was advanced and denied.[80] Now, due to the belief, wholly

---

[75] Messrs. C. P. Williamson and C. W. Pierson. *Ibid.* 2922.

[76] The correspondence is set forth in full in *ibid.* 2920–22.

[77] " If it be thought that cases from the State courts of last resort and those from the circuit courts of appeals should be, as far as may be, on the same plane as respects a review in the Supreme Court, my suggestion would be that those from the State courts, like those from the circuit courts of appeals, be subjected to review only on writ of certiorari. This could be accomplished by a short change in section 237(a) as now set forth in the bill. No other change would be needed to effect it. I regard this as a much better course than to make the review of any cases from the circuit courts of appeals a matter of right." *Ibid.* 2921.   [78] *Ibid.* 2922.

[79] By the Act of Feb. 13, 1925, the amendment became § 240b of the Judicial Code.

[80] See p. 190, *supra.*

speculative, that the federal court would sustain constitutional claims as opposed to the local right, review was provided from the circuit courts of appeals where the constitutional claim was advanced and allowed. Thereby, the Senate " intended to put the two on a perfect parity, allowing a writ of error from the circuit court of appeals under conditions exactly the same, except reversed, and allowing a writ of certiorari in the one case as in the other case, so that the two would be entirely harmonious." [81]

The course of the debate in the Senate threw up a few other and minor amendments. The provisions of the Urgent Deficiency Act of 1913,[82] requiring three judges upon hearing of a motion for a preliminary injunction to restrain the enforcement of a state statute or administrative order, was extended so as to require three judges to sit upon the final hearing for the permanent injunction.[83] The four classes of cases giving direct review to the Supreme Court of the decisions of the district courts, was amended so as to embrace cases under the Stockyard and Packers Act of 1921.[84] To fill up the lacuna, revealed by the recent decision in *Craig* v. *Hecht*,[85] in the confused legislation governing the power

---

[81] Senator Walsh, in 66 CONG. REC. 2923.

[82] Act of Mar. 4, 1913, 37 STAT. 1013.

[83] 66 CONG. REC. 2917. Under § 266 of the Judicial Code, as amended, the requirement for three judges did not apply to any disposition of the issue on its merits. Seaboard Air Line Ry. v. Railroad Comm. of Georgia, 213 Fed. 27 (5th Circ., 1914), aff'd, 240 U. S. 324 (1916); Brown Drug Co. v. United States, 235 Fed. 603 (N. D. Iowa, 1916); Freiberg Co. v. Dawson, 274 Fed. 420, 438 (W. D. Ky., 1920), aff'd, 255 U. S. 288 (1921). Cf. Pacific Tel. & Tel. Co. v. Kuykendall, 265 U. S. 196 (1924); Buck v. Kuykendall, 267 U. S. 307 (1925); Banton v. Belt Line Ry. Corp., 268 U. S. 413 (1925). Contra, Hebe Co. v. Calvert, 246 Fed. 711 (S. D. Ohio, 1917); Marcus Brown Holding Co. v. Feldman, 269 Fed. 306 (S. D. N. Y., 1920), aff'd, 256 U. S. 170 (1921). Consequently under the old procedure where the bill was dismissed on the merits an appeal lay to the Supreme Court under § 238 and not § 266 of the Judicial Code. Shaffer v. Carter, 252 U. S. 37 (1920). Under the new Act the final hearing must be before three judges. Patterson v. Mobile Gas Co., 271 U. S. 131, 136 (1926); Chicago, R. I. & P. Ry. v. United States, 6 F. (2d) 888 (N. D. Tex., 1925); Middlesex Water Co. v. Board of Pub. Util. Commissioners, 10 F. (2d) 519 (D. N. J., 1926). The requirement, however, is not applicable to a case, which had been finally submitted before the Act went into effect. Brooklyn Union Gas Co. v. Prendergast, 7 F. (2d) 628 (E. D. N. Y., 1925).

[84] Act of Aug. 15, 1921, § 317, 42 STAT. 163. 66 CONG. REC. 2917. The amendment became § 238 (5) of the Judicial Code.

[85] 263 U. S. 255 (1923). Cf. United States v. Singer, 5 F. (2d) 966 (3rd Circ., 1925).

to issue writs of *habeas corpus,* an amendment explicitly gave such power to circuit judges.[86]   Finally, the time for applying for review by the circuit courts of appeals over the decisions of the district courts was reduced from six to three months.[87]   With these amendments [88] the bill passed, only one dissenting vote having been recorded against it.[89]

Nothing illustrates more strikingly the failure of the House to exercise responsibility in the enactment of judiciary legislation than its share in the passage of the Judges' Bill. A few minutes of desultory discussion led to its passage in the first instance. On its return from the Senate, the new and important Senate amendments were not only not debated, but were not even brought to the attention of the House by the Chairman of its Judiciary Committee.[90]   Nor did the Senate live up to its best intellectual tradition in considering the most important judiciary measure since 1891. The debate appears meager and uninformed in comparison with the great arguments evoked by judiciary bills in 1825, 1869, 1890.

---

[86] 66 CONG. REC. 2918.

[87] *Ibid.*

[88] An amendment was also added permitting a judge to stay the enforcement of such judgments as were subject to review by the Supreme Court on *certiorari. Ibid.* 2919.

[89] The vote was 76 to 1, Senator Heflin voting in the negative. *Ibid.* 2928.

[90] The following extract from the debate in the House is illuminating:

" Mr. JONES. What changes did the Senate make in the bill?

" Mr. GRAHAM. They made one change to meet the objection of the gentleman from Illinois [Mr. DENISON], made at the time we passed the bill. I had given a promise that I would help him introduce any change that might be necessary to properly safeguard what he was seeking. He went to the committee of judges and the matter was agreed on, and two amendments were inserted, and then there was one formal amendment inserted by the Senator from Massachusetts [*sic*], Mr. WALSH. Otherwise the bill is exactly the same as it passed the House.

" Mr. JONES. What was the other amendment?

" Mr. GRAHAM. The Judiciary Committee considered it and have authorized concurrence in the amendments of the Senate, unanimously.

" Mr. JONES. I understand the amendment that the gentleman from Illinois referred to, in respect to the jurisdiction of the Panama Canal, but what does the other amendment refer to?

" Mr. GRAHAM. I can not point it out as I have not the bill before me, but it is a simple change. It does not involve any organic change or even an important change. It was inserted to satisfy the objection of Senator WALSH.

" The SPEAKER. The question is on agreeing to the Senate amendment.

" The Senate amendment was agreed on."

Ibid. 3005.

This time Van Buren and Webster, Evarts, Edmunds and Hoar had no counterparts. The Senate in 1925, as throughout its history, contained lawyers of distinction and with seasoned experience in federal litigation; but, excepting Senator Walsh of Montana, they hardly intervened in the discussion. This senatorial sterility was due to a number of causes. Some of the ablest lawyers were not on the Judiciary Committee, and so felt no special responsibility for the legislation. The Senate, as a whole, was preoccupied with other issues politically more pressing. Above all, the Senate deferred to the prestige of the Supreme Court and its Chief Justice, whose energetic espousal largely helped to realize the Court's proposal. The opinion of the bar, within and without Congress, accepted the Court's prescription for the Court's needs.

4

Congress gave the Court what it wanted — a very strictly confined jurisdiction. As a matter of right, cases now come to Washington only from three sources: the district courts, the circuit courts of appeals, and the state courts. But even from these courts in only a limited class of cases is review free from grace. To the state courts writs of error run in only two situations; over the district courts review can be exercised in five types of litigation; from the circuit courts of appeals only one contingency gives rise as a matter of course to another review in the Supreme Court. The aim of the Supreme Court, to be allowed to confine its adjudications to issues of constitutionality and other matters of essentially national importance, was thus written into legislation.[91]

---

[91] Act of Feb. 13, 1925, § 14, 43 STAT. 936, 942. The law did not go into effect, however, until May 13, 1925. The Act, due to efforts of the Chief Justice, has been effectively brought to the attention of the profession by numerous writers in recent periodicals. See Paxton Blair, " Federal Appellate Procedure as Affected by the Act of February 13, 1925," 25 COL. L. REV. 393, reprinted in 98 CENT. L. J. 204; Charles W. Bunn, " The New Appellate Jurisdiction in Federal Courts," 9 MINN. L. REV. 309; William J. Hughes, " The New Federal Appellate Jurisdiction Act," 13 GEORGETOWN L. J. 266; Clifford R. Snider, " Important Changes in Federal Appellate Jurisdiction," 31 W. VA. L. Q. 127; William H. Taft, " The Jurisdiction of the Supreme Court under the Act of February 13, 1925," 35 YALE L. J. 1; " New Act Alters Jurisdiction of United States Supreme Court," 2 LAW STUDENT, No. 6, 1;

The entire history of judiciary legislation demonstrates its inevitably empiric character. Jurisdictional problems are too technical and intricate to permit even the most skilled authorship to foresee all possibilities.[92] Even though the Judiciary Act of 1925 was the product of more expert draftsmanship than any of its predecessors, it is not free from omissions and ambiguities. The process of clarifying doubts and filling lacunae by interpretation and supplemental legislation has already begun, and will continue.

The Act of 1925 did not achieve the hope of assembling in a single statute the law defining the appellate power of the United States courts. The authors of the Act convincingly demonstrated the importance to courts, lawyers and litigants of being able to find in one compendious form the authority by which, and the conditions under which, appeal may be sought. All items dealing with this subject should be strung upon the thread of one code. Detached provisions are too easily overlooked. Scientific standards of legislation really demand a comprehensive judicial code, defining the structure of the entire judicial system and bringing the scope of judicial power of the various parts of the judicial hierarchy within the ready understanding of the profession and the public. The Chief Justice has recognized that a " complete revision of the whole Judicial Code . . . would have been better, but such a revision without a corps of assistants, whose time should be exclusively devoted to it, would have been beyond the capacity of the Court with its regular duties to perform." [93] Therefore, the Chief Justice welcomed the Act as a codification of " the entire appellate jurisdiction of the Supreme Court, with the exception of that of the Court of Customs Appeals contained in an amendment to a section of the Judicial Code." [94] Already a further exception must be noted. The Bankruptcy Act of

---

Jacob Trieber, " A Review of the Act of Congress of February 13, 1925," 59 AM. L. REV. 321; " Appellate Procedure of United States Supreme Court and Circuit Court of Appeals," 11 AM. BAR ASSN. J. 145.

[92] " It has generally been regarded as axiomatic in the law that it is beyond human ingenuity or talent to frame statutes or rules suited to every contingency expressed in language concerning the interpretation of which no controversy of substance may arise." Thomas J. Walsh, " Reform of Federal Procedure," SEN. Doc. No. 105, 69th Cong., 1st Sess., at 3.

[93] William H. Taft, *supra*, 35 YALE L. J. at 11.

[94] *Ibid.* 12.

1926 [95] deals with the appellate jurisdiction of the Supreme Court
in bankruptcy matters in such unclear language that we must
await Supreme Court decisions for its meaning.[96]

The Act of 1925 also purported to gather up scattered provisions defining the jurisdiction of the circuit courts of appeals.[97]
Here, too, it did not make an inclusive formulation.[98] The practitioner today must travel outside of the Act of 1925 to ascertain
the full measure of review allotted to these nine courts. Review
of administrative orders by the circuit courts of appeals is scattered in isolated enactments dealing with tribunals such as the
Federal Trade Commission, the Federal Reserve Board, and the
Board of Tax Appeals.[99] As amendments to the Act of 1925 will
be proposed from time to time, it is hoped that Congress will not

---

[95] Despite the fact that the Act of Feb. 13, 1925, § 13, 43 STAT. 936, 942, expressly repealed " so much of sections 24 and 25 of the Bankruptcy Act of July 1,
1898, as regulates the mode of review by the Supreme Court in the proceedings,
controversies, and cases therein named," the Act of May 27, 1926, § 9, 44 STAT. 662,
664, reënacted § 24 with additions, here irrelevant, so as either to nullify the express
repeal contained in the Act of 1925 or to demonstrate that the Act of 1925 needlessly repealed " so much " of § 24, in that the section conferred no appellate jurisdiction inconsistent with the provisions of the Act of 1925. See James A. McLaugh-
lin, " Amendment of the Bankruptcy Act," 40 HARV. L. REV. 341, 344; Ralph F.
Colin, " An Analysis of the 1926 Amendments to the Bankruptcy Act," 26 COL. L.
REV. 789, 796.

[96] Sections 1003–05 of the Revenue Act of Feb. 26, 1926, 44 STAT. 9, 110, also
give the Supreme Court jurisdiction to review upon *certiorari* the decisions of the
circuit courts of appeals reviewing decisions of the Board of Tax Appeals.

[97] The Act of Feb. 13, 1926, § 2, 43 STAT. 936, 939, extended the provisions of
Judicial Code, §§ 239, 240, to cases arising under the Railway Arbitration Act of
1913, the Federal Trade Commission Act of 1914, and the Anti-Trust Act of 1914.
It has since been amended so as to include cases arising under the Railway Labor
Act of May 20, 1926, § 13, 44 STAT. 577, 587.

[98] By the Act of Feb. 7, 1925, 43 STAT. 813, amending Judicial Code, § 128,
appeals could be taken to the circuit courts of appeals from interlocutory decrees in
admiralty. The Act of Feb. 13, 1925, in further amending Judicial Code, § 128,
neglected to take into account the passage of the earlier act and hence succeeded
inadvertently in repealing it. The provisions were thus reënacted by the Act of
Apr. 3, 1926, 44 STAT. 233, as an amendment to Judicial Code, § 129.

[99] See, *e.g.*, review by the circuit courts of appeals over the Federal Trade Commission, Act of Sept. 26, 1914, § 5, 38 STAT. 717, 720; over the orders of the Secretary of Agriculture under the Packers and Stockyards Act of Aug. 15, 1921, § 204,
42 STAT. 159, 162; over the orders of the commission consisting of the Secretary of
Agriculture, the Secretary of Commerce and the Attorney General, under the Grain
Futures Act of Sept. 21, 1922, § 6, 42 STAT. 998, 1001; the enforcement of the orders
of the Interstate Commerce Commission, the Federal Reserve Board and the Federal
Trade Commission under the Act of Oct. 15, 1914, § 11, 38 STAT. 730, 734.

continue the process, already begun,[100] of overlaying a general statute with particular enactments, thereby still further postponing the aim of Mr. Justice Van Devanter to bring together " in a harmonious whole . . . the statutes relating to the appellate jurisdiction of the circuit courts of appeals and of the Supreme Court." [101] Such a process of piecemeal legislation played havoc with the Judicial Code within ten years of its enactment.[102] The mischievous consequences of such anarchic legislative methods ought not to be repeated.

Guided by the desire to define the appellate jurisdiction of the Supreme Court with such scientific precision that no room would be left for doubt, the authors of the Act of 1925 repealed the device adopted by Congress in 1922 [103] whereby, because of the confused state of the law, cases which had come improperly for review before the Supreme Court or a circuit court of appeals could automatically be transferred to the appropriate appellate tribunal without penalizing by dismissal the pardonably wrong guess of counsel.[104] This provision, embodied as Section 238a in the Judicial Code, would, according to Mr. Justice Van Devanter, become " quite unnecessary " [105] once the Judges' Bill became law.[106] Unfortunately, this was a needless sacrifice of a cautionary clause

---

[100] See the Act of Feb. 26, 1926, §§ 1003–05, 44 STAT. 9, 110.

[101] Hearing before a Subcommittee of the Committee on the Judiciary, Senate, 68th Cong., 1st Sess., on S. 2060 and S. 2061, Feb. 2, 1924, at 26.

[102] The Acts of Jan. 28, 1915, 38 STAT. 803, and of Sept. 6, 1916, 39 STAT. 726, contained provisions relating to appellate jurisdiction and procedure which were not drafted so that they amended corresponding sections of the Judicial Code. The Code therefore became a mutilated Code. The same unscientific draftsmanship made many sections of the Judicial Code dealing with review from the insular courts useless. See notes 39–45, *supra*. Such legislation forced the practitioner continually to look outside the Code for the applicable statutes. Similar criticism has aptly been made of the draftsmanship of the present Act. See Paxton Blair, *supra,* 25 COL. L. REV. at 406.

[103] Act of Sept. 14, 1922, 42 STAT. 837.

[104] Six cases were transferred to the circuit courts of appeals during the 1922 Term, 2 during the 1923 Term, 7 during the 1924 Term, and 3 during the 1925 Term.

[105] Hearing before a Subcommittee of the Committee on the Judiciary, Senate, 68th Cong., 1st Sess., on S. 2060 and S. 2061, Feb. 2, 1924, at 33.

[106] The Judges' Bill impliedly repealed § 238a of the Judicial Code. By amendment in the Senate the repeal was made express. Act of Feb. 13, 1925, § 13, 43 STAT. 936, 942; Barr v. McCorkle, 270 U. S. 635 (1926). The repeal does not embrace cases pending in the Supreme Court prior to May 13, 1925. Pascagoula Nat. Bank v. Federal Reserve Bank, 269 U. S. 537 (1925); Salinger v. United States, 272 U. S. 542, 549 (1926).

against the frailties of jurisdictional legislation. In fact, three situations have already arisen in which the Supreme Court was confronted with serious ambiguities in the Act of 1925, leading counsel to appeal to the Supreme Court only to find that they had mistakenly conceived the scope of the provisions allowing direct review of decisions of the district courts.[107] All three cases involved the Senate amendment to the Judges' Bill whereby Section 266 of the Judicial Code, which required a hearing before three judges in suits for an interlocutory injunction against the enforcement of state statutes or administrative orders, was extended to apply " to the final hearing in such suit in the district court; and a direct appeal to the Supreme Court may be taken from a final decree granting or denying a permanent injunction in such suit." [108] The question was presented to the court " whether the phrase ' such suit ' was intended to refer only to a suit in which a preliminary injunction had in fact been sought or to a suit in which an application for such an interlocutory injunction might have been but in fact was not made." [109] The Court, finding that the " general purpose of the Act of February 13, 1925 was to relieve this Court by restricting the right to a review by it," answered that the Act did not purpose " to extend the application of the section with respect to the requirement of three judges or the right of direct appeal to any case in which an interlocutory injunction is not sought." [110] These decisions permit the generalization that the Supreme Court is likely to resolve all doubts against the assumption of obligatory jurisdiction; but they also indicate that the new Act, however much it may have curtailed them, did not wholly still jurisdictional controversies.

One of the most fruitful sources of litigation over jurisdiction has been the language used to describe the basis for review of state court decisions. " Title, right, privilege, or immunity " [111]

---

[107] *Ex parte* Buder, 271 U. S. 461, 465 (1926) ; Moore *v.* Fidelity & Deposit Co., 272 U. S. 317 (1926) ; Smith *v.* Wilson, 47 Sup. Ct. Rep. 385 (1927).

[108] Act of Feb. 13, 1925, § 1, 43 STAT. 936, 938.

[109] Smith *v.* Wilson, *supra*, note 107, at 386.

[110] *Ibid.*

[111] The Act of Sept. 24, 1789, § 25, 1 STAT. 73, 85–86, permitted the Supreme Court to review on writ of error a decision of the highest state court in any case, among others, " where is drawn in question the construction of any clause of the constitution, or of a treaty, or statute of, or commission held under the United

have proved too subtle for definitive judicial determination. The 1916 amendment preserved these categories as grounds for issuing *certiorari*.[112] Cases under that amendment testify to the metaphysical distinctions involved in applying them.[113] The Act of 1925 retains these uncertainties in part, though it minimizes the harm by allowing writs of error and petitions for *certiorari* to perform interchangeable duties.[114] There is every reason for perpetuating legal language which has acquired precise and technical meaning; but, despite its antiquity, the phrase " title, right, privilege, or immunity " has continued to be a mischief-maker. In any future revision of the Judicial Code more scientific language ought to be found to replace these barbed words.[115]

In applying the general principle of restricting obligatory review by the Supreme Court, the Act of 1925 draws a line that cuts across the Court's dominant function as adjudicator of vital con-

---

States, and the decision is against the title, right, privilege or exemption specially set up or claimed by either party, under such clause of the said Constitution, treaty, statute or commission. . . ." The present phraseology is drawn from the revision of § 25 of the Judiciary Act, accomplished by the Act of Feb. 5, 1867, § 2, 14 STAT. 385, 386, providing for review by writ of error from a judgment of a state court in any suit " where any title, right, privilege, or immunity is claimed under the constitution, or any treaty or statute of or commission held, or authority exercised under the United States, and the decision is against the title, right, privilege, or immunity specially set up or claimed by either party under such constitution, treaty, statute, commission, or authority. . . ." This section was carried into the Revised Statutes, § 709, and from there into the Judicial Code, § 237.

112 Act of Sept. 6, 1916, § 2, 39 STAT. 726.

113 See Thomas J. Walsh, " The Overburdened Supreme Court," 1922 VA. BAR ASSN. REP. 216; 62 CONG. REC. 8545; Raymond W. Clifford, " Appellate Procedure through State and Federal Courts," 1924 WASH. BAR ASSN. REP. 187.

114 Act of Feb. 13, 1925, § 1, 43 STAT. 936, 937, amending § 237 of the JUDICIAL CODE. The Senate amendment of paragraph (b) of § 237 makes *certiorari* a proper method for invoking review in every case, even though review might also be had in such case by writ of error. Paragraph (c) of § 237 permits the Court to regard a writ of error as a petition for *certiorari* in cases where review has been improperly invoked on writ of error and the only means of securing review is by petition for *certiorari*. Due to the difficulty of determining the exact lines of demarcation between *certiorari* and writ of error, where review is sought on writ of error, and the case presents doubt as to whether error or *certiorari* is the appropriate means of invoking the Court's jurisdiction, it will not be unlikely that the practice will grow up whereby the papers upon which the writ of error is allowed will include a brief argument for urging the Court to take jurisdiction of the case on *certiorari* in the event that error may be an inappropriate means of securing review. Some such practice will supplant the former mode of seeking review both by writ of error and by petition for *certiorari*. See Longest *v.* Langford, 47 Sup. Ct. Rep. 668 (1927), and Paxton Blair, 25 COL. L. REV. 393, 396.   115 See *ibid.* 395–96.

stitutional issues. Under Section 240b of the Judicial Code, as amended by the Act of 1925,[116] a decision adverse to the constitutionality of federal legislation cannot be taken from the circuit courts of appeals except on *certiorari.*[117] To be sure, there is little likelihood that the Supreme Court would withhold permissive review of a case in which a circuit court of appeals invalidated an act of Congress. But a scientifically framed judicial code ought to give formal as well as practical expression to the governing ideas of a judicial system. If the invalidation of an act of Congress by a lower federal court is, as a matter of fact, one of the clearest cases for invoking the judgment of the Supreme Court, the opportunity for review should be explicit and not left to discretion. This formal discrimination against federal legislation is emphasized by the fact that a declaration by a circuit court of appeals of the unconstitutionality of state legislation is subject to review as of right by the Supreme Court.[118]

5

A change so drastic as that wrought by the new Act in the discretionary powers of the Court must await its vindication from

---

[116] Act of Feb. 13, 1925, § 1, 43 Stat. 936, 939.

[117] *E.g.*, neither of two such profoundly important constitutional cases as Myers *v.* United States, 272 U. S. 52 (1926), and McGrain *v.* Daugherty, 273 U. S. 135 (1927), could have reached the Court save on *certiorari*.

[118] Section 240b, a Senate amendment, sought to introduce equality of review between state and federal courts. See note 76, *supra*. It does not. A decision by a state court denying the validity of a federal act on the ground of constitutionality may be taken to the Supreme Court as of right; a decision upholding its validity may be reviewed on *certiorari*. Decisions by the circuit courts of appeals, whether denying or upholding the validity of a federal act, may only be reviewed on *certiorari*. A decision by a state court upholding a state law against attack on the ground of repugnancy to the Constitution, laws or treaties of the United States, may be taken to the Supreme Court on error or *certiorari*; if the state law is held invalid upon the same ground, review lies by *certiorari*. A decision by the circuit courts of appeals denying the validity of a state statute because of repugnancy to the Constitution, laws or treaties of the United States may be reviewed only by error and not by *certiorari*; a decision upholding its validity upon the same grounds may be reviewed only by *certiorari*. Further, the language of § 240b leaves it uncertain whether its provisions are to be taken to apply to the Court of Appeals of the District of Columbia and thereby follow the general principle embodied in § 240a of likening review from that court to review from the circuit courts of appeals. *Cf.* § 5 of the Act of 1925, dispelling the doubts created by Swift & Co. *v.* Hoover, 242 U. S. 107 (1916).

actual practice. New perplexities are raised by the great volume of petitions for *certiorari* which are coming to the Court under the new dispensation. The Court is keenly alive to the importance of having its discretionary reviewing power exercised by the application of well-defined legal criteria. The general rules which determine the fate of petitions have not been left to scattered observations in cases dealing with *certiorari*; they have now been formulated in the Revised Rules of the Court framed to give effect to the Act of February 13, 1925.[119] Rule 35 indicates with great clarity the character of " special and important reasons " by which the " sound judicial discretion " of the Court will be guided.[120] Such a petition is taken under advisement by the whole Court, and may issue if only a substantial minority " are impressed with the propriety " of taking the case.[121] But when, as has already happened, the Court is confronted with 500 petitions at a single term,[122] the objective standards governing the exercise of discretion may unwittingly fail in numerous instances. The reports make abundantly clear that because of the quantity of these petitions and the conditions under which they must be scrutinized, they are sometimes granted when they should have been denied.[123] Is it not likely, too, that petitions are occasionally denied when they should have been granted? Their disposition rests inescapably upon judgment, and it is familiar experience that judgment is less sure in the later stages of a long series.[124]

---

[119] Adopted June 8, 1925. See 266 U. S. 653. The rules were revised by the same committee of the Court, with Mr. Justice Van Devanter at its head, that framed the Act of 1925. See William H. Taft, *supra*, 35 YALE L. J. at 12.

[120] Rule 35, paragraph 5, 266 U. S. 681. See also Chief Justice Taft in Hearing before the Committee on the Judiciary, House of Representatives, 67th Cong., 2nd Sess., on H. R. 10479, Mar. 30, 1922, at 3.

[121] Mr. Justice Van Devanter in Hearing before a Subcommittee of the Committee on the Judiciary, Senate, 68th Cong., 1st Sess., on S. 2060 and S. 2061, Feb. 2, 1924, at 29.

[122] During the 1925 Term, 539 petitions for *certiorari* were considered. See Table I, *infra*, p. 295.

[123] See United States *v.* Rimer, 220 U. S. 547 (1911) ; Furness, Withy & Co. *v.* Yang-Tsze Ins. Ass'n, 242 U. S. 430 (1917) ; Layne & Bowler Corp. *v.* Western Well Works, Inc., 261 U. S. 387 (1923) ; Keller *v.* Adams-Campbell Co., 264 U. S. 314 (1924) ; Davis *v.* Currie, 266 U. S. 182 (1924) ; Missouri Pacific R. R. *v.* Hanna, 266 U. S. 184 (1924) ; Erie R. R. *v.* Kirkendall, 266 U. S. 185 (1924).

[124] It is important that the bar, generally, do not come to share the following view of Senator Walsh: " Whatever may be said touching the degree of care with which such applications are considered, it is impossible to resist the conclusion that

If experience should disclose that these are serious risks, the Court through its rules can fashion corrective measures. Thus it has been suggested that a short oral statement would enable the Court to penetrate more readily the true issues embedded in a petition.[125] Against this it is urged that considerable time would be consumed by such oral appearances.[126] Two other modifications in the traditional procedure for disposing of petitions for *certiorari* are open. According to the established routine, they are ordinarily disposed of during a week after their submission. Their volume varies from week to week.[127] It might be feasible to regulate their flow by limiting the maximum number of petitions considered in any one week. Secondly, the very heavy burden which now rests upon the Chief Justice alone in reporting on these petitions to the Court might, perhaps, be shared with the Associate Justices. Undoubtedly, the responsibility for

---

in the vast majority of cases they can have nothing more than the most cursory and superficial examination." Thomas J. Walsh, *supra,* 1922 VA. BAR ASSN. REP. at 229; 62 CONG. REC. 8545, 8548.

[125] 66 CONG. REC. 2753 (Jan. 31, 1925). See also Thomas J. Walsh, *supra,* 1922 VA. BAR ASSN. REP. 216; 62 CONG. REC. 8545. The suggestion was also made that an oral hearing be had upon the petition before a single Justice: " Mr. WALSH. . . . Would it be practicable to permit a brief hearing before a single justice in support of the application which he files for a writ of certiorari?

" Mr. BECK. That is a very interesting suggestion and I would not, on the spur of the moment, either concur in or dissent from it. I would not hastily concur in the suggestion for this reason: The judges being human beings, there is a manifest difference in temperament between them. Some would be liberal in allowing certioraris and others would be less generous. The advantage of taking the composite mind of the court upon whether the case is of sufficient importance to be one of the favored cases to be heard by that court results in every litigant getting the same composite impression, whereas if you allow one judge to hear them, in the first place, the disappointed litigant would say: ' Well, if I had gone before Mr. Justice Smith or had I only been heard by Mr. Justice Brown, I think I would have gotten that certiorari.' I believe, in the long run, my superficial impression is that it would not work." Hearing before the Committee on the Judiciary, House of Representatives, 67th Cong., 2nd Sess., on H. R. 10479, Apr. 18 and 27, 1922, at 16.

[126] William H. Taft, *supra,* 35 YALE L. J. at 12. A suggestion has also been advanced for the appointment of commissioners who would prepare the petitions for *certiorari* for ready disposition by the Court. See Jacob Trieber, " Further Relief for the United States Supreme Court," 12 AM. BAR ASSN. J. 167; " The Delays in the Courts," 57 AM. L. REV. 24, 38.

[127] Thus, for the week ending Oct. 12, 1925, 64 petitions were disposed of; 50 for the week ending Oct. 19, 1925; 48 for the week ending Oct. 26, 1925; 8 for the week ending Nov. 16, 1925; 18 for the week ending Nov. 23, 1926; 5 for the week ending Nov. 30, 1925.

granting or denying a petition now rests with the entire Court. But if the present number continues or increases, experiment might show that more effective scrutiny would be secured if petitions for *certiorari* were assigned for reporting to individual members of the Court, as is true in writing opinions. Eventually, also, the bar might be educated to conserve the Court's time by withholding unmeritorious petitions. In any event, the difficulties that experience may disclose are within the control of the Court's own flexible procedure.

While the new Act lessened the number of cases from the lower federal courts, with a single exception it did nothing to narrow the scope of the Court's review in cases that were allowed to come to it. Since the Act of 1789, review by the Supreme Court of cases from the state courts has been rigorously restricted to the federal issues in the record. A different rule was evolved by the Court as to cases coming to it from the federal courts. All questions in the case, both state and federal, were open.[128] This practice continued to be applied by the Court after 1891 in reviewing decisions of the circuit courts of appeals. As a result, while in cases from state courts rulings on state law were final, a litigation begun in the federal courts solely because a federal issue was raised, might bring to the Supreme Court technical questions of local statutes and local common law. The Court's members are not experts in the statute and common law of the forty-eight states, and yet they are frequently called upon to determine such local questions without the guidance of state court decisions.[129] An inordinate demand is thus made on the Court's time in a peculiarly treacherous realm of knowledge, essentially foreign to its duties. The Act of 1925 only partly corrects this evil. As to the one class of cases for which a second review by the Supreme Court is granted as a matter of right, after a decision by the circuit court of appeals, it is expressly provided

---

[128] See Siler *v.* Louisville & Nashville R. R., 213 U. S. 175, 191 (1909).

[129] *Cf., e.g.,* City of Winchester *v.* Winchester Water Works Co., 251 U. S. 192 (1920) ; Risty *v.* Chicago, R. I. & P. Ry., 270 U. S. 378 (1926).

As to the difficulty felt by the Supreme Court in construing a state statute without the guiding construction of a state court, see Dorchy *v.* Kansas, 264 U. S. 286 (1924). Compare Groves *v.* Slaughter, 15 Pet. (U. S.) 449 (1841), with Rowan *v.* Runnels, 5 How. (U. S.) 134 (1847), as to the difficulties involved in anticipating the interpretation of state legislation by a state court.

that such review " shall be restricted to an examination and decision of the Federal questions presented in the case." [130]   Even such a restriction does not wholly remove the necessity for passing upon questions of state law in advance of decisions by state courts entrusted with the ultimate determination of their local law.[131] But it does remove the necessity for deciding such questions when not essential to the disposition of the federal question in the record.   As to the large number of cases, however, which will come to the Supreme Court from the circuit courts of appeals on *certiorari*,[132] the old scope of review remains and the Court will have to deal with all the questions presented by the record.   This ought not to be.   Conservation of the Court's energy for the disposition of issues specially pertinent to its functions can be achieved, without further reduction of its appellate jurisdiction, by the simple device of restricting review to the federal questions in the case.[133]

Another source of needless and time-consuming perplexity for the Court results from the present necessity of passing on issues of fact.   Not merely is the Supreme Court subject to the usual psychological difficulty involved in reading, as against hearing, evidence.   The Justices are out of touch with the circumstances and details and judgments which go to make up evidence.   They ought not to be asked to disentangle confused testimony, nor ought a Court, charged with keeping our constitutional system in equilibrium, be compelled to pass on disputations over evidence.   The ascertainment of principles governing authenticated facts, accommodations between conflicting principles, adaptations of old principles to new situations — only issues of such moment are meet to invoke the judgment of our ultimate tribunal.   The credibility of witnesses, the reconciliation of conflicting testimony, the proof of underlying facts, the reliability of experts —

---

130 JUDICIAL CODE, § 240b.

131 *Cf.* American Ry. Express Co. *v.* Levee, 263 U. S. 19 (1923); Appleby *v.* New York, 271 U. S. 364 (1926).

132 During the 1925 Term petitions for *certiorari* to the circuit courts of appeals were granted in 53 cases.

133 An obvious exception to the principle of denying review save where a federal question is presented is illustrated by one of the grounds set forward by the Court for awarding *certiorari*, namely where a circuit court of appeals " has decided an important question of local law in a way probably in conflict with applicable local decisions." Rule 35, 266 U. S. 681. *Cf.* Benedict *v.* Ratner, 268 U. S. 353 (1925).

all the data from which principles are derived and to which they are applied — ought to have been sifted and formulated as findings in the stages of the judicial process preceding review by the Supreme Court. This is the theory upon which review of decisions of the Court of Claims,[134] as well as review of common law actions without a jury,[135] has already been based. It surely ought to be possible to devise rules of appellate practice whereby the Supreme Court will be relieved from quarrying the facts out of a confused mass of evidence.[136] In tax cases, in rate

---

[134] Rule 1 of Appeals from the Court of Claims; Rule 38 of 1925 Supreme Court Rules, 266 U. S. 683. "For the purposes of our review the findings of that court are to be treated like the verdict of a jury, and we are not at liberty to refer to the evidence, any more than to the opinion, for the purpose of eking out, controlling, or modifying their scope." Brothers v. United States, 250 U. S. 88, 93 (1919). *Cf.* Hathaway & Co. v. United States, 249 U. S. 460, 463 (1919); Portsmouth Harbor Land & Hotel Co. v. United States, 260 U. S. 327 (1922); Luckenbach S. S. Co. v. United States, 272 U. S. 533 (1926). The evidence cannot be certified to the Supreme Court. United States v. Société Anonyme des Anciens Establissements Cail, 224 U. S. 309, 329 (1912). But in the event that the findings are deficient or that no such special findings have been made as were requested, the case may be remanded to the Court of Claims for additional findings. Ripley v. United States, 222 U. S. 144 (1911); Fidelity & Deposit Co. v. United States, 259 U. S. 296 (1922). The same requirement for special findings is demanded of district courts when acting upon claims against the United States under the provisions of the Tucker Act. See Act of Mar. 3, 1887, § 7, 24 STAT. 505, 506.

[135] The findings by the trial court when a jury has been waived may be either general or special. REV. STAT. § 649. "It is, however, only when the finding is special, that the review of this court can extend to the determination of the sufficiency of the facts found to support the judgment." Dickinson v. Planters' Bank, 16 Wall. (U. S.) 250, 257 (1872). *Cf.* Meath v. Board of Mississippi Commissioners, 109 U. S. 268 (1883); British Queen Mining Co. v. Baker Silver Mining Co., 139 U. S. 222 (1891). The results of waiver of a jury have thus been condensed by the Court: " (1) If the verdict be a general verdict, only such rulings of the court, *in the progress of the trial,* can be reviewed as are presented by bill of exceptions, or as may arise on the pleadings. (2) In such cases, a bill of exceptions cannot be used to bring up the whole testimony for review any more than in a trial by jury. (3) That if the parties desire a review of the law involved in the case, they must either get the court to find a special verdict, which raises the legal propositions, or they must present to the court their propositions of law, and require the court to rule on them. (4) That objection to the admission or exclusion of evidence, or to such ruling on the propositions of law as the party may ask, must appear by bill of exceptions." Norris v. Jackson, 9 Wall. (U. S.) 125, 128–29 (1869); Insurance Co. v. Sea, 21 Wall. (U. S.) 158, 160 (1874). *Cf.* Insurance Co. v. Folsom, 18 Wall. (U. S.) 237, 248–50 (1873). See Edward F. Treadwell, "Some Pitfalls in Federal Practice," 15 CAL. L. REV. 113.

[136] Where there is a conflict of evidence the Court will generally accept the concurrent findings of fact by the two lower courts. Luckenbach v. McCahan

cases,[137] in cases under the Sherman law, a needless and awkward duty is cast upon the Court in passing upon evidence, instead of requiring carefully framed findings of fact as a foundation for review.

With the minor exception relating to federal corporations, the efforts which culminated in the Act of 1925 did not seek to explore ways and means of shutting off at its sources litigation that eventually finds its way to the Supreme Court. Neither the Court nor Congress attempted to reconsider the wisdom of continuing the wide range of controversies to which the district courts are open. But any effort to relieve an overburdened federal judiciary may well, for instance, reëxamine the justification of the existing jurisdiction resting solely on diversity of citizenship. The plea for withdrawal from federal courts of litigation solely concerned with local matters has been reinforced by the vast increase of essentially federal litigation and the vigorous movement for state judicial reforms. A systematic revision of the Judicial Code should certainly consider the desirability of continuing the present sanction given to incorporation in foreign states merely for the purpose of gaining access to the federal courts.[138] Future federal judicial legislation will also have to scrutinize the justification of the load which the federal courts now carry in their administration, through receivership proceedings, of local public utilities and ordinary business corporations, particularly in view of the

---

Sugar Co., 248 U. S. 139, 145 (1918); Thomas v. Kansas City Southern Ry., 261 U. S. 481, 484 (1923); American Bank & Trust Co. v. Federal Reserve Bank, 262 U. S. 643, 645 (1923); Charleston Mining & Mfg. Co. v. United States, 273 U. S. 220 (1927). Cf. Pan American Petroleum & Transport Co. v. United States, 47 Sup. Ct. Rep. 416 (1927).

[137] Cf., e.g., the difficulties presented in determining the scope of the lower court's holding in McCardle v. Indianapolis Water Co., 272 U. S. 400 (1926). See Donald R. Richberg, " Value — By Judicial Fiat," 40 HARV. L. REV. 567, 581.

[138] " It is perfectly well known that innumerable corporations have been organized under the laws of States other than those in which they contemplate operating for no reason except to enjoy a choice of having their legal controversies determined as their interests would seem best subserved, either in the State or the Federal courts, while the scandal of 'tramp' corporations, the incorporators of which are residents of the State in which they do business under charters from distant States, sued out in order to escape the jurisdiction of the local courts, is a reproach to our judicial system." See Thomas J. Walsh, supra, 1922 VA. BAR. ASSN. REP. at 234; 62 CONG. REC. 8545, 8549.

tempting facility afforded by the doctrine of *Re Metropolitan Railway Receivership.*[139]

Heretofore the area of federal police legislation has been extended with little consideration of the consequences entailed on the effective functioning of the federal courts in enforcing such legislation. The huge number of prosecutions under the Volstead Act has sharply challenged attention to the recent preoccupation of the federal courts with misconduct of an essentially local nature, widely different in its practical incidence from the kind of transactions which in the past have invoked the federal criminal law. Particularly in the large cities are the federal courts diverted from disposition of cases uniquely federal in character to the prosecution of offenses which theretofore have been left for state action.[140] Liquor violations, illicit dealing in narcotics, thefts of interstate freight and automobiles, schemes to defraud essentially local in their operation but involving a minor use of the mails, these and like offenses have brought to the federal courts a volume of business which, to no small degree, endangers their capacity to dispose of distinctively federal litigation and to maintain the quality which has heretofore characterized the United States courts. The burden of vindicating the interests behind this body of recent litigation should, on the whole, be assumed by the states. At the least, the expedient of entrusting state courts with the enforcement of federal laws of this nature, like state enforcement of the Federal Employers' Liability Act, deserves to be thoroughly canvassed. [141] Another alternative is the withdrawal of the petty criminal business from the federal district courts by devising an appropriate method of summary procedure.[142] One thing is clear. The relief of the district courts from this avoidable litigation, which eventually has its reflex upon the Supreme Court's work, is an insistent problem of federal jurisdiction.[143]

---

[139] 208 U. S. 90 (1908). *Cf.* Pusey & Jones Co. *v.* Hanssen, 261 U. S. 491 (1923); Lion Bonding Co. *v.* Karatz, 262 U. S. 77 (1923).

[140] See Report of Special Committee on Congested Calendars, 1926 YEAR BOOK OF ASSOCIATION OF THE BAR OF THE CITY OF NEW YORK, 330; Report of the Committee on Jurisprudence and Law Reform, 51 AM. BAR ASSN. REP. 428.

[141] See Charles Warren, " Federal Criminal Laws and the State Courts," 38 HARV. L. REV. 545.

[142] See Felix Frankfurter and Thomas G. Corcoran, " Petty Federal Offenses and the Constitutional Guaranty of Trial by Jury," 39 HARV. L. REV. 917.

[143] A real burden has been taken from the district judges by the Act of June 8,

The Act of 1925 thus still leaves us with major problems of federal jurisdiction. They remain because the federation remains. Technical issues of jurisdiction will continue to reveal the interaction of political forces divided between States and Nation. The Act of 1925 concerned itself solely with furthering the efficiency of the Supreme Court and defining more accurately the exercise of federal appellate power. Drafted and sponsored as it was by the Court, it could not enter into the political field of apportioning judicial power between state and United States courts. How well the present judicial machinery has been adjusted, and how adequately its component parts have been freed for their proper spheres of action, only experience with the new Act can tell. It does, however, represent the considered attempt of the Supreme Court to secure through its own initiative an appellate jurisdiction which the Court deemed appropriate to its high functions.

1926, 44 STAT. 709, authorizing the designation of examiners to conduct the preliminary hearings upon petitions for naturalization, and limiting the judges' function to action upon the findings submitted by the examiners. See Report of the Committee on Jurisprudence and Law Reform, 51 AM. BAR ASSN. REP. 428; HOUSE REPORT, No. 1328, SEN. REP., No. 837, 69th Cong., 1st Sess.

TABLE I

CASES DISPOSED OF BY THE SUPREME COURT OF THE UNITED STATES
1916–1925

OBLIGATORY JURISDICTION

TERM	STATE COURTS	CIRCUIT COURTS OF APPEALS	DISTRICT COURTS	COURT OF CLAIMS	COURT OF APPEALS OF DISTRICT OF COLUMBIA	SUPREME COURT OF PHILIPPINE ISLANDS	DISTRICT COURT OF PORTO RICO	SUPREME COURT OF PORTO RICO	DISTRICT COURT OF ALASKA	SUPREME COURT OF HAWAII	TOTALS
1916	157	29	80	5	4	2	1	6		1	285
1917	150	48	78	10	6	4	1	1			298
1918	132	48	73	23	3	7					286
1919	101	25	70	26	7						229
1920	75	43	73	30	12				1		234
1921	105	38	94	21	18	2			1		279
1922	85	65	104	34	9		1				298
1923	76	44	91	18	9						238
1924	96	30	100	34	11						271
1925	75	41	78	52	27						273
Total	1052	411	841	253	106	15	3	7	2	1	2691

DISCRETIONARY JURISDICTION

TERM	STATE COURTS CERTIORARI	CIRCUIT COURTS OF APPEALS — CERTIORARI	CIRCUIT COURTS OF APPEALS — CERTIFICATE	COURT OF APPEALS OF D.C. — CERTIORARI	COURT OF APPEALS OF D.C. — CERTIFICATE	COURT OF CUSTOMS APPEALS CERTIORARI	SUPREME COURT OF PHILIPPINE ISLANDS CERTIORARI	COURT OF CLAIMS CERTIORARI	TOTALS
1916		33	3	2		14			52
1917		41	6	2	1				50
1918	13	29	9	1		4			56
1919	12	38	2	2			1		55
1920	22	28	6	7	2	1			66
1921	14	24	7	1		1	3		50
1922	18	46	5				1		70
1923	18	54	5		1		1		79
1924	20	42	10	1	4	1			78
1925	25	34	9	2			3	1	74
Total	142	369	62	18	8	21	9	1	630

PETITIONS FOR CERTIORARI

TERM	GRANTED	DENIED	POSTPONED	DISMISSED	PENDING	WITHDRAWN	TOTALS
1916	53	217					270
1917	49	225	6	1			281
1918	55	267	11		3		336
1919	46	246	11				303
1920	50	250	7				307
1921	58	267	7	9	1		342
1922	85	323	12	7	2		429
1923	72	293	22	5		14	406
1924	68	364	11	8	3	2	456
1925	100	428	3	8			539
Total	636	2880	90	38	9	16	3669

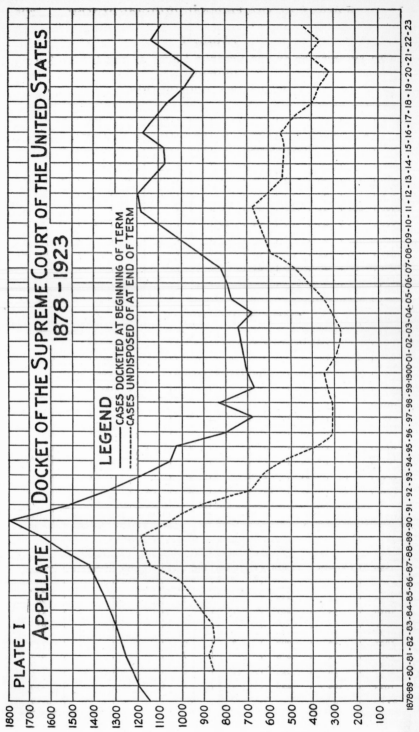

PLATE I

APPELLATE DOCKET OF THE SUPREME COURT OF THE UNITED STATES
1878 – 1923

LEGEND
———— CASES DOCKETED AT BEGINNING OF TERM
------------ CASES UNDISPOSED OF AT END OF TERM

1800
1700
1600
1500
1400
1300
1200
1100
1000
900
800
700
600
500
400
300
200
100

1878·79·80·81·82·83·84·85·86·87·88·89·90·91·92·93·94·95·96·97·98·99·1900·01·02·03·04·05·06·07·08·09·10·11·12·13·14·15·16·17·18·19·20·21·22·23

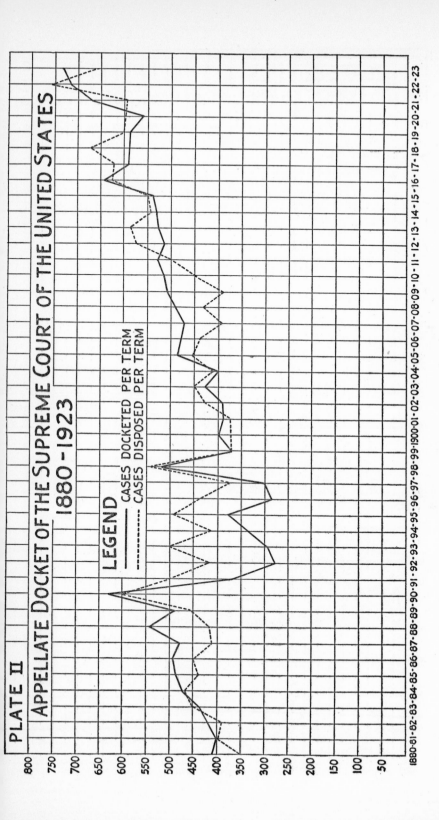

PLATE II

APPELLATE DOCKET OF THE SUPREME COURT OF THE UNITED STATES
1880 - 1923

LEGEND

CASES DOCKETED PER TERM
CASES DISPOSED PER TERM

800 750 700 650 600 550 500 450 400 350 300 250 200 150 100 50

1880·81·82·83·84·85·86·87·88·89·90·91·92·93·94·95·96·97·98·99·1900·01·02·03·04·05·06·07·08·09·10·11·12·13·14·15·16·17·18·19·20·21·22·23

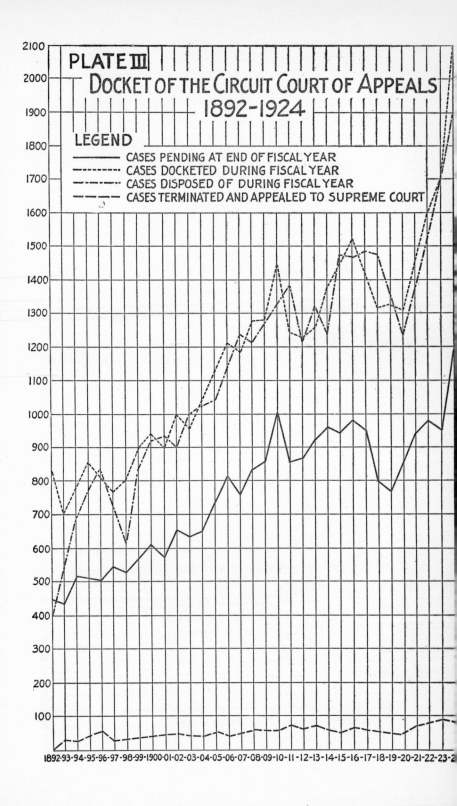

PLATE III

DOCKET OF THE CIRCUIT COURT OF APPEALS
1892-1924

LEGEND
——————— CASES PENDING AT END OF FISCAL YEAR
--------- CASES DOCKETED DURING FISCAL YEAR
—·—·—·— CASES DISPOSED OF DURING FISCAL YEAR
— — — — CASES TERMINATED AND APPEALED TO SUPREME COURT

1892·93·94·95·96·97·98·99·1900·01·02·03·04·05·06·07·08·09·10·11·12·13·14·15·16·17·18·19·20·21·22·23·2

CHAPTER VIII
THE FUTURE
OF
SUPREME COURT LITIGATION

I

FOR a hundred years the range of Supreme Court litigation remained practically unchanged. The same types of cases which in 1789 the framers of the Judiciary Act had designated for review by the Supreme Court continued to come before it till 1891. Despite the vast transformation of thirteen seaboard colonies into a great nation, with all that this implied in the growth of judicial business and the emergence of new controversies of vast proportions, a heavy stream of petty litigation reached the Supreme Court. We have reviewed the long struggle that preceded relief for the Court from business inappropriate to its true functions. The Act of 1891 was only the beginning of a steady curtailment of cases originally assigned to the Court. With increase rather than abatement in the sources of federal litigation, a further drastic restriction of cases that could go to the Supreme Court was again made in 1916. Finally, less than ten years later further barriers had to be established against access to the Court. Increase in the Court's business has always heretofore been met with decrease in its jurisdiction. But in future, when the Court's business expands, relief can hardly come from further contraction of the right to resort to the Court.

The Act of 1925 has cut the Supreme Court's jurisdiction to the bone. A still wider use of *certiorari* has been suggested, whereby all cases from the state courts and the circuit courts of appeals could be reviewed only at the Supreme Court's discretion.[1] Such a step is highly improbable. The analysis of the Act of 1925 has shown that the limited class of cases which can now go to Washington as of right are cases which concern issues of far-reaching public importance. Their disposition is precisely the

---

[1] See, *e.g.*, the suggestions of Taft, C. J., in 66 CONG. REC. 2920–22.

raison d'être of the Supreme Court. That the review of such issues should be made to depend on grace and not on right is not within the limits of likely Congressional action. An even less probable device for relieving the Supreme Court is the establishment of another appellate tribunal intermediate between the Supreme Court and the circuit courts of appeals, or an enlargement of the personnel of the Supreme Court to sit in banc or in divisions. These proposals have been amply canvassed in the past and found wanting. Relief must be sought elsewhere.

The opinion has been ventured that a reëxamination of the present scope of federal litigation is called for with a view to shutting off at its sources business that eventually reaches the Supreme Court. This involves relinquishing of federal concern over conduct more appropriately left to state action as well as providing for trial in state courts of cases now exclusively entrusted to United States courts. The directions which such restrictions upon jurisdiction may profitably take have been indicated in our last chapter. Other aids to the effective dispatch of the business of the Supreme Court, looking toward prevention as well as relief of its future congestion, depend on a more critical realization of the demands which Supreme Court litigation makes upon the legal profession. A better understanding is needed of the intrinsic character of the issues involved in Supreme Court cases and of the materials entering into their decision, a bar better equipped to deal with these issues, as the necessary collaborator with the Court, and a better technique for formulating and resolving the issues.

We have seen that, broadly speaking, the Supreme Court is now confined in its adjudications to questions of constitutionality and like problems of essentially national importance. In large measure, the cases center about the interplay of government and economic enterprise. It was not always thus. But the abstract categories of jurisdiction lack vividness of meaning unless translated into the concrete terms of the specific issues upon which the cases turn. Only a detailed analysis of the nature of the litigation now engaging the attention of the Court, as compared with a similar analysis of the work of the Court fifty and one hundred years ago, can give an adequate conception of the stuff of present-day controversies, and of the changes in the subject-matter of litigation at different stages in the Court's history.

Table I shows [2] how striking is the mere increase in the volume of business before the Supreme Court. In 1825 circuit riding was a feasible duty to impose upon Justices who rendered but 26 opinions during the year; of these almost half were in suits between individuals involving applications of recognized principles of the common law. That three cases out of 26 arose out of the slave trade is not an insignificant index of the Supreme Court's concern a hundred years ago. Notable are the changes wrought in the volume as well as in the variety of litigation fifty years later. An increase from 26 opinions to 193 brought with it those far-reaching modifications in the activities of the Court which ended circuit riding and culminated in the establishment of the circuit courts of appeals. But the issues in litigation remained predominantly common law topics and federal specialties like admiralty, bankruptcy, patents, claims against the government and legislation concerning the public domain. These absorbed 130 cases out of a total of 193 in the 1875 Term. Technical questions of statutory construction and of federal jurisdiction, reflecting vast increase in legislative activity, account for 46 more cases. Thus, only 17 cases, less than ten per cent of the total dispositions of the term, dealt with questions of constitutionality, taxation, and other aspects of public law.

For the next fifty years the Court's business is comparable in volume to that of 1875, but the complexion of the litigation progressively changes. The content of the reports for the 1925 Term is radically different from the reports for the 1875 Term. The reader finds himself in a different world of ideas as he turns from 91 U. S. and 92 U. S. to 269 U. S., 270 U. S. and 271 U. S. Nearly half of the opinions relate to control of economic enterprise, taxa-

---

[2] This table is based on cases disposed of by written opinions. Decisions *per curiam*, of which there were 83 during the 1925 Term, are excluded; so also decisions granting or denying petitions for *certiorari*. Furthermore, the classification proceeds on the basis of opinions and not cases. Thus, one opinion may dispose of several cases involving the same issues. Such an analysis as is here attempted must necessarily make its own classifications. One opinion may often deal with a variety of issues; but for our purpose the issue that seems to be the most significant determined the character of the case. The table purports only to show trends, rather than to furnish complete statistics of the content of the Court's business.

TABLE I

COMPARATIVE ANALYSIS OF SUPREME COURT BUSINESS
1825, 1875, 1925

	1825 Term	1875 Term	1925 Term
Admiralty..	2	5	8
Anti-trust Legislation	0	0	2
Bankruptcy.....................................	0	13	9
Bill of Rights (other than Due Process)...........	0	2	3
Commerce Clause			
1. Constitutionality of Federal Regulation.......	0	0	2
2. Constitutionality of State Regulation.........	0	2	2
3. Construction of Federal Legislation..........	0	0	29
Common Law Topics............................	10	81	11
Construction of Miscellaneous Statutes			
1. Federal..................................	2	14	15
2. State...................................	2	2	0
Due Process			
1. Regulation of Economic Enterprise...........	0	0	20
2. Relating to Procedure......................	0	2	3
Impairment of Contract.........................	0	1	4
Indians..	0	0	7
International Law, War and Peace................	2	5	6
Jurisdiction, Practice and Procedure			
1. Supreme Court............................	0	19	9
2. Inferior Courts............................	4	11	20
Land Legislation................................	0	11	3
Patents and Trademarks.........................	1	8	4
Slave Trade....................................	3	0	0
Suits against Government in Contract.............	0	12	17
Suits by States.................................	0	0	8
Taxation			
1. Federal..................................	0	2	19
2. State...................................	0	3	8
Totals.................................	26	193	209

tion, and interstate adjustments.   Common law controversies are
in process of atrophy.   Of these there were 81 in the 1875 Term
and only 11 in the 1925 Term — a shrinkage from 43 per cent to
5 per cent.   Of the federal specialties there were 48 cases during
the 1925 Term.   But the Judiciary Act of 1925 was passed to
relieve the Court from these sources of jurisdiction.   Thus, during
the 1925 Term, 17 of the cases which have been classified under
federal specialties were contract claims against the government
which no longer come to the Supreme Court save through the rare
exercise of *certiorari*.   So also, resort to the Supreme Court in the
classes of cases involving ordinary common law or statutory issues
which had to be considered in the 1925 Term will hereafter be
shut off by making decisions in the circuit courts of appeals final.
Consequently, analysis of the litigation for the 1925 Term gives
a subnormal picture of the color and complexion of the future
business of the Court.   Even during the 1926 Term the Court disposed of litigation that arose prior to the Act of 1925 and to which
its terms were not applicable.   Not until the 1927 Term will the
nature of the Court's business reflect the full force of that Act.
In view of the trend of the litigation before the Court and the aims
of the legislation framed by the Court itself to control the character of its business, inevitably the future statistics of the Court's
work will show a continuing growth in the volume of business
dealing with control over economic enterprise and kindred public
controversies, and a still more striking decrease in ordinary private litigation.

The nature of contemporary Supreme Court litigation is not
only in marked contrast with that which was before the Court in
earlier periods; it differs essentially from the stuff of issues which
are the preoccupation of the supreme courts of the states.   The
accompanying tables give an analysis of the subject matter of reported decisions, during 1925, of New York, Wisconsin and Colorado, chosen as representative of the variety and volume of state
litigation.   The judgments of the House of Lords and the Privy
Council, during 1925, give additional bases for comparison.[3]   The

---

[3] See Tables II and III.   The terms of court differ markedly in different states,
and in turn differ from the period of time, the judicial year 1925–26, embraced by
the 1925 Term of the Supreme Court.   Consequently, the analysis in these tables
covers the cases disposed of by state courts during the year 1925, rather than
during their specific terms of court.   The tables also proceed on the basis of opinions

TABLE II

COMPARATIVE ANALYSIS OF BUSINESS OF SELECTED STATE
AND BRITISH COURTS

1925

	New York	Wisconsin	Colorado	House of Lords	Privy Council
Administrative Law..........	10	3	5	1	0
Admiralty..................	0	0	0	1	0
Bankruptcy.................	0	0	0	1	0
Commercial Arbitration......	6	1	0	0	0
Common Law Topics					
1. Agency................	4	1	6	0	0
2. Bills and Notes........	8	5	6	0	0
3. Contract and Sale......	69	23	34	5	1
4. Corporations and Partnerships............	14	7	9	2	0
5. Criminal Law..........	35	7	13	0	0
6. Damages..............	2	1	2	0	1
7. Domestic Relations.....	9	9	6	2	0
8. Evidence..............	6	13	20	0	0
9. Insurance..............	16	5	5	2	1
10. Municipal Corporations.	8	11	6	0	1
11. Property..............	33	22	31	2 *	1
12. Quasi-Contract.........	1	3	0	0	0
13. Suretyship.............	2	3	2	0	0
14. Torts.................	71	51	15	3	1
15. Trusts................	8	4	3	0	0
16. Water Rights..........	3	0	6	0	0
17. Wills and Administration	14	15	6	0	0
Constitutional Questions......	9	8	5	0	5
Disbarment.................	2	1	0	0	0
International Law, War and Peace	3	0	0	0	0
Jurisdiction.................	3	1	6	0	0
Practice, Pleading and Procedure	81	24	56	0	1
Public Utilities..............	5	10	1	0	0
Search and Seizure...........	0	6	1	0	0
Statutory Construction.......	14	23	6	3	6
Taxation...................	23	10	8	7	0
Workmen's Compensation.....	21	21	13	1	1
Totals..............	480	288	271	30	19

* This figure embraces one case involving a claim to peerage.

TABLE III

COMPARATIVE ANALYSIS ON PERCENTAGE BASIS OF BUSINESS
OF SELECTED STATE AND BRITISH COURTS

1925

	New York	Wisconsin	Colorado	House of Lords	Privy Council
	%	%	%	%	%
Administrative Law.........	2.5	1.0	1.8	3.3	0
Admiralty..................	0	0	0	3.3	0
Bankruptcy................	0	0	0	3.3	0
Commercial Arbitration.......	1.3	.3	0	0	0
Common Law Topics					
1. Agency...............	.8	.3	2.2	0	0
2. Bills and Notes........	1.7	1.7	2.2	0	0
3. Contract and Sale......	14.4	8.0	12.5	16.7	5.3
4. Corporations and Part- nerships.............	2.9	2.4	3.4	6.7	0
5. Criminal Law.........	7.3	2.4	4.8	0	0
6. Damages.............	.4	.3	.7	0	5.3
7. Domestic Relations.....	1.9	3.1	2.2	6.7	0
8. Evidence.............	1.3	4.5	7.4	0	0
9. Insurance............	3.3	1.7	1.8	6.7	5.3
10. Municipal Corporations.	1.7	3.8	2.2	0	5.3
11. Property.............	6.9	7.6	11.4	6.7	5.3
12. Quasi-Contract........	.2	1.0	0	0	0
13. Suretyship............	.4	1.0	.7	0	0
14. Torts................	14.8	17.7	5.5	10.0	5.3
15. Trusts...............	1.7	1.4	1.1	0	0
16. Water Rights.........	.6	0	2.2	0	0
17. Wills and Administration	2.9	5.2	2.2	0	0
Constitutional Questions......	1.9	2.8	1.8	0	26.3
Disbarment.................	.4	.3	0	0	0
International Law...........	.6	0	0	0	0
Jurisdiction................	.6	.3	2.2	0	0
Practice, Pleading and Procedure	16.9	8.3	20.7	0	5.3
Public Utilities..............	1.0	3.5	.4	0	0
Search and Seizure...........	0	2.1	.4	0	0
Statutory Construction.......	2.9	8.0	2.2	10.0	31.4
Taxation...................	4.8	3.5	3.0	23.3	0
Workmen's Compensation.....	4.4	7.3	4.8	3.3	5.3

difference between the content of Supreme Court cases and those in the state courts and the House of Lords is striking. As against 34 cases out of 209 primarily involving constitutionality before the Supreme Court during the 1925 Term, the New York Court of Appeals was confronted with such issues in only 9 cases out of 480; the Wisconsin Supreme Court in 8 cases out of 288; and the Colorado Supreme Court in 5 cases out of 271. Moreover, constitutionality in state cases frequently concerns not weighty questions of policy, but the observance of technical formalities required by state constitutions. Equally startling is the recurrence of familiar common law issues before the state courts and the House of Lords, compared with their slight and diminishing appearance before the Supreme Court. Thus, as against 5.4 per cent of common law litigation at the 1925 Term of the Supreme Court,[4] common law causes in New York, Wisconsin, Colorado

---

and not cases, and an opinion disposing of more than one case but the same issues is counted as one. Cases are classified under their dominant issues. For example, a criminal appeal may concern itself mainly with the correctness of the trial court's rulings on evidence rather than questions of substantive criminal law. The New York Court of Appeals is accustomed to dispose of many cases by memoranda decisions. Where a memorandum sufficiently discloses the character of the case, it has been included in the analysis. It must also be remembered that the Privy Council disposes of numerous appeals without rendering any opinion; these are omitted from the analysis of its business. Thus, these tables also purport merely to reveal trends; they are not inclusive statistics of the total business of the various courts.

[4] The following table presents an analysis of the common law litigation before the Supreme Court of the United States:

	1825 Term	1875 Term	1925 Term
Bills and Notes	1	4	1
Conflicts	2	0	0
Contracts	1	12	0
Corporations	0	11	1
Damages	0	3	0
Domestic Relations	0	1	0
Equity	1	6	4
Evidence	0	5	0
Insurance	1	4	1
Municipal Corporations	0	15	0
Pleading, Practice and Procedure	2	4	1
Property	2	10	2
Suretyship	0	1	0
Torts	0	1	0
Trusts	0	3	1
Wills and Administration	0	1	0
Totals	10	81	11
Percentage of total business of the Court	38%	43%	5%

and the House of Lords, represented, respectively, 63.2 per cent, 62.3 per cent, 62.5 per cent and 53.5 per cent of the reported business of the various courts. This vivid difference between Supreme Court adjudications and those comprising the staple business of other courts receives added color from an analysis of the causes that came before the Privy Council. They are, to be sure, few in number. But such as they are, they reflect the fact that the Privy Council performs a function for the British Commonwealth of Nations comparable to the part played in our federal scheme by the Supreme Court.[5] The Privy Council is the legal mechanism for adjusting differences within the dominions and the dependencies, and between the local parliaments and Westminster.[6] Out of 19 cases that came before the Privy Council in 1925, 5 turned on what Americans call constitutionality, of which one at least stirred issues of great moment in the relations of Canada to Great Britain.[7]

2

The Supreme Court has ceased to be a common law court. What then are the characteristics of its business? It ought to be a needless platitude to say that there are many kinds of "law" as administered by the courts, but unfortunately it is not. The fact that the single term "law" should cover the rule against perpetuities as well as the unconstitutionality of ticket-scalping legislation is a prolific source of confusion. Here, unlike on the Continent, the common speech of lawyers does not indicate the differences in the content of the material, the nature of the interests, and the technique of adjudication between the two types of cases represented by the broad classification of "private law" and "public law." Rigorous practical consequences in the exercise of judicial power depend upon these differences in the types of litigation presented to courts. The issues which normally come before

---

[5] Viscount Haldane, "The Work for the Empire of the Judicial Committee of the Privy Council," 1 CAMB. L. J. 143.

[6] Berriedale Keith, "The Privy Council and the Canadian Constitution," 7 J. COMP. LEG. (3rd series) 61. And see Berriedale Keith, "The Imperial Conference, 1926," 9 *ibid.* 68.

[7] Toronto Elec. Commissioners *v.* Snider, [1925] A. C. 396; and see debate thereon in the Canadian Parliament, 60 Hansard (Can. 1925) 300, 302 *et seq.* See also leader in London *Times* ("A Privy Council Decision") for Jan. 22, 1925, and Berriedale Keith, *supra,* 7 J. COMP. LEG. (3rd series) 61.

the Supreme Court are not the ordinary legal questions in the multitudinous lawsuits of *Smith* v. *Jones* before other courts. The Supreme Court is the final authority in adjusting the relationships of the individual to the separate states, of the individual to the United States, of the forty-eight states to one another, and of the states to the United States. It mediates between the individual and government; it marks the boundaries between state and national action.

Constitutional interpretation is most frequently invoked by the broad and undefined clauses of the Constitution. Their scope of application is relatively unrestricted, and the room for play of individual judgment as to policy correspondingly broad. A few simple terms like " liberty " and " property," phrases like " regulate Commerce . . . among the several States " and " without due process of law " are invoked in judgment upon the engulfing mass of economic, social and industrial facts. Phrases like " due process of law," as Judge Hough reminded us, are of " convenient vagueness." [8] Their content is derived from without, not revealed within the Constitution. The power of states to enact legislation restricting an owner's use of natural resources,[9] providing a living wage for women workers,[10] limiting the rents chargeable by landlords,[11] fixing standard weights for bread,[12] prohibiting the use of shoddy in comfortables,[13] prescribing building zones,[14] requiring the sterilization of mental defectives,[15] — these powers hinge on the Court's reading of the due process clause. The Stockyards Act,[16] the Grain Futures Act,[17] the West Virginia Natural Gas Act,[18] the Recapture Clause of the Transportation Act,[19] the First

---

[8] Charles M. Hough, " Due Process of Law — Today," 32 HARV. L. REV. 218.

[9] *Cf.* Walls *v.* Midland Carbon Co., 254 U. S. 300 (1920); West *v.* Kansas Natural Gas Co., 221 U. S. 229 (1911); New York *ex rel.* Silz *v.* Hesterberg, 211 U. S. 31 (1908); Geer *v.* Connecticut, 161 U. S. 519 (1896).

[10] Adkins *v.* Children's Hospital, 261 U. S. 525 (1923).

[11] Block *v.* Hirsh, 256 U. S. 135 (1921); Marcus Brown Holding Co. *v.* Feldman, 256 U. S. 170 (1921). *Cf.* Chastleton Corp. *v.* Sinclair, 264 U. S. 543 (1924).

[12] Jay Burns Baking Co. *v.* Bryan, 264 U. S. 504 (1924).

[13] Weaver *v.* Palmer Bros. Co., 270 U. S. 402 (1926).

[14] Village of Euclid *v.* Amber Realty Co., 272 U. S. 365 (1926).

[15] Buck *v.* Bell, 47 Sup. Ct. Rep. 584 (1927).

[16] Stafford *v.* Wallace, 258 U. S. 495 (1922).

[17] Chicago Board of Trade *v.* Olsen, 262 U. S. 1 (1923). *Cf.* Hill *v.* Wallace, 259 U. S. 44 (1922).   [18] Pennsylvania *v.* West Virginia, 262 U. S. 553 (1923).

[19] Dayton-Goose Creek Ry. *v.* United States, 263 U. S. 456 (1924).

Child Labor Law,[20] all involved "interpretation" of the commerce clause; but the fate of these laws depended on adequate information before the Court, on the economic and industrial data which underlay this legislation, and judgment on these facts by the Court. Again, the *Steel Trust* case,[21] the *Shoe Machinery* case,[22] the *Duplex* case,[23] the *Bedford Cut Stone* case,[24] all involved "interpretation" of the Anti-Trust Acts. But the interpretation of this legislation was decided by the facts of industrial life as seen by the Court. The conflicting opinions of the Justices in the recent series of cases involving the activities of trade associations [25] are not due to any differences in their reading of the Sherman Law *in vacuo*. The differences are attributable to the economic data which they deemed relevant to their judgment and the use which they made of them. What constitutes a "spur track," [26] when public convenience justifies a railroad extension or abandonment,[27] under what conditions one railroad must permit use of its facilities by a rival,[28] how far the requirement of a state for the abolition of grade-crossings depends on approval by the Interstate Commerce Commission,[29] these and like questions cannot be answered by the most alert reading of the Transportation Act. Their solution implies a wide knowledge of railroad economics, of railroad practices and the history of transportation, as well as a political philosophy concerning the respective rôles of national control and state authority.[30]

---

[20] Hammer *v.* Dagenhart, 247 U. S. 251 (1918). *Cf.* Child Labor Tax Case, 259 U. S. 20 (1922).

[21] United States *v.* United States Steel Corp., 251 U. S. 417 (1920).

[22] United States *v.* United Shoe Machinery Co., 247 U. S. 32 (1918).

[23] Duplex Printing Press Co. *v.* Deering, 254 U. S. 443 (1921).

[24] Bedford Cut Stone Co. *v.* Journeymen Stone Cutters' Ass'n, 47 Sup. Ct. Rep. 522 (1927).

[25] *Cf.* American Column & Lumber Co. *v.* United States, 257 U. S. 377 (1921); United States *v.* American Linseed Oil Co., 262 U. S. 371 (1923); Maple Flooring Manufacturers Ass'n *v.* United States, 268 U. S. 563 (1925); Cement Manufacturers Protective Ass'n *v.* United States, 268 U. S. 588 (1925); United States *v.* Trenton Potteries Co., 47 Sup. Ct. Rep. 377 (1927).

[26] Texas & Pacific Ry. *v.* Gulf, C. & S. F. Ry., 270 U. S. 266 (1926).

[27] Colorado *v.* United States, 271 U. S. 153 (1926).

[28] *Cf.* Alabama & Vicksburg Ry. *v.* Jackson & Eastern Ry., 271 U. S. 244 (1926); Chicago, I. & L. Ry. *v.* United States, 270 U. S. 287 (1926).

[29] Erie R. R. *v.* Board of Pub. Util. Commissioners, 254 U. S. 394 (1921), in connection with Railroad Commission *v.* Southern Pacific Co., 264 U. S. 331, 341 (1924).

[30] *Cf.* Napier *v.* Atlantic Coast Line R. R., 272 U. S. 605 (1926). See Bran-

These are tremendous and delicate problems. But the words
of the Constitution on which their solution is based are so unrestrained by their intrinsic meaning, or by their history, or by
tradition, or by prior decisions, that they leave the individual
Justice free, if indeed they do not compel him, to gather meaning
not from reading the Constitution but from reading life. It is
most revealing that members of the Court are frequently admonished by their associates not to read their economic and social
views into the neutral language of the Constitution.[31] But the
process of constitutional interpretation compels the translation of
policy into judgment, and the controlling conceptions of the Justices are their " idealized political picture " of the existing social
order.[32] Only the conscious recognition of the nature of this exercise of the judicial process will protect policy from being narrowly
construed as the reflex of discredited assumptions or the abstract
formulation of unconscious bias.

3

That its business is of a different order from the common run
of litigation has been recognized by the Court in the aids which it
has called to its assistance, in the mode of arguments which it

---

deis, J., dissenting in New York Cent. R. R. *v.* Winfield, 244 U. S. 147, 154 (1917);
McReynolds, J., dissenting in George W. Bush & Sons Co. *v.* Maloy, 267 U. S.
317, 325 (1925); McReynolds and Sutherland, JJ., dissenting in Oregon-Washington
R. R. & Nav. Co. *v.* Washington, 270 U. S. 87, 103 (1926).

[31] " The Fourteenth Amendment does not enact Mr. Herbert Spencer's Social
Statics." Holmes, J., dissenting in Lochner *v.* New York, 198 U. S. 45, 75 (1905).
" Under the guise of interpreting the Constitution we must take care that we do
not import into the discussion our own personal views of what would be wise, just
and fitting rules of government to be adopted by a free people and confound them
with constitutional limitations." Moody, J., in Twining *v.* New Jersey, 211 U. S.
78, 106–07 (1908). " But it is not the function of this Court to hold congressional
acts invalid simply because they are passed to carry out economic views which the
Court believes to be unwise or unsound." Taft, C. J., dissenting in Adkins *v.*
Children's Hospital, 261 U. S. 525, 562 (1923). " If the Fourteenth Amendment
were now before us for the first time I should think that it ought to be construed
more narrowly than it has been construed in the past. But even now it seems to
me not too late to urge that in dealing with state legislation upon matters of substantive law we should avoid with great caution attempts to substitute our judgment for that of the body whose business it is in the first place, with regard to
questions of domestic policy that fairly are open to debate." Holmes, J., dissenting in Schlesinger *v.* Wisconsin, 270 U. S. 230, 241 (1926).

[32] See Roscoe Pound, " The Theory of Judicial Decision," 36 Harv. L. Rev.
641, 651 *et seq.*

entertains, and in the extra-legal authorities upon which it relies. Thus, in the *Employers' Liability Cases*,[33] the litigation was in form between Damselle Howard and the Illinois Central Railroad Company to vindicate the private right of Damselle Howard against her husband's employer for the loss of his life. In essence, however, the right of Congress to legislate about the agents and instruments of interstate commerce was at stake, as well as the appropriate area of authority in the distribution of political power between the Federal Government and the states. The Court, therefore, did not rely for the elucidation of these governmental issues upon the private litigants, but heard the United States " through the Attorney General as a friend of the court."[34] A still more striking recognition by the Court that at the heart of these constitutional problems is usually a " politico-legal ques-tion "[35] is furnished by the recent *Myers* case.[36] In form, this was a suit by a postmaster for the recovery of his back salary. In fact, the real issue was the historic contest between President and Congress for control over the tenure of federal officeholders. Here was a problem of statecraft of the first magnitude, and the Court treated it as such. As soon as the original argument dis-closed the fact that the real issue was a challenge to the Senate's power, the case was set down for re-argument with an invitation by the Court to the Senate to present its position at the bar of the Court.[37] In ordinary controversies, where individual interests

---

[33] 207 U. S. 463 (1908).

[34] *Ibid.* at 490. In the Second Employers' Liability Cases, 223 U. S. 1 (1912), where the litigation was again in form between private litigants the Attorney General, by leave of Court, again appeared as *amicus curiae* to represent the inter-est of the United States. In *Ex parte* Grossman, 267 U. S. 87, 108 (1925), involv-ing the power of the President to pardon for criminal contempt, in form a petition for *habeas corpus* to release the petitioner from confinement despite the pardon, " Special counsel, employed by the Department of Justice, appear for the respond-ent to uphold the legality of the detention. The Attorney General of the United States, as *amicus curiae,* maintains the validity and effectiveness of the President's action. The petitioner, by his counsel, urges his discharge from imprisonment."

[35] Carpenter, J., in United States *v.* Grossman, 1 F. (2d) 941, 952 (N. D. Ill. 1924). See Address of Lawrence Maxwell, Jr., 1921 PROC. KY. BAR ASSN. 150, 168.

[36] Myers *v.* United States, 272 U. S. 52 (1926).

[37] " Apparently, after some review of the arguments in the proceeding, the court became convinced that the rights and prerogatives of the Senate were so deeply involved that the legislative department should be given the right of ap-pearance. Accordingly, a rehearing was ordered and the matter was brought to the attention of Senator Albert B. Cummins, as President of the Senate, who conferred

are dominantly at stake, courts rely upon counsel for the parties in interest. Decisions are influenced not inconsiderably by those chances which determine the selection of counsel. In the *Myers* case, by calling for argument on behalf of the Senate, the Supreme Court gave weighty evidence of its belief that a practice which works well enough in everyday litigation is inadequate and likely to be disastrous when great issues of state are before the Court.[38]

Since the Court's business is rooted in judgment on materials outside of technical law books, the technique for assuring itself an adequate knowledge and understanding of such data assumes a primary rôle in the Court's work. With an empiricism characteristic of Anglo-American lawyers, methods for adjudication in these cases have not been systematically pursued.[39] Constitutional problems are still presented haphazardly, and too much in the atmosphere and with the attitude of conventional appellate arguments. But consciousness of the need for a specialized technique has definitely emerged. In various forms the Court has indicated that these public causes call for difference in treatment by counsel and court from what is appropriate to mere private litigation.

At least five modes of proof have been relied on for the facts relevant to the characteristic business of the Court. The duty of ascertaining the need for corrective legislation is the essential function of legislatures. Deference to the legislative judgment

---

with Chairman George S. Graham, Pennsylvania, of the House Judiciary Committee, with a view to arranging Congressional representation." See *N. Y. Times,* Feb. 3, 1925. On Feb. 2, 1925, however, the Chief Justice announced that Senator George Wharton Pepper of Pennsylvania had been invited to appear as a friend of the Court to present upon re-argument the right of Congress to impose limitations upon the executive's power of removal. *Ibid.*

[38] " Before closing this opinion, we wish to express the obligation of the Court to Mr. Pepper for his able brief and argument as a friend of the Court. Undertaken at our request, our obligation is none the less if we find ourselves obliged to take a view adverse to his. The strong presentation of arguments against the conclusion of the Court is of the utmost value in enabling the Court to satisfy itself that it has fully considered all that can be said." Taft, C. J., in Myers *v.* United States, 272 U. S. at 176–77.

[39] See Roscoe Pound, " Legislation as a Social Function," 7 PUB. AM. SOCIOL. SOC. 148, 161; Felix Frankfurter, " Hours of Labor and Realism in Constitutional Law," 29 HARV. L. REV. 353, 364–73; Henry W. Biklé, " Judicial Determination of Questions of Fact Affecting the Constitutional Validity of Legislative Action," 38 HARV. L. REV. 6.

that circumstances exist warranting a change in the policy of law, is a postulate of all judicial review when the constitutionality of legislation is assailed.[40] But the mere fact that the legislature has spoken, provided that its opinion is not " manifestly absurd," [41] ought to, and sometimes does, save legislation.[42] Again, with a view to advising the Court, modern legislation shows some striking illustrations of recitals embodying the considerations for its enactment. These have been relied upon by the Court in upholding laws.[43] More frequently, however, courts support legislative policy by drawing on information based on common knowledge or in books of reference. Courts use such material on their own initiative on the theory of " judicial notice." [44] But this is a tenuous basis for informing the judicial mind. It places an undue burden of independent investigation on judges who are limited in

---

[40] " The judicial function therefore with respect to the invalidation of a legislative act does not consist merely in comparing the determination evinced by such act with that reached by the court and the substitution of the latter for the former whenever they happen to differ. On the contrary, the ultimate judicial question is not whether the court construes the constitution as permitting the act, but whether the constitution permits the court to disregard the act; a question that is not to be conclusively tested by the court's judgment as to the constitutionality of the act, but by its conclusion as to what judgment was permissible to that department of the government to which the constitution has committed the duty of making such judgment." Garrison, J., in Wilson v. McGuinness, 78 N. J. L. 346, 373, 75 Atl. 455, 462 (1910). See James B. Thayer, " The Origin and Scope of the American Doctrine of Constitutional Law," 7 HARV. L. REV. 129, reprinted in LEGAL ESSAYS, 1.

[41] See Holmes, J., dissenting in Weaver v. Palmer Bros. Co., 270 U. S. 402, 415 (1926).

[42] " I suppose that this act was passed because the operatives, or some of them, thought that they were often cheated out of a part of their wages under a false pretence that the work done by them was imperfect, and persuaded the Legislature that their view was true. If their view was true, I cannot doubt that the Legislature had the right to deprive the employers of an honest tool which they were using for a dishonest purpose, and I cannot pronounce the legislation void, as based on a false assumption, since I know nothing about the matter one way or the other." Holmes, J., dissenting in Commonwealth v. Perry, 155 Mass. 117, 124, 28 N. E. 1126, 1127 (1891). See, e.g., Hadacheck v. Sebastian, 239 U. S. 394, 413 (1915), and State of Ohio v. Deckebach, 47 Sup. Ct. Rep. 630 (1927).

[43] See Stafford v. Wallace, 258 U. S. 495, 520 (1922); Dayton-Goose Creek Ry. v. United States, 263 U. S. 456, 476 (1924); Buck v. Bell, 47 Sup. Ct. Rep. 584 (1927). The Court has also on occasion had resort to the report of legislative committees in charge of a measure to discover its purposes. E.g., James Everard's Breweries v. Day, 265 U. S. 545, 561 (1924); Omaechevarria v. Idaho, 246 U. S. 343 (1918).

[44] Jacobson v. Massachusetts, 197 U. S. 11 (1905). See, e.g., Brandeis, J., dissenting in Jay Burns Baking Co. v. Bryan, 264 U. S. 504, 517 (1924), and in Adams v. Tanner, 244 U. S. 590, 597 (1917).

their facilities and still more limited by the pressure of business. Therefore, extra-legal facts which determine constitutionality have in recent years been brought to the Supreme Court's attention in briefs of counsel. Such weighty presentation of the experience which underlies challenged legislation has been welcomed by the Court and relied on in its adjudications.[45] Finally, the warrant for legislation has been made an issue for proof to be established by evidence, like matters in ordinary litigation.[46] This method of testimonial proof, calling into formal issue the actual or presumed findings of the legislature, was rejected by the Court in an earlier phase of the development of modern constitutional interpreta-

---

[45] The method begins with the brief filed by Louis D. (now Mr. Justice) Brandeis in Muller v. Oregon, 208 U. S. 412 (1908). See Felix Frankfurter, *supra*, 29 HARV. L. REV. at 364. The effect of such a presentation of the issue is shown by the following passage from Mr. Justice Brewer's opinion in Muller v. Oregon, 208 U. S. at 419–21: " It may not be amiss, in the present case, before examining the constitutional question, to notice the course of legislation as well as expressions of opinion from other than judicial sources. In the brief filed by Mr. Louis D. Brandeis, for the defendant in error, is a very copious collection of all these matters, an epitome of which is found in the margin. . . . The legislation and opinions referred to in the margin may not be, technically speaking, authorities, and in them is little or no discussion of the constitutional question presented to us for determination, yet they are significant of a widespread belief that woman's physical structure, and the functions she performs in consequence thereof, justify special legislation restricting or qualifying the conditions under which she should be permitted to toil. Constitutional questions, it is true, are not settled by even a consensus of present public opinion, for it is the peculiar value of a written constitution that it places in unchanging form limitations upon legislative action, and thus gives a permanence and stability to popular government which otherwise would be lacking. At the same time, when a question of fact is debated and debatable, and the extent to which a special constitutional limitation goes is affected by the truth in respect to that fact, a widespread and long continued belief concerning it is worthy of consideration. We take judicial cognizance of all matters of general knowledge." The method has since been followed in Bunting v. Oregon, 243 U. S. 426 (1917); Stettler v. O'Hara, 243 U. S. 629 (1917); Adkins v. Children's Hospital, 261 U. S. 525 (1923). *Cf.* People v. Schweinler Press, 214 N. Y. 395, 108 N. E. 639 (1915), where the court upon " new and additional knowledge " came to a different conclusion upon a statute regulating night-work of women in factories from their former decision in People v. Williams, 189 N. Y. 131, 81 N. E. 778 (1907).

[46] Chastleton Corp. v. Sinclair, 264 U. S. 543 (1924), where the Court reversed the case with directions to the lower court to discover whether the exigency necessary for rent regulation still existed. In Buck v. Bell, 47 Sup. Ct. Rep. 584 (1927), specific findings were made by a state court upon the necessity for compulsory sterilization of mental defectives. As to the determination " either by the court or the jury " of conditions on which constitutional validity of the application of a statute may, under the due process clauses, turn, see concurring opinion of Brandeis, J., in Whitney v. California, 47 Sup. Ct. Rep. 641 (1927).

tion.[47] It raises, indeed, far-reaching questions of policy in the accommodation of the respective functions of court and legislature. One thing is clear. The legal profession has not yet put its mind to devising the necessary method and machinery by which knowledge of those facts, which are the foundation of constitutional judgment, may be formally at the service of courts. Here, as elsewhere, the inventive powers of lawyers will have to experiment consciously with different procedures, in order to evolve the technique best adapted to the elucidation of these politico-legal issues, or to formulate a variety of methods appropriate to different situations.

This brings into focus the part played by the bar in constitutional litigation. An adequately equipped professional bar is the mainstay of the Anglo-American legal order, for it is a necessary adjunct of our courts. If the bar is to fulfill its duties in this most important domain of law, it must realize the nature of issues raised by constitutional controversies and be capable of assisting courts in their solution. The intellectual direction of the bar will certainly in the future be decided by the law schools. The aims and atmosphere of our law schools, the ideas and philosophy which underlie their curricula, the breadth of scholarship and understanding of their faculties, will determine the quality of our lawyers. With legal education rests the responsibility for training men fitted for constitutional adjudications.

Promising efforts to lift the level of the lawyer's technical training are under way. Undoubtedly the standards of legal education have been notably raised in recent years.[48] As befits our national needs, about a dozen really important centers of legal education are in process of making. Law schools ample in number and adequate in resources for the training of a competent bar will be sustained in their purposes by the increasing imposition of higher professional requirements for admission to the bar.[49] But a bar

---

[47] Jacobson *v.* Massachusetts, 197 U. S. 11 (1905).

[48] See, *e.g.*, REDLICH, COMMON LAW AND THE CASE METHOD IN AMERICAN UNIVERSITY LAW SCHOOLS (Carnegie Foundation for the Advancement of Teaching, Bull. No. 8) ; " Tendencies in Legal Education," Annual Report of Dean Harlan F. Stone of Columbia Law School, 1921.

[49] See Proceedings of the National Conference of Bar Associations on Legal Education at Washington, D. C., in Feb., 1922, 8 AM. BAR ASSN. REP. 137; In the Matter of Requirements for Admission to the New York Bar, Report of Committee

better trained merely in technical legal learning will not in itself produce fitness for participation in the work of the Supreme Court. The admonition addressed by Elihu Root in 1916 to the American bar is increasingly pertinent:

" To deal with American law as it is, however, is but half the problem. We are in the midst of a process of rapid change in the conditions to which the principles of law are to be applied, and if we are to have a consistent system that change must be met not at haphazard but by constructive development. The industrial and social changes of our time have been too swift for slowly forming custom. Old rules, applied to new conditions never dreamed of when the rules were stated, prove inadequate too suddenly for the courts readily to overtake them with application of the principles out of which the rules grew. We have only just begun to realize the transformation in industrial and social conditions produced by the wonderful inventions and discoveries of the past century." [50]

The form of litigation reveals the forces of this transformation in detached and isolated instances. But the individual case will be given dwarfed and distorted significance unless it is related to the deeper controversies of which it is a part. Mr. Root proceeded to indicate the tasks which now confront the law:

" The vast increase of wealth resulting from the increased power of production is still in the first stages of the inevitable processes of distribution. The power of organization for the application of capital and labor in the broadest sense to production and commerce has materially changed the practical effect of the system of free contract to the protection of which our law has been largely addressed. The interdependence of modern life, extending not merely to the massed city community but to the farm and mine and isolated factory, which depend for their markets and their supplies upon far distant regions and upon complicated processes of transportation and exchange, has deprived the individual largely of his power of self-protection, and has opened new avenues through which, by means unknown to the ancient law, fatal injuries may be inflicted upon his rights, his property, his health, his liberty of action, his life itself. We have not yet worked out the *formulae* through which old principles are to be applied to these new

---

on Character and Fitness, First Department, 1926; Order of N. Y. Court of Appeals, June 7, 1927, relative to admission to bar, (N. Y. Times, June 8, 1927, p. 14); Rules of Colorado Supreme Court, 13 Am. Bar Assn. J. 423.

[50] ROOT, ADDRESSES ON GOVERNMENT AND CITIZENSHIP, 532–33. Also Elihu Root, " Public Service by the Bar," 41 AM. BAR ASSN. REP. 355, 366.

conditions — the new forms perhaps through which the law shall continue to render its accustomed service to society." [51]

Unless the lawyer is equipped to penetrate to the core of these issues, to move freely in the world of ideas and knowledge which they imply, his technical training will be either futile or obstructive to the overwhelming enterprise of governing modern society by law. New facts must be able to find a ready access to his mind. " Improvement," Lord Acton quotes from Mill, " consists in bringing our opinions into clearer agreement with facts; and we shall not be likely to do this while we look at facts only through glasses colored by those very opinions." [52] The powers and *esprit* thus demanded of the bar the universities alone can cultivate.

Only a bar so trained will furnish a judiciary with ample horizon. But for a seat on the Supreme Bench still greater qualities are demanded. Throughout its history the Supreme Court has called for statesmanship — the gifts of mind and character fit to rule nations. The capacity to transcend one's own limitations, the imagination to see society as a whole, come, except in the rarest instance, from wide experience. Only the poetic insight of the philosopher can replace seasoned contact with affairs.[53] Lord Haldane's comments on the personnel of the Judicial Committee of the Privy Council reflect the same considerations which have largely determined selection for the Supreme Court:

" It is not always that the King can be safely advised to interfere with what belongs to the constitutions or systems of government of the countries of the Empire, and so the Judges of the Judicial Committee have been selected because of their training, not only in the law, but because in the case of most of them they have had experience elsewhere — in the House of Commons or in the House of Lords as members of it, or as Chancellors or ex-Chancellors, or by training calculated to give what is called the statesmanlike outlook to the Judge — that is to say, the outlook which makes him remember that with a growing Constitution things are always changing and developing, and that you cannot be sure that what was right ten years ago will be right to-day." [54]

---

[51] ROOT, *op. cit. supra* note 50, at 533.

[52] ACTON, LECTURE ON THE STUDY OF HISTORY, 84, n. 27.

[53] See Felix Frankfurter, " Twenty Years of Mr. Justice Holmes' Constitutional Opinions," 36 HARV. L. REV. 909, 919.

[54] Viscount Haldane, *supra*, 1 CAMB. L. J. at 148. Mr. John Maynard Keynes'

Not by chance have the most influential Chief Justices been drawn from the world of affairs. Jay and Marshall and Taney, Chase and White and Taft were summoned to preside over the Court not merely because they were lawyers. The accents of statesmen are the recurring motif of Supreme Court opinions. From the beginning, the Court had to resolve what were essentially political issues — the proper accommodation between the states and the central government. These political problems will persist as long as our federalism endures; and the Supreme Court will remain the ultimate arbitrator between Nation and States. Now the still more subtle conflicts of economic forces also press for answers from the nine Justices in Washington. To wisdom in political adjustment, talent for industrial statesmanship must be joined. No graver responsibilities ever confronted a judicial tribunal; no more searching equipment was ever exacted from judges.

---

recipe for a master-economist is illuminating, *mutatis mutandis*, for an understanding of the qualities demanded of a great justice of the Supreme Court:

"The study of economics does not seem to require any specialised gifts of an unusually high order. Is it not, intellectually regarded, a very easy subject compared with the higher branches of philosophy and pure science? Yet good, or even competent, economists are the rarest of birds. An easy subject, at which very few excel! The paradox finds its explanation, perhaps, in that the master-economist must possess a rare *combination* of gifts. He must reach a high standard in several different directions and must combine talents not often found together. He must be mathematician, historian, statesman, philosopher — in some degree. He must understand symbols and speak in words. He must contemplate the particular in terms of the general, and touch abstract and concrete in the same flight of thought. He must study the present in the light of the past for the purposes of the future. No part of man's nature or his institutions must lie entirely outside his regard. He must be purposeful and disinterested in a simultaneous mood; as aloof and incorruptible as an artist, yet sometimes as near the earth as a politician." Memorials of Alfred Marshall, edited by A. C. Pigou, Pt. I, In Memoriam, by J. M. Keynes, 1, 12.

TABLE OF CASES

TABLE OF CASES

TABLE OF STATUTES

TABLE OF UNITED STATES STATUTES

INDEX

INDEX